# THE
# BEST
# BUSINESS
# WRITING
# 2012

Columbia Journalism Review Books

COLUMBIA JOURNALISM REVIEW BOOKS
Series Editors: Victor Navasky, Evan Cornog, Mike Hoyt, and the editors of the *Columbia Journalism Review*

For more than fifty years, the *Columbia Journalism Review* has been the gold standard for media criticism, holding the profession to the highest standards and exploring where journalism is headed, for good and for ill.

Columbia Journalism Review Books expands upon this mission, seeking to publish titles that allow for greater depth in exploring key issues confronting journalism, both past and present, and pointing to new ways of thinking about the field's impact and potential.

Drawing on the expertise of the editorial staff at the *Columbia Journalism Review* as well as the Columbia Journalism School, the series of books will seek out innovative voices as well as reclaim important works, traditions, and standards. In doing this, the series will also incorporate new ways of publishing made available by the Web and e-books.

*Second Read: Writers Look Back at Classic Works of Reportage*, edited by James Marcus and the Staff of the Columbia Journalism Review

*The Story So Far: What We Know About the Business of Digital Journalism*, Bill Grueskin, Ava Seave, and Lucas Graves

*The Best Business Writing 2012*, edited by Dean Starkman, Martha M. Hamilton, Ryan Chittum, and Felix Salmon

*The Art of Making Magazines: On Being an Editor and Other Views from the Industry*, edited by Victor S. Navasky and Evan Cornog

# Contents

**Part II. The Financial System and
Its Discontents**

**Part III. Over There**

**Part IV. Politics and Money**

**Part VI.   Corporate Stories**

# Introduction
## Dean Starkman

I n the wake of the financial crisis of 2008, Damian Tambini, a professor at the London School of Economics, wrote a paper that asked a pretty basic question: "What Is Financial Journalism For?"

As it happens, Tambini found that no one could really agree what business and financial journalism is for, or even *who* it's for: Is it for investors? Markets? Or is it for everybody, the public?

We believe we know the answer: Yes.

Welcome to *Best Business Writing 2012*, the first in an annual series that will collect the best English-language writing on business, finance, and economics. For the past several months, the editors have conducted a thorough, and thoroughly unscientific, search for what we believe is "the best." We start out with a good vantage point. I run "The Audit," the business-press section of the *Columbia Journalism Review*, and part of our job is to read as much of the business press as we can and comment on the good, the bad, and the ugly (hey, it's a living). Beyond that, our fearless panel scoured the Internet, approached traditional and nontraditional news organizations for what *they* thought was their best, and asked people in our networks what they had read and liked. We also asked Twitter and received some of our strongest entries. We didn't care about medium. This book has newspapers, magazines, blogs, radio, even a movie. I'm sure *some* great business writing has gotten by us, but not much.

The result is a collection of nonfiction writing of the highest caliber. Never mind the subject, these are fantastic stories. You will find a riveting yarn of executive-suite intrigue at a major multinational corporation (psst, it's Pfizer); fascinating behind-the-scenes profiles of business behaving badly (Countrywide, Massey), business behaving brilliantly (Ford), and business behaving weirdly (Ikea). You'll read trenchant critiques of failed policy makers (yes, Greenspan is there) and business boners (Netflix, Hewlett Packard). You'll find penetrating looks at a distorted market (psychotropic drugs) and searing investigations. We have insightful think pieces on subjects including the rise of the new elite, Steve Jobs's genius, and Google's omnipresence.

And authors? We've got the incomparable James Stewart, Gretchen Morgenson, Paul Krugman, John Gapper, Marcia Angell, Martin Wolf, Chrystia Freeland, David Cay Johnston, not to mention noted business reporters Hugh Grant and Warren Buffett. *Rolling Stone*'s Matt Taibbi? Of course. (If not *all* of those names are familiar to you, that's okay; that's what we're here for.) But so, too, are people less well known but probably not for long: Michael Hudson, Raquel Rutledge and Rick Barrett, Max Chafkin, and Nick Davies, who for several years has been driving the story about phone hacking and other misdeeds at Rupert Murdoch's News Corp.

For us, the value of a collection of great business and financial writing is self-evident. But we think this book is more than a good idea, more even than a collection of great reading.

In some ways, our times demand it.

The Great Crash of 2008 was, of course, a watershed event—in financial history but also in the history of the United States and the whole world. The financial crisis rocked great financial institutions, drained public treasuries, fomented political upheaval, triggered a crisis in Europe, and plunged much of the world into a long economic winter. Its total economic and human cost is beyond measure. While historians will be debating the causes for decades, a consensus has formed around one thing: the degree to which the collapse took "everyone"—financial professionals, regulators, journalists, and, certainly, the public—by surprise.

I put "everyone" in quotes because a disparate group of professionals—an economist here, a handful of Wall Street traders there, a couple of hedge funds, even a journalist or two—has been identified as having duly warned of, or at least profited from, the great crash centered on the U.S. mortgage market. Indeed, a minidebate has emerged in business-news circles (in which I played some role via a lengthy critical review of precrash reporting, ["Power Problem," *CJR*, May/June 2009]) over the performance of the business press in its watchdog role over financial institutions that it purports to cover.

But beyond who-wrote-what-story-when, the crash and ongoing crisis remind us that, in a democracy, it's not enough to understand only political events and actors. We need to know economic and financial ones as well. The debate can't be left to experts and cognoscenti (clearly) and must be opened to as wide a swath of society as possible, even people who don't normally think of business news as their bag. Put another way: hopeful ignorance about matters business and financial is no longer an option, if it ever was.

In assessing the early-twentieth-century Muckrakers, the historian Richard Hofstadter said their importance lay in the fact that their sweeping, investigative style of journalism allowed "any literate citizen to know what barkeepers, district attorneys, ward heelers, prostitutes, police court magistrates, reporters and corporation lawyers had always come to know in the course of their business." That certainly describes Ida Tarbell's sober, fact-laden nineteen-part expose of Standard Oil, which became a national phenomenon and changed the national discussion about industrial consolidation, the great economic issue of that era. What insiders already knew, Muckrakers revealed to the general public. They were the great connectors.

That role is now played, more or less, by the business press, supplemented by the general press when it ventures into business, economics, and finance (e.g. *The Atlantic, Rolling Stone, This American Life*). The definition of the business press has changed radically in the last decade or so. It has exploded with the rise of new media and has also shrunk as industrial-era news-gathering institutions—particularly great metropolitan dailies including the *Los Angeles Times* and the *Washington Post*—have seen once-formidable business desks hollowed out. For now, the public still relies to a great extent on what are known as "legacy" news organizations for news gathering and investigations, supplemented by a gusher of economic, financial, and business commentary and analysis from new players, some of it quite fantastic (examples of which are included here).

So for those who read the business press regularly, this book is for you. Skim the table of contents and marvel at how much great stuff you missed in the last year or so. But for those who don't read it regularly, this book is for you, too.

It's true, business news has an image problem. Many believe it's too technical or geared to insiders and people already in the know. There's some truth to the perception. Business news began as form of elite communications, a pragmatic messaging tool to aid investors and markets, and, until not so long ago, that's all it was. Indeed, the book you are holding is a result of business news's long, tortured fight from the cultural margins to the mainstream.

Business news as we understand it arose in the late seventeenth century and gained traction in the early eighteenth century, accompanying the rise of capitalism and early publicly traded companies, like the notorious South Seas Trading Company, which flourished—until it crashed. The economist Robert J. Shiller pointedly notes that the history of financial bubbles coincided with the advent of financial media (you can insert your own CNBC joke here).

The business press expanded to chronicle the Industrial Revolution, notably including *The Economist*, founded in 1843 and edited by businessman and essayist Walter Bagehot, considered the granddaddy of modern business news. In the United States, many early American newspapers, in fact, *were* commercial papers until technological improvements made it cheap enough to provide general news for a broader audience in the penny press. And while the early commercial press is credited with helping propel the growth of markets and industry and with providing the very language of capitalism, no one would mistake it for James B. Stewart. For most of its history, extending well into the twentieth century, business news was a dreary, incoherent jumble of earnings, prices, and government data. Put it this way: there is a reason there is no book called *Best Business Writing 1912*.

The great broadening of business news came incrementally, then suddenly. Publications conceived during the go-go 1920s (poorly timed, as it turned out: *BusinessWeek* started in 1929) were aimed at a growing managerial and entrepreneurial class. Henry Luce staffed his new magazine, *Fortune* (launched 1930), with poets and novelists, including Archibald MacLeish, James Agee, and Dwight MacDonald, on the theory that it was "easier to turn poets into business journalists than it was to turn bookkeepers into writers" (and isn't *that* the truth?). *Fortune* in the early and mid-1930s produced a spate of business writing so radical—including a scathing series on U.S. Steel by MacDonald, then a Trotskyite sympathizer—that Luce by the mid-1930s had to retake control and install a new editor. Still, the mainstreamed *Fortune* helped to pioneer in-depth business reporting with the "corporation story," the classic corporate profile that became a minor art form, a tradition represented in this volume (see: "Inside Pfizer's Palace Coup," by Peter Elkind and Jennifer Reingold, with Doris Burke).

The real breakthrough in American business news came in 1941. That's when the *Wall Street Journal,* undistinguished editorially and in desperate shape financially, elevated to managing editor a thirty-two-year-old DePauw graduate with a deft writing touch, an easygoing manner, and a clear vision of what business news could be. Bernard S. Kilgore was a midcentury, middle-American executive out of a Frank Capra movie. A devoted family man, he rode the commuter train from Princeton, marking up that morning's *Journal,* and for relaxation changed the engine of the family Ford.

But he took business-news convention and basically tore it up. He ignored the inverted pyramid. He expanded story length, installed a new narrative writing style, and threw out hide-bound definitions of what was and wasn't a "business story." He created a system that would be able to produce two long-form stories a day that would take readers into corners of the economy they had never before seen: a salad-oil swindle in New Jersey, Lyndon Johnson's wife's broadcasting empire, slave-labor camps in Houston. Eventually, *Journal* reporters transcended business reporting—or one could argue, expanded it—to broach almost any subject of interest. The *Journal* found relevant to business readers the secret shame of illiterates, the Cabrini Green housing projects, the Falun Gong, you name it. Business news was now about a lot more than just what General Electric said yesterday.

After a tense few years waiting for the new format to take hold, success and acclaim followed. By the late 1950s, *Harper's* would pronounce the *Journal*'s rise the "outstanding phenomenon in American daily journalism in the past two decades," adding that "whether the (journalistic) broadening brought success or vice verse is an open question." When Kilgore took over the paper in 1941, its circulation was 35,000. By the time he died in 1967, it was more than a million; by the late 1970s, it would top 1.7 million, passing the *New York Daily News* to become the largest-circulation paper in the United States, a place it has held off and on ever since.

Kilgore's expansive journalistic vision, copied elsewhere, created a permanent argument in business newsrooms over the very purpose of business news and its intended audience—hence the disagreements Dr. Tambini found in his study. These tensions are, for the most part, healthy.

Much is made about the need to improve Americans' "financial literacy"—nuts-and-bolts tools such as knowing which mutual fund to buy, how to avoid banking fees, and so on. But the Kilgore revolution was concerned with a more important pedagogical job: nothing less than the democratization of financial and economic knowledge. While it's nice to know about financial and consumer products and services, it's much more important to know about financial and corporate *institutions* and *actors* because they shape the world we live in. That's the kind of "financial literacy" that counts.

Much of the business press today is built on a foundation laid by Kilgore. In a way, this book is another of his legacies.

Of course, business news, like the rest of the media, has continued to evolve. The mid-1990s saw an explosion of business news to accompany Americans' stampede into the stock market (much later than many imagine). In 1996, by one count, twenty-two new business publications were launched. CNBC rose from cable TV afterthought to cultural icon. The 2000s brought even more dramatic changes—the tech wreck, a severe advertising recession, and the rise of the Internet started a great unraveling of institutional media and triggered the emergence of new journalism forms. We are now in a transitional moment: weakened legacy institutions bobbing in a vibrant, conversational, chaotic, and atomized digital sea. The degree to which what was lost from mainstream media is offset by gains in new media is a debate for another day.

The important thing is that great business journalism is going strong in both new and old forms and media. In this volume, the point is forcefully driven home by Zach Carter and Ryan Grim's X ray of the Washington debate on bankcard swipe fees for *Huffington Post* and by Jesse Eisinger and Jake Bernstein's expose of crimes and misdemeanors at Merrill Lynch for *ProPublica*, which won the first Pulitzer Prize awarded to a piece that never appeared in print. Morgan Housel's deconstruction of bubble-era policymakers "Greenspan, Rubin, and a Roomful of Hypocrites," (*The Motley Fool*) obviously represents the tip of a huge iceberg of amazing online economic commentary and analysis.

It's not going overboard to say that great business writing is the vital link between the public and the institutions that shape our economic lives. That's why we're proud to present *Best Business Writing 2012* and even prouder to do it now when the economic currents are so complex and the stakes are so high.

And besides, these are just such great reads. Thanks for picking us up.

# Acknowledgments

The editors would like to thank *CJR*'s agent, the indispensible Deirdre Mullane, who came up with the idea of a Best Business Writing series then tirelessly shepherded the process of obtaining rights to all the works, no small job. We also, of course, thank our contributors, who did the real work and did it brilliantly. And we gratefully acknowledge the support of Nicholas Lemann, dean of the Columbia Journalism School, Victor Navasky, chairman of the *Columbia Journalism Review*; Peter Osnos, the magazine's vice chairman; its board, Stephen Adler, Neil Barsky (chairman), Nathan S. Collier, Cathleen Collins, Wade Greene, Joan Konner, Kenneth Lerer, William Lilley III, Herbert Winokur, Emily Bell, Sheila Coronel, Howard W. French, and Michael Schudson; and major funders: the Adams Cowan Foundation, the Atlantic Philanthropies, Maria Moors Cabot Fund, the Challenge Fund for Journalism, Kingsford Capital Management, Peter Lowy, Omidyar Network, Open Society Institute, the Saul and Janice Poliak Center for the Study of First Amendment Issues, Rockefeller Family Fund, M & T Weiner Foundation, the Schumann Foundation, Gary Lutin, and Ted Weschler.

Dean Starkman would like to thank his wife, Alex, and his parents, Stanley and Regina Starkman. Ryan Chittum thanks Anna, Clara, and Nina. Felix would like to thank Jim, Jim, and Chrystia.

THE

BEST

BUSINESS

WRITING

2012

Part I

# Bad Business

***Rolling Stone***

With convincing reporting and authoritative writing, Jeff Goodell paints a compelling portrait of Massey Energy's former chief executive Don Blankenship as, quite simply, "the embodiment of everything that's wrong with the business and politics of energy in America today." Massey Energy owned and operated the Upper Big Branch Mine in West Virginia where twenty-nine miners were killed in April 2010. Blankenship, Goodell writes, is a man who "pursues naked self-interest and calls it patriotism, who buys judges like cheap hookers, treats workers like dogs, blasts mountains to get at a few inches of coal and uses his money and influence to ensure that America remains enslaved to the nineteenth-century idea that burning coal equals progress." Bold words, backed up.

# 1. The Dark Lord of Coal Country

One balmy night this fall, a black BMW 750LI—a German luxury sedan that costs more than a typical coal miner makes in a year—pulls into the parking lot of the shaggy country club in Bluefield, West Virginia. Bluefield is a fading coal town in a state that is full of fading coal towns. Seventy-five years ago, when the Pocahontas coal seam was one of the richest veins in America, and tooling up for the twentieth century required massive tonnage of coal, there was money here, and hope. But now the coal is mined out, the buildings downtown are vacant, and shiny new Beemers are about as common as flying saucers.

The driver—a young, tan, L.A.-surfer-boy type—jumps out and opens the rear door. A tall man, sixty, with a thin mustache and a double chin emerges: Don Blankenship, the CEO of Massey Energy, the largest and most powerful coal company in central Appalachia. He grabs his dark-blue suit jacket, which is folded on the tan leather seat beside him, and slips it on. He wears a red-and-yellow silk tie and tasseled leather loafers. His hands are chubby and white—no calluses, not a speck of coal dust. Accountant's hands. His eyes are black and inexpressive.

Unless you live in West Virginia, you've probably never heard of Don Blankenship. You might not know that he grew up in the coal fields of West Virginia, received an accounting degree from a local college, and, through a combination of luck, hard work, and coldblooded ruthlessness, transformed himself into the embodiment of everything that's wrong with the business and politics of energy in America today—a man who pursues naked self-interest and calls it patriotism, who buys judges like cheap hookers, treats workers like dogs, blasts mountains to get at a few inches of coal, and uses his money and influence to ensure that America remains enslaved to the nineteenth-century idea that burning coal equals progress. And for this, he earns $18 million a year—making him the highest-paid CEO in the coal industry—and flies off to vacations on the French Riviera.

As Blankenship walks into the country club, heads turn. A hundred executives from the coal industry have gathered for a two-day conference on mine safety—a topic that has taken on added urgency since April, when twenty-nine men were killed in an explosion at the Upper Big Branch mine run by Massey Energy. The blast, fueled by high levels of methane in the mine, was so powerful that it twisted the steel rail tracks on the mine's floor and killed men more than a mile away. It was the worst mining tragedy in forty years, but nobody in the room seems to hold that against Blankenship. As he strides to the podium, he is greeted by applause and whistles. A handful of students from Virginia Tech rush up to get their picture taken with him as his fellow coal executives stand aside, resentment and awe mixed on their faces.

Blankenship is a lousy speaker, using the same deadpan tone whether he's talking about quarterly earnings or busting a union. But he does not mince words. After laughing off global warming as a "hoax," he moves on to the meat of his talk: the tragedy at Upper Big Branch. Instead of acknowledging any responsibility for the disaster, Blankenship argues that the explosion was an act of God, caused by a buildup of methane that had seeped in through a fifty-foot crack in the ground. He blames the federal Mine Safety and Health Administration for contributing to the accident by altering the mine's ventilation system. "You remember Watergate?" he says. "Today what you have is MSHA-Gate." He even accuses Joe Main, the respected head of the agency, of giving false testimony to Congress to cover up MSHA's culpability in the explosion. "What is the difference between Roger Clemens and Joe Main?" he asks, referring to the former Red Sox pitcher who denied using steroids. "We don't know if Roger lied to Congress. But we know Joe did."

The line gets a big laugh, but it's pure horseshit. The entire speech, in fact, is nothing but a desperate attempt to shift blame for the tragedy and obscure the fact that twenty-nine men died violent deaths in large part because Don Blankenship ran what amounted to an outlaw coal mine, racking up more than 500 safety violations and nearly $1 million in fines last year alone. But if any of the coal executives assembled in the country club see it that way, no one speaks up. They want to believe that the coal industry has a bright future, and that Blankenship is nothing more than a tough-talking local boy made good. As he finishes his rant, they give him a standing ovation.

"The thing I admire most about Don Blankenship is that he's not afraid to tell the truth," Ben Parker, an engineering student, tells me as the applause fades. "He's just like Sarah Palin."

·　　　·　　　·

For the past two decades, Don Blankenship has been the undisputed king of coal in West Virginia. Other Big Coal CEOs who operate in Appalachia are business-school types who have offices in other states and leave the dirty work to their minions. Blankenship, by contrast, is a rich hillbilly who believes that God put coal in the ground so that he could mine it, and anyone—or any law—that stands in his way needs to be beaten down, bought off, or tied up in court. Blankenship is hated, feared, and respected, but nobody wants to tangle with him. "He's a throwback to the old coal barons of the nineteenth century," says Cecil Roberts, the head of the United Mine Workers of America, who has battled Blankenship for nearly thirty years.

From a strictly business point of view, it's hard to argue with Blankenship's success: He has taken a sleepy old coal company and built it into the most powerful economic and political machine in Appalachia. Massey Energy and its subsidiaries operate 56 mines in the region, employing nearly 6,000 workers and producing some 40 million tons of coal a year. Even after the disaster at Upper Big Branch hammered the company's stock, it's still worth about $4 billion. To the degree that West Virginia's future is tied to coal, it is also tied to Blankenship: His company owns more than a third of the remaining coal reserves in the region.

Blankenship has never hidden the fact that, when it comes to mining coal, he'll do whatever it takes to make a buck. "It's like a jungle, where a jungle is survival of the fittest," he told a documentary filmmaker in the 1980s. "Unions, communities, people—everybody's gonna have to learn to accept that in the United States you have a capitalist society, and that capitalism, from a business standpoint, is survival of the most productive."

In Blankenship's view, being productive means getting coal out of the ground as fast and cheap as possible, no matter the cost to workers or the environment. "He has been hugely influential in the coal industry in Appalachia," says a rival coal executive. "He basically transformed a gentlemanly, Democratic, union-based industry, where deals were done on a handshake, into the aggressive, partisan industry that we know today." Blankenship helped popularize the style of mining known as mountaintop removal, in which the mountains are removed from the coal, rather than the coal from the mountains—a practice that has destroyed 2,000 miles of streams and damaged more than a million acres of forest. He has fought labor unions and federal regulators at every turn, exposing miners to dangerous conditions. And he has injected toxic coal slurry near underground aquifers, a practice that has allegedly sickened hundreds of residents.

"All in all, Blankenship has probably caused more suffering than any other human being in Appalachia," says Roberts.

A right-wing Republican in a traditionally Democratic state, Blankenship has also used his wealth and influence to go after anyone who opposes him. "Unlike the old coal barons, who mostly shunned the limelight, Blankenship is a very flamboyant character," says Robert Rupp, professor of political science at West Virginia Wesleyan College. When it comes to politics, Blankenship doesn't waste time twisting arms: Massey spent less than $20,000 on federal lobbying last year and has contributed only $300,000 to federal candidates since 1990. Instead, he goes for a more direct bang for his buck. He spent more than $3 million electing a state Supreme Court judge who would provide a favorable verdict in a lawsuit, funneled nearly $1 million into advertising this year to improve coal's image, and served on the boards of the U.S. Chamber of Commerce and the National Mining Association, which has attacked the Obama administration for waging a "regulatory jihad" against coal.

The real reason that the coal industry in West Virginia is slowly dying has nothing to do with government regulation. After 150 years of mining, most of the good, easy-to-get coal in Appalachia is simply gone. Coal production in the region plunged 13 percent last year—one of the biggest drops in fifty years. But to Blankenship, the true enemies are the environmental "greeniacs" who recognize that burning coal has dangerously overheated the planet. In his view, even something as innocuous as energy conservation is nothing but a communist plot. "Turn down your thermostats?" he once scoffed. "Buy a smaller car? Conserve? I have spent quite a bit of time in Russia and China, and that's the first stage. You go from having your own car to carpooling to riding the bus to mass transit. You eventually get to where you're going by walking. That's what socialism and the elimination of capitalism and free enterprise is all about."

But it was the disaster at Upper Big Branch that brought Blankenship into the national spotlight. "It was his coming-out party," says Jeff Biggers, author of *Reckoning at Eagle Creek*, who has written widely about the coal industry. "People in the coal fields had been dealing for years with the brutal repercussions of how Blankenship operates. Now the rest of the country was getting a look." In a Rose Garden speech not long after the disaster, President Obama seemed to point his finger directly at Blankenship. "This tragedy was triggered by a failure, first and foremost, of management," Obama said. Massey's stock price plunged, cutting the value of the company by at least $2 billion, and a group of powerful shareholders filed a lawsuit against Blankenship and Massey's board, accusing them of mismanagement. On top of everything, the Justice Department announced a criminal investigation into the Upper Big Branch explosion. As a senior official in the Labor Department told me flat-out: "We would like to see Don Blankenship go to jail."

·     ·     ·

Blankenship lives in Mingo County, West Virginia, just a few miles from where he grew up. It's one of the poorest, sickest, most economically depressed regions in America. Blankenship's house, which sits near the polluted waters of the Tug Fork, is an oasis of money and privilege in a landscape of rusting 4x4s and abandoned appliances. From the road, it looks like an estate in the Hamptons, with neatly trimmed hedges and a broad curving drive. The property is surrounded by a high steel fence, with cameras mounted near the automatic gate. The house itself, fittingly enough, is an old mining superintendent's building, built back in the days when coal barons like Blankenship hired armed guards to mow down striking miners with machine guns. Nearby is a helicopter landing pad, as well as a spacious garage for Blankenship's vehicles, which reportedly include a Bentley. Across the river, perched on the mountaintop like a castle, is Blankenship's corporate party house, a baronial estate where he entertains industry executives and politicians with superb views of his broken world.

Blankenship was born just down the road in Stopover, Kentucky, a tiny collection of shacks and mobile homes. His mother, Nancy, was a McCoy, a descendant of the infamous mountain clan that was always warring with the Hatfields. Soon after Blankenship was born, his mother divorced her husband, who was serving in Korea, and moved across the border to Delorme, West Virginia. She used her divorce settlement to buy a convenience store and gas station, where she worked for the next forty years.

Today, Delorme is more a memory than a town—a few houses scattered along the banks of the Tug Fork, a tiny post office, a vinyl-sided Pentecostal church, and a sagging building by the railroad tracks where you can drive up and buy beer. The trailer that Blankenship and his three siblings grew up in is long gone, as is his mother's store, both wiped out by occasional floods and constant poverty. But back in the 1950s, when Blankenship was a kid, the Norfolk and Western Railway still rumbled through, and it was a lively place. "There were seven bars in town," says Jack Murphy, who grew up with Blankenship. "It got rough sometimes." Blankenship watched bar fights from his living-room window, sometimes climbing up on the roof of a nearby barbershop to get closer to the action.

Blankenship takes pride in the fact that he grew up in such a hardscrabble place. "I have trapped muskrats for fifty cents and hunted two-cent pop bottles in order to buy a one-dollar baseball," he told a rally of West Virginians last year, trying to establish his street cred as a boy from the hollows. But his biggest influence was clearly his mother, who worked nearly one hundred hours a week. Blankenship often helped her in the store, adding up sales numbers in his head. From her, he learned his first lesson in Darwinian economics: In a place as tough as West Virginia, only the strongest survive.

"He was a very competitive kid—he didn't like to fail," says Eddie Croaff, a childhood friend. "He loved baseball and was a pretty good shortstop." Croaff, a former coal miner himself, says that even as a kid Blankenship liked to calculate the odds of risky behavior—like the chances of being killed if he went around a blind corner on the wrong side of the road in his black Chevy Camaro. "He was always trying to figure out what he could get away with."

Blankenship was president of his high school class and enrolled in Marshall University in Huntington, where he majored in accounting and earned his degree in just three years. He worked in a Kentucky coal mine one summer, but was "a mediocre miner," says Darrell Ratliff, his foreman at the time. "I don't want to say he was lazy, but I had to make him move once in a while." After graduation, Blankenship took a job as an accountant for the Keebler cookie company in Macon, Georgia. He got married, had two kids, settled down. Then in 1982, at a moment when he was in between jobs, he got a call from Massey offering him a job as an office manager. Blankenship, who was thirty-one at the time, accepted. He would later say that it felt like predestination.

Blankenship went to work at a Massey subsidiary called Rawl Sales & Processing, located just a few miles down the road from where he had grown up in Delorme. A.T. Massey, as the company was then called, was founded in 1920, and it reflected the patriarchal benevolence of its era; its executives were known for their genteel manners and their generous donations to local philanthropies. It was also deeply antiunion. In 1984, Massey tried to break the United Mine Workers by announcing that each of its mines would be treated as separate companies—a move that would effectively enable them to reopen as nonunion operations.

Determined to hold Massey accountable for its subsidiaries, the union went on strike that fall. Blankenship, who by then had been named president of Rawl, found himself in the middle of an epic battle in the coal fields of West Virginia.

As a local boy, Blankenship might have been expected to be sympathetic to local workers who were trying to improve safety in the mines and feed their families. But as president of Rawl, Blankenship put profits before people. To him, the union was nothing but a drag on Rawl's profitability—and he quickly turned the mine into a flash point in the larger strike. Blankenship erected two miles of chain-link fence around the facility, brought in dogs and armed guards, and ferried nonunion workers through the union's blockades. The strike, which lasted more than a year, grew increasingly violent—strikers took up baseball bats against the workers trying to take their jobs, and a few even fired shots at the scabs. A volley of bullets zinged into Blankenship's office and smashed into an old TV. Frightened for his safety, Blankenship slept in a different bed every night. But in the end, he proved stronger than the union: In 1985, the United Mine Workers gave in.

The strike marked a turning point in the decades-old struggle between coal barons and their workers. "The union tried to make a stand and failed," says Les Leopold, director of the Labor Institute in New York. "After that, their power in the region declined." For years afterward, Blankenship kept the TV with a bullet hole through it in his office as a souvenir—and a reminder to others of what a tough motherfucker he is.

•    •    •

Blankenship's success as a union buster, combined with his mastery of financial arcana, catapulted him through the ranks at Massey. "Don could always tell you exactly what the numbers were," recalled E. Morgan Massey, the grandson of the company's founder. "The numbers drive every decision he makes." In 1992, only a decade after starting out at Massey, Blankenship was appointed chairman and CEO.

At the time, Appalachia's coal industry faced increasing competition from big Western mines and from natural gas, which is cheaper and cleaner. To cut costs, Blankenship started blowing up mountains to get at the coal, since blasting is cheaper than digging. He also used Massey's financial strength to buy up smaller coal companies that were having a rough time, often at fire-sale prices. "Blankenship is a master at recognizing and taking advantage of distressed assets," says Bruce Stanley, a lawyer who grew up in Mingo County not far from Blankenship. In 1997, hoping to sell more of a special type of premium-priced coal used in steelmaking, Blankenship set his sights on a small outfit called Harman Mining.

First, Blankenship bought the company that processed Harman's coal and broke its contract with the smaller firm. "I didn't know it at the time, but his goal was to replace my coal with cheaper, lower-quality coal from his own mine," says Hugh Caperton, who served as president of Harman. Then, after offering to buy out Harman, Blankenship used information he had obtained during the negotiations to buy up the coal reserves around Harman's mine, effectively making the company unattractive to other buyers. "His goal was to drive me into bankruptcy, so he could buy me for nothing," Caperton says.

Caperton lost a company he had spent ten years building, and his 150 employees lost their jobs. Not long afterward, Blankenship stopped in to see his vanquished rival. "It was one of the strangest conversations I've ever had," Caperton recalls. "He just walked into my office, and if I would have had a couch, he would have laid down on it. He said, 'I don't understand why people don't like me anymore. In high school, I played ball. I was really popular.'" Then Blankenship abruptly stood up and left.

Despite Blankenship's power, Caperton decided to fight back. He sued Massey, arguing that the company had set out to destroy him. In 2002, a jury awarded Caperton $50 million in damages.

Blankenship was furious. "He took this fight personally," says Stanley, who represented Caperton in the case. "His whole persona is based on the idea that if you mess around with Don, he will take you to the wall." Massey appealed the verdict to the state's Supreme Court. But rather than trusting in the wisdom of the justice system, Blankenship tried to rig the outcome in his favor. In 2004, he spent $3 million—an enormous sum in West Virginia politics—to finance a political hit machine to take down Justice Warren McGraw, who was likely to serve as the swing vote in the court's decision. The group deployed every sleazy trick in the book, accusing McGraw of letting child rapists out of prison and putting them to work in local schools. The smear tactics worked: McGraw was defeated, replaced by an industry-friendly judge backed by Blankenship. In 2007, the court overturned the $50 million verdict against Blankenship by a vote of three to two. His $3 million investment had saved him $47 million.

"Don didn't put $3 million into the election because he wanted a fair and balanced court system," says Robert Rupp, the political science professor. "He wanted to buy himself a favorable verdict."

But Caperton kept fighting. Then in January 2008, he got a mysterious break: A plain brown envelope was delivered to his attorney by an unknown person. In it were photographs of Blankenship and Spike Maynard, the chief justice of the state Supreme Court, vacationing together on the French Riviera. "The photos were visual evidence of what everyone suspected," says Caperton. "Blankenship was again trying to influence the court."

The photos prompted the court to rehear the case. This time around, Maynard agreed to recuse himself—but so did another justice, who had publicly called Blankenship a "clown." The court once again found in favor of Blankenship. But this time, the case attracted national attention—especially after a crew from ABC

News tried to interview Blankenship outside his office. "If you're going to start taking pictures of me," he told the crew, shoving the camera away, "you're liable to get shot."

Last year, Caperton won a major victory in the case. Citing "extreme" conflict of interest, the U.S. Supreme Court ruled that the state judge whose election was backed by Blankenship should have recused himself from the case. "It was a huge victory for one of the most basic aspects of the rule of law—the right to a fair hearing," said James Sample of the Brennan Center for Justice at the New York University School of Law. Yet last year, when the state Supreme Court took up the issue for a third time, it once again found in Blankenship's favor—this time citing a legal technicality to rule that the West Virginia courts had no jurisdiction in the case.

"It was a travesty of justice at every level," says Caperton, who has refiled the case in Virginia. In fact, the whole case was so outlandish that John Grisham used it as the basis for the plot in his novel *The Appeal*. As Grisham told Matt Lauer on the *Today Show*: "A guy owned a coal company, he got tired of getting sued. He elected his guy to the Supreme Court—and now he didn't worry about getting sued."

·  ·  ·

Blankenship often argues that he is the embodiment of a successful capitalist—that the jobs he provides put food on people's tables and allow them to buy houses and cars and all the other necessities of modern life. But there is a larger question he doesn't address: Why, if the coal industry is so good for West Virginia, is there so much sickness, death, and economic decline in the state—especially in the very area where Blankenship lives?

David Joe Mollett lives up in Lick Creek, just a few miles from Blankenship's well-manicured estate. His father went to work in the coal mines when he was thirteen years old. The small house where Mollett lives with his sister and his brother is pretty much all that their father left them after decades in the mines. On the once idyllic ridge behind them, a huge Massey operation has begun removing the top of the mountain.

As a kid in the 1980s, Mollett remembers filling up a glass of water at the kitchen sink and seeing black stuff floating in it. "Sometimes it smelled of rotten egg, sometimes it had a rainbow on top," he recalls. The water came from a well out back; families in the area had been drinking water out of the ground for generations. Now, all of a sudden, they started to get sick. In high school, Mollett got rashes, bad ones, on his back and arms. He had diarrhea, stomachaches. In 2000, he was bombing around on his four-wheeler when he suddenly passed out completely. He was rushed to the hospital, where doctors discovered he was in complete kidney failure. He spent three years on dialysis, then finally had a transplant. "The doctor told me that my kidney failed because of the water I'd been drinking," he says. In addition, two of his sisters suffer from severe kidney problems.

The Molletts aren't the only ones getting sick. More than 700 people in the immediate vicinity have reported health problems that they believe are related to water from their wells, and four have died from their ailments. Symptoms range from rashes and ruined kidneys to birth defects and brain cancer.

According to a lawsuit filed by Mollett and his neighbors, the cause of their sickness is clear: Massey, they say, poisoned their drinking water. Back when Blankenship was running Rawl Sales, he needed a cheap, quick way to get rid of millions of gallons of coal slurry—the toxic runoff that comes from washing coal to remove impurities. The slurry is laden with a host of heavy metals known to be deadly to humans—arsenic, lead, cadmium, manganese.

"Blankenship decided it would be simpler and cheaper to inject the slurry into old coal mines underground," says Kevin Thompson, a lawyer representing Mollett and others in the community.

During the 1980s, the company injected more than 1.4 billion gallons of slurry underground—seven times the amount of oil spilled into the Gulf of Mexico during the BP disaster this spring. According to the lawsuit, Massey knew that the ground around the injection sites was cracked, which would allow the toxic waste to leach into nearby drinking water. But injecting the slurry underground saved Massey millions of dollars a year. "The BP oil spill was an accident," says Thompson. "This was an intentional environmental catastrophe." Massey denies any wrongdoing in the case. But after Blankenship started pumping the slurry underground, he took steps to make sure that he and his family did not suffer. Around the time that his neighbors were starting to get sick, Massey paid to build a waterline to bring clean, treated water directly to Blankenship's house from Matewan, a few miles away. Yet he never offered to provide the water to his neighbors, some of whom can see his house from their windows.

Nor was the epidemic in West Virginia the only catastrophe caused by the way Blankenship disposed of coal slurry. In October 2000, a large slurry pond at a Massey subsidiary in Martin County, Kentucky, broke open and spilled 300 million gallons of black, toxic sludge into surrounding creeks. It was one of the nation's worst man-made environmental disasters. Massey paid $3.5 million in state fines for the breach, but only $5,600 in federal penalties.

Mollett, a tall, quiet guy in his late thirties with hair down to his shoulders, says his life has been destroyed by the company's toxic waste. The drugs he takes for his kidney ailments have made him a diabetic, and he can't walk far without his leg swelling up. "Massey should have done more studying before they did this," he says, leaning against the kitchen counter in his small, dark house. "They don't care about people, about what happens to them."

·     ·     ·

On the evening of January 19, 2006, Blankenship was at a reception with some railroad executives at the Greenbrier, the grandest resort hotel in the state. The Greenbrier is one of his favorite haunts, a place where he can have a drink and unwind with his fellow CEOs. Sometime around six P.M., Drexel Short, a senior vice president at Massey, motioned to Blankenship to step into the hallway. There had been a devastating fire at a coal mine run by Aracoma Coal, a Massey subsidiary. Ten men working in the deepest section of the mine had donned their respirators and managed to grope their way to safety through the smoke-filled tunnels. But two men who had become separated from the group were missing.

Blankenship talked briefly with Short about how to handle the situation. Then he went back into the reception at the posh resort and rejoined his pals. Two days later, the two men—Don Bragg, thirty-three, and Elvis Hatfield, forty-six—were found dead in the mine, overcome by the smoke.

Blankenship went to the church where families of the miners were holding vigil, but he didn't offer his condolences. "He didn't say a word to me," recalled Bragg's wife, Delorice, a mother of two who worked as a nurse at the local hospital. "In fact, he avoided looking at me." It was the only time she saw him during the entire ordeal.

Delorice had been born and raised in coal country; she understood that mining was a dangerous job. But in the weeks after Bragg's death, she heard from friends who worked in the mines that Massey was always cutting corners on safety, pushing for more coal. A subsequent investigation showed that the fire had been caused by an improperly maintained conveyor belt. In the previous year, Massey had racked up more than ninety safety violations at the mine. "It wasn't a mine fire that killed my husband," Delorice told me not long after the disaster, her eyes hardening. "It was greed."

Massey offered Delorice a small settlement, but she took the company to court, believing that management should be forced to pay for its negligence. During the proceedings, her lawyer unearthed two revealing memos. The first indicated that Blankenship knew personally that there had been a problem with a conveyor belt nearly a week before the fire broke out. In the second, dated three months before the disaster, Blankenship appeared to order the superintendents of Massey's mines to ignore safety concerns in favor of increasing production. "If any of you have been asked by your group presidents, your supervisors, engineers or anyone else to do anything other than run coal (i.e., build overcasts, do construction jobs, or whatever), you need to ignore them and run coal," Blankenship told them. "This memo is necessary only because we seem not to understand that the coal pays the bills."

The memo created a furor in the mining community. "Throughout Appalachia, there's tremendous support for the coal industry," says Rupp, the political science professor. "But one thing that they will not tolerate is any compromise to the safety of miners. That is where they draw the line. In West Virginia, if you are seen as someone who willfully puts miners at risk to make a buck, then you are in trouble. It's political dynamite."

In the end, Aracoma Coal pleaded guilty to ten criminal charges in the disaster, including one felony, and paid $4.2 million in penalties. The company also admitted that one of the violations—the failure to replace a key ventilation wall—"resulted in the deaths" of Bragg and Hatfield. But as part of the plea deal, prosecutors agreed not to pursue any charges against any Massey executives, including Blankenship.

Delorice Bragg was furious—and not just because Blankenship had shown up for his deposition in his Bentley. In her view, prosecutors had given him a get-out-of-jail-free card. "If Massey executives have done nothing wrong and bear no criminal responsibility for the fire that killed Don and Elvis, then why do they need the deal?" she asked when the plea bargain was announced in court. To Delorice, the message was clear: In West Virginia, nobody messes with Don Blankenship.

.　　　　.　　　　.

The entrance to the Upper Big Branch mine is just off a twisting, narrow road that cuts through the Coal River Valley near Whitesville, West Virginia. It is one of the most valuable underground mines that Massey owns, not only because the coal seam is six feet thick—a rarity in Appalachia these days, when many seams have been mined out—but because its high-grade coal commands a premium on the market. Massey employed nearly 200 miners to work in three shifts around the clock, running an enormous, high-tech machine that moves back and forth across the mine's wall like a giant meat slicer, shearing off coal. "They mined a million dollars worth of coal a day in there," says Gary Quarles, a Massey miner whose son worked at Upper Big Branch.

With so much profitable coal to be had, the focus was on productivity at any cost. The safety record at the mine was abysmal—and it was getting worse. Last year, citations by the Mine Safety Health Administration at Upper Big Branch doubled to more than 500—including 200 for "significant and substantial" violations that MSHA considers "reasonably likely to result in a reasonably serious injury or illness." Most telling of all, MSHA issued sixty-one withdrawal orders at the mine, temporarily shutting down parts of the operation fifty-four times in 2009 and seven times in 2010. Such a high number of withdrawal orders is virtually unheard of in the industry—yet federal inspectors, not known for being tough on outlaw coal operations, failed to close down the mine. "It's like someone driving drunk sixty-one times," said Celeste Monforton, a former policy adviser at MSHA.

The most serious violations involved the ventilation system, a complex operation that requires miners to constantly move curtains around to funnel fresh air into the mine. But at Upper Big Branch, supervisors pushed miners to cut corners and evade inspectors. "When an MSHA inspector came to the section, we'd hang the curtain—but as soon as the inspector left, the curtain came down again," miner Jeffrey Harris later testified. "Some people would tell the inspectors about these kinds of ventilation changes, which were made for their benefit. But the inspectors told us, 'We need to catch it,' and that didn't happen very often." In parts of the mine, Harris added, "the air was so thick you could hardly see in front of you."

The explosion occurred just as miners were changing shifts around three P.M. on Monday, April 5. The force of the blast, which was likely caused by high levels of methane ignited by a spark, ripped apart massive mining machines as if they were a child's toys. The fire turned ninety-degree corners and rounded a block of coal 1,000 feet wide, killing everyone in its path. The destruction was so bad that rescuers walked past the bodies of four missing miners on the first day without noticing them.

In the days after the disaster, Blankenship could be seen heading in and out of the company building where families waited for news, his eyes fixed on the ground, a mix of what looked like guilt and anger on his hangdog face. His presence only served to enrage family members. "He just stood there and let others do the talking," says Quarles, whose son died in the explosion. In interviews, Blankenship denied that his mines are more dangerous than others, and dismissed the high number of safety citations at Upper Big Branch. "Violations are unfortunately a normal part of the mining process," he said.

For the first time in his life, Blankenship suddenly found himself in the midst of a crisis that he could not buy his way out of. The media coverage of the disaster was relentless, and industry insiders wondered openly if he would have to step down as CEO of Massey. Even longtime champions of Big Coal began to use him as a punching bag. During a Senate hearing on the tragedy, Sen. Robert Byrd of West Virginia—perhaps the single most valuable ally the coal industry had—took the extraordinary step of personally rebuking Blankenship for his recklessness and hypocrisy. "I cannot fathom how an American business could practice such disgraceful health and safety policies while simultaneously boasting about its commitment to the safety of its workers," Byrd said. "The Upper Big Branch mine had an alarming—an alarming—record. Shame!"

Blankenship took the abuse from Byrd—and then got on with the business of being Don Blankenship. He recruited a team of heavyweight consultants from the Bush era, including lawyer Robert Luskin, who represented Karl Rove in the Valerie Plame spy case; a PR firm called Public Strategies, run by former Bush communications chief Dan Bartlett; and Dave Lauriski, the head of MSHA under Bush. Together, they cobbled together a survival strategy that Tom Sanzillo, a financial analyst who specializes in coal, calls a "blood war" against MSHA. "His goal," says Sanzillo, "is to turn the tables on investigators and turn the Upper Big Branch disaster into a referendum against the federal government."

The first prong of the strategy is to delay and discredit the investigation. Massey tried to challenge MSHA for refusing to allow the company into the mine to collect its own evidence, but a judge dismissed the complaint as grandstanding; it was as if a murder suspect had demanded that police grant him access to a crime scene so he could examine the bloodstains himself. But the ruse allowed Blankenship to suggest that MSHA was conducting the investigation in a secretive way—a charge that fit well into the larger narrative he was constructing about the disaster.

The story that Blankenship is peddling has taken several turns. First he argued that MSHA itself was responsible for the explosion at Upper Big Branch because its ventilation plan didn't allow methane that had accumulated in the mine to be removed quickly enough. Then, on November 17, he suddenly theorized that the explosion had been caused not by methane but by natural gas, which is rarely a problem in coal mines. In short, he suggested, the disaster had been unavoidable.

It's a good story—but it has little to do with reality. For starters, testimony from miners makes clear that high levels of methane were a persistent problem at Upper Big Branch. Two miners told the *New York Times* that the mine had been evacuated for dangerously high methane levels three times in the previous two months. "Finding explosive levels of methane regularly," one miner wrote nine months before the explosion, documenting conditions in the mine. "Section has low air. Company constantly trying to fool inspectors."

What's more, Blankenship's version of events conveniently ignores the role of coal dust in amplifying the explosion. Coal dust is a constant problem in underground mines. It's usually handled by good housekeeping, and by scattering limestone dust in problem areas to neutralize the coal's volatility. Shane Harvey, the general counsel for Massey, insists that Upper Big Branch was adequately dusted before the blast. But of 1,800 samples collected by MSHA after the explosion, only 400 had been properly treated for coal dust. Even more damning, logs of inspections by mine employees show that eight conveyor belts contained excessive amounts of coal dust only hours before the explosion.

All of which raises a legitimate question about federal regulators: If Upper Big Branch was a disaster waiting to happen—full of coal dust, choked with dangerous levels of methane, a tinderbox waiting to ignite—why didn't federal inspectors shut the mine down? "Because nobody shuts one of Don Blankenship's mines down," says miner Gary Quarles. "It has never happened. Everyone knows when mine inspectors are coming, you clean things up for a few minutes, make it look good, then you go back to the business of running coal. That's how things work at Massey. When inspectors write a violation, the company lawyers challenge it in court. It's all just a game. Don Blankenship does what he wants."

But if the mine was so dangerous, why didn't the miners themselves speak out? Because if they did, they would lose their jobs. "No one felt they could go to management and express their fears," a miner named Stanley Stewart testified after the disaster. "We knew that we'd be marked men and the management would look for ways to fire us. Maybe not that day, or that week, but somewhere down the line, we'd disappear. We'd seen it happen. I told my wife I felt like I was working for the Gestapo at times."

•　　•　　•

Ten days after the disaster, MSHA released a preliminary report that suggested the obvious: The blast was likely caused by an explosive combination of methane and coal dust. It will be months before the agency concludes its investigation, and even longer before federal prosecutors decide whether to pursue criminal charges against Massey. But it is highly unlikely that Blankenship will ever see the inside of a prison cell. The coal industry has more than a century of experience in structuring its companies to shield its executives from criminal liability, and Blankenship continues to disavow any responsibility for the deadly explosion at Upper Big Branch. Although he refused to talk with *Rolling Stone* for this article, Blankenship recently told industry analysts that he has "a totally clear conscience" about the tragedy and does not believe that Massey "contributed in any way" to the disaster.

But whatever happens in court, Blankenship's days as the king of coal are over. The era of Big Coal is coming to a close in West Virginia. Even Senator Byrd, the biggest booster the industry has ever known, admitted as much before his death earlier this year. "The greatest threats to the future of coal do not come from possible constraints on mountaintop-removal mining or other environmental regulations," Byrd warned, "but rather from rigid mind-sets, depleting coal reserves and the declining demand for coal as more power plants begin shifting to biomass and natural gas as a way to reduce emissions. West Virginians can choose to anticipate change and adapt to it, or resist and be overrun by it."

Blankenship still holds an iron grip on Massey's board of directors. "He's the embodiment of an imperial CEO," says one expert on corporate governance. But the board may soon find itself forced to choose between Blankenship and the company's survival. In early November, the Labor Department moved to shut down a Massey mine in Kentucky that has racked up nearly 2,000 safety violations in the past two years. Pressure from environmental activists has forced big lenders like JP Morgan Chase to decline financing for mountaintop-removal operations, which could hurt Massey's bottom line. And big shareholders are beginning to turn against the company. "The mine disaster was an eye-opening event for us," says Brian Bartow, general counsel for the California State Teachers' Retirement System, a large pension fund that is a major holder in Massey stock. "We re-examined the risks that the company was running in the way it does business. In our view, it has a lot in common with the subprime mortgage crisis—there are a lot of risks here that Massey is not acknowledging."

I ask Bartow if he believes Blankenship should resign. "He should," he says. "He clearly doesn't get it."

Blankenship could still orchestrate a smooth exit for himself, perhaps by selling Massey to a rival company. But however his career comes to an end, his story is a deeply tragic one. Given his local roots and his business acumen, he might have helped West Virginia turn toward the future and imagine itself as something more than a landscape to be raped and pillaged by greedy industrialists. Instead, he has become just another coal baron, a symbol of all the worst impulses of American capitalism.

"One thing that is hard to take about Don Blankenship is how he betrayed his own people," says Bruce Stanley, the lawyer who grew up in Mingo County. "West Virginians have always looked at their plight and blamed outsiders: 'It's the coal barons and lumber kings from the North who have come in and stolen our resources, left us poor and broken.' But Blankenship is a Mingo County boy. He took over control of a coal company and rose to the top—and it turned him into an asshole. Blankenship could have easily been a hero, not a villain. He could have said to the people of Appalachia, 'Let me show you how to pick yourself up by your bootstraps. Let me show you how to make something of yourself.' Instead he said, 'Fuck it—I'm king.'"

If any of this troubles Blankenship, he doesn't let on. By his own accounting, the bottom line provides all the proof he needs of his virtue. "I don't care what people think," he once said during a talk to a gathering of Republican Party leaders in West Virginia. "At the end of the day, Don Blankenship is going to die with more money than he needs."

## The Guardian

As recently as last July, it wasn't entirely clear who in the United Kingdom was the more powerful: the British prime minister or Rupert Murdoch, whose vast media properties hold enormous sway over the country's political life. Politicians, even prime ministers, kowtowed to him to the point that Murdoch himself would testify, "I wish they'd leave me alone." Today, it is clear who is the more powerful, thanks in large part to reporter Nick Davies and his editors at the *Guardian*. For years, Davies and his colleagues dug into allegations of phone hacking and other misdeeds at the notorious *News of the World*, Murdoch's largest and most feared tabloid. One story, in particular, gripped the public's imagination and boosted the years-long hacking probe, which in the end triggered a cascade of official investigations, parliamentary hearings, and social-media uproar that many believe has permanently altered Britain's cloistered political culture. Davies revealed that among the thousands of the paper's hacking victims was a missing thirteen-year-old girl who at the time was the subject of a nationwide police search. She later turned up murdered. And in an ironic twist, the endless series of phone-hacking investigations has now revealed that *NotW* hirelings might not have deleted some of Dowler's messages after all. But there's no doubt that the full scope of Murdoch's hacking would never have become clear without Davies's assiduous reporting.

Nick Davies and
Amelia Hill

# 2. Missing Milly Dowler's Voicemail Was Hacked by *News of the World*

The *News of the World* illegally targeted the missing schoolgirl Milly Dowler and her family in March 2002, interfering with police inquiries into her disappearance, an investigation by the *Guardian* has established.

Scotland Yard is investigating the episode, which is likely to put new pressure on the then editor of the paper, Rebekah Brooks, now Rupert Murdoch's chief executive in the UK; and the then deputy editor, Andy Coulson, who resigned in January as the prime minister's media adviser.

The Dowlers' family lawyer, Mark Lewis, this afternoon issued a statement describing the *News of the World*'s activities as "heinous" and "despicable." He said this afternoon the Dowler family was now pursuing a damages claim against the *News of the World*.

Milly Dowler disappeared at the age of thirteen on her way home in Walton-on-Thames, Surrey, on 21 March 2002.

Detectives from Scotland Yard's new inquiry into the phone hacking, Operation Weeting, are believed to have found evidence of the targeting of the Dowlers in a collection of 11,000 pages of notes kept by Glenn Mulcaire, the private investigator jailed for phone hacking on behalf of the *News of the World*.

In the last four weeks the Met officers have approached Surrey police and taken formal statements from some of those involved in the original inquiry, who were concerned about how *News of the World* journalists intercepted—and deleted—the voicemail messages of Milly Dowler.

The messages were deleted by journalists in the first few days after Milly's disappearance in order to free up space for more messages. As a result friends and relatives of Milly concluded wrongly that she might still be alive. Police feared evidence may have been destroyed.

The *Guardian* investigation has shown that, within a very short time of Milly vanishing, *News of the World* journalists reacted by engaging in what was standard practice in their newsroom: they hired private investigators to get them a story.

Their first step was simple, albeit illegal. Paperwork seen by the *Guardian* reveals that they paid a Hampshire private investigator, Steve Whittamore, to obtain home addresses and, where necessary, ex-directory phone numbers for any families called Dowler in the Walton area. The three addresses Whittamore found could be obtained lawfully on the electoral register. The two ex-directory numbers, however, were "blagged" illegally from British Telecom's confidential records by one of Whittamore's associates, John Gunning, who works from a base in Wiltshire. One of the ex-directory numbers was attributed by Whittamore to Milly's family home.

Then, with the help of its own full-time private investigator, Glenn Mulcaire, the *News of the World* started illegally intercepting mobile phone messages. Scotland Yard is now investigating evidence that the paper hacked directly into the voicemail of the missing girl's own phone. As her friends and parents called and left messages imploring Milly to get in touch with them, the *News of the World* was listening and recording their every private word.

But the journalists at the *News of the World* then encountered a problem. Milly's voicemail box filled up and would accept no more messages. Apparently thirsty for more information from more voicemails, the paper intervened—and deleted the messages that had been left in the first few days after her disappearance. According to one source, this had a devastating effect: when her friends and family called again and discovered that her voicemail had been cleared, they concluded that this must have been done by Milly herself and, therefore, that she must still be alive. But she was not. The interference created false hope and extra agony for those who were misled by it.

The Dowler family then granted an exclusive interview to the *News of the World* in which they talked about their hope, quite unaware that it had been falsely kindled by the newspaper's own intervention. Sally Dowler told the paper: "If Milly walked through the door, I don't think we'd be able to speak. We'd just weep tears of joy and give her a great big hug."

The deletion of the messages also caused difficulties for the police by confusing the picture when they had few leads to pursue. It also potentially destroyed valuable evidence.

According to one senior source familiar with the Surrey police investigation: "It can happen with abduction murders that the perpetrator will leave messages, asking the missing person to get in touch, as part of their efforts at concealment. We need those messages as evidence. Anybody who destroys that evidence is seriously interfering with the course of a police investigation."

The paper made little effort to conceal the hacking from its readers. On 14 April 2002 it published a story about a woman allegedly pretending to be Milly Dowler who had applied for a job with a recruitment agency: "It is thought the hoaxer even gave the agency Milly's real mobile number . . . the agency used the number to contact Milly when a job vacancy arose and left a message on her voicemail . . . it was on March 27, six days after Milly went missing, that the employment agency appears to have phoned her mobile."

The newspaper also made no effort to conceal its activity from Surrey police. After it had hacked the message from the recruitment agency on Milly's phone, the paper informed police about it.

It was Surrey detectives who established that the call was not intended for Milly Dowler. At the time, Surrey police suspected that phones belonging to detectives and to Milly's parents also were being targeted.

One of those who was involved in the original inquiry said: "We'd arrange landline calls. We didn't trust our mobiles."

However, they took no action against the *News of the World*, partly because their main focus was to find the missing schoolgirl and partly because this was only one example of tabloid misbehavior. As one source close to the inquiry put it: "There was a hell of a lot of dirty stuff going on." Two earlier Yard inquiries had failed to investigate the relevant notes in Mulcaire's logs.

In a statement, the family's lawyer said the Dowlers were distressed at the revelation. "It is distress heaped upon tragedy to learn that the *News of the World* had no humanity at such a terrible time. The fact that they were prepared to act in such a heinous way that could have jeopardized the police investigation and give them false hope is despicable," Lewis said.

The *News of the World*'s investigation was part of a long campaign against pedophiles championed by the then editor, Rebekah Brooks. The Labour MP Tom Watson last week told the House of Commons that four months after Milly Dowler's disappearance the *News of the World* had targeted one of the parents of the two ten-year-old Soham girls, Jessica Chapman and Holly Wells, who were abducted and murdered on 4 August 2002.

The behavior of tabloid newspapers became an issue in the trial of Levi Bellfield, who last month was jailed for life for murdering Milly. A second charge, that he had attempted to abduct another Surrey schoolgirl, Rachel Cowles, had to be left on file after premature publicity by tabloids was held to have made it impossible for the jury to reach a fair verdict. The tabloids, however, focused their anger on Bellfield's defense lawyer, complaining that the questioning had caused unnecessary pain to Milly Dowler's parents.

Surrey police referred all questions on the subject to Scotland Yard, who said they could not discuss it.

The *News of the World*'s parent company News International, part of Murdoch's media empire, said: "We have been co-operating fully with Operation Weeting since our voluntary disclosure in January restarted the investigation into illegal voicemail interception. This particular case is clearly a development of great concern and we will be conducting our own inquiry as a result. We will obviously co-operate fully with any police request on this should we be asked."

**The Guardian**

In this lucid discussion of the significance of revelations of systemic wrongdoing at *News of the World*, the press critic Jay Rosen puts his finger on something important: namely, that the culture of Murdoch's News Corp. is different from that of other public companies in that denial is engrained and woven into its ethos. Moreover, he writes, it deploys its journalism for purposes that are unique to News Corp. and have nothing to do with informing the public.

Jay Rosen

# 3. Phone-Hacking Crisis Shows News Corp Is No Ordinary News Company

Watching the phone hacking crisis crack wide open over the last few weeks has left me puzzled about its ultimate causes: what is it about News Corp. that has produced these events?

I don't think we understand very much about this. We can say things like, "Ultimate responsibility goes to the man at the top," meaning Rupert Murdoch, chairman and CEO. And that sounds right, but it still doesn't explain how any of it happened. "The key people are criminals, liars, or willfully blind . . ." We could say that, but then we would have to explain how so many of them ended up at one company.

Puzzles like these have led many people to the conclusion that there's a culture inside News Corp. that is in some way responsible, and I basically agree with that. Mark Lewis, lawyer for the family of Milly Dowler, said after Rebekah Brooks resigned: "This is not just about one individual but about the culture of an organization." Carl Bernstein agrees.

He wrote this in *Newsweek* a few days ago:

As anyone in the business will tell you, the standards and culture of a journalistic institution are set from the top down, by its owner, publisher, and top editors. Reporters and editors do not routinely break the law, bribe policemen, wiretap, and generally conduct themselves like thugs unless it is a matter of recognized and understood policy.

Private detectives and phone hackers do not become the primary sources of a newspaper's information without the tacit knowledge and approval of the people at the top, all the more so in the case of newspapers owned by Rupert Murdoch, according to those who know him best."

Bernstein tells us that one of his sources is a former executive at News Corp., who says: "Murdoch invented and established this culture in the newsroom, where you do whatever it takes to get the story, take no prisoners, destroy the competition, and the end will justify the means."

I think this is correct as far as it goes, but now I want to introduce my theory of how this culture works and why it exists in the first place.

When the news broke that the Murdochs had hired the Edelman firm to handle public relations in the UK, I thought to myself, "Edelman has a crisis response practice, but do they have a denial division?"

Because to me that is the most striking thing about the way News Corp. has reacted to these events from the beginning. Denial! Not only in the sense of deflecting questions with "move along, nothing to see here . . ." (when, in fact, there is something) but that deeper sense of denial we invoke when we say that a woman is in denial about her unfaithful husband or a man about his coming mortality.

Denial is somehow built into the culture of News Corp., more so than any normal company. It isn't normal for the CEO to say, as Murdoch said on July 15, that his company had handled the crisis "extremely well in every way possible," making just "minor mistakes," when the next day the executive in charge (Rebekah

Brooks) resigns, then a day later gets arrested, followed by Murdoch's closest aide, Les Hinton, who also resigned in hopes of reversing the tide of defeats.

Your top people don't quit for minor mistakes, but no one in News Corp. seemed troubled by that July 15 statement. The *Wall Street Journal* reported it without raising an eyebrow. Murdoch was confronted with his "minor mistakes" quote in Tuesday's parliamentary hearing but he turned down the chance to take it back. Where does denial so massive come from?

Here's my little theory: News Corp. is not a news company at all, but a global media empire that employs its newspapers—and in the United States, Fox News—as a lobbying arm. The logic of holding these "press" properties is to wield influence on behalf of the rest of the (much bigger and more profitable) media business and also to satisfy Murdoch's own power urges.

However, this fact, fairly obvious to outside observers, is actually concealed from the company by its own culture. So here we find the source for the river of denial that runs through News Corp.

Fox News and the newspapers Murdoch owns are described by News Corp., and understood by most who work there as "normal" news organizations. But they aren't, really. What makes them different is not that they have a more conservative take on the world—that's the fiction in which opponents and supporters join—but rather: news is not their first business. Wielding influence is.

Scaring politicians into going along with News Corp.'s plans. Building up an atmosphere of fear and paranoia, which then admits Rupert into the back door of 10 Downing Street.

But none of these facts can be admitted into company psychology, because the flag that its news-related properties fly, the legend on the license, doesn't say "lobbying arm of the Murdoch empire." No. It says "First Amendment" or "Journalism" or "Public Service" or "news and information."

In this sense the company is built on a lie, but a necessary lie to preserve certain fictions that matter to Murdoch and his heirs. And that, I believe, explains how it got itself into this phone hacking mess. All the other lies follow from that big one.

Strangely, I do not think that News Corp. people like Rebekah Brooks and James Murdoch are being insincere when they pledge allegiance to the values of good journalism. On the contrary, they believe that this is what their newspapers are all about. And this is the sense in which denial is constitutive of the company, a built-in feature that cannot be acknowledged by any of the major players because self-annihilation would be the result.

**The New Statesman**

After his car broke down in the English countryside in late 2010, Hugh Grant, the leading man known for his insouciant charm in such films as *Love Actually* and *About a Boy*, found himself approached by a man getting out of a white van. Help on the way? Just the opposite: it was a former *News of the World* reporter and freelance paparazzo, Paul McMullan, camera in hand. But, after a chat, Grant accepted an invitation to visit McMullan at his pub in Dover, and he turned the tables on the former reporter, secretly taping a conversation in which McMullan's freely discusses his career as a phone hacker. The result is a hilarious transcript that could well have been written for the Theater of the Absurd.

# 4. The Bugger, Bugged

When I broke down in my midlife crisis car in remotest Kent just before Christmas, a battered white van pulled up on the far carriageway. To help, I thought. But when the driver got out he started taking pictures with a long-lens camera. He came closer to get better shots and I swore at him. Then he offered me a lift the last few miles to my destination. I suspected his motives and swore at him some more. (I'm not entirely sympathetic towards paparazzi.) Then I realized I couldn't get a taxi and was late. So I had to accept the lift.

He turned out to be an ex–*News of the World* investigative journalist and paparazzo, now running a pub in Dover. He still kept his camera in the car's glove box for just this kind of happy accident.

More than that, he was Paul McMullan, one of two ex-*NoW* hacks who had blown the whistle (in the *Guardian* and on Channel 4's *Dispatches*) on the full extent of phone hacking at the paper, particularly under its former editor Andy Coulson. This was interesting, as I had been a victim—a fact he confirmed as we drove along. He also had an unusual defense of the practice: that phone hacking was a price you had to pay for living in a free society. I asked how that worked exactly, but we ran out of time, and next thing we had arrived and he was asking me if I would pose for a photo with him, "not for publication, just for the wall of the pub."

I agreed and the picture duly appeared in the *Mail* on Sunday that weekend with his creative version of the encounter. He had asked me to drop into his pub some time. So when, some months later, Jemima asked me to write a piece for this paper, it occurred to me it might be interesting to take him up on his invitation.

I wanted to hear more about phone hacking and the whole business of tabloid journalism. It occurred to me just to interview him straight, as he has, after all, been a whistleblower. But then I thought I might possibly get more, and it might be more fun, if I secretly taped him, The bugger bugged, as it were. Here are some excerpts from our conversation.

ME:     So, how's the whistleblowing going?

HIM:    I'm trying to get a book published. I sent it off to a
        publisher who immediately accepted it and then
        it got legal and they said, "This is never going to get
        published."

ME:     Why? Because it accuses too many people of
        crime?

HIM:    Yes, as I said to the parliamentary commission,
        Coulson knew all about it and regularly ordered
        it. . . . He [Coulson] rose quickly to the top; he
        wanted to cover his tracks all the time. So he
        wouldn't just write a story about a celeb who'd done
        something. He'd want to make sure they could
        never sue, so he wanted us to hear the celeb like you
        on tape saying, "Hello, darling, we had lovely sex
        last night." So that's on tape—OK, we've got that
        and so we can publish. . . . Historically, the way it
        went was, in the early days of mobiles, we all had
        analogue mobiles and that was an absolute joy. You
        know, you just . . . sat outside Buckingham Palace

with a £59 scanner you bought at Argos and get
Prince Charles and everything he said.

ME: Is that how the Squidgy tapes [of Diana's phone
conversations] came out? Which was put down to
radio hams, but was in fact . . .

HIM: Paps in the back of a van, yes . . . I mean, politicians
were dropping like flies in the nineties because it
was so easy to get stuff on them. And, obviously,
less easy to justify is celebrities. But yes.

ME: And . . . it wasn't just the *News of the World*. It was,
you know—the *Mail*?

HIM: Oh absolutely, yeah. When I went freelance in 2004
the biggest payers—you'd have thought it would
be the *NoW*, but actually it was the *Daily Mail*.
If I take a good picture, the first person I go to
is—such as in your case—the *Mail* on Sunday.
Did you see that story? The picture of you, breaking
down . . . I ought to thank you for that. I got £3,000.
Whooo!

ME: But would they [the *Mail*] buy a phone-hacked
story?

HIM: For about four or five years they've absolutely been
cleaner than clean. And before that they weren't.
They were as dirty as anyone. . . . They had the most
money.

ME: So everyone knew? I mean, would Rebekah Wade
have known all this stuff was going on?

HIM: Good question. You're not taping, are you?

ME: [slightly shrill voice] No.

HIM: Well, yeah. Clearly she . . . took over the job of
[a journalist] who had a scanner who was trying to
sell it to members of his own department. But it
wasn't a big crime. [NB: Rebekah Brooks has always
denied any knowledge of phone hacking. The

current police investigation is into events that took place after her editorship of the *News of the World*.]

It started off as fun—you know, it wasn't against the law, so why wouldn't you? And it was only because the MPs who were fiddling their expenses and being generally corrupt kept getting caught so much they changed the law in 2001 to make it illegal to buy and sell a digital scanner. So all we were left with was—you know—finding a blag to get your mobile [records] out of someone at Vodafone. Or, when someone's got it, other people swap things for it.

ME: So they all knew? Wade probably knew all about it all?

HIM: [ . . . ] Cameron must have known—that's the bigger scandal. He had to jump into bed with Murdoch as everyone had, starting with Thatcher in the seventies . . . Tony Blair . . . [tape is hard to hear here] Maggie openly courted Murdoch, saying, you know, "Please support me." So when Cameron, when it came his turn to go to Murdoch via Rebekah Wade . . . Cameron went horse riding regularly with Rebekah. I know, because as well as doorstepping celebrities, I've also doorstepped my ex-boss by hiding in the bushes, waiting for her to come past with Cameron on a horse . . . before the election to show that—you know—Murdoch was backing Cameron.

ME: What happened to that story?

HIM: The Guardian paid for me to do it and I stepped in it and missed them, basically. They'd gone past—not as good as having a picture.

ME: Do you think Murdoch knew about phone hacking?

HIM: Errr, possibly not. He's a funny bloke given that he owns the *Sun* and the *Screws* . . . quite puritanical. Sorry to talk about Divine Brown, but when that came out . . . Murdoch was furious: "What are you putting that on our front page for? You're bringing down the tone of our papers." [Indicating himself] That's what we do over here.

ME: Well, it's also because it was his film I was about to come out in.

HIM: Oh. I see.

ME: Yeah. It was a Fox film.

[A pause here while we chat to other customers, and then—]

HIM: So anyway, let me finish my story.

ME: Murdoch, yes . . .

HIM: So I was sent to do a feature on *Moulin Rouge!* at Cannes, which was a great send anyway. Basically my brief was to see who Nicole Kidman was shagging—what she was doing, poking through her bins and get some stuff on her. So Murdoch's paying her five million quid to big up the French and at the same time paying me £5.50 to fuck her up. . . . So all hail the master. We're just pawns in his game. How perverse is that?

ME: Wow. You reckon he never knew about it?

HIM: [pause] I don't even think he really worried himself too much about it.

ME: What's his son called?

HIM: James. They're all mates together. They all go horse riding. You've got Jeremy Clarkson lives here [in Oxfordshire]. Cameron lives here, and Rebekah Wade is married to Brooks's son [the former racehorse trainer Charlie Brooks]. Cameron gets dressed up as the Stig to go to Clarkson's fiftieth birthday party [NB: it was actually to record a video message for the party]. Is that demeaning for a prime minister? It should be the other way round, shouldn't it? So basically, Cameron is very much in debt to Rebekah Wade for helping him not quite win the election. . . . So that was my submission to Parliament—that Cameron's either a liar or an idiot.

ME: But don't you think that all these prime ministers deliberately try to get the police to drag their feet about investigating the whole [phone hacking] thing because they don't want to upset Murdoch?

HIM: Yeah. There's that . . . You also work a lot with policemen as well . . . One of the early stories was [and here he names a much-loved TV actress in her sixties] used to be a street walker—whether or not she was, but that's the tip.

ME AND
CHUM: MLTVA?!

ME: I can't believe it. Oh no!

CHUM: Really??

HIM: Yeah. Well, not now . . .

CHUM: Oh, it'd be so much better if it was now.

HIM: So I asked a copper to get his hands on the phone files, but because it's only a caution it's not there any more. So that's the tip . . . it's a policeman ringing up a tabloid reporter and asking him for ten grand because this girl had been cautioned right at the start of his career. And then I ask another policemen to go and check the records. . . . So that's happening regularly. So the police don't particularly want to investigate.

ME: But do you think they're going to have to now?

HIM: I mean—20 per cent of the Met has taken back-handers from tabloid hacks. So why would they want to open up that can of worms? . . . And what's wrong with that, anyway? It doesn't hurt anyone particularly. I mean, it could hurt someone's career—but isn't that the dance with the devil you have to play?

ME: Well, I suppose the fact that they're dragging their feet while investigating a mass of phone hacking—which is a crime—some people would think is a bit depressing about the police.

HIM: But then—should it be a crime? I mean, scanning never used to be a crime. Why should it be? You're transmitting your thoughts and your voice over the airwaves. How can you not expect someone to just stick up an aerial and listen in?

ME: So if someone was on a landline and you had a way of tapping in . . .

HIM: Much harder to do.

ME: But if you could, would you think that was illegal? Do you think that should be illegal?

HIM: I'd have to say quite possibly, yeah. I'd say that should be illegal.

ME: But a mobile phone—a digital phone . . . you'd say it'd be all right to tap that?

HIM: I'm not sure about that. So we went from a point where anyone could listen in to anything. Like you, me, journalists could listen in to corrupt politicians, and this is why we have a reasonably fair society and a not particularly corrupt or criminal prime minister, whereas other countries have Gaddafi. Do you think it's right the only person with a decent digital scanner these days is the government? Whereas twenty years ago we all had a go? Are you comfortable that the only people who can listen in to you now are—is it MI5 or MI6?

ME:     I'd rather no one listened in, to be honest. And I might not be alone there. You probably wouldn't want people listening to your conversations.

HIM:    I'm not interesting enough for anyone to want to listen in.

ME:     Ah . . . I think that was one of the questions asked last week at one of the parliamentary committees. They asked Yates [John Yates, acting deputy commissioner of the Metropolitan Police] if it was true that he thought that the *NoW* had been hacking the phones of friends and family of those girls who were murdered . . . the Soham murder and the Milly girl [Milly Dowler].

HIM:    Yeah. Yeah. It's more than likely. Yeah . . . It was quite routine. Yeah—friends and family is something that's not as easy to justify as the other things.

ME:     But celebrities you would justify because they're rich?

HIM:    Yeah. I mean, if you don't like it, you've just got to get off the stage. It'll do wonders.

ME:     So I should have given up acting?

HIM:    If you live off your image, you can't really complain about someone . . .

ME:     I live off my acting. Which is different to living off your image.

HIM:    Yeah, but you're still presenting yourself to the public. And if the public didn't know you—

ME:     They don't give a shit. I got arrested with a hooker and they still came to my films. They don't give a fuck about your public image. They just care about whether you're in an entertaining film or not.

HIM:    That's true . . . I have terrible difficulty with him [points to pap shot of Johnny Depp]. He's really difficult. You know, I was in Venice and he was a nightmare to do because he walks around looking like Michael Jackson. And the punchline was . . . after leading everyone a merry dance the film was shot on an open balcony—I mean, it was like—he was standing there in public.

ME: And you don't see the difference between the two situations?

CHUM: He was actually working at this time? As opposed to having his own private time?

HIM: You can't hide all the time.

ME: So you're saying, if you're Johnny Depp or me, you don't deserve to have a private life?

HIM: You make so much more money. You know, most people in Dover take home about £200 and struggle.

ME: So how much do you think the families of the Milly and Soham girls make?

HIM: OK, so there are examples that are poor and you can't justify—and that's clearly one of them.

ME: I tell you the thing I still don't get—if you think it was all right to do all that stuff, why blow the whistle on it?

HIM: Errm . . . right. That's interesting. I actually blew the whistle when a friend of mine at the *Guardian* kept hassling me for an interview. I said, "Well if you put the name of the Castle [his pub] on the front page of the *Guardian*, I'll do anything you like." So that's how it started.

ME: So, have you been leant on by the *NoW*, News International, since you blew the whistle?

HIM: No, they've kept their distance. I mean, there's people who have much better records—my records are nonexistent. There are people who actually have tapes and transcripts they did for Andy Coulson.

ME:     And where are these tapes and transcripts? Do you think they've been destroyed?

HIM:    No, I'm sure they're saving them till they retire.

ME:     So did you personally ever listen to my voice messages?

HIM:    No, I didn't personally ever listen to your voice messages. I did quite a lot of stories on you, though. You were a very good earner at times.

Those are the highlights. As I drove home past the white cliffs, I thought it was interesting—apart from the fact that Paul hates people like me, and I hate people like him, we got on quite well. And, absurdly, I felt a bit guilty for recording him.

And he does have a very nice pub. The Castle Inn, Dover, for the record. There are rooms available, too. He asked me if I'd like to sample the honeymoon suite some time: "I can guarantee your privacy."

## Milwaukee Journal Sentinel

"We were told to keep things running at all costs," said a former employee of a family-owned health care products firm where Food and Drug Administration inspectors found multiple violations of good manufacturing procedures. When the shutdown finally came, it was too late for a two-year-old boy and his family. Raquel Rutledge and Rick Barrett of the *Journal Sentinel* document the failures that led to a sadly preventable death in a meticulously reported and beautifully written account that won the Silver Award in the annual Barlett & Steele contest, which recognizes outstanding investigative reporting focused on business.

Raquel Rutledge and
Rick Barrett

# 5. A Case of Shattered Trust

Houston—In the photograph, they walk together through the hospital hallway, two-year-old Harrison Kothari smiling as he reaches up to hold his parents' hands, his blue gown nearly touching the floor. Mom and Dad gaze down at the "little angel" they tried for two years to conceive.

"I would give anything to go back to that day," says Shanoop Kothari, the boy's father. "Anything."

Days later, Harry would be sleeping.

The hospital is quiet. Shanoop, an investment banker, sits by Harry's bed doing paperwork. His wife of thirteen years, Sandy, has gone home to get some sleep. She will be coming in the morning to bring Harry home. He is well, the doctors and nurses say, recovering from a low-risk surgery.

Harry stirs. It is about ten P.M. He becomes agitated and begins to throw up.

The nurses give him some medicine and don't seem too worried. *Probably a food bug*, Shanoop thinks. But Harry's temperature shoots to 102. He asks for water. Lies back down. Then sits up for more water. He starts to hit his hands against his head.

About one A.M. Shanoop calls Sandy: "I think you need to come down."

Harry clutches his dad's shirt in desperation. "Da, Da," he says. Then his eyes roll back in his head and he has a seizure. He's never had a seizure before, but he has another one. Doctors give him antiseizure drugs.

It's just 3.2 miles from the Kotharis' house to Memorial Hermann Hospital in Houston. Sandy races through the empty streets.

It is November 29, 2010.

### A Strangely Urgent Inspection

That same day, some 1,200 miles away, three investigators and a consumer safety officer with the U.S. Food and Drug Administration are dispatched to a pharmaceutical company on the edge of a suburban office park in Hartland, Wis.

The Triad Group sells an array of health care products, including cough syrups, suppositories, creams, and ointments. Its sister company, H&P Industries, manufactures the products.

H&P also makes alcohol and iodine wipes used to clean skin before injections and surgical incisions. The family-owned firm, started in 1976, has grown into one of the nation's largest manufacturers of wipes and swabs, supplying hundreds of millions each year to hospitals and drugstore chains.

FDA investigators have been to the factory before, but this time is different. They bring cameras and other equipment. They take notes continually.

"I had never seen an audit like that before," said a former employee who did not want his name published out of fear of reprisal. "Usually they would come in, point out a few things."

This time, investigators came back the next day. And the next. They stayed for weeks.

"They weren't fooling around," the longtime employee said. "I think they knew exactly what they were looking for."

What they were looking for—and found—was a dangerous bacterium. And they would find dozens of other serious problems: children's cold medicine being made without its active ingredient; workers packaging acne pads with their bare hands; a water supply that could contaminate products; dirty utensils and equipment.

They found workers who changed the specifications of products when the products didn't meet the proper standards and sent them out anyway. The plant did not have a microbiologist on staff. And inspectors found that some employees could not read or write English, raising questions about whether they had followed directions in making products.

Each of the four investigators was familiar with the plant. FDA records show they found major problems there six months earlier—including workers not following proper procedures to sterilize alcohol wipes and suppositories containing metal shavings. They also had found problems the previous year.

In fact, the FDA—the federal agency tasked with protecting public health—had known about critical issues at the company for at least a decade but failed to take any enforcement action, an investigation by the *Journal Sentinel* has found.

Instead, inspectors gave verbal warnings and repeatedly accepted the company's promises to correct problems. And tainted products landed on store shelves and in hospital supply rooms.

"What's alarming . . . is the FDA had evidence that Triad was screwing up, talked to them about it, but did not force the issue," said Larry Smith, president of the Institute for Crisis Management, a Louisville, Ky., consulting firm not affiliated with Triad or the H&P manufacturing operation.

In January, five weeks after launching its probe, the FDA announced the firm's voluntary recall of Triad's alcohol wipes and swabsticks, citing concerns about potential contamination with deadly bacteria . But the assembly lines continued to churn out other products—one of which would later be recalled as well.

The plant would not be shut down until April.

### A Seemingly Routine Surgery

Harry Kothari was a healthy boy last August when he fell off a couch and conked his head on the wood floor of his home on Houston's southwest side. He rode a tricycle, stacked blocks, and said all the words a not-quite-two-year-old typically says: mama, airplane, thank you. He even spoke a little Spanish, thanks to the housekeeper.

The fall didn't change anything, but Sandy worried about the lump on Harry's head, so the family pediatrician ordered a scan to ensure he hadn't fractured his skull. The scan showed something else. Harry had not fractured his skull, but had a cyst on the other side of his head. If left untreated, the benign cyst had the potential to cause speech and other problems.

The Kotharis consulted three surgeons. All said the cyst was treatable and the risk of surgery was very low. So the Kotharis decided to go ahead.

In September, Stephen Fletcher, head of pediatric neurosurgery at the University of Texas Medical School, removed the cyst. All appeared to go well, according to medical records, and Harry was sent home a week later.

He celebrated his second birthday on October 23. A photo shows him happily perched on his mom's hip. A cake decorated with a giant airplane sits on the table in front of them. Home videos show him running around the house playing with his seven-year-old sister, Hannah. The next week, he went trick-or-treating dressed up as a UPS driver. He walked to a few houses but soon became bored.

"I remember thinking, 'Next year will be the perfect year. He'll be three and he'll be all excited,'" Sandy said.

At a follow-up visit, Fletcher noticed cerebrospinal fluid—the fluid that cushions the brain and circulates into the spinal cord—leaking at the site of Harry's surgical incision on his forehead.

Medication didn't stop the leakage, so on November 8, he was admitted to Memorial Hermann Hospital to have a lumbar drain inserted. The small catheter in his lower back would relieve pressure from the fluid, allowing the incision to heal.

Tests of the fluid showed no signs of infection. Doctors surmised Harry had an allergic reaction to the adhesive used during surgery to glue his skin back together. During the next three weeks, nurses regularly drew cerebrospinal fluid from the lumbar drain to test for any infection.

Before drawing the samples—following typical protocol—they wiped the area around the drain with what they assumed were sterile alcohol wipes.

## In Colorado, Alarming Infections

In October, weeks before Harry would be readmitted to the Houston hospital, officials at the Children's Hospital in Aurora, Colo., noticed strange infections cropping up.

A child with leukemia became gravely ill after hospital workers implanted an IV port in his chest. Then an infant with congenital heart disease developed a fever and was having trouble breathing a few days after doctors replaced an IV tube. Blood cultures from both patients revealed something alarming: *Bacillus cereus*, a cousin to the more widely known and feared *Bacillus antracis*, or anthrax.

*Bacillus cereus* (pronounced buh-sil-us seer-ee-uhs) is often associated with food-borne illness. While common in the soil and elsewhere in the environment, it rarely causes infections in hospitals.

"It seemed unusual," said Sue Dolan, an epidemiologist at the hospital. "The patients were pretty ill, pretty quickly."

Dolan and a team of infection-prevention experts launched an investigation to pinpoint the source. They looked at each patient, at each procedure, and sought common factors. They sorted through all the products the patients came in contact with, looking for matches.

They narrowed the possible culprit to three products, all disposable and all found in hospitals everywhere: syringes, applicators, and alcohol wipes.

The syringes and applicators tested negative for any bacterial contamination. Lab tests showed the alcohol wipes were tainted with *Bacillus cereus.*

Hospital investigators found forty of sixty wipes from about ten different lots were contaminated with the bacteria or related species. According to Dolan, all the wipes came from one company: Triad Group.

"We began pulling the alcohol prep wipes immediately that day," she said. "We didn't wait for a recall."

Hospital investigators also notified the Colorado Department of Public Health and Environment.

It was November 18, eleven days before Harry Kothari grew suddenly ill in Houston. The state health department took no immediate action. Instead, it waited until the following week to alert the U.S. Centers for Disease Control and Prevention and the FDA.

Children's Hospital "notified us they had a suspicion," said Wendy Bamberg, medical epidemiologist with the Colorado health department. "At that point the information was very preliminary.

"When we talked the following week, they had really confirmed they were getting positive results."

Yet even then, the findings didn't trigger a nationwide alert as they would have if the hospital had confirmed an outbreak of, for example, smallpox or botulism.

Six more weeks would pass before Triad and the FDA announced a voluntary Class II recall of the wipes. Class II recalls are meant for products in which adverse health effects are considered "temporary and reversible."

## Bacterium with Deadly Potential

*Bacillus cereus* is a spore-forming bacterium undaunted by heat or high concentrations of alcohol. It lingers dormant in the soil but springs to life when it finds nourishment. If ingested, it typically causes vomiting or diarrhea before the body's natural defenses knock it out.

Most people survive the usual types of exposure to *Bacillus cereus*, microbiologists and other medical experts say.

But when *Bacillus cereus* enters the blood or cerebrospinal fluid and finds a host—such as a tube or valve—it thrives. It sets up shop feeding on simple sugars and proteins, spewing out deadly toxins. And it acts quickly.

"It's got to find a niche in the body where it can multiply," said David Warshauer, deputy director of communicable disease with the Wisconsin State Laboratory of Hygiene. "Then you're going to see some serious complications."

Antibiotics such as ciprofloxacin can—but don't always—kill it.

"These are bugs that don't cause diseases unless they get somewhere where they shouldn't be," said Alex Kallen, a medical officer with the Centers for Disease Control.

It's impossible to know the true scope of such infections and where they occur because *Bacillus cereus* is not an infection the CDC recommends that hospitals report. And states—which set their own reporting requirements—don't usually notify the CDC unless they discover an outbreak.

Furthermore, the discovery of *Bacillus cereus* outbreaks is fairly rare, and particularly challenging. That's partly because hospitals don't typically track incidental products used in patients' care. A patient's record doesn't include the brand of gloves a nurse was wearing when blood was drawn or a shot was given.

Improved tracking, like retailers use with bar codes, would be helpful in identifying tainted products, Kallen said. "It would require an unbelievable amount of work," he said. "But having as much information as to what every patient is exposed to is important."

## The Role of Purchasing Groups

The way some disposable products wind up in hospitals depends on purchasing contracts for thousands of items.

Years ago, operating room nurses and other hospital staff were more involved in making decisions about which products and supplies they should buy. Hospitals today often use group purchasing organizations to buy things ranging from expensive lab equipment to antiseptic wipes.

Purchasing groups represent multiple hospitals and negotiate prices. They rely on manufacturers and the FDA to ensure product quality and safety. If something is labeled sterile, they trust it's sterile. And when there is little difference in functionality, as with an alcohol wipe, more emphasis is placed on price.

Hospitals don't visit manufacturing plants to assess quality. Purchasing organizations don't typically do that either. "I don't really see it as our place to go into a plant," said Curtis Rooney, president of the Health Industry Group Purchasing Association, a national trade group.

Spokeswoman Elizabeth Whitehead from the Children's Hospital in Colorado said her hospital has a "Value Analysis Multidisciplinary team" that reviews products on a regular basis. Input from infection-prevention staff is included, she said.

She wouldn't say what, if anything, the hospital is doing differently now to ensure it doesn't get another batch of bad products. And Whitehead would not say what company now supplies the hospital with alcohol wipes. She would only reiterate: They are "not manufactured by the Triad Group."

## As Business Grew, so Did Complaints

For decades, H&P and Triad flew below the radar of consumers and even hospital staffs. At various times H&P operated plants in Franklin, Mukwonago, Pewaukee, and Hartland. It churned out all sorts of items from suppositories to cough syrup, often generically so distributors and retailers could affix their own labels.

When founder Richard Haertle died in 1988, his three adult children, Eric Haertle, David Haertle, and Donna Petroff, took over as co-owners. His wife, Joanne, also helped run the business. "Our family came together from all over and banded together to try and keep this company going," Eric Haertle, chief operating officer, said in an interview with the *Journal Sentinel* in April. "We worked there every summer through high school and college."

The siblings continued to expand the business in the early 1990s, but it didn't take long for trouble to surface. At first, the problems centered on worker safety at the plant in Franklin.

In 1991, the federal Occupational Safety and Health Administration fined H&P for "willful, repeat, and serious" health and safety violations. As the company grew, opening a plant in Mukwonago in 1992 and adding employees to locations in Brookfield and Pewaukee, more worker-safety issues arose.

In 1998, OSHA again found workplace health and safety violations, this time at the Mukwonago plant.

In recent *Journal Sentinel* interviews, former employees said the Mukwonago plant wasn't clean—especially troublesome because it made medical products. They complained to supervisors about conditions in the bathrooms, including broken toilet seats, sewage on the floor, and no hot water. They complained about alcohol-wipe machines not being properly sanitized.

"There was nothing sanitary there at all," Ed Westrick, a seven-year machine repairman, said of the Mukwonago plant. Westrick, who left his job in 2007, said the production room was always filled with a red cloud from manufacturing iodine prep pads and swabs. The company hired people who didn't know how to run the machines, he said. Making matters worse, safety switches on the machines were often bypassed to keep lines moving, he said.

"You might come into work and find a finger that somebody lost the night before," he said. Westrick wasn't exaggerating; he knew of at least two workers who lost fingers.

While OSHA inspects factories for worker-safety issues, it does not examine product safety. That task falls to the FDA.

Quality-control employees said they also complained to managers about sloppy manufacturing practices. "They (the Haertles) had plenty of people telling them the right things to do, but they just didn't do them," said Frances Lee, a microbiologist who headed up Triad's quality/regulatory/product development unit for three years ending in 2002.

Lee said she left the company over disputes about the manufacturing process. She and others said previous president and co-owner David Haertle showed little concern for keeping the plants sterile.

"I can't make the president of the company stop eating a banana and drinking coffee on the production line," Lee said.

### Family's World Turns Upside-Down

When Sandy Kothari arrives at Hermann Memorial Hospital, her husband, Shanoop, is slumped in the corner of Harry's room, crying. Doctors and nurses are in panic mode, crowded around Harry's bed.

Sandy can't get to him. She can't even see him. Minutes pass. They rush Harry out and down the hall for a brain scan. Sandy grabs the bedrail and runs alongside.

Harry's body is under siege. Nobody has any idea what is ravaging his insides, shutting down his system. Tiny bacteria are waging a full attack on Harry's mitochondria—the power plants of his cells. As the bacteria grow and multiply, their potent poison shuts down energy production. Without power, none of Harry's organs can function.

His breathing becomes labored. Doctors insert a tube in his mouth, forcing his lungs to work. They hook him to an IV and start antibiotics. His brain swells. They give him drugs to boost his blood pressure and steroids to try to stop the swelling.

Nothing works. His brain continues to swell. They take blood and spinal fluid samples and send them to the lab.

Harry's thirty-five-pound body is losing the fight. Machines keep his heart pumping and lungs inflating. Tests confirm he is brain-dead.

"That was it," said Sandy. A boy who was walking around, eating, playing, happy, hours before, is gone.

Results from the lab come back that afternoon: *Bacillus cereus*. Like the doctors, the Kotharis have no idea how it got into Harry's body.

Hannah, too, cannot understand what has happened. Nothing makes sense. He is her baby brother. She used to run across the hall to his crib every morning. They chased around the house, took baths together. On Harry's second birthday, a month earlier, Hannah gave him a talking teddy bear and showered him with kisses.

"Why can't we just keep him on the machine?" she asks. "Just don't take him off the machine," she pleads.

Sandy and Shanoop try to explain that Harry is broken and they can't fix him.

The next day, Hannah lays her head on Harry's chest as all life support is turned off. "His heart stopped," she whispers.

## Inspection Reports Redacted

It's impossible for the public to know when regulators first discovered *Bacillus cereus* at H&P's plant because the FDA heavily redacted details from a decade's worth of inspection reports provided to the *Journal Sentinel* under the Freedom of Information Act.

Records do show inspectors found the bacterium—which was the basis for the January recall of the alcohol wipes—during their weeks-long inspection starting November 29. That was revealed only after the newspaper challenged the redaction.

The newspaper's review shows H&P had serious problems including trouble with cleanliness—and that FDA inspectors knew it—as far back as 2000.

Medikmark Inc., an Illinois company that sold medical kits that included Triad products, alleges Triad was aware of sterility issues as early as 2002 and continuing until the recent product recalls. "The products Medikmark purchased from Triad were unreasonably and inherently dangerous," according to a lawsuit Medikmark filed this year after the nationwide recall of antiseptic wipes.

Triad has strongly denied the allegations, saying its products met FDA requirements. "We would not be manufacturing for more than thirty years if we did not take quality seriously," Eric Haertle told the *Journal Sentinel* in April.

From 2000 through 2003, inspection records show the FDA noted fourteen violations of good manufacturing practices at H&P's plants, including not properly testing its water supply for purity and mislabeling products. The labeling is important to make sure rejected products don't get mixed with approved ones or that unsterile products aren't marked as sterile.

In a two-year period, from 2002 to 2003, the company received more than 250 complaints from customers voicing concerns about product-related rashes and dry antiseptic wipes and swabs.

FDA inspectors found the company did not adequately investigate the complaints. Yet the agency took no enforcement action.

In October 2004, Triad began receiving a higher than usual number of complaints, this time about moldy cosmetic wipes. Yet it took more than two months for the company to notify the FDA and announce a recall, according to a February 2005 FDA inspection report. In addition, the company failed to recall all affected lots and didn't log all customer complaints, as required.

Inspector Jeffry A. Bernhardt wrote: "I questioned [the vice president of quality assurance] why none of the lots with associated complaints were being recalled and why none of the recalled lots have complaints in the file. He stated that he was new in his position at the time the complaints came in and he did not handle them as formal complaints." Bernhardt suggested the company improve its complaint tracking system and took no enforcement action.

Around that same time, in 2004 and 2005, a cluster of people in Beverly Hills sued Triad after they had liposuction procedures, alleging the company's lubrication jelly used in the process had caused infections. The sixteen people settled the case out of court. Terms were not disclosed.

In 2006, customers began reporting odd colors on alcohol prep wipes. When an FDA inspector went to the plant, he wrote up the company for "failure to adequately address potential contamination in Raw Material." Again, the violation resulted in no penalties.

## Employees Concerned

When H&P opened the Hartland factory in 2007—consolidating operations from Mukwonago, Brookfield, and Pewaukee—Eric Haertle told Hartland officials it would be a "world class" manufacturing plant . Yet Kathleen Smith and other former employees interviewed by the *Journal Sentinel* say it didn't turn out that way.

Smith, a former quality-control inspector at the Hartland plant, predicted Triad's products might kill someone someday. The company's inspectors were threatened with their jobs if they tried to stop a production line because it was not properly sanitized or if they complained about employees having dirt under their fingernails, according to Smith and other former employees.

After working two stints at H&P covering about eight months in 2009 and 2010, Smith said she was fired for unsatisfactory work performance. She believes it was because she complained about things such as employees sneaking food and personal items into areas of the factory that made sterile products.

"Oh, God, people knew what was going on," Smith said. "We called attention to problems constantly." When an employee cut her finger while packing alcohol wipe packets, according to Smith, the wipes were shipped with blood inside and outside the box. Smith said she brought it to the attention of a supervisor but nothing was done.

"We were told to keep things running at all cost. But I asked, at the cost of what? People's lives? You don't care if people die?

"I should have gone to the FDA and told them what was going on," Smith said. "But they were there and knew it. And they kept letting them run and letting them run."

In 2009, the FDA found serious problems at the Hartland plant. The inspectors—Marie A. Fadden, Sandra A. Hughes, and Joel D. Hustedt—noted twenty-one violations of good manufacturing practices, a set of guidelines used to assure public safety. For example, drugs that didn't meet product specifications were tagged as being acceptable; equipment was dirty; products were left uncovered. The firm had not been reporting health-related complaints to the FDA and it was not able to produce any documentation that bottles and tubes of lubricating jelly were sterile.

Still, the FDA took no enforcement action. "This is an area that should be covered in depth during the next inspection," inspectors wrote about proof of sterilization.

In May 2010, Hughes and Hustedt went back to the plant along with another inspector, Justin A. Boyd, and found the company still wasn't able to verify it had sterilized the lubricating jelly. This time they found evidence the sterilization process the company used was not adequate, according to documents.

After the inspection, Triad recalled hundreds of cases of suppositories with the Walgreen's label on them. The recall was initiated because of potential contamination and involved nearly 750 cases of products. The recall notice didn't specify the contaminant, but a partially unredacted FDA document shows they were tainted by aluminum and stainless steel shavings. H&P spokeswoman Christy Maginn said that none of the suppositories in question ever reached the public and that the company has installed a metal detector.

Again, the investigators took no enforcement action and left with only promises that improvements would be made.

## Feds Finally Shut Plant

Six months after that inspection, word came from the Colorado health department: A hospital had discovered Triad's alcohol wipes were contaminated with *Bacillus cereus*. And on November 29, the same four inspectors who had been at the plant in 2009 and earlier in 2010 were sent back to 700 W. North Shore Drive in Hartland. They scoured the plant for weeks and found forty-six violations of good manufacturing practices.

A bucket labeled "purified water" was actually deionized water used to rinse equipment after cleaning. Water pipes leading to vats that made batches of mouth rinse and glycerin suppositories had microbial contamination.

And there, listed as "Observation 7" on page five of the thirty-page report by FDA inspectors, is the one violation most devastating to the Kothari family: "Sterile alcohol prep wipes were found to be contaminated with *Bacillus cereus* organisms and were released for shipment after confirmation of the results," the inspection report noted.

In the copy of the inspection report initially provided to the *Journal Sentinel*, the FDA redacted the name of the specific organisms that contaminated the wipes saying it was considered trade secret and confidential information. After the newspaper appealed, the agency on Friday provided a new version that included the *Bacillus cereus* reference.

"The name of the bacteria is obviously a public health issue" rather than a trade secret, said Sidney Wolfe, a physician and official with Public Citizen, a nonprofit consumer advocacy group. "It isn't as though the company invented this bacteria."

Maginn, the H&P spokeswoman, said Friday the wipes contained only a "trace amount" of *Bacillus cereus*. She acknowledged some of the product was shipped—inadvertently—but said it did not reach the public.

Six months earlier, the same inspectors had noted that H&P employees were not following proper procedures for sterilizing alcohol wipes. The specifics of that violation were also redacted.

On January 3, Triad voluntarily recalled all lots of its alcohol wipes and swab sticks—saying it was taking the action "out of an abundance of caution" and contending that no link had been made to an illness. A separate announcement by the FDA identified the potential contaminant as *Bacillus cereus*.

H&P assembly lines kept making other products, including iodine wipes that would later be recalled after inspectors found lots at the factory contaminated with another dangerous bacterium.

No investigation was conducted to identify the source of the contamination, according to a March 28 report. The raw material and foil were identified as potential sources of contamination of the alcohol wipes, the report said. Moreover, FDA investigators found *Bacillus cereus* in benzalkonium chloride towelettes, an antiseptic wipe.

Finally, on April 4, FDA regulators took a rare step and sought the help of U.S. marshals, who swept into the factory and seized $6 million worth of products, effectively shutting the plant down.

"The firm was certainly aware of the [Colorado] hospital's findings and the CDC's findings," said Michael Rogers, acting director of the FDA's Office of Regional Operations. "If a firm disagrees with our belief that products should be removed from the market, then we have to take more aggressive steps."

Eric Haertle defended his company's decision to keep production going even after the discovery of contaminated alcohol wipes in Colorado, Harry's death, and the FDA's findings. The company shut its alcohol products production line one day after the FDA said there was potential contamination, Haertle said in a written statement last week in response to questions from the newspaper. "The info provided [from Colorado] was all verbal without any supporting proof other than their word. We immediately opened up an investigation to assess the complaint and, without receiving any further information from the FDA, decided to be proactive and shut down our [alcohol] pad manufacturing lines," Haertle said. He said it takes weeks to get some microbial test results.

"At no time did the company knowingly allow contaminated material to leave the factory or release products slated for hold due to various reasons," he said. "In the case of shipments mistakenly sent, product was immediately recalled."

When the marshals arrived, H&P employees were told to go to the lunchroom. Marshals searched the building to make sure no one was still at a work station. They guarded the doors to the lunchroom.

Eric Haertle told employees the plant was being asked to close—at least temporarily. Then employees were told to go home. "I have people who are very hurt by what has transpired," Haertle said in April. "When I had to look them in the eye and tell them that we were done for the time being, it wasn't easy."

### FDA Defends Prior Leniency

Under its own rules, the FDA could have acted sooner and with more force at H&P. The agency could have issued warning letters demanding that problems with contamination and sterilization be corrected. Those letters become a public blemish on a company's record. The FDA also could have sought a court order to shut the plant. And it has the authority to seek criminal prosecution that could result in jail time and fines.

According to an FDA manual, when inspectors find even one problem that jeopardizes the "quality, identity, strength and purity" of products, they should classify the report as "official action indicated"—the precursor to formal agency action.

Inspectors didn't do that, according to inspection reports from 2000 to 2010. Instead they classified the reports as "voluntary action indicated" or "no action indicated," even when they found the company wasn't properly testing its water and when batches of products didn't meet specifications.

In an interview in May, Rogers of the FDA defended the agency's oversight of H&P, including the lack of warning letters and other corrective measures. He said the agency took action as soon as officials believed there was a true threat to public safety. That was four months after Harry Kothari died.

"The actions that we take have to be supported with evidence," Rogers said. "And in this case when we obtained that evidence, we immediately approached the firm about removing unsafe products from the market."

The FDA expected H&P would live up to its promises to correct problems in the plant, according to Rogers. Eventually, he said, "We got to a point where we felt the firm was not living up to their obligations."

The FDA took weeks to gather evidence at the plant. It was a time-consuming process, according to the agency, because it involved sampling of products and an assessment of the company's practices and procedures, employee training methods, and how the company handled its manufacturing from raw materials to finished products.

Voluntary recalls of Triad products, including alcohol wipes, iodine wipes, and lubrication jelly, were adequate, Rogers said.

Several weeks later, though, the FDA admitted it should have at least issued a warning letter.

The lengthy investigation leading up to a recall is understandable considering the agency's case has to hold up in court, said Ed Elder, director of the pharmaceutical experiment station at University of Wisconsin–Madison. Elder worked for sixteen years in the pharmaceutical industry, mostly in drug research.

Product recalls are not strictly a public-safety issue; they include a mix of business, legal, and publicity decisions, according to Elder. "There are a lot of downsides. It costs a lot of money to recall a product; sales are going to be lost and negative publicity is going to occur," he said. "Yet if you don't make that call, and someone gets sick or dies, that's an even bigger downside."

## Triad Denies Liability in Death

Triad officials deny their products had anything to do with Harry Kothari's death and have vowed to fight all allegations raised in at least six lawsuits, including one filed by the Kotharis. In its March 28 response, the business denies its wipes were contaminated with *Bacillus cereus* and contends any contamination came after the products left the company's control.

"They're disgusting," Sandy Kothari said. "I am just so angry. These people can go on and they have no idea what the loss is. They have no idea."

In addition to suing Triad and H&P, the Kotharis have named a hospital group-purchasing organization, a raw-material supplier, and a sterilization equipment and services company in their lawsuit, which seeks up to $40 million. They are not suing the

Houston hospital. Hospital officials declined to comment about the case, other than to say they removed Triad alcohol wipes and swabs from all their facilities.

The Kotharis also blame the FDA and say there must be greater accountability and higher standards for health care products. "This company would have sold products forever until somebody put two and two together," Shanoop said. "I think there are some other people who have gone through some pain and haven't put two and two together. . . . They had no idea. They just walked out of the hospital and had to deal with it."

A fifty-five-year-old Tennessee man has filed a $30 million lawsuit against Triad, saying he is permanently disabled after he developed a *Bacillus cereus* infection from Triad's alcohol wipes and had to undergo open-heart surgery.

Triad's future is unclear. The week after the alcohol wipes recall in January, David Haertle registered for a new limited liability company called Trivaria. A company spokeswoman wouldn't answer questions about why the new company is being created.

Meanwhile, the FDA laid out a list of strict protocols for H&P to follow to resume production.

The conditions, outlined in a June 10 consent decree, cover virtually every aspect of the company's manufacturing process and would cost the company millions of dollars. Violations could result in the company being permanently shut down by the FDA.

"This is the all-important first step in resuming our manufacturing operations," Eric Haertle said at the time. "We are fully committed to addressing FDA's concerns and rebuilding the confidence of the customers we have served for so many years."

### Grieving Mom Learns of Recall

The house in Houston is empty now. Striped shades still hang on the windows in Harry's bedroom, but the monkeys and other jungle animals that decorated the pale green walls have come down. The carpet is worn where his crib and changing table once stood.

It's early May.

Sandy looks around the room for the last time. She remembers Harry climbing on the rocking chair and peering out the window with his big brown eyes. She pictures his little clothes filling the armoire in the corner. She doesn't want to leave him behind. But she can't stay.

"We just had to get out . . . ," she says. "You could paint it a different color, you could put all different, new furniture in it, but it won't . . ."

Sometimes, she and her husband look at the photo, the one taken in the hospital, the one that marks a day they desperately long to return to, before *Bacillus cereus* and Triad. But what they learned on a different day drives them now.

About five weeks after Harry's death, still wondering how Harry had been infected, Sandy was talking with her aunt on the telephone. The aunt, a teacher, said she had just read about an FDA recall of alcohol wipes. The reason: *Bacillus cereus*.

Sandy went straight to Harry's room where she had kept a box of alcohol wipes sent home with Harry when he was first discharged from the hospital. She turned over the box. The label matched.

It was the first time Sandy had ever heard of the Triad Group.

Part II

# The Financial System and Its Discontents

**ProPublica**

When the protesters in the Occupy Wall Street movement gathered in New York's Zuccotti Park in the fall of 2011, they probably didn't have in mind this particular story by *ProPublica*, the nonprofit investigative group. But they might well have. In the third installment of a series that won the 2011 Pulitzer Prize for National Reporting, Jake Bernstein and Jesse Eisinger show the extent to which Wall Street pay incentives perverted the financial system toward destructive ends. With remarkable clarity, the story shows that in 2006, as the housing market cooled, executives at a Merrill Lynch unit that made mortgage bonds resorted to paying off members of another unit to buy securities that they realized would soon collapse. The sole purpose: to keep the money-machine going and earn bonuses, no matter what the eventual cost to the firm or to society.

Jake Bernstein and
Jesse Eisinger

# 6. The "Subsidy"

## How a Handful of Merrill Lynch Bankers Helped Blow Up Their Own Firm

Two years before the financial crisis hit, Merrill Lynch confronted a serious problem. No one, not even the bank's own traders, wanted to buy the supposedly safe portions of the mortgage-backed securities Merrill was creating.

Bank executives came up with a fix that had short-term benefits and long-term consequences. They formed a new group within Merrill, which took on the bank's money-losing securities. But how to get the group to accept deals that were otherwise unprofitable? They paid them. The division creating the securities passed portions of their bonuses to the new group, according to two former Merrill executives with detailed knowledge of the arrangement.

The executives said this group, which earned millions in bonuses, played a crucial role in keeping the money machine moving long after it should have ground to a halt.

"It was uneconomic for the traders"—that is, buyers at Merrill—"to take these things," says one former Merrill executive with knowledge of how it worked.

Within Merrill Lynch, some traders called it a "million for a billion"—meaning a million dollars in bonus money for every billion taken on in Merrill mortgage securities. Others referred to it as "the subsidy." One former executive called it bribery. The group was being compensated for how much it took, not whether it made money.

The group, created in 2006, accepted tens of billions of dollars of Merrill's Triple A–rated mortgage-backed assets, with disastrous results. The value of the securities fell to pennies on the dollar and helped to sink the iconic firm. Merrill was sold to Bank of America, which was in turn bailed out by taxpayers.

What became of the bankers who created this arrangement and the traders who took the now-toxic assets? They walked away with millions. Some still hold senior positions at prominent financial firms.

Washington is now grappling with new rules about how to limit Wall Street bonuses in order to better align bankers' behavior with the long-term health of their bank. Merrill's arrangement, known only to a small number of executives at the firm, shows just how damaging the misaligned incentives could be.

ProPublica has published a series of articles throughout the year about how Wall Street kept the money machine spinning. Our examination has shown that as banks faced diminishing demand for every part of the complex securities known as collateralized debt obligations, or CDOs, Merrill and other firms found ways to circumvent the market's clear signals.

The mortgage securities business was supposed to have a firewall against this sort of conflict of interest.

Banks like Merrill bought pools of mortgages and bundled them into securities, eventually making them into CDOs. Merrill paid upfront for the mortgages, but this outlay was quickly repaid as the bank made the securities and sold them to investors. The bankers doing these deals had a saying: We're in the moving business, not the storage business.

Executives producing the securities were not allowed to buy much of their own product; their pay was calculated by the revenues they generated. For this reason, decisions to hold a Merrill-created security for the long term were made by independent traders who determined, in essence, that the Merrill product was as good or better than what was available in the market.

By creating more CDOs, banks prolonged the boom. Ultimately the global banking system was saddled with hundreds of billions of dollars worth of toxic assets, triggering the 2008 implosion and throwing millions of people out of work and sending the global economy into a tailspin from which it has not yet recovered.

Executives who oversaw Merrill's CDO buying group dispute aspects of this account. One executive involved acknowledges that fees were shared but says it was not a "formalized arrangement" and was instead done on a "case-by-case basis." Calling the arrangement bribery "is ridiculous," he says.

The executives also say the new group didn't drive Merrill's CDO production. In fact, they say the group was part of a plan to reduce risk by consolidating the unwanted assets into one place. The traders simply provided a place to put them. "We were managing and booking risk that was already in the firm and couldn't be sold," says one person who worked in the group.

A month before the group was created, Merrill Lynch owned $7.2 billion of the seemingly safe investments, according to an internal risk-management report. By the time the CDO losses started mounting in July 2007, that figure had skyrocketed to $32.2 billion, most of which was held by the new group.

The origins of Merrill's crisis came at the beginning of 2006, when the bank's biggest customer for the supposedly safe assets— the giant insurer AIG—decided to stop buying the assets, known as "super-senior," after becoming worried that perhaps they weren't so safe after all.

The super-senior was the top portion of CDOs, meaning investors who owned it were the first to be compensated as homeowners paid their mortgages and last in line to take losses should people become delinquent. By the fall of 2006, the housing market was dipping, and big insurance companies, pension funds, and other institutional investors were turning away from any investments tied to mortgages.

Until that point, Merrill's own traders had been making money on purchases of super-senior debt. The traders were careful about their purchases. They would buy at prices they regarded as attractive and then make side bets—what are known as hedges—that would pay off if the value of the securities fell. This approach allowed the traders to make money for Merrill while minimizing the bank's risk.

It also was personally profitable. Annual bonuses for traders—which can make up more than 75 percent of total compensation—are largely based on how much money each individual makes for the firm.

By the middle of 2006, the Merrill traders who bought mortgage securities were often clashing with the powerful division, run by Harin De Silva and Ken Margolis, which created and sold the CDOs. At least three traders began to refuse to buy CDO pieces created by De Silva and Margolis's division, according to several former Merrill employees. (De Silva and Margolis didn't respond to requests for comment.)

In late September, Merrill created a $1.5 billion CDO called Octans, named after a constellation in the southern sky. It had been built at the behest of a hedge fund, Magnetar, and filled with some of the riskier mortgage-backed securities and CDOs. (As we reported in April with Chicago Public Radio's *This American Life* and NPR's *Planet Money*, Magnetar had helped create more than $40 billion worth of CDOs with a variety of banks and bet against many of those CDOs as part of a strategy to profit from the decline in the housing market.)

In an incident reported by the *Wall Street Journal* in April 2008, a Merrill trader looked over the contents of Octans and refused to buy the super-senior, believing that he should not be buying what no one else wanted. The trader was sidelined and eventually fired. (The same *Journal* article also reported that the new group had taken the majority of Merrill's super-seniors.)

The difficulty in finding buyers should have been a warning signal: If the market won't buy a product, maybe the bank should stop making it.

Instead, a Merrill executive, Dale Lattanzio, called a meeting, attended by, among others, the heads of the CDO sales group—Margolis and De Silva—and a trader, Ranodeb Roy. According to a person who attended the meeting, they discussed creating a special group under Roy to accept super-senior slices. (Lattanzio didn't respond to requests for comment.)

The head of the new group, Roy, had arrived in the United States early in the year, having spent his whole career in Asia. He had little experience either with the American capital markets or mortgages. His new unit was staffed with three junior people drawn from various places in the bank. The three didn't have the stature within the firm to refuse a purchase and, more troubling, had little expertise in evaluating CDOs, former Merrill employees say.

Roy had reservations about purchasing the super-senior pieces. In August 2006, he sent a memo to Lattanzio warning that Merrill's CDO business was flawed. He wrote that holding super-senior positions disregarded the "systemic risk" involved.

When younger traders complained to him, Roy agreed it was unwise to retain the position. But he also told these traders that it was good for one's career to try to get along with people at Merrill, according to a former employee.

But Roy and his team needed to be paid. As they were setting up the trading group, Roy raised the issue of compensation. "The CDO guys said this helps our business and said don't worry about it—we will take care of it," recalls a person involved in the discussions.

The agreement, according to a former executive with direct knowledge of it, generally worked like this: Each time Merrill's CDO salesmen created a deal, they shared part of the fee they generated with the special group that had been created to "buy" some of the CDO. A billion-dollar CDO generated about $7 million in fees for Merrill's CDO sales group. The new group that bought the CDO would usually be credited with a profit between $2 million and $3 million—despite the fact that the trade often lost money.

Sharing the bonus money for a deal or trade is common on Wall Street, arrangements known as "soft P&L," for "profit and loss." But it is not typical, or desirable, to pay a group to do something against their financial interests or those of the bank.

Roy made about $6 million for 2006, according to former Merrill executives. He was promoted out of the group in May 2007 but then fired in November of that year. He now is a high-level executive for Morgan Stanley in Asia. The co-heads of Merrill's CDO sales group, Ken Margolis and Harin De Silva, pulled down about $7 million each in 2006, according to those executives. De Silva is now at the investment firm PIMCO.

By early summer 2007, many former executives now realize, Merrill was a dead firm walking. As the mortgage securities market imploded, high-level executives embarked on an internal investigation to get to the bottom of what had happened. It did not take them long to discover the subsidy arrangement.

Executives made a sweep of the firm to see if there were other similar deals. We "made a lot of noise" about the Roy subsidy to root out any other similarly troublesome arrangements, said one of the executives involved in the internal investigation. "I'd never seen it before and have never seen it again," he says.

In early October 2007, Merrill began to purge executives and, slowly, to reveal its losses. The heads of Merrill's fixed income group, including Dale Lattanzio, were fired.

Days later, the bank announced it would write down $5.5 billion worth of CDO assets. Less than three weeks after that, Merrill raised the estimate to $8.4 billion. Days later, the board fired Merrill's CEO, Stan O'Neal.

Eventually, Merrill would write down about $26 billion worth of CDOs, including most of the assets that Ranodeb Roy and his team had taken from De Silva and Margolis.

After Merrill revised its estimate of losses in October 2007, the Securities and Exchange Commission began an investigation to discover if the firm's executives had committed securities fraud or misrepresented the state of its business to investors.

But then the financial crisis began in earnest. By March 2008, Bear Stearns had collapsed. By the fall of 2008, Merrill was sold to Bank of America. In a controversial move, Merrill paid bonuses out to its top executives despite its precarious state. The SEC turned its focus on Merrill and BofA's bonuses and sued, alleging failures to properly disclose the payments.

As for the original SEC probe into Merrill Lynch's CDO business in 2007, nothing ever came of it.

*ProPublica research director Lisa Schwartz and Karen Weise contributed reporting to this story.*

If the previous article by *ProPublica* doesn't get your blood boiling, try this one by Michael Hudson. Here the muckraking reporter takes up a vital question: Just where did all the mortgages for those toxic mortgage bonds come from? Hudson's story is a damning peek behind the scenes at Countrywide Financial through the eyes of a former executive who discovered that fraud was systemic at the lender and was punished for trying to blow the whistle. Her revelations are eye-popping. But Hudson, who has been reporting on the subprime industry's excesses since the early 1990s, tracks down no fewer than thirty former executives who confirm that Countrywide, once the nation's largest mortgage lender, either encouraged or protected fraud on borrowers.

Michael Hudson

# 7. Countrywide Protected Fraudsters by Silencing Whistleblowers, Say Former Employees

In the summer of 2007, a team of corporate investigators sifted through mounds of paper pulled from shred bins at Countrywide Financial Corp. mortgage shops in and around Boston.

By intercepting the documents before they were sliced by the shredder, the investigators were able to uncover what they believed was evidence that branch employees had used scissors, tape and Wite-Out to create fake bank statements, inflated property appraisals, and other phony paperwork. Inside the heaps of paper, for example, they found mock-ups that indicated to investigators that workers had, as a matter of routine, literally cut and pasted the address for one home onto an appraisal for a completely different piece of property.

Eileen Foster, the company's new fraud investigations chief, had seen a lot of slippery behavior in her two-plus decades in the banking business. But she'd never seen anything like this.

"You're looking at it and you're going, Oh my God, how did it get to this point?" Foster recalls. "How do you get people to go to work every day and do these things and think it's okay?"

More surprises followed. She began to get pushback, she claims, from company officials who were unhappy with the investigation.

One executive, Foster says, sent an e-mail to dozens of workers in the Boston region, warning them the fraud unit was on the case and not to put anything in their e-mails or instant messages that might be used against them. Another, she says, called her and growled into the phone: "I'm g—d—ed sick and tired of these witch hunts."

Her team was not allowed to interview a senior manager who oversaw the branches. Instead, she says, Countrywide's Employee Relations Department did the interview and then let the manager's boss vet the transcript before it was provided to Foster and the fraud unit.

In the end, dozens of employees were let go and six branches were shut down. But Foster worried some of the worst actors had escaped unscathed. She suspected, she says, that something wasn't right with Countrywide's culture—and that it was going to be rough going for her as she and her team dug into the methods used by Countrywide's sales machine.

By early 2008, she claims, she'd concluded that many in Countrywide's chain of command were working to cover up massive fraud within the company—outing and then firing whistleblowers who tried to report forgery and other misconduct. People who spoke up, she says, were "taken out."

By the fall of 2008, she was out of a job too. Countrywide's new owner, Bank of America Corp., told her it was firing her for "unprofessional conduct."

Foster began a three-year battle to clear her name and establish that she and other employees had been punished for doing the right thing. Last week, the U.S. Department of Labor ruled that Bank of America had illegally fired her as payback for exposing fraud and retaliation against whistleblowers. It ordered the bank to reinstate her and pay her some $930,000.

Bank of America denies Foster's allegations and stands behind its decision to fire her. Foster sees the ruling as a vindication of her decision to keep fighting.

"I don't let people bully me, intimidate me, and coerce me," Foster told *iWatch News* during a series of interviews. "And it's just not right that people don't know what happened here and how it happened."

## Greedy People

This is the story of Eileen Foster's fight against the nation's largest bank and what was once the nation's largest mortgage lender. It is also the story of other former Countrywide workers who claim they, too, fought against a culture of corruption that protected fraudsters, abused borrowers, and helped land Bank of America in a quagmire of legal and financial woes.

In government records and in interviews with *iWatch News*, thirty former employees charge that Countrywide executives encouraged or condoned fraud. The misconduct, they say, included falsified income documentation and other tactics that helped steer borrowers into bad mortgages.

Eighteen of these ex-employees, including Foster, claim they were demoted or fired for questioning fraud. They say sales managers, personnel executives and other company officials used intimidation and firings to silence whistleblowers.

A former loan-underwriting manager in northern California, for example, claimed Countrywide retaliated against her after she sent an e-mail to the company's founder and chief executive, Angelo Mozilo, about questionable lending practices. The ex-manager, Enid Thompson, warned Mozilo in March 2007 that "greedy unethical people" were pressuring workers to approve loans without regard for borrowers' ability to pay, according to a lawsuit in Contra Costa Superior Court.

Within twelve hours, Thompson claimed, Countrywide executives began a campaign of reprisal, reducing her duties and transferring staffers off her team. Corporate minions, she charged, ransacked her desk, broke her computer, and removed her printer and personal things.

Soon after, she said, she was fired. Her lawsuit was resolved last year. The terms were not disclosed.

Bank of America officials deny Countrywide or Bank of America retaliated against Foster, Thompson, or others who reported fraud. The bank says Foster's firing was based only on her "management style." It says it takes fraud seriously and never punishes workers who report wrongdoing up the corporate ladder.

When fraud happens, Bank of America spokesman Rick Simon says, "the lender is almost always a victim, even if the fraud is perpetrated by individual employees. Fraud is costly, so lenders necessarily invest heavily in both preventing and investigating it."

When it uncovers fraud, Simon says, the bank takes "appropriate actions," including firing the employees involved and cooperating with law-enforcement authorities in criminal investigations.

Mozilo's attorney, David Siegel, told *iWatch News* it was "unlikely that Mr. Mozilo either would have had a direct role with, or would recall, specific employee grievances, and it would be inappropriate for him to comment on individual employment issues in any event." Siegel added that "any implication that he ever would have tolerated much less condoned to any extent misconduct or fraudulent activity in loan production and underwriting . . . is utterly baseless."

In closed-door testimony a year ago, the ex-CEO defended his company, telling the federal Financial Crisis Inquiry Commission that Countrywide "probably made more difference in society, in the integrity of our society, than any company in the history of America."

Foster says that, in her experience, Mozilo urged managers to crack down on fraud. If he saw an e-mail about a fraudster within the ranks, she says, he would hit "reply all" and type, "Track the bastard down and fire him."

She says, though, that others within the company often screened his e-mails, and it's likely Mozilo never saw Thompson's e-mail or many other messages about fraud.

"My sense is they kept things from Angelo," she says.

## An Old Matter

When Bank of America announced in January 2008 that it was going to buy Countrywide at a fire-sale price, some analysts thought it was a great move, one that would leave the bank well positioned once the home-loan market recovered.

Almost three years later, defaults on loans originated by Countrywide have soared and Bank of America's stock price has plunged as investors and government agencies have pursued mortgage-related claims totaling tens of billions of dollars.

Federal and state officials are pressing Bank of America and other big players to settle charges they used falsified documents to speed homeowners through foreclosure. Lawsuits filed on behalf of investors claim Countrywide lied about the quality of the pools of mortgages that the lender sold them during the home-loan boom.

Bank of America says issues related to Countrywide are old news. Last year a spokesman described fraud claims by state officials as "water under the bridge," noting that the bank settled with dozens of states soon after buying Countrywide.

When federal officials announced Foster's victory last week, Bank of America dismissed the case as "an old matter dating from 2008."

Accounts from Foster and other former employees, however, put the bank in an uncomfortable position. These accounts, as well as lawsuits pushed by investors, borrowers, and government agencies, raise questions about how diligently the bank has worked to clean up the mess caused by Countrywide—and whether the bank has tried to curtail its legal liability by papering over the history of corruption at its controversial acquisition.

In Foster's case, the Labor Department notes that two senior Bank of America officials—not former Countrywide executives—made the decision to fire her.

The agency says the investigations led by Foster found "widespread and pervasive fraud" that, Foster claimed, went beyond misconduct committed at the branch level and reached into Countrywide's management ranks.

Foster told the agency that instead of defending the rights of honest employees, Countrywide's employee relations unit sheltered fraudsters inside the company. According to the Labor Department, Foster believed Employee Relations "was engaged in the systematic cover-up of various types of fraud through terminating, harassing, and otherwise trying to silence employees who reported the underlying fraud and misconduct."

In government records and in interviews with *iWatch News*, Foster describes other top-down misconduct:

- She claims Countrywide's management protected big loan producers who used fraud to put up big sales numbers. If they were caught, she says, they frequently avoided termination.

- Foster claims Countrywide's subprime lending division concealed from her the level of "suspicious activity reports." This in turn reduced the number of fraud reports Countrywide gave to the U.S. Treasury's Financial Crimes Enforcement Network.

- Foster claims Countrywide failed to notify investors when it discovered fraud or other problems with loans that it had sold as the underlying assets in "mortgage-backed" securities.

When she created a report designed to document these loans on a regular basis going forward, she says, she was "shut down" by company officials and told to stop doing the report.

In Foster's view, Countrywide lost its way as it became a place where everyone was expected to bend to the will of salespeople driven by a whatever-it-takes ethos.

The attitude, she says, was: "The rules don't matter. Regulations don't matter. It's our game and we can play it the way we want."

Bank of America declined to answer detailed questions about Foster's allegations. Simon, the bank spokesman, told *iWatch News* "we are certain" that Foster's claims "were properly and fully investigated by Countrywide and appropriate actions were taken."

And not all former Countrywide workers say that fraud was condoned by management.

Frank San Pedro, who worked as a manager within the investigations unit from 2004 to 2008, told the Financial Crisis Inquiry Commission the company worked hard "to root out all the fraud that we could possibly find. We continued to get better and better at it."

He said most of the fraud was "external"—outsiders trying to rip off the lender—and in-house sales staffers who tried to push through fraudulent loans "seldom got away with it."

Gregory Lumsden, former head of Countrywide's subprime division, Full Spectrum Lending, says there are thousands of ex-Countrywiders who can vouch for the company's honesty. When bad actors were caught, he says, Countrywide took swift action.

"I don't care if you're Microsoft or you're the Golf Channel or Dupont or MSNBC: companies are going to make some mistakes," Lumsden told *iWatch News*. "What you hope is that companies will deal with employees that do wrong. That's what we did."

## The American Dream

In February 2003, Countrywide's founder and CEO, Angelo Mozilo, gave a lecture hosted by Harvard's Joint Center for Housing Studies titled "The American Dream of Homeownership: From Cliché to Mission."

Mozilo, the Bronx-born son of a butcher, had started Countrywide with a partner in 1969 and built it into a home-loan empire that was now on the verge of becoming the nation's largest home lender.

But he saw trouble on the horizon. Before his audience of academics and business people, he complained that a "regulatory mania" was hurting Countrywide and other "reputable" mortgage lenders. Overreaching predatory-lending laws, he said, were threatening shut the door to homeownership for hard-working low-income and minority families. Industry and citizenry needed to work together to prevent government from strangling the mortgage market, he said.

It wasn't, Mozilo added, that he was against cracking down on bad apples that took advantage of vulnerable borrowers.

"These lenders," the CEO said, "deserve unwavering scrutiny and, when found guilty, an unforgiving punishment."

Around the time Mozilo was giving his speech back east, one of his employees was finding what she later claimed to be evidence of serious fraud at Countrywide's Roseville, Calif., branch.

Employees were falsifying loan applicants' salaries in mortgage paperwork and forging their names on loan documents, according to a lawsuit filed by Michele Brunelli, who was a loan processor and later a branch operations manager for Countrywide. In March 2003, Brunelli recalled, she used the company's "ethics hotline" and lodged what she thought was a confidential complaint.

Immediately after, Brunelli claimed, her regional manager yelled at her for calling the hotline. Then, she said, her immediate supervisor called her in and reprimanded her for making the complaint.

"Not everyone's hands are clean in this office," the branch manager said, according to Brunelli. "Are you ready for that?"

Brunelli didn't back down. She continued reporting evidence of fraud to the executives above her, her lawsuit said. They dismissed her concerns, she said, saying she was having "emotional outbursts" and accusing her of being "on a witch hunt."

In court papers, the company flatly denied her allegations, accusing Brunelli of acting in "bad faith." Her lawsuit was resolved in 2010.

Two other former Countrywide workers, Sabrina Arroyo and Linda Court, claimed they lost their jobs in 2004 after they complained supervisors were directing them to forge borrowers' signatures on loan paperwork. After they informed Employee Relations about the forgeries, the company quickly fired them, they claimed.

"Corporate came in. We told them the story. We told them everything," Arroyo told iWatch News. "They said don't worry, whatever you say, you're going to be covered. A month or so later, I was let go."

Arroyo and Court sued Countrywide in state court in Sacramento, but Countrywide won an order forcing the case into arbitration. They decided to drop their claim because the odds are stacked against workers in arbitration, their attorney, William Wright, said.

Some ex-employees say they went high up Countrywide's chain of command to raise red flags about fraud. Mark Bonjean, a former operations unit manager in Arizona, complained to a divisional vice president, according to a lawsuit in state court in Maricopa County. Within two hours of sending the VP an e-mail about what he believed were violations of the state's organized crime and fraud statutes, the suit said, he was placed on administrative leave. The next day, according to the lawsuit, he was fired.

Another ex-Countrywider, Shahima Shaheem, claimed she took her complaints to the very top. Like Enid Thompson before her, she said she wrote an e-mail directly to Mozilo, the CEO, about fraud and retaliation. She never heard back from Mozilo, according to her lawsuit in Contra Costa Superior Court. Instead, the suit said, she was subjected to a campaign of harassment by company executives and human-resources representatives that forced her to leave her job.

Shaheem's case was settled out of court, her attorney said.

A Bank of America spokesman declined to respond to questions about allegations by Shaheem, Bonjean and other former Countrywide employees, noting that their claims "are related to situations and investigations that took place at Countrywide prior to Bank of America acquiring the company."

Countrywide had been slower than many other mortgage lenders to fully embrace making subprime loans to borrowers with modest incomes or weak credit. By 2004, though, Countrywide had become a player in the market for subprime deals and many other nontraditional mortgages, including loans that didn't require much documentation of borrowers' income and assets.

These loans were part of the plan for meeting its CEO's audacious goal of growing his company from a giant to a colossus. Mozilo had vowed that his company would double its share of the home-loan market to 30 percent by 2008.

Some former Countrywide employees say the pressure to push through more and more loans encouraged an anything-goes attitude. Questionable underwriting practices often helped risky loans sail through the lender's loan-approval process, they say.

In one example, Countrywide approved a loan for a borrower whose application listed him as a dairy foreman earning $126,000 a year, according to a legal claim later filed by Mortgage Guaranty Insurance Co., a mortgage insurer. It turned out that the borrower actually milked cows at the dairy and earned $13,200 a year, the lawsuit alleged.

The borrower provided the correct information, but the lender booked the loan based on data that inflated his wages by more than 800 percent, the legal claim said.

In another instance, according to a former manager cited as a "confidential witness" in shareholders' litigation against the company, employees appeared to be involved in a "loan flipping" scheme, persuading borrowers to refinance again and again, giving them little new money, but piling on more fees and ratcheting up their debt. The witness recalled that when the scheme was pointed out to Lumsden, Countrywide's subprime loan chief, the response from Lumsden was "short and sweet": "Fund the loans."

Such episodes weren't uncommon, the witness said. In early 2004, he claimed, he discovered that Nick Markopoulos, a high-producing loan officer in Massachusetts, had cut and pasted information from the Internet to create a fake verification of employment for a loan applicant. Markopoulos left the company of his own accord, the witness said, but he was soon rehired as a branch manager.

The witness said he contacted a regional vice president to object to rehiring an employee with a history of fraud. But he said the regional VP—citing Markopoulos's high productivity— overruled his objections.

Markopoulos couldn't be reached for a response. Lumsden says he doesn't recall any incident involving "loan flipping" allegations.

Eileen Foster knew little about Countrywide's fraud problems when she took a job with the company in September 2005.

For Foster, the move seemed like a natural progression. She'd accumulated twenty-one years' experience in the banking business, starting out as a teller at Great Western Bank and working her way up to vice president for fraud prevention and investigation at First Bank Inc.

Countrywide brought her on as a first vice president and put her in charge of a high-priority project: an overhaul of how the company handled customer complaints.

The company's systems for handling complaints, Foster recalls, were disjointed and ineffective. Various divisions had differing policies and there wasn't much effort to ensure that complaints got addressed. Things had gotten so bad, she says, federal banking regulators ordered the company to do something about the problem. Foster's task was to standardize the company's procedures and ensure that people with complaints didn't get brushed off.

As she set about fixing the problems, she says, she encountered things that gave her pause.

The company's mortgage fraud investigation unit, Foster says, refused to share data about the complaints it received. Each time she requested the stats, she says, she hit a brick wall.

Foster says she also ran into a hitch when she began distributing a monthly report that broke down complaint data for each of the companies' operating divisions.

Countrywide Home Loans Servicing, which collected borrowers' payments each month, was the subject of complaints about its foreclosure practices and other issues. The volume of serious complaints involving the servicing unit topped 1,000 per month, dwarfing the number for other divisions.

This upset officials with the servicing unit, Foster recalls. The complaints weren't "real complaints," the servicing execs argued, and Foster was making the unit look bad by including them in her reports.

The upshot: Foster was ordered, she says, not to include many of the complaints about the servicing unit in her reports. She thought it was odd, she says, but she didn't think it was evidence of a larger pattern. She figured it was mostly an exercise in backside covering.

"When we lost at the meeting, I was like, 'OK, they want to just cover this up,'" Foster says. "But it wasn't anything to the scale that I thought it would cause great harm."

Only later—after she took over the mortgage fraud investigation unit—did she realize, she says, that cover-ups were part of the culture of Countrywide, and that efforts to paper over problems had less to do with bureaucratic infighting and more to do with hiding something darker within the company's culture.

"What I came to find out," she says, "was that it was all by design."

State law enforcers would later charge that Countrywide executives designed fraud into the lender's systems as a way of boosting loan production. During the mortgage boom, critics say, Countrywide and other lenders didn't worry about the quality of the loans they were making because they often sold the loans to Wall Street banks and investors. So long as borrowers made their first few payments, the investors were usually the ones who took the hit if homeowners couldn't keep up with payments.

Countrywide treated borrowers, California's attorney general later claimed, "as nothing more than the means for producing more loans," manipulating them into signing up for loans with little regard for whether they could afford them.

Countrywide's drive to boost loan production encouraged fraud, for example, on loans that required little or no documentation of borrowers' finances, according to a lawsuit by the Illinois attorney general. One former employee, the suit said, estimated that borrowers' incomes were exaggerated on 90 percent of the reduced-documentation loans sold out of his branch in Chicago.

One way that Countrywide booked loans was by paying generous fees to independent mortgage brokers who steered customers its way. Countrywide gave so little scrutiny to these deals that borrowers often ended up in loans that they couldn't pay, the state of Illinois' suit said.

In Chicago, the suit said, Countrywide's business partners included a mortgage broker controlled by a five-time convicted felon. One Source Mortgage Inc.'s owner, Charles Mangold, had served time for weapons charges and other crimes, the suit said.

One Source received as much as $100,000 per month in fees from Countrywide, banking as much as $11,000 for each loan it steered to the lender. Mangold, in turn, showered a Countrywide branch manager and other employees with expensive gifts, including flowers and Coach handbags, the suit said.

Countrywide in turn funded a stream of loans arranged by One Source, the suit said, even as the broker misled borrowers about how much they'd be paying on their loans and falsified information on their loan applications. One borrower provided pay stubs and tax returns showing he earned no more than $48,000 per year, but One Source listed his income as twice that much, according to the suit.

Mangold couldn't be reached for comment. His attorney said in 2007 that Mangold denied all of the state's allegations against him.

Countrywide, the state's suit said, kept up its partnership with One Source for more than three years. It didn't end the relationship until the state sued One Source for fraud and slapped Countrywide with a subpoena seeking documents relating to the broker.

As questionable practices continued, Countrywide's fraud investigation unit had trouble keeping up, according to Larry Forwood, who worked as a California-based fraud investigator for Countrywide in 2005 and 2006, before Foster took over the fraud unit. His personal caseload totaled as many as one hundred cases at a time, many of them involving dozens or hundreds of loans each.

Some cases involved mortgage brokers or in-house staffers who pressured real-estate appraisers to inflate property values. The company maintained a "do not use" list of crooked appraisers who'd been caught falsifying home values, but the sales force often ignored the list and used these appraisers anyway, Forwood says.

Countrywide's fraud investigation unit did have some successes during Forwood's tenure. It shut down a branch in the

Chicago area, he said, after a rash of quick-defaulting loans sparked a review that uncovered evidence of bogus appraisals and forged signatures on loan paperwork. One manager, Forwood says, tried to rationalize the fraud, telling investigators: What was the big deal if, say, five out of every thirty loans was fraudulent?

When the unit shut down a branch in southern California after uncovering similar evidence of fraud, Forwood recalls, it got some pushback. It came all the way from the top, he says, via a phone call to the fraud unit from Mozilo.

"He got very upset," Forwood says. "He basically got on the phone and said: 'Next time you need to do that, clear it with me.'"

Mozilo's attorney didn't respond to questions from *iWatch News* about Forwood's account.

***Bloomberg News***

This next piece is about accounting—but don't skip it just yet. Bloomberg News's Jonathan Weil shows here how he turns bookkeeping issues like tangible common equity into something you actually enjoy reading. Weil looks at Bank of America's books to show how the stock market places a far lower value on the company and its assets than its own accountants do. In other words, investors think Bank of America is hiding losses, and that poses a serious risk to the financial system less than three years after taxpayers bailed out the bank.

Jonathan Weil

# 8. Curse the Geniuses Who Gave Us Bank of America

Ask anyone what the most immediate threats to the global financial system are, and the obvious answers would be the European sovereign-debt crisis and the off chance that the United States won't raise its debt ceiling in time to avoid a default. Here's one to add to the list: the frightening plunge in Bank of America Corp.'s stock price.

At $9.85 a share, down 26 percent this year, Bank of America finished yesterday with a market capitalization of $99.8 billion. That's an astonishingly low 49 percent of the company's $205.6 billion book value, or common shareholder equity, as of June 30. As far as the market is concerned, more than half of the company's book value is bogus, due to overstated assets, understated liabilities, or some combination of the two.

That perception presents a dangerous situation for the world at large, not just the company's direct stakeholders. The risk is that with the stock price this low, a further decline could feed on itself and spread contagion to other companies, regardless of the bank's statement this week that it is "creating a fortress balance sheet."

It isn't only the company's intangible assets, such as goodwill, that investors are discounting. (Goodwill is the ledger entry a company records when it pays a premium to buy another.) Consider Bank of America's calculations of tangible common equity, a bare-bones capital measure showing its ability to absorb future losses. The company said it ended the second quarter with tangible common equity of $128.2 billion, or 5.87 percent of tangible assets.

### Investor Doubts

That's about $28 billion more than the Charlotte, North Carolina–based company's market cap. Put another way, investors doubt Bank of America's loan values and other numbers, too, not just its intangibles, the vast majority of which the company doesn't count toward regulatory capital or tangible common equity anyway.

So here we have the largest U.S. bank by assets, fresh off an $8.8 billion quarterly loss, which was its biggest ever. And the people in charge of running it have a monstrous credibility gap, largely of their own making. Once again, we're all on the hook.

As recently as late 2010, Bank of America still clung to the position that none of the $4.4 billion of goodwill from its 2008 purchase of Countrywide Financial Corp. had lost a dollar of value. Chief executive officer Brian Moynihan also was telling investors the bank would boost its penny-a-share quarterly dividend "as fast as we can" and that he didn't "see anything that would stop us." Both notions proved to be nonsense.

### Acquisition Disaster

The goodwill from Countrywide, one of the most disastrous corporate acquisitions in U.S. history, now has been written off entirely, via impairment charges that were long overdue. And, thankfully, Bank of America's regulators in March rejected the company's dividend plans, in an outburst of common sense.

Last fall, Bank of America also was telling investors it probably would incur $4.4 billion of costs from repurchasing defective mortgages that were sold to investors, though it did say more were possible. Since then the company has recognized an additional $19.2 billion of such expenses, with no end in sight.

The crucial question today is whether Bank of America needs fresh capital to strengthen its balance sheet. Moynihan emphatically says it doesn't, pointing to regulatory-capital measures that would have us believe it's doing fine. The market is screaming otherwise, judging by the mammoth discount to book value. Then again, for all we know, the equity markets might not be receptive to a massive offering of new shares anyway, even if the bank's executives were inclined to try for one.

## No Worries

We can only hope Bank of America's regulators are tracking the market's fears closely and have contingency plans in place should matters get worse. Yet to believe Moynihan, there's nary a worry from them. When asked by one analyst during the company's earnings conference call this week whether there was any "pressure to raise capital from a regulatory side of things," Moynihan replied, simply, "no."

If that's true, the banking regulators should share blame with Moynihan for the current mess. It would be impossible for any lender to have too much capital in the event that Europe's debt problems, for example, morph into another global banking crisis. It's also hard to believe Bank of America has enough capital now, given that the market doesn't believe it.

There undoubtedly are plenty of brave investors eyeing Bank of America's stock price who trust the numbers on the company's books and see a buying opportunity. Perhaps they'll even be proven right. We should hope so, for our own sakes. There's more at stake here, however, than whether Bank of America's shares are a "buy" or a "sell."

The main thing the rest of us care about is the continuing menace this company and others like it pose to the financial system, knowing we never should have let ourselves be put in the position where a collapse in confidence at a single bank could wreak havoc on the world's economy. Here we are again, though. Curse the geniuses who brought us this madness.

***Rolling Stone***

Matt Taibbi's 5,000-word exposé of document shredding at the Securities and Exchange Commission is just a magnificent piece of journalism. In a piece that caused Senator Chuck Grassley to push for an in-depth investigation into possible SEC wrongdoing, Taibbi reveals that instead of trying to catch companies and individuals who broke the law, the SEC did everything in its power—in the face of explicit federal document-disposal regulations ordering otherwise—to shred as much evidence as it could. If the SEC ever does manage to reclaim the respect and fear it once projected on Wall Street, Taibbi will deserve a lot of the credit.

# 9. Is the SEC Covering Up Wall Street Crimes?

I magine a world in which a man who is repeatedly investigated for a string of serious crimes, but never prosecuted, has his slate wiped clean every time the cops fail to make a case. No more Lifetime channel specials where the murderer is unveiled after police stumble upon past intrigues in some old file—"Hey, chief, didja know this guy had *two* wives die falling down the stairs?" No more burglary sprees cracked when some sharp cop sees the same name pop up in one too many witness statements. This is a different world, one far friendlier to lawbreakers, where even the *suspicion* of wrongdoing gets wiped from the record.

That, it now appears, is exactly how the Securities and Exchange Commission has been treating the Wall Street criminals who cratered the global economy a few years back. For the past two decades, according to a whistle-blower at the SEC who recently came forward to Congress, the agency has been systematically destroying records of its preliminary investigations once they are closed. By whitewashing the files of some of the nation's worst financial criminals, the SEC has kept an entire generation of federal investigators in the dark about past inquiries into insider trading, fraud, and market manipulation against companies like Goldman Sachs, Deutsche Bank, and AIG. With a few strokes of the keyboard, the evidence gathered during thousands of investigations—"18,000 . . . including Madoff," as one high-ranking SEC official put it during a panicked meeting about the destruction—has apparently disappeared forever into the wormhole of history.

Under a deal the SEC worked out with the National Archives and Records Administration, all of the agency's records—"including case files relating to preliminary investigations"—are supposed to be maintained for at least twenty-five years. But the SEC, using history-altering practices that for once actually deserve the overused and usually hysterical term "Orwellian," devised an elaborate and possibly illegal system under which staffers were directed to dispose of the documents from any preliminary inquiry that did not receive approval from senior staff to become a full-blown, formal investigation. Amazingly, the wholesale destruction of the cases—known as MUIs, or "Matters Under Inquiry"—was not something done on the sly, in secret. The enforcement division of the SEC even spelled out the procedure in writing, on the commission's internal website. "After you have closed a MUI that has not become an investigation," the site advised staffers, "you should dispose of any documents obtained in connection with the MUI."

Many of the destroyed files involved companies and individuals who would later play prominent roles in the economic meltdown of 2008. Two MUIs involving con artist Bernie Madoff vanished. So did a 2002 inquiry into financial fraud at Lehman Brothers, as well as a 2005 case of insider trading at the same soon-to-be-bankrupt bank. A 2009 preliminary investigation of insider trading by Goldman Sachs was deleted, along with records for at least three cases involving the infamous hedge fund SAC Capital.

The widespread destruction of records was brought to the attention of Congress in July, when an SEC attorney named Darcy Flynn decided to blow the whistle. According to Flynn, who was responsible for helping to manage the commission's records, the SEC has been destroying records of preliminary investigations since at least 1993. After he alerted NARA to the problem, Flynn reports, senior staff at the SEC scrambled to hide the commission's improprieties.

As a federally protected whistle-blower, Flynn is not permitted to speak to the press. But in evidence he presented to the SEC's inspector general and three congressional committees earlier this summer, the thirteen-year veteran of the agency paints a startling picture of a federal police force that has effectively been conquered by the financial criminals it is charged with investigating. In at least one case, according to Flynn, investigators at the SEC found their desire to bring a case against an influential bank thwarted by senior officials in the enforcement division—whose director turned around and accepted a lucrative job from the very same bank they had been prevented from investigating. In another case, the agency farmed out its inquiry to a private law firm—one hired by the company under investigation. The outside firm, unsurprisingly, concluded that no further investigation of its client was necessary. To complete the bureaucratic laundering process, Flynn says, the SEC dropped the case and destroyed the files.

Much has been made in recent months of the government's glaring failure to police Wall Street; to date, federal and state prosecutors have yet to put a single senior Wall Street executive behind bars for any of the many well-documented crimes related to the financial crisis. Indeed, Flynn's accusations dovetail with a recent series of damaging critiques of the SEC made by reporters, watchdog groups, and members of Congress, all of which seem to indicate that top federal regulators spend more time lunching, schmoozing, and job-interviewing with Wall Street crooks than they do catching them. As one former SEC staffer describes it, the agency is now filled with so many Wall Street hotshots from oft-investigated banks that it has been "infected with the Goldman mindset from within."

The destruction of records by the SEC, as outlined by Flynn, is something far more than an administrative accident or bureaucratic fuck-up. It's a symptom of the agency's terminal brain damage. Somewhere along the line, those at the SEC responsible for policing America's banks fell and hit their head on a big pile of Wall Street's money—a blow from which the agency has never recovered. "From what I've seen, it looks as if the SEC might have sanctioned some level of case-related document destruction," says Sen. Chuck Grassley, the ranking Republican on the Senate Judiciary Committee, whose staff has interviewed Flynn. "It doesn't make sense that an agency responsible for investigations would want to get rid of potential evidence. If these charges are true, the agency needs to explain why it destroyed documents, how many documents it destroyed over what time frame, and to what extent its actions were consistent with the law."

How did officials at the SEC wind up with a faithful veteran employee—a conservative, midlevel attorney described as a highly reluctant whistle-blower—spilling the agency's most sordid secrets to Congress? In a way, they asked for it.

On May 18 of this year, SEC enforcement director Robert Khuzami sent out a mass e-mail to the agency's staff with the subject line "Lawyers Behaving Badly." In it, Khuzami asked his subordinates to report any experiences they might have had where "the behavior of counsel representing clients in . . . investigations has been questionable."

Khuzami was asking staffers to recount any stories of *outside* counsel behaving unethically. But Flynn apparently thought his boss was looking for examples of lawyers "behaving badly" anywhere, including *within* the SEC. And he had a story to share he'd kept a lid on for years. "Mr. Khuzami may have gotten something more than he expected," Flynn's lawyer, a former SEC whistleblower named Gary Aguirre, later explained to Congress.

Flynn responded to Khuzami with a letter laying out one such example of misbehaving lawyers within the SEC. It involved a case from very early in Flynn's career, back in 2000, when he was working with a group of investigators who thought they had a "slam-dunk" case against Deutsche Bank, the German financial giant. A few years earlier, Rolf Breuer, the bank's CEO, had given an interview to *Der Spiegel* in which he denied that Deutsche was involved in *übernahmegespräche*—takeover talks—to acquire a rival American firm, Bankers Trust. But the statement was apparently untrue—and it sent the stock of Bankers Trust tumbling, potentially lowering the price for the merger. Flynn and his fellow SEC investigators, suspecting that investors of Bankers Trust had been defrauded, opened a MUI on the case.

A Matter Under Inquiry is just a preliminary sort of look-see—a way for the SEC to check out the multitude of tips it gets about suspicious trades, shady stock scams and false disclosures, and to determine which of the accusations merit a formal investigation. At the MUI stage, an SEC investigator can conduct interviews or ask a bank to send in information voluntarily. Bumping a MUI up to a formal investigation is critical because it enables investigators to pull out the full law-enforcement ass-kicking measures—subpoenas, depositions, everything short of hot pokers and waterboarding. In the Deutsche case, Flynn and other SEC investigators got past the MUI stage and used their powers to collect sworn testimony and documents indicating that plenty of *übernahmegespräche* indeed had been going on when Breuer spoke to *Der Spiegel*. Based on the evidence, they sent an "Action Memorandum" to senior SEC staff, formally recommending that the agency press forward and file suit against Deutsche.

Breuer responded to the threat as big banks like Deutsche often do: He hired a former SEC enforcement director to lobby the agency to back off. The ex-insider, Gary Lynch, launched a creative and inspired defense, producing a linguistic expert who argued that *übernahmegespräche* only means "advanced stage of discussions." Nevertheless, the request to proceed with the case was approved by several levels of the SEC's staff. All that was needed to move forward was a thumbs-up from the director of enforcement at the time, Richard Walker.

But then a curious thing happened. On July 10, 2001, Flynn and the other investigators were informed that Walker was mysteriously recusing himself from the Deutsche case. Two weeks later, on July 23, the enforcement division sent a letter to Deutsche that read, "Inquiry in the above-captioned matter has been terminated." The bank was in the clear; the SEC was dropping its fraud investigation. In contradiction to the agency's usual practice, it provided no explanation for its decision to close the case.

On October 1 of that year, the mystery was solved: Dick Walker was named general counsel of Deutsche. Less than ten weeks after the SEC shut down its investigation of the bank, the agency's director of enforcement was handed a cushy, high-priced job at Deutsche.

Deutsche's influence in the case didn't stop there. A few years later, in 2004, Walker hired none other than Robert Khuzami, a young federal prosecutor, to join him at Deutsche. The two would remain at the bank until February 2009, when Khuzami joined the SEC as Flynn's new boss in the enforcement division. When Flynn sent his letter to Khuzami complaining about misbehavior by Walker, he was calling out Khuzami's own mentor.

The circular nature of the case illustrates the revolving-door dynamic that has become pervasive at the SEC. A recent study by the Project on Government Oversight found that over the past five years, former SEC personnel filed 789 notices disclosing their intent to represent outside companies before the agency—sometimes within *days* of their having left the SEC. More than half of the disclosures came from the agency's enforcement division, who went to bat for the financial industry four times more often than ex-staffers from other wings of the SEC.

Even a cursory glance at a list of the agency's most recent enforcement directors makes it clear that the SEC's top policemen almost always wind up jumping straight to jobs representing the banks they were supposed to regulate. Lynch, who represented Deutsche in the Flynn case, served as the agency's enforcement chief from 1985 to 1989, before moving to the firm of Davis Polk, which boasts many top Wall Street clients. He was succeeded by

William McLucas, who left the SEC in 1998 to work for Wilmer-Hale, a Wall Street defense firm so notorious for snatching up top agency veterans that it is sometimes referred to as "SEC West." McLucas was followed by Dick Walker, who defected to Deutsche in 2001, and he was in turn followed by Stephen Cutler, who now serves as general counsel for JP Morgan Chase. Next came Linda Chatman Thomsen, who stepped down to join Davis Polk, only to be succeeded in 2009 by Khuzami, Walker's former protégé at Deutsche Bank.

This merry-go-round of current and former enforcement directors has repeatedly led to accusations of improprieties. In 2008, in a case cited by the SEC inspector general, Thomsen went out of her way to pass along valuable information to Cutler, the former enforcement director who had gone to work for JP Morgan. According to the inspector general, Thomsen signaled Cutler that the SEC was unlikely to take action that would hamper JP Morgan's move to buy up Bear Stearns. In another case, the inspector general found, an assistant director of enforcement was instrumental in slowing down an investigation into the $7 billion Ponzi scheme allegedly run by Texas con artist R. Allen Stanford—and then left the SEC to work for Stanford, despite explicitly being denied permission to do so by the agency's ethics office. "Every lawyer in Texas and beyond is going to get rich on this case, OK?" the official later explained. "I hated being on the sidelines."

Small wonder, then, that SEC staffers often have trouble getting their bosses to approve full-blown investigations against even the most blatant financial criminals. For a fledgling MUI to become a formal investigation, it has to make the treacherous leap from the lower rungs of career-level staffers like Flynn all the way up to the revolving-door level at the top, where senior management is composed largely of high-priced appointees from the private sector who have strong social and professional ties to the very banks they are charged with regulating. And if senior management didn't approve an investigation, the documents often wound up being destroyed—as Flynn would later discover.

After the Deutsche fiasco over Bankers Trust, Flynn continued to work at the SEC for four more years. He briefly left the agency to dabble in real estate, then returned in 2008 to serve as an attorney in the enforcement division. In January 2010, he accepted new responsibilities that included helping to manage the disposition of records for the division—and it was then he first became aware of the agency's possibly unlawful destruction of MUI records.

Flynn discovered a directive on the enforcement division's internal website ordering staff to destroy "any records obtained in connection" with closed MUIs. The directive appeared to violate federal law, which gives responsibility for maintaining and destroying all records to the National Archives and Records Administration. Over a decade earlier, in fact, the SEC had struck a deal with NARA stipulating that investigative records were to be maintained for twenty-five years—and that if any files were to be destroyed after that, the shredding was to be done by NARA, not the SEC.

But Flynn soon learned that the records for thousands of preliminary investigations no longer existed. In his letter to Congress, Flynn estimates that the practice of destroying MUIs had begun as early as 1993 and has resulted in at least 9,000 case files being destroyed. For all the thousands of tips that had come in to the SEC, and the thousands of interviews that had been conducted by the agency's staff, all that remained were a few perfunctory lines for each case. The mountains of evidence gathered were no longer in existence.

To read through the list of dead and buried cases that Flynn submitted to Congress is like looking through an infrared camera at a haunted house of the financial crisis, with the ghosts of missed prosecutions flashing back and forth across the screen. A snippet of the list:

| Party | MUI # | Opened / Closed | Issue |
|-------|-------|-----------------|-------|
| Goldman Sachs | MLA-01909 | 6/99–4/00 | Market Manipulation |
| Deutsche Bank | MHO-09356 | 11/01–7/02 | Insider Trading |
| Deutsche Bank | MHO-09432 | 2/02–8/02 | Market Manipulation |
| Lehman Brothers | MNY-07013 | 3/02–7/02 | Financial Fraud |
| Goldman Sachs | MNY-08198 | 11/09–2/09 | Insider Trading |

One MUI—case MNY-08145—involved allegations of insider trading at AIG on September 15, 2008, right in the middle of the insurance giant's collapse. In that case, an AIG employee named Jacqueline Millan reported irregularities in the trading of AIG stock to her superiors, only to find herself fired. Incredibly, instead of looking into the matter itself, the SEC agreed to accept "an internal investigation by outside counsel or AIG." The last note in the file indicates that "the staff plans to speak with the outside attorneys on Monday, August 24th [2009], when they will share their findings with us." The fact that the SEC trusted AIG's lawyers to investigate the matter shows the basic bassackwardness of the agency's approach to these crash-era investigations. The SEC formally closed the case on October 1, 2009.

The episode with AIG highlights yet another obstacle that MUIs experience on the road to becoming formal investigations. During the past decade, the SEC routinely began allowing financial firms to investigate themselves. Imagine the LAPD politely asking a gang of Crips and their lawyers to issue a report on whether or not a drive-by shooting by the Crips should be brought before a grand jury—that's basically how the SEC now handles many preliminary investigations against Wall Street targets.

The evolution toward this self-policing model began in 2001, when a shipping and food-service conglomerate called Seaboard aggressively investigated an isolated case of accounting fraud at one of its subsidiaries. Seaboard fired the guilty parties and made sweeping changes to its internal practices—and the SEC was so impressed that it instituted a new policy of giving "credit" to companies that police themselves. In practice, that means the agency simply steps aside and allows companies to slap themselves on the wrists. In the case against Seaboard, for instance, the SEC rewarded the firm by issuing no fines against it.

According to Lynn Turner, a former chief accountant at the SEC, the Seaboard case also prompted the SEC to begin permitting companies to hire their own counsel to conduct their own inquiries. At first, he says, the process worked fairly well. But then President Bush appointed the notoriously industry-friendly Christopher Cox to head up the SEC, and the "outside investigations" turned into whitewash jobs. "The investigations nowadays are probably not worth the money you spend on them," Turner says.

Harry Markopolos, a certified fraud examiner best known for sounding a famously unheeded warning about Bernie Madoff way back in 2000, says the SEC's practice of asking suspects to investigate themselves is absurd. In a serious investigation, he says, "the last person you want to trust is the person being accused or their lawyer." The practice helped Madoff escape for years. "The SEC took Bernie's word for everything," Markopolos says.

At the SEC, having realized that the agency was destroying documents, Flynn became concerned that he was overseeing an illegal policy. So in the summer of last year, he reached out to NARA, asking them for guidance on the issue.

That request sparked a worried response from Paul Wester, NARA's director of modern records. On July 29, 2010, Wester sent a letter to Barry Walters, who oversees document requests for the SEC. "We recently learned from Darcy Flynn . . . that for the past 17 years the SEC has been destroying closed Matters Under Inquiry files," Wester wrote. "If you confirm that federal records have been destroyed improperly, please ensure that no further such disposals take place and provide us with a written report within 30 days."

Wester copied the letter to Adam Storch, a former Goldman Sachs executive who less than a year earlier had been appointed as managing executive of the SEC's enforcement division. Storch's appointment was not without controversy. "I'm not sure what's scarier," Daniel Indiviglio of *The Atlantic* observed, "that this guy worked at an investment bank that many believe has questionable ethics and too cozy a Washington connection, or that he's just 29." In any case, Storch reacted to the NARA letter the way the SEC often does—by circling the wagons and straining to find a way to blow off the problem without admitting anything.

Last August, as the clock wound down on NARA's thirty-day deadline, Storch and two top SEC lawyers held a meeting with Flynn to discuss how to respond. Flynn's notes from the meeting, which he passed along to Congress, show the SEC staff wondering aloud if admitting the truth to NARA might be a bad idea, given the fact that there might be criminal liability.

"We could say that we do not believe there has been disposal inconsistent with the schedule," Flynn quotes Ken Hall, an assistant chief counsel for the SEC, as saying.

"There are implications to admit what was destroyed," Storch chimed in. It would be "not wise for me to take on the exposure voluntarily. If this leads to something, what rings in my ear is that Barry [Walters, the SEC documents officer] said: This is serious, could lead to criminal liability."

When the subject of how many files were destroyed came up, Storch answered: "18,000 MUIs destroyed, including Madoff."

Four days later, the SEC responded to NARA with a hilariously convoluted nondenial denial. "The Division is not aware of any specific instances of the destruction of records from any other MUI," the letter states. "But we cannot say with certainty that no such documents have been destroyed over the past 17 years." The letter goes on to add that "the Division has taken steps . . . to ensure that no MUI records are destroyed while we review this issue."

Translation: Hey, maybe records were destroyed, maybe they weren't. But if we did destroy records, we promise not to do it again—for now.

The SEC's unwillingness to admit the extent of the wrongdoing left Flynn in a precarious position. The agency has a remarkably bad record when it comes to dealing with whistle-blowers. Back in 2005, when Flynn's attorney, Gary Aguirre, tried to pursue an insider-trading case against Pequot Capital that involved John Mack, the future CEO of Morgan Stanley, he was fired by phone while on vacation. Two Senate committees later determined that Aguirre, who has since opened a private practice representing whistle-blowers, was dismissed improperly as part of a "process of reprisal" by the SEC. Two whistle-blowers in the Stanford case, Julie Preuitt and Joel Sauer, also experienced retaliation—including reprimands and demotions—after raising concerns about superficial investigations. "There's no mechanism to raise these issues at the SEC," says another former whistle-blower. Contacting the agency's inspector general, he adds, is considered "the nuclear option"—a move "well-known to be a career-killer."

In Flynn's case, both he and Aguirre tried to keep the matter in-house, appealing to SEC chairman Mary Schapiro with a promise not to go outside the agency if she would grant Flynn protection against reprisal. When no such offer was forthcoming, Flynn went to the agency's inspector general before sending a detailed letter about the wrongdoing to three congressional committees.

One of the offices Flynn contacted was that of Sen. Grassley, who was in the midst of his own battle with the SEC. Frustrated with the agency's failure to punish major players on Wall Street, the Iowa Republican had begun an investigation into how the SEC follows up on outside complaints. Specifically, he wrote a letter to FINRA, another regulatory agency, to ask how many complaints it had referred to the SEC about SAC Capital, the hedge fund run by reptilian billionaire short-seller Stevie Cohen.

SAC has long been accused of a variety of improprieties, from insider trading to harassment. But no charge in recent Wall Street history is crazier than an episode involving a SAC executive named Ping Jiang, who was accused in 2006 of enacting a torturous hazing program. According to a civil lawsuit that was later dropped, Jiang allegedly forced a new trader named Andrew Tong to take female hormones, come to work wearing a dress and lipstick, have "foreign objects" inserted in his rectum, and allow Jiang to urinate in his mouth. (I'm not making this up.)

Grassley learned that over the past decade, FINRA had referred nineteen complaints about suspicious trades at SAC to federal regulators. Curious to see how many of those referrals had been looked into, Grassley wrote the SEC on May 24, asking for evidence that the agency had properly investigated the cases.

Two weeks later, on June 9, Khuzami sent Grassley a surprisingly brusque answer: "We generally do not comment on the status of investigations or related referrals, and, in turn, are not providing information concerning the specific FINRA referrals you identified." Translation: We're not giving you the records, so blow us.

Grassley later found out from FINRA that it had actually referred sixty-five cases about SAC to the SEC, making the lack of serious investigations even more inexplicable. Angered by Khuzami's response, he sent the SEC another letter on June 15 demanding an explanation, but no answer has been forthcoming.

In the interim, Grassley's office was contacted by Flynn, who explained that among the missing MUIs he had uncovered were at least three involving SAC—one in 2006, one in 2007, and one in 2010, involving charges of insider trading and currency manipulation. All three cases were closed by the SEC, and the records apparently destroyed.

On August 17, Grassley sent a letter to the SEC about the Flynn allegations, demanding to know if it was indeed true that the SEC had destroyed records. He also asked if the agency's failure to produce evidence of investigations into SAC Capital were related to the missing MUIs.

The SEC's inspector general is investigating the destroyed MUIs and plans to issue a report. NARA is also seeking answers. "We've asked the SEC to look into the matter and we're awaiting their response," says Laurence Brewer, a records officer for NARA. For its part, the SEC is trying to explain away the illegality of its actions through a semantic trick. John Nester, the agency's spokesman, acknowledges that "documents related to MUIs" have been destroyed. "I don't have any reason to believe that it hasn't always been the policy," he says. But Nester suggests that such documents do not "meet the federal definition of a record," and therefore don't have to be preserved under federal law.

But even if SEC officials manage to dodge criminal charges, it won't change what happened: The nation's top financial police destroyed more than a decade's worth of intelligence they had gathered on some of Wall Street's most egregious offenders. "The SEC not keeping the MUIs—you can see why this would be bad," says Markopolos, the fraud examiner famous for breaking the Madoff case. "The reason you would want to keep them is to build a pattern. That way, if you get five MUIs over a period of twenty years on something similar involving the same company, you should be able to connect five dots and say, 'You know, I've had five MUIs—they're probably doing something. Let's go tear the place apart.'" Destroy the MUIs, and Wall Street banks can commit the exact same crime over and over, without anyone ever knowing.

Regulation isn't a panacea. The SEC could have placed federal agents on every corner of lower Manhattan throughout the past decade, and it might not have put a dent in the massive wave of corruption and fraud that left the economy in flames three years ago. And even if SEC staffers from top to bottom had been fully committed to rooting out financial corruption, the agency would still have been seriously hampered by a lack of resources that often forces it to abandon promising cases due to a shortage of manpower. "It's always a triage," is how one SEC veteran puts it. "And it's worse now."

But we're equally in the dark about another hypothetical. Forget about what might have been if the SEC had followed up in earnest on *all* of those lost MUIs. What if even a handful of them had turned into real cases? How many investors might have been saved from crushing losses if Lehman Brothers had been forced to reveal its shady accounting way back in 2002? Might the need for taxpayer bailouts have been lessened had fraud cases against Citigroup and Bank of America been pursued in 2005 and 2007? And would the U.S. government have doubled down on its bailout of AIG if it had known that some of the firm's executives were suspected of insider trading in September 2008?

It goes without saying that no ordinary law-enforcement agency would willingly destroy its own evidence. In fact, when it comes to garden-variety crooks, more and more police agencies are catching criminals with the aid of large and well-maintained databases. "Street-level law enforcement is increasingly data-driven," says Bill Laufer, a criminology professor at the University of Pennsylvania. "For a host of reasons, though, we are starved for good data on both white-collar and corporate crime. So the idea that we would take the little data we do have and shred it, without a legal requirement to do so, calls for a very creative explanation."

We'll never know what the impact of those destroyed cases might have been; we'll never know if those cases were closed for good reasons or bad. We'll never know exactly who got away with what because federal regulators have weighted down a huge sack of Wall Street's dirty laundry and dumped it in a lake, never to be seen again.

**The New York Times**

During his acceptance speech after wining the 2011 Oscar for best documentary, the filmmaker Charles Ferguson famously noted that not a single financial executive had yet gone to jail as a result of the crisis, adding, "And that's wrong." That remains true as we go to press. Here, Gretchen Morgenson, one of the most accomplished financial reporters of her generation, and rising star Louise Story explain that government prosecutors and regulators ignored lessons of past financial crackups and failed even to muster a collective government-wide effort to get to the bottom of potential wrongdoing. While acknowledging the legal and factual complexities of financial prosecutions, Morgenson and Story also point to key decisions by top policy makers under both the Bush and Obama administrations that have hamstrung federal criminal probes. In doing so, they provide an answer to one of the most vexing questions lingering after the crisis.

Gretchen Morgenson
and Louise Story

# 10. In Financial Crisis, No Prosecutions of Top Figures

It is a question asked repeatedly across America: why, in the aftermath of a financial mess that generated hundreds of billions in losses, have no high-profile participants in the disaster been prosecuted?

Answering such a question—the equivalent of determining why a dog did not bark—is anything but simple. But a private meeting in mid-October 2008 between Timothy F. Geithner, then president of the Federal Reserve Bank of New York, and Andrew M. Cuomo, New York's attorney general at the time, illustrates the complexities of pursuing legal cases in a time of panic.

At the Fed, which oversees the nation's largest banks, Mr. Geithner worked with the Treasury Department on a large bailout fund for the banks and led efforts to shore up the American International Group, the giant insurer. His focus: stabilizing world financial markets.

Mr. Cuomo, as a Wall Street enforcer, had been questioning banks and rating agencies aggressively for more than a year about their roles in the growing debacle, and also looking into bonuses at AIG.

Friendly since their days in the Clinton administration, the two met in Mr. Cuomo's office in Lower Manhattan, steps from Wall Street and the New York Fed. According to three people briefed at the time about the meeting, Mr. Geithner expressed concern about the fragility of the financial system.

His worry, according to these people, sprang from a desire to calm markets, a goal that could be complicated by a hard-charging attorney general.

Asked whether the unusual meeting had altered his approach, a spokesman for Mr. Cuomo, now New York's governor, said Wednesday evening that "Mr. Geithner never suggested that there be any lack of diligence or any slowdown." Mr. Geithner, now the treasury secretary, said through a spokesman that he had been focused on AIG "to protect taxpayers."

Whether prosecutors and regulators have been aggressive enough in pursuing wrongdoing is likely to long be a subject of debate. All say they have done the best they could under difficult circumstances.

But several years after the financial crisis, which was caused in large part by reckless lending and excessive risk taking by major financial institutions, no senior executives have been charged or imprisoned, and a collective government effort has not emerged. This stands in stark contrast to the failure of many savings and loan institutions in the late 1980s. In the wake of that debacle, special government task forces referred 1,100 cases to prosecutors, resulting in more than 800 bank officials going to jail. Among the best-known: Charles H. Keating Jr., of Lincoln Savings and Loan in Arizona, and David Paul, of Centrust Bank in Florida.

Former prosecutors, lawyers, bankers, and mortgage employees say that investigators and regulators ignored past lessons about how to crack financial fraud.

As the crisis was starting to deepen in the spring of 2008, the Federal Bureau of Investigation scaled back a plan to assign more field agents to investigate mortgage fraud. That summer, the Justice Department also rejected calls to create a task force devoted to mortgage-related investigations, leaving these complex cases understaffed and poorly funded, and only much later established a more general financial crimes task force.

Leading up to the financial crisis, many officials said in interviews, regulators failed in their crucial duty to compile the information that traditionally has helped build criminal cases. In effect, the same dynamic that helped enable the crisis—weak regulation—also made it harder to pursue fraud in its aftermath.

A more aggressive mind-set could have spurred far more prosecutions this time, officials involved in the S&L cleanup said.

"This is not some evil conspiracy of two guys sitting in a room saying we should let people create crony capitalism and steal with impunity," said William K. Black, a professor of law at University of Missouri, Kansas City, and the federal government's director of litigation during the savings and loan crisis. "But their policies have created an exceptional criminogenic environment. There were no criminal referrals from the regulators. No fraud working groups. No national task force. There has been no effective punishment of the elites here."

Even civil actions by the government have been limited. The Securities and Exchange Commission adopted a broad guideline in 2009—distributed within the agency but never made public—to be cautious about pushing for hefty penalties from banks that had received bailout money. The agency was concerned about taxpayer money in effect being used to pay for settlements, according to four people briefed on the policy but who were not authorized to speak publicly about it.

To be sure, Wall Street's role in the crisis is complex, and cases related to mortgage securities are immensely technical. Criminal intent in particular is difficult to prove, and banks defend their actions with documents they say show they operated properly.

But legal experts point to numerous questionable activities where criminal probes might have borne fruit and possibly still could.

Investigators, they argue, could look more deeply at the failure of executives to fully disclose the scope of the risks on their books during the mortgage mania or the amounts of questionable loans they bundled into securities sold to investors that soured.

Prosecutors also could pursue evidence that executives knowingly awarded bonuses to themselves and colleagues based on overly optimistic valuations of mortgage assets—in effect, creating illusory profits that were wiped out by subsequent losses on the same assets. And they might also investigate whether executives cashed in shares based on inside information, or misled regulators and their own boards about looming problems.

Merrill Lynch, for example, understated its risky mortgage holdings by hundreds of billions of dollars. And public comments made by Angelo R. Mozilo, the chief executive of Countrywide Financial, praising his mortgage company's practices were at odds with derisive statements he made privately in e-mails as he sold shares; the stock subsequently fell sharply as the company's losses became known.

Executives at Lehman Brothers assured investors in the summer of 2008 that the company's financial position was sound, even though they appeared to have counted as assets certain holdings pledged by Lehman to other companies, according to a person briefed on that case. At Bear Stearns, the first major Wall Street player to collapse, a private litigant says evidence shows that the firm's executives may have pocketed revenues that should have gone to investors to offset losses when complex mortgage securities soured.

But the Justice Department has decided not to pursue some of these matters—including possible criminal cases against Mr. Mozilo of Countrywide and Joseph J. Cassano, head of financial products at AIG, the business at the epicenter of that company's collapse. Mr. Cassano's lawyers said that documents they had given to prosecutors refuted accusations that he had misled investors or the company's board. Mr. Mozilo's lawyers have said he denies any wrongdoing.

Among the few exceptions so far in civil action against senior bankers is a lawsuit filed last month against top executives of Washington Mutual, the failed bank now owned by JPMorgan Chase. The Federal Deposit Insurance Corporation sued Kerry K. Killinger, the company's former chief executive, and two other officials, accusing them of piling on risky loans to grow faster and increase their compensation. The SEC also extracted a $550 million settlement from Goldman Sachs for a mortgage security the bank built, though the SEC did not name executives in that case.

Representatives at the Justice Department and the SEC say they are still pursuing financial-crisis cases, but legal experts warn that they become more difficult as time passes.

"If you look at the last couple of years and say, 'This is the big-ticket prosecution that came out of the crisis,' you realize we haven't gotten very much," said David A. Skeel, a law professor at the University of Pennsylvania. "It's consistent with what many people were worried about during the crisis, that different rules would be applied to different players. It goes to the whole perception that Wall Street was taken care of, and Main Street was not."

## The Countrywide Puzzle

As nonprosecutions go, perhaps none is more puzzling to legal experts than the case of Countrywide, the nation's largest mortgage lender. Last month, the office of the United States attorney for Los Angeles dropped its investigation of Mr. Mozilo after the SEC extracted a settlement from him in a civil fraud case. Mr. Mozilo paid $22.5 million in penalties, without admitting or denying the accusations.

White-collar crime lawyers contend that Countrywide exemplifies the difficulties of mounting a criminal case without assistance and documentation from regulators—the Office of the Comptroller of the Currency, the Office of Thrift Supervision, and the Fed, in Countrywide's case.

"When regulators don't believe in regulation and don't get what is going on at the companies they oversee, there can be no major white-collar crime prosecutions," said Henry N. Pontell, professor of criminology, law, and society in the School of Social Ecology at the University of California, Irvine. "If they don't understand what we call collective embezzlement, where people are literally looting their own firms, then it's impossible to bring cases."

Financial crisis cases can be brought by many parties. Since the big banks' mortgage machinery involved loans on properties across the country, attorneys general in most states have broad criminal authority over most of these institutions. The Justice Department can bring civil or criminal cases, while the SEC can file only civil lawsuits.

All of these enforcement agencies traditionally depend heavily on referrals from bank regulators, who are more savvy on complex financial matters.

But data supplied by the Justice Department and compiled by a group at Syracuse University show that over the last decade, regulators have referred substantially fewer cases to criminal investigators than previously.

The university's Transactional Records Access Clearinghouse indicates that in 1995, bank regulators referred 1,837 cases to the Justice Department. In 2006, that number had fallen to 75. In the four subsequent years, a period encompassing the worst of the crisis, an average of only 72 a year have been referred for criminal prosecution.

Law enforcement officials say financial-case referrals began declining under President Clinton as his administration shifted its focus to health care fraud. The trend continued in the Bush administration, except for a spike in prosecutions for Enron, WorldCom, Tyco, and others for accounting fraud.

The Office of Thrift Supervision was in a particularly good position to help guide possible prosecutions. From the summer of 2007 to the end of 2008, OTS-overseen banks with $355 billion in assets failed.

The thrift supervisor, however, has not referred a single case to the Justice Department since 2000, the Syracuse data show. The Office of the Comptroller of the Currency, a unit of the Treasury Department, has referred only three in the last decade.

The comptroller's office declined to comment on its referrals. But a spokesman, Kevin Mukri, noted that bank regulators can and do bring their own civil enforcement actions. But most are against small banks and do not involve the stiff penalties that accompany criminal charges.

Historically, Countrywide's bank subsidiary was overseen by the comptroller, while the Federal Reserve supervised its home loans unit. But in March 2007, Countrywide switched oversight of both units to the thrift supervisor. That agency was overseen at the time by John M. Reich, a former banker and Senate staff member appointed in 2005 by President George W. Bush.

Robert Gnaizda, former general counsel at the Greenlining Institute, a nonprofit consumer organization in Oakland, Calif., said he had spoken often with Mr. Reich about Countrywide's reckless lending.

"We saw that people were getting bad loans," Mr. Gnaizda recalled. "We focused on Countrywide because they were the largest originator in California and they were the ones with the most exotic mortgages."

Mr. Gnaizda suggested many times that the thrift supervisor tighten its oversight of the company, he said. He said he advised Mr. Reich to set up a hotline for whistle-blowers inside Countrywide to communicate with regulators.

"I told John, 'This is what any police chief does if he wants to solve a crime,'" Mr. Gnaizda said in an interview. "John was uninterested. He told me he was a good friend of Mozilo's."

In an e-mail message, Mr. Reich said he did not recall the conversation with Mr. Gnaizda, and his relationships with the chief executives of banks overseen by his agency were strictly professional. "I met with Mr. Mozilo only a few times, always in a business environment, and any insinuation of a personal friendship is simply false," he wrote.

After the crisis had subsided, another opportunity to investigate Countrywide and its executives yielded little. The Financial Crisis Inquiry Commission, created by Congress to investigate the origins of the disaster, decided not to make an in-depth examination of the company—though some staff members felt strongly that it should.

In a January 2010 memo, Brad Bondi and Martin Biegelman, two assistant directors of the commission, outlined their recommendations for investigative targets and hearings, according to Tom Krebs, another assistant director of the commission. Countrywide and Mr. Mozilo were specifically named; the memo noted that subprime-mortgage executives like Mr. Mozilo received hundreds of millions of dollars in compensation even though their companies collapsed.

However, the two soon received a startling message: Countrywide was off-limits. In a staff meeting, deputies to Phil Angelides, the commission's chairman, said he had told them Countrywide should not be a target or featured at any hearing, said Mr. Krebs, who said he was briefed on that meeting by Mr. Bondi and Mr. Biegelman shortly after it occurred. His account has been confirmed by two other people with direct knowledge of the situation.

Mr. Angelides denied that he had said Countrywide or Mr. Mozilo were off-limits. Chris Seefer, the FCIC official responsible for the Countrywide investigation, also said Countrywide had not been given a pass. Mr. Angelides said a full investigation was done on the company, including forty interviews, and that a hearing was planned for the fall of 2010 to feature Mr. Mozilo. It was canceled because Republican members of the commission did not want any more hearings, he said.

"It got as full a scrub as AIG, Citi, anyone," Mr. Angelides said of Countrywide. "If you look at the report, it's extraordinarily condemnatory."

## An FBI Investigation Fizzles

The Justice Department in Washington was abuzz in the spring of 2008. Bear Stearns had collapsed, and some law enforcement insiders were suggesting an in-depth search for fraud throughout the mortgage pipeline.

The FBI had expressed concerns about mortgage improprieties as early as 2004. But it was not until four years later that its officials recommended closing several investigative programs to free agents for financial fraud cases, according to two people briefed on a study by the bureau.

The study identified about two dozen regions where mortgage fraud was believed rampant, and the bureau's criminal division created a plan to investigate major banks and lenders. Robert S. Mueller III, the director of the FBI, approved the plan, which was described in a memo sent in spring 2008 to the bureau's field offices.

"We were focused on the whole gamut: the individuals, the mortgage brokers and the top of the industry," said Kenneth W. Kaiser, the former assistant director of the criminal investigations unit. "We were looking at the corporate level."

Days after the memo was sent, however, prosecutors at some Justice Department offices began to complain that shifting agents to mortgage cases would hurt other investigations, he recalled. "We got told by the DOJ not to shift those resources," he said. About a week later, he said, he was told to send another memo undoing many of the changes. Some of the extra agents were not deployed.

A spokesman for the FBI, Michael Kortan, said that a second memo was sent out that allowed field offices to try to opt out of some of the changes in the first memo. Mr. Kaiser's account of pushback from the Justice Department was confirmed by two other people who were at the FBI in 2008.

Around the same time, the Justice Department also considered setting up a financial fraud task force specifically to scrutinize the mortgage industry. Such task forces had been crucial to winning cases against Enron executives and those who looted savings and loans in the early 1990s.

Michael B. Mukasey, a former federal judge in New York who had been the head of the Justice Department less than a year when Bear Stearns fell, discussed the matter with deputies, three people briefed on the talks said. He decided against a task force and announced his decision in June 2008.

Last year, officials of the Financial Crisis Inquiry Commission interviewed Mr. Mukasey. Asked if he was aware of requests for more resources to be dedicated to mortgage fraud, Mr. Mukasey said he did not recall internal requests.

A spokesman for Mr. Mukasey, who is now at the law firm Debevoise & Plimpton in New York, said he would not comment beyond his FCIC testimony. He had no knowledge of the FBI memo, his spokesman added.

A year later—with precious time lost—several lawmakers decided that the government needed more people tracking financial crimes. Congress passed a bill, providing a $165 million budget increase to the FBI and Justice Department for investigations in this area. But when lawmakers got around to allocating the budget, only about $30 million in new money was provided.

Subsequently, in late 2009, the Justice Department announced a task force to focus broadly on financial crimes. But it received no additional resources.

## A Break for Eight Banks

In July 2008, the staff of the SEC received a phone call from Scott G. Alvarez, general counsel at the Federal Reserve in Washington.

The purpose: to discuss an SEC investigation into improprieties by several of the nation's largest brokerage firms. Their actions had hammered thousands of investors holding the short-term investments known as auction-rate securities.

These investments carry interest rates that reset regularly, usually weekly, in auctions overseen by the brokerage firms that sell them. They were popular among investors because the interest rates they received were slightly higher than what they could earn elsewhere.

For years, companies like UBS and Goldman Sachs operated auctions of these securities, promoting them as highly liquid investments. But by mid-February 2008, as the subprime mortgage crisis began to spread, investors holding hundreds of billions of dollars of these securities could no longer cash them in.

As the SEC investigated these events, several of its officials argued that the banks should make all investors whole on the securities, according to three people with knowledge of the negotiations but who were not authorized to speak publicly, because banks had marketed them as safe investments.

But Mr. Alvarez suggested that the SEC soften the proposed terms of the auction-rate settlements. His staff followed up with more calls to the SEC, cautioning that banks might run short on capital if they had to pay the many billions of dollars needed to make all auction-rate clients whole, the people briefed on the conversations said. The SEC wound up requiring eight banks to pay back only individual investors. For institutional investors— like pension funds—that bought the securities, the SEC told the banks to make only their "best efforts."

This shift eased the pain significantly at some of the nation's biggest banks. For Citigroup, the new terms meant it had to redeem $7 billion in the securities for individual investors—but it was off the hook for about $12 billion owned by institutions. These institutions have subsequently recouped some but not all of their investments. Mr. Alvarez declined to comment, through a spokeswoman.

An SEC spokesman said: "The primary consideration was remedying the alleged wrongdoing and in fashioning that remedy, the emphasis was placed on retail investors because they were suffering the greatest hardship and had the fewest avenues for redress."

A similar caution emerged in other civil cases after the bank bailouts in the autumn of 2008. The SEC's investigations of financial institutions began to be questioned by its staff and the agency's commissioners, who worried that the settlements might be paid using federal bailout money.

Four people briefed on the discussions, who spoke anonymously because they were not authorized to speak publicly, said that in early 2009, the SEC created a broad policy involving settlements with companies that had received taxpayer assistance. In discussions with the Treasury Department, the agency's division of enforcement devised a guideline stating that the financial health of those banks should be taken into account when the agency negotiated settlements with them.

"This wasn't a political thing so much as, 'We don't know if it makes sense to bring a big penalty against a bank that just got a check from the government,'" said one of the people briefed on the discussions.

The people briefed on the SEC's settlement policy said that while it did not directly affect many settlements, it slowed down the investigative work on other cases. A spokesman for the SEC declined to comment.

## Attorney General Moves On

The final chapter still hasn't been written about the financial crisis and its aftermath. One thing has been especially challenging for regulators and law enforcement officials: balancing concerns for the state of the financial system even as they pursued immensely complicated cases.

The conundrum was especially clear back in the fall of 2008 when Mr. Geithner visited Mr. Cuomo and discussed AIG. Asked for details about the meeting, a spokesman for Mr. Geithner said: "As AIG's largest creditor, the New York Federal Reserve installed new management at AIG in the fall of 2008 and directed the new CEO to take steps to end wasteful spending by the company in order to protect taxpayers."

Mr. Cuomo's office said, "The attorney general went on to lead the most aggressive investigation of AIG and other financial institutions in the nation." After that meeting, and until he left to become governor, Mr. Cuomo focused on the financial crisis, with mixed success. In late 2010, Mr. Cuomo sued the accounting firm Ernst & Young, accusing it of helping its client Lehman Brothers "engage in massive accounting fraud."

To date, however, no arm of government has sued Lehman or any of its executives on the same accounting tactic.

Other targets have also avoided legal action. Mr. Cuomo investigated the 2008 bonuses that were paid out by giant banks just after the bailout, and he considered bringing a case to try to claw back some of that money, two people familiar with the matter said. But ultimately he chose to publicly shame the companies by releasing their bonus figures.

Mr. Cuomo took a tough stance on Bank of America. While the SEC settled its case with Bank of America without charging any executives with wrongdoing, Mr. Cuomo filed a civil fraud lawsuit against Kenneth D. Lewis, the former chief executive, and the bank's former chief financial officer. The suit accuses them of understating the losses of Merrill Lynch to shareholders before the deal was approved; the case is still pending.

Last spring, Mr. Cuomo issued new mortgage-related subpoenas to eight large banks. He was interested in whether the banks had misled the ratings agencies about the quality of the loans they were bundling and asked how many workers they had hired from the ratings agencies. But Mr. Cuomo did not bring a case on this matter before leaving office.

Part III

# Over There

Martin Wolf

# 11. Time for Germany to Make Its Fateful Choice

"Perhaps future historians will consider Maastricht a decisive step towards the emergence of a stable, European-wide power. Yet there is another, darker possibility.... The effort to bind states together may lead, instead, to a huge increase in frictions among them. If so, the event would meet the classical definition of tragedy: *hubris* (arrogance), *ate* (folly); *nemesis* (destruction)."

I wrote the above in the *Financial Times* almost twenty years ago. My fears are coming true. This crisis has done more than demonstrate that the initial design of the eurozone was defective, as most intelligent analysts then knew; it has also revealed—and, in the process, exacerbated—a fundamental lack of trust, let alone sense of shared identity, among the peoples locked together in what has become a marriage of inconvenience.

The extent of the breakdown was not brought home to me by the resignation of Germany's Jürgen Stark from the board of the European Central Bank, nor by the looming Greek default, nor by new constraints imposed by the German constitutional court. What brought it home to me was a visit to Rome.

This is what I heard from an Italian policy maker: "We gave up the old safety valves of inflation and devaluation in return for lower interest rates, but now we do not even have the low interest rates." Then: "Some people seem to think we have joined a currency board, but Italy is not Latvia." And, not least: "It would be better to leave than endure thirty years of pain." These remarks speak of a loss of faith in both the project and the partners.

In his latest press conference, Jean-Claude Trichet, outgoing president of the European Central Bank, pointed to the bank's stellar counter-inflationary record, far better than the Bundesbank's. But the low inflation masked the emergence of profound imbalances within the zone and the lack of means—or will—to resolve them. As a result, a default by a major government, a break-up of the eurozone, or both is now conceivable. The consequent flight to safety, which must include attempts to hedge cross-border exposures in a supposedly integrated currency area, threatens a meltdown. We are witnessing a lethal interplay between fears of sovereign insolvency, emerging sovereign illiquidity, and financial stress.

As designed the eurozone lacked essential institutions, the most important being a central bank able and willing to act as lender of last resort in all important markets, a rescue fund large enough to ensure liquidity in sovereign bond markets, and effective ways of managing an interconnected web of sovereign insolvencies and banking crises.

In the absence of strong institutions, the attitudes and policies of the core country have become crucial. Along with everybody else, I admire the political and economic reconstruction of Germany after the Second World War and again after unification, the commitment to economic stability, and its first-class manufactured exports. Unfortunately, these are insufficient. German policy makers persist in viewing the world through the lens of a relatively small, open, and highly competitive economy. But the eurozone is not a small open economy; it is a large and relatively closed one. The core country of such a union must either provide a buoyant market for less creditworthy countries when the latter can no longer finance their deficits, or it has to finance them. If the private sector will not provide the needed finance, the public sector must do so. If the latter fails to act, a wave of private- and public-sector defaults will occur. These are sure to damage the financial sector and exports of the core country itself, as well.

The failure of Germany's leaders to explain these facts at home makes it impossible to solve the current crisis. Instead, they indulge in the fantasy that everybody can be a lender, simultaneously. For small open economies such as Latvia and Ireland, regaining competitiveness and growth through deflation might work. For a big country such as Italy, it is too painful to be credible. Wolfgang Schäuble, Germany's finance minister, may call for such austerity. It will not happen.

Today, raging fire must be put out. Only then can attempts at building a more fireproof eurozone begin. The least bad option would be for the ECB to ensure liquidity for solvent governments and financial institutions, without limit. It should not, in fact, be intellectually difficult to argue that buying bonds is compatible with continued monetary stability, since broad money has been growing at a mere 2 percent a year. It is sure to be politically hard, however, particularly for Mario Draghi, the incoming Italian ECB president. Yet it is what has to be done given the inadequate size of the European financial stability facility if called on to help larger beleaguered euro-member countries. Politicians must then dare to support such action.

What should happen if the German government decided that it could not support such a bold step? The ECB should go ahead anyway rather than let a cascading collapse unfold. It would then be up to Germany to decide whether to leave, perhaps with Austria, the Netherlands and Finland. The German people should be made aware that the results would include a soaring exchange rate, a massive decline in the profitability of Germany's exports, a huge financial shock, and a sharp fall in gross domestic product. All this would be apart from the failure of two generations of efforts to build a strong European framework around Germany itself.

Germany possesses a binding veto over efforts to expand official fiscal support. But it is losing control over its central bank. In a crisis so menacing to Europe and the world, the one European institution with the capacity to act on the requisite scale should dare to do so, since the costs of not doing so are bound to prove devastating. That will surely create a political crisis, but this would be better than the financial crisis unleashed by a failure to try.

In the end Germany must choose between a eurozone disturbingly different from the larger Germany it expected or no eurozone at all. I recognize how much its leaders and people must hate having been forced into a position in which they have to make this choice. But it is the one they confront. Chancellor Angela Merkel must now dare to make that choice, clearly and openly.

*Inc.*

If you were going to build an entrepreneurial paradise from scratch, you might well make it look a lot like Norway—a place with high taxes, a strong social safety net, and regulations that make it very hard to fire workers. Max Chafkin does a fantastic job of explaining this counterintuitive conclusion in his tour of Norway's entrepreneurs—who, like entrepreneurs anywhere else in the world, are not actually motivated primarily by money. In fact, it turns out that if you give your population a strong net to support those who fall, many more of them will take the risks that drive growth.

Max Chafkin

# 12. In Norway, Start-Ups Say Ja to Socialism

Wiggo Dalmo is a classic entrepreneurial type: the Working-Class Kid Made Good.

Dalmo, who is thirty-nine, with sandy blond hair and an easy smile, grew up in modest circumstances in a blue-collar town dominated by the steel industry. After graduating from high school, he apprenticed as an industrial mechanic and got a job repairing mining equipment.

He liked the challenge of the work but not the drudgery of working for someone else. "I never felt like there was a place for me as an employee," Dalmo explains as we drive past spent chemical drums and enormous mounds of scrap metal on the road that leads to his office. When he needed an inexpensive part to complete a repair, company rules required Dalmo to fill out a purchase order and wait days for approval, when he knew he could simply walk into a hardware store and buy one. He resented this on a practical level—and as an insult to his intelligence. "I wanted more responsibility at my job, more control," he says. "I wanted freedom."

In 1998, Dalmo quit his job, bought a used pickup truck, and started calling on clients as an independent contractor. By year's end, he had six employees, all mechanics, and he was making more money than he ever had. Within three years, his new company, Momek, was booking more than $1 million a year in revenue and quickly expanding into new lines of business. He built a machine shop and began manufacturing parts for oil rigs, and he started bidding on and winning contracts to staff oil-drilling sites and mines throughout the country. He kept hiring, kept bidding, and when he looked around a decade later, he had a $44 million company with 150 employees.

As his company grew, Dalmo adopted the familiar habits of successful entrepreneurs. He bought a Porsche, a motorcycle, and a wardrobe of polo shirts with his corporate logo on the chest. As rock music blasts from the speakers in his office, Dalmo tells me that he is proud of the company he has created. "We tried to build a family, and we have succeeded," he says. "I have no friends outside this company."

This is exactly the kind of pride I often hear from the CEOs I have met while working at *Inc.*, but for one important difference: Whereas most entrepreneurs in Dalmo's position develop a retching distaste for paying taxes, Dalmo doesn't mind them much. "The tax system is good—it's fair," he tells me. "What we're doing when we are paying taxes is buying a product. So the question isn't how you pay for the product; it's the quality of the product." Dalmo *likes* the government's services, and he believes that he is paying a fair price.

This is particularly surprising, because the prices Dalmo pays for government services are among the highest in the world. He lives and works in the small city of Mo i Rana, which is about seventeen miles south of the Arctic Circle in Norway. As a Norwegian, he pays nearly 50 percent of his income to the federal government, along with a substantial additional tax that works out to roughly 1 percent of his total net worth. And that's just what he pays directly. Payroll taxes in Norway are double those in the United States. Sales taxes, at 25 percent, are roughly triple.

Last year, Dalmo paid $102,970 in personal taxes on his income and wealth. I know this because tax returns, like most everything else in Norway, are a matter of public record. Anyone anywhere can log on to a website maintained by the government and find out what kind of scratch a fellow Norwegian taxpayer makes—be he Ole Einar Bjørndalen, the famous Norwegian bi-athlete, or Ole the next-door neighbor. This, Dalmo explains, has a chilling effect on any desire he might have to live even larger. "When you start buying expensive stuff, people start to talk," says Dalmo. "I have to be careful, because some of the people who are judging are my potential customers."

Welcome to Norway, where business is radically transparent, militantly egalitarian, and, of course, heavily taxed. This is socialism, the sort of thing your average American CEO has nightmares about. But not Dalmo—and not most Norwegians. "The capitalist system functions well," Dalmo says. "But I'm a socialist in my bones."

·　　·　　·

Norway, population five million, is a very small, very rich country. It is a cold country and, for half the year, a dark country. (The sun sets in late November in Mo i Rana. It doesn't rise again until the end of January.) This is a place where entire cities smell of drying fish—an odor not unlike the smell of rotting fish—and where, in the most remote parts, one must be careful to avoid polar bears. The food isn't great.

Bear strikes, darkness, and whale meat notwithstanding, Norway is also an exceedingly pleasant place to make a home. It ranked third in Gallup's latest global happiness survey. The unemployment rate, just 3.5 percent, is the lowest in Europe and one of the lowest in the world. Thanks to a generous social welfare system, poverty is almost nonexistent.

Norway is also full of entrepreneurs like Wiggo Dalmo. Rates of start-up creation here are among the highest in the developed world, and Norway has more entrepreneurs per capita than the United States, according to the latest report by the Global Entrepreneurship Monitor, a Boston-based research consortium. A 2010 study released by the U.S. Small Business Administration reported a similar result: Although America remains near the top of the world in terms of entrepreneurial aspirations—that is, the percentage of people who want to start new things—in terms of actual start-up activity, our country has fallen behind not just Norway but also Canada, Denmark, and Switzerland.

If you care about the long-term health of the American economy, this should seem strange—maybe even troubling. After all, we have been told for decades that higher taxes are without-a-doubt, no-question-about-it Bad for Business. President Obama recently bragged that his administration had passed "sixteen different tax cuts for America's small businesses over the last couple years. These are tax cuts that can help America—help businesses . . . making new investments right now."

Since the Reagan Revolution, which drastically cut tax rates for wealthy individuals and corporations, we have gotten used to hearing these sorts of announcements from our leaders. Few have dared to argue against tax cuts for businesses and business owners. Questioning whether entrepreneurs really need tax cuts has been like asking if soldiers really need weapons or whether teachers really need textbooks—a possible position, sure, but one that would likely get you laughed out of the room if you suggested it. Or thrown out of elected office.

Taxes in the United States have fallen dramatically over the past thirty years. In 1978, the top federal tax rates were as follows: 70 percent for individuals, 48 percent for corporations, and almost 40 percent on capital gains. Americans as a whole paid the ninth-lowest taxes among countries in the Organization for Economic Cooperation and Development, a group of thirty-four of the largest democratic, market economies. Today, the top marginal tax rates are 35 percent, 35 percent, and 15 percent, respectively. (Even these rates overstate the level of taxation in America. Few large corporations pay anywhere near the 35 percent corporate tax; Warren Buffett has famously said that he pays 18 percent in income tax.) Only two countries in the OECD—Chile and Mexico—pay a lower percentage of their gross domestic product in taxes than we Americans do.

But there is precious little evidence to suggest that our low taxes have done much for entrepreneurs—or even for the economy as a whole. "It's actually quite hard to say how tax policy affects the economy," says Joel Slemrod, a University of Michigan professor who served on the Council of Economic Advisers under Ronald Reagan. Slemrod says there is no statistical evidence to prove that low taxes result in economic prosperity. Some of the most prosperous countries—for instance, Denmark, Sweden, Belgium, and, yes, Norway—also have some of the highest taxes. Norway, which in 2009 had the world's highest per-capita income, avoided the brunt of the financial crisis: From 2006 to 2009, its economy grew nearly 3 percent. The American economy grew less than one-tenth of a percent during the same period. Meanwhile, countries with some of the lowest taxes in Europe, like Ireland, Iceland, and Estonia, have suffered profoundly. The first two nearly went bankrupt; Estonia, the darling of antitax groups like the Cato Institute, currently has an unemployment rate of 16 percent. Its economy shrank 14 percent in 2009.

Moreover, the typical arguments peddled by business groups and in the editorial pages of the *Wall Street Journal*—the idea, for instance, that George W. Bush's tax cuts in 2001 and 2003 created economic growth—are problematic. The unemployment rate rose following the passage of both tax-cut packages, and economic growth during Bush's eight years in office badly lagged growth during the Clinton presidency, before the tax cuts were passed.

And so the case of Norway—one of the most entrepreneurial, most heavily taxed countries in the world—should give us pause. What if we have been wrong about taxes? What if tax cuts are nothing like weapons or textbooks? What if they don't matter as much as we think they do?

I'm sure I've already pissed off some people with that question— and not just the rich ones. It's hard these days to say anything positive about taxes without being accused of economic treason. President Barack Obama's health care plan and his proposal to allow certain Bush tax cuts to expire in 2012—a move that would cause the top marginal tax rate on individuals to go up by 4.6 basis points, to the rate that prevailed in the late 1990s—have caused the administration to be eviscerated by business groups and their allies. "We are essentially undoing the very thing that has made America exceptional: the free enterprise system," wrote congressional candidate (and now a Republican congressman from New York) Richard Hanna in a letter published by the National Federation of Independent Business. "We can no longer devalue the energy of the entrepreneur this way." Newt Gingrich, a presidential hopeful and the former Speaker of the House, has called Obama's presidency the first step toward "European socialism and secularism," which he has suggested is a greater threat to our country than Islamic terrorism.

The idea that Americans should be more terrified of Norwegian economists than of al Qaeda bomb makers is pretty nutty, but I couldn't help wondering: How bad would European socialism really be? What if President Obama's health care and tax policies—which so far have been modest by European standards—are just the beginning? What if his proposal to allow the income tax rate on the richest Americans to rise by several basis points is just the first step? What if, say, by some crazy backdoor dealing involving Joe Biden, Nancy Pelosi, and the Ghost of Ted Kennedy, liberals manage something more sweeping: taxes of 50 percent, a government-run health care system, an expansion of Social Security, and sweeping regulations on business?

In other words, instead of some American version of European socialism, what if we got the genuine article? What if the nightmare scenario were real? What if you woke up tomorrow as a CEO in a socialist country?

•    •    •

To answer this question, I spent two weeks in Norway, seeking out entrepreneurs in all sorts of industries and circumstances.

I met fish farmers in the country's northern hinterlands and cosmopolitan techies in Oslo, the capital. I met start-up founders who were years away from having to worry about making money and then paying taxes on it, and I met established entrepreneurs who every year fork over millions of dollars to the authorities. (Norway's currency is the kroner. I have converted all figures in this article to dollars.)

The first thing I learned is that Norwegians don't think about taxes the way we do. Whereas most Americans see taxes as a burden, Norwegian entrepreneurs tend to see them as a purchase, an exchange of cash for services. "I look at it as a lifelong investment," says Davor Sutija, CEO of Thinfilm, a Norwegian start-up that is developing a low-cost version of the electronic tags retailers use to track merchandise.

Sutija has a unique perspective on this matter: He is an American who grew up in Miami and, twenty years ago, married a Norwegian woman and moved to Oslo. In 2009, as an employee of Thinfilm's former parent company, he earned about $500,000, half of which he took home and half of which went to the Kingdom of Norway. (The country's tax system is progressive, and the highest tax rates kick in at $124,000. From there, the income tax rate, including a national insurance tax, is 47.8 percent.) If he had stayed in the United States, he would have paid at least $50,000 less in taxes, but he has no regrets. (For a detailed comparison, see "How High Is Up?") "There are no private schools in Norway," he says. "All schooling is public and free. By being in Norway and paying these taxes, I'm making an investment in my family."

For a modestly wealthy entrepreneur like Sutija, the value of living in this socialist country outweighs the cost. Every Norwegian worker gets free health insurance in a system that produces longer life expectancy and lower infant mortality rates than our own. At age sixty-seven, workers get a government pension of up to 66 percent of their working income, and everyone gets free education, from nursery school through graduate school.

(Amazingly, this includes colleges outside the country. Want to send your kid to Harvard? The Norwegian government will pick up most of the tab.) Disability insurance and parental leave are also extremely generous. A new mother can take forty-six weeks of maternity leave at full pay—the government, not the company, picks up the tab—or fifty-six weeks off at 80 percent of her normal wage. A father gets ten weeks off at full pay.

These are benefits afforded to every Norwegian, regardless of income level. But it should be said that most Norwegians make about the same amount of money. In Norway, the typical starting salary for a worker with no college education is a very generous $45,000, while the starting salary for a Ph.D. is about $70,000 a year. (This makes certain kinds of industries, such as textile manufacturing, impossible; on the other hand, technology businesses are very cheap to run.) Between workers who do the same job at a given company, salaries vary little, if at all. At Wiggo Dalmo's company, everyone doing the same job makes the same salary.

The result is that successful companies find other ways to motivate and retain their employees. Dalmo's staff may consist mostly of mechanics and machinists, but he treats them like Google engineers. Momek employs a chef who prepares lunch for the staff every day. The company throws a blowout annual party—the tab last year was more than $100,000. Dalmo supplements the standard government health plan with a $330-per-employee-per-year private insurance plan that buys employees treatment in private hospitals if a doctor isn't immediately available in a public one. These benefits have kept turnover rates at Momek below 2 percent, compared with 7 percent in the industry.

But it takes more than perks to keep a worker motivated in Norway. In a country with low unemployment and generous unemployment benefits, a worker's threat to quit is more credible than it is in the United States, giving workers more leverage over employers. And though Norway makes it easy to lay off workers in cases of economic hardship, firing an employee for cause typically takes months, and employers generally end up paying at least three months' severance. "You have to be a much more democratic manager," says Bjørn Holte, founder and CEO of bMenu, an Oslo-based start-up that makes mobile versions of websites. Holte pays himself $125,000 a year. His lowest-paid employee makes more than $60,000. "You can't just treat them like machines," he says. "If you do, they'll be gone."

If the Norwegian system forces CEOs to be more conciliatory to their employees, it also changes the calculus of entrepreneurship for employees who hope to start their own companies. "The problem for entrepreneurship in Norway is it's so lucrative to be an employee," says Lars Kolvereid, the lead researcher for the Global Entrepreneurship Monitor in Norway. Whereas in the U.S., about one-quarter of start-ups are founded by so-called necessity entrepreneurs—that is, people who start companies because they feel they have no good alternative—in Norway, the number is only 9 percent, the third lowest in the world after Switzerland and Denmark, according to the Global Entrepreneurship Monitor.

This may help explain why entrepreneurship in Norway has thrived, even as it stagnates in the United States. "The three things we as Americans worry about—education, retirement, and medical expenses—are things that Norwegians don't worry about," says Zoltan J. Acs, a professor at George Mason University and the chief economist for the Small Business Administration's Office of Advocacy. Acs thinks the recession in the United States has intensified this disparity and is part of the reason America has slipped in the past few years. When the U.S. economy is booming, the absence of guaranteed health care isn't a big concern for aspiring founders, but with unemployment near double digits, would-be entrepreneurs are more cautious. "When the middle class is shrinking, the pool of entrepreneurs is shrinking," says Acs.

·       ·       ·

The downside to Norway's security, of course, is that it is expensive. Norway has substantial oil reserves—but most of the proceeds are invested abroad in a sovereign wealth fund. Norway's generous social benefits are financed largely from taxes that fall heavily on the country's richest people. The most controversial of these taxes is a wealth tax, a 1.1 percent annual levy on the entirety of a person's holdings above about $117,000, including stock in private companies held by the owner.

In search of an opinion on how such soak-the-successful policies affect the truly successful, I visited the tiny town of Misvær, a mountain hamlet in the country's interior, thirty-eight miles north of the Arctic Circle. To get to Misvær, I took a small plane from Oslo to Bodø, where I was met by a gorgeous twentysomething blonde in a flight suit. She was, I somehow knew instantly, the pilot for Inger Ellen Nicolaisen, the country's answer to Donald Trump and the most flamboyant character in a country that prefers its wealthy to go about their business modestly.

After a short helicopter ride over a fjord and some mountains, we touch down in a snow-covered backyard, where we are greeted by a positively feudal scene: Nicolaisen trots out from the house, a modernistic structure perched far above the rest of the town like some enormous suburban castle, followed by five dogs—two great danes, two toy poodles, and a bulldog. She has shoulder-length platinum blond hair and wears teal contact lenses and knee-high boots, looking entirely unlike the fifty-two-year-old mother of three that she is. "Welcome to Miami," she yells above the roar of the helicopter.

She leads me inside, where we are attended by a pair of servants who bring us coffee, pastries, and, though it's not quite noon, champagne. Nicolaisen's husband—her second, a thirty-nine-year-old former professional soccer player— eventually shows up and immediately begins assisting the servants. Later, he shows me around the grounds on a six-wheel all-terrain vehicle. There are the grazing sheep, the three teepees equipped with heat, electricity, and full bars—Nicolaisen uses the structures for corporate retreats—and the pack of Icelandic horses. As we rumble around on the ATV, it seems clear to me that these are the sort of people who should be animated by the wealth tax—and who won't mind saying so.

But they aren't, not really. Although Nicolaisen considers herself a conservative, she told me the issue that most animates her is poverty, not taxes. "Yeah, the wealth tax is a problem," she says. "But you have to make a choice. You can live in the Cayman Islands and pay no tax. But I don't want to live in the Cayman Islands. To live in Norway, you have to do what you have to. I think it's worth it."

Nicolaisen is famous for being the host of the country's version of *The Apprentice* and for founding Nikita, the largest chain of hair salons in Scandinavia. Over twenty-six years, Nikita has expanded into a hair-care conglomerate called Raise, whose concerns include a line of private-label products and 120 salons in Norway and Sweden. Nicolaisen owns the $60 million company outright. Her story, which she tells in a best-selling memoir, *Drivkraft*—Norwegian for driving force—is a triumph of scrappiness. Nicolaisen dropped out of high school at fourteen, when she became pregnant. In her late teens, she supported herself and her daughter, Linda, by hawking handmade children's clothes. In her early twenties, she moved to Bodø and got a job as the receptionist in a hair salon. She took up with the salon's owner, they eventually married, and she got hooked on the hair business.

Nicolaisen was never much of a stylist, but her entrepreneurial ambitions quickly outstripped her husband's. "My first goal was five salons—that seemed like a big goal," says Nicolaisen. She would eventually divorce her husband and take over the business completely. By 2000, she had expanded to fifty salons, and she found herself at a crossroads. She was booking $21 million in revenue a year, and the company was throwing off enough cash to allow her to live well. "I had to decide: Should I relax, stop growing, and just earn a lot of money, or should I expand?" she says. "I realized I couldn't stop there, so I set the next goal at 500. Because, you know—5, 50, 500—it made sense."

I would have thought that Norway's tax system would discourage this kind of thinking, but it doesn't seem to have been a factor. When I asked her why she bothered growing, she said simply, "I'm an entrepreneur. It's in my backbone."

This was the attitude of even those entrepreneurs who strenuously objected to the Norwegian tax regimen, which I learned when I traveled to Stokmarknes and visited the region's best-known entrepreneur, Inge Berg. Berg's company, a fish-farming enterprise called Nordlaks, is a half-hour's flight north of Bodø. The cold North Atlantic waters there make for ideal spawning grounds for salmon, cod, and herring.

We hop into an inflatable skiff and, with Berg in the cockpit, motor across the fjord to one of the company's twenty-three fish farms. There are three floating pens, barely visible from a distance, each housing 50,000 teenage salmon jostling to catch the food pellets that are being blown over the pens from a nearby barge. When Berg started as a fish farmer, it was his job to hand-feed the fish, dumping bucket after bucket of feed over the pens.

From the farm, we take the boat back to Berg's slaughterhouse and packing facility, where the same salmon will eventually meet their demise at a breathtaking rate of one fish per second. "One of the reasons we've been successful is that we've focused exclusively on salmon and trout farming—some other companies tried to expand to the tourist industry or the cod industry," Berg says over the din of the machines. "We invest everything in improving the process." Berg proudly catalogues a number of innovations— a flash-freezing process, a robotic packing system, and a fish oil plant that ensures that no fish scrap is wasted. For now, the oil is mainly used in livestock feed, but Berg brags that he has made sure it is approved for human consumption, then proves his point by pouring me a shot of the viscous pink liquid. (It smelled and tasted awful, but to his point, I did not die.)

In 2009, Nordlaks pulled in $62 million in profits on revenue of $207 million, making Berg, the sole owner, a very rich man.

Although the Norwegian wealth tax includes generous deductions that allow Berg to report a net worth of about $30 million, far less than he would net if he sold his company, his tax bill is still substantial. Even if Nordlaks made no profits, paid no dividends, and paid its owner no salary, Berg would owe the Norwegian government a third of a million dollars a year. "Every year, I have to take a dividend, just to pay the tax," he says, sounding genuinely angry.

Berg is successful enough that paying the wealth tax is no hardship—in 2009, he took a dividend of nearly $10 million—but when a company slips into the red, entrepreneurs can find themselves in trouble. "If a company grows to a large size and then has two bad years in a row, the founder may be forced to sell some stock," says Erlend Bullvåg, a business-school professor at the University of Nordland and an adviser to the Norwegian central bank. But none of the entrepreneurs I spoke with had been forced to sell stock to pay their taxes—and Bullvåg, who has interviewed dozens of entrepreneurs on behalf of the Norwegian central bank, hasn't encountered a case personally. Berg told me that he hadn't given much thought to the wealth tax; he didn't even know exactly how it was calculated. "I get so pissed sometimes," he says. "But you just have to look forward, and it passes."

·　　·　　·

The posting of tax returns online makes tax evasion nearly impossible in Norway, but it doesn't stop the very rich from fleeing the country altogether. The best-known example is John Fredriksen, a shipping tycoon worth $7.7 billion and at one time the richest Norwegian. In 2006, Fredriksen, who had kept most of his personal assets outside the country to avoid taxes, renounced his Norwegian citizenship. He became the richest man in Cyprus.

Fredriksen's past is murky—he is reputed to have been one of the only exporters willing to do business with Iran after the revolution—and he rarely gives interviews. But in 2008, he told the *Wall Street Journal*, "It's almost impossible to do business in Norway today." Norway's prime minister, Jens Stoltenberg, dismissed the defection as no great loss—Fredriksen hadn't paid personal taxes in Norway for decades, and his companies continue to pay taxes in the country. Even so, Fredriksen is something of a folk hero to the entrepreneurs in his former home.

"He is cool," says Jan Egil Flo, chief financial officer of Moods of Norway, a $35 million clothing company in Stryn. I visited Moods of Norway's offices on my last day in Norway and chatted with Flo and his cofounders, Simen Staalnacke and Peder Børresen. The three were able to start their company, which makes fashionable sportswear and suits, largely thanks to the beneficence of the Norwegian socialist system. In 2004, they received a $20,000 start-up grant from the Norwegian equivalent of the Small Business Administration. Staalnacke and Børresen enrolled in a local college because doing so meant the government would cover most of their living expenses. This may be why, when I ask the three founders if they might become Cypriots anytime soon, they protest. "No, no, no," says Børresen. "We've received a lot from Norway and Norwegian society. Giving back is not a problem."

Moods of Norway operates ten boutiques, which, in a country of five million, means the company has saturated its home market. Two years ago, it opened its first store in the United States, a 2,500-square-foot space in Beverly Hills, and Flo is in negotiations to open stores in New York City's SoHo neighborhood and the Mall of America in Minnesota. It has been more challenging than he expected. "It's much easier to do business in Norway," Flo says. "The U.S. isn't one country; it's fifty countries." Although Norway may be more heavily regulated than America, the regulations are uniform across the country and are less apt to change drastically when the political winds blow.

In addition to regulatory stability, Flo pointed to a number of other advantages his company enjoys in Norway. Although personal taxes on entrepreneurs are high, the tax rate on corporate profits is low—28 percent, compared with an average of about 40 percent in combined federal and state taxes in the United States. A less generous depreciation schedule and higher payroll taxes in Norway more than make up for that difference—Norwegian companies pay 14.1 percent of the entirety of an employee's salary, compared with 7.65 percent of the first \$106,800 in the U.S.—but that money pays for benefits such as health care and retirement plans. "There's no big difference in cost," Flo says. In fact, his company makes more money, after taxes, on items sold in Norway than it does on those sold in its California shop.

Flo is pushing his business into America for reasons that have nothing to do with our tax structure. He wants Moods of Norway to be here because America is the largest, most influential market in the world. "There are more Norwegians in the Minneapolis area than in Norway," Flo says excitedly. "If you can get known in America, then the whole world knows you."

I heard this sort of sentiment from lots of the entrepreneurs I spoke with in Norway. They talked about the ambition and aggressiveness of American culture, which can't help breeding success. The younger entrepreneurs yearned for our tradition of mentoring, whereby seasoned entrepreneurs help nascent ones, with money or advice or both.

The more time I spent with Norwegian entrepreneurs, the more I became convinced that the things that make the United States a great country for entrepreneurs have little to do with the fact that we enjoy relatively low taxes. Kenneth Winther, the founder of the Oslo management consultancy MoonWalk, regaled me for hours about the virtues of Norway—security, good roads, good schools. But at the end of our interview, he confessed that he had been hedging his bets: He intended to apply to the American green-card lottery in January. "Why not try?" he said with a shrug.

I also became convinced of this truth, which I have observed in the smartest American and the smartest Norwegian entrepreneurs: It's not about the money. Entrepreneurs are not hedge fund managers, and they rarely operate like coldly rational economic entities. This theme runs through books like Bo Burlingham's *Small Giants*, about company owners who choose not to maximize profits and instead seek to make their companies great, and it can be found in the countless stories, many of them told in this magazine, of founders who leave money on the table in favor of things they judge to be more important.

At one point, I asked Wiggo Dalmo why he was still working so hard to expand his company: Why not just have a nice life—especially given that the authorities would take a hefty chunk of whatever additional money he made? "For me personally, building something to change the world is the kick," he says. "The worst thing to me is people who chose the easiest path. We should use our wonderful years to do something on this earth."

.    .    .

When I got back to the United States, I had a beer with Bjørn Holte, the CEO of bMenu, whom I'd first met in Oslo. It was early November—days after the congressional elections—and Holte had just arrived in New York City, where he is opening a new office. We talked about the commercial real estate market, the amazing cultural diversity in a city that has twice as many people as his entire country, and the current debate in the United States about the role of government. Holte was fascinated by this last topic, particularly the angry opposition to President Obama's health care reform package. "It makes me laugh," he says. "Americans don't understand that you can't have a functioning economy if people aren't healthy."

Holte's American subsidiary pays annual health care premiums that make his head spin—more than $23,000 per employee for a family plan—and that make the cost of employing a software developer in the United States substantially higher than it is in Norway, even after taxes. (For a full breakdown, see "Making

Payroll.") Holte is no pinko—he finds many aspects of Norwegian socialism problematic, particularly regulations about hiring and firing—but when he looks at the costs and benefits of taxes in each country, he sees no contest. Norway is worth the cost.

Of course, that's only half the question when it comes to taxes. The other, more divisive question is, What is fair? Is it right to make rich people pay more than poor people? Would paying a greater percentage of our income for more government services make us less free? "I'd rather be in the U.S., where you can enjoy the fruit of your labor, rather than a country like Norway, where your hard work is confiscated by the government," says Curtis Dubay, senior tax policy analyst at the Heritage Foundation, a Washington, D.C., think tank that advocates for lower taxes.

These are important moral issues, but, in America, they are often the only ones we are willing to consider. We have, as Holte suggests, become religious about economic policy. We are unable or unwilling to make the kind of cool-headed calculations about costs and benefits that I saw in Norway. "There's a disconnect in the way people think about paying taxes and funding public services that's worse here than in any other country," says Donald Bruce, a tax economist at the University of Tennessee. "We refuse to believe that taxes can be used for anything productive. But then we say, 'Stay out of my Social Security. And my Medicare. And don't cut defense or national parks.'"

Our collective inability to have a rational conversation about taxes will have consequences. In 2010, the American budget deficit hit $1.3 trillion, or 10 percent of GDP. By 2035, the deficit could be close to 16 percent of GDP, according to the report issued late last year by the National Commission on Fiscal Responsibility and Reform. That report prescribed dramatic spending cuts and tax increases. But just weeks after it was released, President Obama and congressional Republicans unveiled a new package of tax cuts, which will add an extra $800 billion to the deficit over two years.

Obama has said he hopes to allow these cuts to expire in 2012 and for income tax rates to revert to levels of the 1990s, and that is only one of many revenue-generation ideas kicking around in policy circles. There are also proposals for a tax on millionaires, a national sales tax, and even a dreaded, Norwegian-style wealth tax.

When lawmakers inevitably take up these issues, it's a sure thing that those who oppose raising revenue through tax hikes will make the argument that higher taxes will hurt entrepreneurs. They will make it sound as if even a modest tax increase would represent a death knell for American business. But the case of Norway suggests that Americans should view these arguments with skepticism—and that American entrepreneurs could stand to be less dogmatic about the role of government in society.

This isn't to say that entrepreneurs don't have a right to get angry about taxes—or to fight tax increases in the same way they might fight any price increase by a supplier. It is to say only that, despite what you hear from Washington politicians and activist groups, the tax rate is probably far from the most important issue facing your business. Entrepreneurs can thrive under almost any regime, even the scourge of European socialism. "Taxes matter, but their effect is small in magnitude," says Bruce. "In the end, decisions entrepreneurs make are about more important things: Is there a market for what you're making? Are you doing something relevant for the economy? If the answer is no, then taxes don't matter much."

Part IV

# **Politics and Money**

**The Huffington Post**

This *Huffington Post* story takes us inside the fierce lobbying battle between Big Retail and Big Banks over debit-card fees, in the process providing a revealing look at why the American political system has become so dysfunctional. With billions of dollars at stake, banks pushed hard to overturn a Dodd-Frank provision capping their so-called swipe fees. They would eventually fall short, not so much because of congressional concerns about consumers or monopoly pricing power but because another powerful, well-financed lobby took them on. Zach Carter and Ryan Grim show how the deep pockets and political clout of these two interests put the swipe-fee fight at the top of the Washington agenda while the country faced far more pressing concerns.

Zach Carter and
Ryan Grim

# 13. Swiped

## Banks, Merchants,
and Why Washington
Doesn't Work for You

harlie Chung runs Cups & Co., a coffee and sandwich shop in the basement of the Russell Senate Office Building. Known on Capitol Hill simply as "Cups," the shop—a rickety twenty-second train ride away from the elevator to the Senate floor—is always swarmed with lobbyists, staffers, and the occasional senator.

If customers flash an American Express card to buy a banana, Chung waves them off: "Just take the banana. Don't give me the card."

Chung has run Cups for about a decade and says that plastic has allowed him to better serve a hurried and harried clientele. But Chung is still routinely frustrated with the card networks—Visa, MasterCard, and American Express—that dictate the fees storeowners like himself must pay to process credit and debit card transactions. Why charge for a banana when card fees make it a losing proposition?

Fees are annoying, Chung says, but not debilitating. "They're just like a phone company," he says. "Delivery surcharge. Paper charge. Equipment charge." There's an additional fee for using cards from banks outside his contract, but Chung says he has no way of knowing until he's gotten his bill how much of that pricier plastic has been swiped.

The fees Chung pays are a tiny fraction of Wall Street's swipe-fee windfall; banks take in a combined $48 billion a year from these "interchange" fees on debit and credit cards, according to analysts at the *Nilson Report*. That money comes out of the pockets of consumers as well as merchants, as stores pass on whatever costs they can to their customers.

Major retailers—the Walmarts, Home Depots, and the Targets of the world—complain that card fees are one of their biggest annual expenses, and they've entered into a Capitol Hill battle royale against card companies to roll back the lucrative fee regime. Last year's financial reform bill ordered the Federal Reserve to crack down on debit card swipe fees, a $16 billion pool of money from which $8 billion flows to just ten banks. As a concession to Wall Street, credit card fees were left unscathed.

But the clock never ticks down to zero in Washington: one year's law is the next year's repeal target. Politicians, showered with cash from card companies and giant retailers alike, have been moving back and forth between camps, paid handsomely for their shifting allegiances.

The swipe-fee spat is generating huge business for K Street: A full 118 ex-government officials and aides are currently registered to lobby on behalf of banks in the fee fight, according to data compiled for this story by the Sunlight Foundation, a nonpartisan research group. Retailers have signed up at least 124 revolving-door lobbyists. And at least one lobbyist has switched sides during the melee. Republican Thomas Shipman of Cornerstone Government Affairs registered to lobby for the merchant's leading player, Walmart, in 2010, only to move over to Visa in 2011.

"Oh man, this is unbelievable. You've got the banking community, the financial community, pitted against the retail community," says Sen. Mike Johanns (R-Neb.). "They've both been in my office and I'm a clear yes vote on this . . . so you can only imagine those who are trying to figure this out or are still on the fence. They must be getting flooded."

The flood fills the hallways with lobbyists and deluges the airwaves with ads. For weeks, Washington's Metro system has been papered with pro-plastic ads on trains and station walls. It's a way for card networks to flex their muscles, to put lawmakers and lobbyists on notice that they're willing to spend big to win. "Where does Washington's $12 billion gift to giant retailers come from? YOUR DEBIT CARD," blares one ad. This being Washington, a poster on the Metro was hacked by a swipe-fee reform supporter, who crossed out "YOUR DEBIT CARD" and penned in "BANKS."

The swipe-fee debate, as mundane as it may appear, is emblematic of how Washington works today—and helps explain why Congress hasn't passed an appropriations bill in years, can't write an annual budget, is flirting with defaulting on the country's debt, and effectively gave up on job-creation efforts in the midst of a brutal economic downturn. There are, to be sure, a variety of reasons that Congress is zombified, but one of the least understood explanations is also one of the simplest: The city is too busy refereeing disputes between major corporate interest groups.

As swipe fees dominate the Congressional agenda, a handful of other intracorporate contests consume most of what remains on the Congressional calendar: a squabble over a jet engine, industry tussling over health-care spoils, and the never-ending fight over the corporate tax code.

The endless meetings and evenings devoted to arbitrating duels between big businesses destroy time and energy that could otherwise be spent on higher priorities. In America today, over 13 million people are out of work and millions more are underemployed. One out of every seven is living on food stamps. One out of every five American children lives in poverty. Yet the most consuming issue in Washington—according to members of Congress, Hill staffers, lobbyists, and Treasury officials—is determining how to slice up the $16 billion debit-card swipe-fee pie for corporations.

"Every time we go in to an office and tell them we're here to talk about interchange, they cringe," says Dennis Lane, who makes regular lobbying trips to Washington and has owned a Massachusetts 7-Eleven for thirty-seven years. "I think there's been more lobbying—there's been more hours and minutes spent on Capitol Hill discussing interchange reform—than there has been talking about a shutdown of the government."

The combination of high financial stakes and scant public attention to the faceoff between card companies and retailers has blurred party lines. Dozens of unlikely and influential figures have rushed to random sides of the swipe fee trough: Anti-tax advocate Grover Norquist, hip-hop mogul Russell Simmons, the Christian Coalition, teachers unions, Koch-funded think tanks, the NAACP, Karl Rove, Dick Morris, Walmart, and Google. Even Mickey Mouse has made an appearance.

In Washington, the easiest way to derail somebody else's good idea is to suggest delaying it while experts conduct a study. In the Senate, Tester is joined by Bob Corker, a Republican from Tennessee, in pushing the plan to postpone Durbin's fee caps. West Virginia Republican Shelley Moore Capito is carrying a similar bill in the House, cosponsored by Florida Democrat Debbie Wasserman Schultz. When corporate interests are at stake, such bipartisanship tends to be much easier to secure.

In the first quarter of 2011, members of the Electronic Payments Coalition—the bank lobby fighting swipe fee reform—gave more than $2 million to members of Congress and the two parties and more than $250,000 to cosponsors of Capito's bill, according to an analysis done by the Sunlight Foundation for this story.

And that's just direct contributions. Both sides have spent lavishly on TV and radio ads and face-to-face lobbying. After all, a mere month of swipe-fee revenue amounts to more than the total sum a presidential campaign will spend between now and next November. Many of the ads openly attack big business, while giving no hints about their own corporate backing.

"Everybody and their grandmother's lobbying on this," says Sen. Lindsey Graham (R-S.C.). Graham, who supported Durbin last year, hasn't made up his mind on the Tester bill, but says the ongoing swipe-fee fight is one of the "top ten" most brutal and well-funded battles he's seen in the Senate.

Not all of the interests in the fee fight are powerful. But small business owners like Chung who might benefit from swipe-fee reform would be sharing in a victory that the big-box retailers are funding. This, in the end, may be the best little guys can hope for in Washington: to have their interests roughly align with those of powerful players.

One frustrated moderate Democratic senator asks to remain anonymous so he can speak freely about his legislative education. "I'm surprised at how much of our time is spent trying to divide up the spoils between various economic interests. I had no idea. I thought we'd be focused on civil liberties, on education policy, energy policy, and so on," the senator says. "The fights down here can be put in two or three categories: The big greedy bastards against the big greedy bastards; the big greedy bastards against the little greedy bastards; and some cases even the other little greedy bastards against the other little greedy bastards."

## Time Is Money

Although a hotly contested issue in Washington, swipe fees barely register as a concern to most Americans. A merchant-sponsored poll last month of the issue found that nearly half of respondents were completely unfamiliar with it. Once it was explained to them, however, 70 percent backed Fed action to cut the fees.

In December, the Fed proposed to reduce the average debit-card swipe fee by nearly 75 percent—down from an average of forty-four cents per swipe to just twelve cents.

For every month the law is postponed, banks will make $1.35 billion on debit cards, according to *Nilson Report* data. That makes for a very motivated lobby. "The merchants had the ad-vantage last year of caring only about this in the bill while the banks were worried about trying to kill the consumer bill and the other stuff," says Rep. Barney Frank (D-Mass.), former chairman of the House Financial Services Committee. "This is now as important to the banks—in fact, it's more important to the banks than to the average merchant, which is what shifted this."

Indeed, the American Bankers Association, JPMorgan Chase, and Regions Bank count a total of eight new lobbying shops working on swipe fees in 2011, according to lobbying disclosure forms.

Banks began issuing cash cards in the 1970s as a tactic to automate services and cut labor costs—more ATMs meant fewer bank tellers and check processing costs. When swipe machines were first introduced in stores, banks actually paid some merchants to accept debit cards. Later, swipes became free, and once debit cards had become ingrained in consumer culture, banks began charging merchants, and the costs keep going up.

The fees incense many merchants. Sheetz Corp. operates nearly 400 gas stations and convenience stores from Ohio to North Carolina, and CEO Stan Sheetz is pressing lawmakers hard to lower swipe fees. But unlike most retailers, Sheetz also serves on the board of a small bank that makes a fortune from fees. "From the bank's standpoint . . . it's all gravy," says Sheetz. "It's a cash cow."

Credit and debit swipe fees cost Sheetz $5 million a month, second only to labor costs. "I am a die-hard capitalist pig," Sheetz tells HuffPost. "That's why Visa and MasterCard piss me off. . . . They treat us like shit. The arrogance is unbelievable."

Target Corp. spokesperson Morgan O'Malley says interchange is its second-biggest expense after labor, amounting to "hundreds of millions of dollars a year." The retailers have taken the banks to court over the fees at least four times with little success. But one merchant has done more for the cause than any other.

Banks argue that merchants are not required to accept debit cards and that multiple judges have found that the companies are not violating antitrust laws. The merchants will pocket the money they'll save rather than pass it on to customers, the banks say, insisting that there is no justification for government intervention.

Money flows freely around the fee battle. Political action committees organized by members of the Electronic Payments Coalition, a cadre of banking trade groups, dumped more than $500,000 into campaign coffers during January and February alone, according to data compiled by the nonpartisan Sunlight Foundation. During those same months, PACs for Walmart and Home Depot gave a total of $75,000 to twenty-six senators, along with $45,000 to political parties, while Target dropped an additional $54,000.The National Franchise Association, the Society of Independent Gasoline Marketers of America, the Society of American Florists, the Petroleum Marketers Association of America, and the Food Marketing Institute—all traditionally small-time players in Washington—contributed a combined $78,500 in the first two months of 2011.

But that's just the money groups have to disclose. In the wake of the Supreme Court's controversial Citizens United decision, an enormous share of corporate money in politics is now spent secretly, moving through anonymous front groups with vague names like "Americans for Job Security."

## "The Banks Aren't Happy"

Plenty of lawmakers are anguished about their swipe-fee position, but largely because they're worried about falling out of favor with good friends in the corporate world.

"I've got friends on both sides of it and, you know, it is what it is," says a visibly anguished Sen. Saxby Chambliss (R-Ga.) when asked about the bill to delay swipe-fee reform. Home Depot, headquartered in Atlanta, is a leading player on the merchant side, and both the company and its cofounder, Bernard Marcus, have invested heavily in Chambliss's Senate career. "I voted to support it and I'm gonna continue to support it."

HuffPost asks what he says to the bankers. "I've voted. And I'm sticking with it," he says. "Oooh, the bankers aren't happy."

Chambliss's fellow Georgia Republican, Sen. Johnny Isakson, is also staying with Home Depot. "It's part of the job," Isakson says of resisting the bank pressure. "That's why they pay us the big bucks."

Mike Lux, a vocally liberal Democrat who is doing PR on behalf of the merchants, has written on the issue for HuffPost.

"I figured I'd rather have mainstream businesses, even if some are ones I don't like, like Walmart, have the [swipe fee] money than the big six banks," he says.

He also sees a broader threat. "Barney Frank and other folks who are inclined to see the swipe fee adjusted, they're playing with fire. There's the potential to add in bigger changes," warns Lux. Republicans, he says, "would like to reopen the whole financial reform bill and they're debating whether to use the swipe fee bill to do it."

But while Walmart won over Lux, the Arkansas-based mega-retailer is having a harder time corralling lawmakers from its home state. Republican Sen. John Boozman, Democratic Sen. Mark Pryor, and Democratic Rep. Mike Ross all tell HuffPost they're undecided on rolling back the swipe-fee laws, in spite of the retailer's enormous lobbying push.

"Walmart's a huge employer in our state. It's a consideration, but it's one of many considerations," says Pryor, who is known on the Hill as one of two "senators from Walmart."

What kind of consideration could be a bigger concern for an Arkansas senator than Walmart? "We have a lot of banks and credit unions in our state as well," he explains.

Walmart declined multiple opportunities to participate in this story.

### "I Know the Zip Code for Wall Street"

Jon Tester defeated his gaffe-prone opponent by fewer than 3,000 votes in 2006, a year that saw popular national support for Democrats. He was recruited by Dick Durbin's longtime housemate, Sen. Chuck Schumer (D-N.Y.), who was then the head of the Senate Democratic campaign operation. And like Schumer, Tester has become a Wall Street courtier. He's hauled in over $821,000 from the finance, insurance, and real estate industries since entering office, according to the Center for Responsive Politics. In the first quarter of 2011, he raised total funds of $1.16 million—double his GOP opponent—including more than $100,000 from PACs representing the finance, insurance, and real estate industry (That total only counts PAC money, not contributions from executives).

Schumer has largely refrained from operating too visibly on behalf of the banks in the swipe-fee fight. But bank lobbyists tell HuffPost he had made it clear from the beginning he was on their side and was working behind the scenes to gather support for the Tester bill that seeks to undermine Durbin's fee-capping effort.

That suspicion was confirmed at a "Politico Playbook Breakfast" sponsored by Bank of America on April 6, when Schumer was asked about the Tester effort to delay Durbin's reform.

"Well, you know, it was passed rather quickly," began Schumer. The Durbin amendment "didn't have all the hearings and everything else that lots of the rest of the [financial reform] bill" did, Schumer went on. "On this particular issue, because there wasn't study, there is some momentum, led by Senator Tester, who's done a great job, to at least delay it." He predicted a vote on Tester's amendment before the end of the year.

Durbin doesn't hold back on his longtime housemate when asked by HuffPost about Schumer's remark. "Listen, I know the zip code for Wall Street and I know what state it's in," he says.

The swipe-fee faceoff is a major test of whether Wall Street's post-crash power has any limits. It's one thing for a few large corporations to run roughshod over consumer groups on Capitol Hill. It's quite another to take on a team of deep-pocketed corporate opponents with well-established relationships, armed with strong pro-consumer arguments. Wall Street isn't just targeting guileless subprime borrowers on swipe fees—it's taking on what economists call "the real economy"—the world beyond complex financial deal making where actual goods are bought and sold.

But there has been little serious attention paid to the effects swipe fees have beyond the corporate world. Only one major economic study has attempted to quantify how much swipe fees cost U.S. consumers in terms of higher prices—a February 2010 paper by respected economist Robert Shapiro and analyst Jiwon Vellucci, which found that 56 percent of all swipe fees are passed on to consumers, raising costs for the average household by about $230 a year.

That extra $230 isn't a burden for affluent families accustomed to paying for convenience. Still, for families living below the poverty line, that money translates into two weeks worth of groceries or the monthly heating bill.

Yet the poor have no voice in Washington. Even the Shapiro and Vellucci study would never have been conducted without major corporate backing—it was funded by Consumers for Competitive Choice, a front group for telecommunications giants, which tried to kill last year's financial reform bill at the same time it was pushing for the swipe fee crackdown included in the bill.

Whatever the ultimate cost of swipe fees for consumers, there's no question that the resulting higher prices hit the poor hardest of all. Affluent consumers are more likely to pay with plastic, and both credit cards and debit cards frequently come with rewards programs that bestow frequent flyer miles, Amazon.com discounts, trips to Disney World, and a host of other benefits upon card users. So while swipe fees cause higher prices for everyone, affluent consumers get some of that money back in the form of rewards. The result is an effective transfer of wealth from poor shoppers to wealthier consumers: stores charge higher prices for goods in order to cover higher swipe fees, and those higher swipe fees are converted into rewards programs. According to an August study by the Boston Federal Reserve, the perks associated with plastic lead to an average wealth transfer of $771 from families making less than $20,000 a year to households earning $150,000 or more.

## The Russians Are Coming!

Outside of Washington, companies have started pleading their fee case before their own customers, and some haven't shied away from statistical hysterics to argue their cases. Earlier this month, Walmart sent an e-mail to shoppers warning of dire economic fallout, citing "US Federal Reserve" estimates that a two-year delay of swipe-fee caps would cost consumers $24 billion and kill 200,000 jobs.

All very scary, of course. But the Fed hasn't made any such estimates, according to a central bank spokeswoman. Walmart declined to comment on the bogus statistics.

Big banks have been deploying similar tactics. In January 2010, TCF Bank, which pioneered free checking in the 1980s, announced it would begin charging a monthly fee in response to Federal Reserve rules restricting overdraft charges. The move was regularly cited during the 2010 swipe-fee fracas as evidence of the harm that would befall consumers if Durbin didn't back off. It's the argument that forms the basis of the bank-sponsored movement to "Save My Debit Card." This January, TCF brought back free checking after losing customers.

In October, Bank of America responded to the passage of the Durbin amendment by taking a $10.4 billion writedown on its card business, a move that many political observers saw as a political gesture. While the sheer size of the writedown generated headlines in the business press, it had very little actual impact on BofA's operations; no cash actually went out the door. Instead, the company merely revised its estimate of what its card business is worth.

Banks are even blasting the Internet with ads warning of "the Soviets" and asking whether Congress will "take away" the debit card. There is, of course, no risk that banks will stop issuing debit cards, however the swipe-fee fracas ends.

One day before the Senate was expected to vote on delaying reform, Chase went nuclear: Thanks to the Durbin amendment, thousands of Chase customers were warned, your kid can forget about that trip to Disney World. "Congress recently enacted a new law known as the Durbin Amendment that significantly impacts debit cards," reads the letter. "As a result of this law, we will be changing our debit rewards program. After July 21, 2011 you will no longer earn Disney Dream Reward Dollars when you use your Disney Rewards Debit Card."

Investors get the same treatment. JPMorgan Chase's CEO, Jamie Dimon, singled out the Durbin amendment in an April 5 speech before the Council of Institutional Investors, saying it was "downright idiotic" and "passed in the middle of the night and had nothing to do with the crisis."

Durbin blasted back in a letter to Dimon, which the senator asked to be sent to the company's shareholders, ripping Dimon's eye-popping paydays and the financial excess on Wall Street that pushed the economy into a deep recession.

"Last year Chase had $17.4 billion in profits—up 48 percent from the previous year—and a 15 percent profit margin," Durbin wrote Dimon, noting that Dimon's own personal compensation "jumped nearly 1,500 percent to $20.8 million in 2010."

"There is no need for you to threaten your customers with higher fees when you and your bank are already making money hand over fist," Durbin continued. "And there is no need to make such threats in response to reform that simply tries to spare consumers."

With a vigor that would make Tom DeLay proud, Durbin has confronted just about anybody who is taking the other side of his swipe-fee issue, including lobbyists, civil rights organizations, editorial boards, and public interest groups. Even the NAACP was on the receiving end of his ire, an official there says. An assistant Senate majority leader lobbying interest groups to switch sides may seem backward, but it reflects a Washington reality in which lobbyists, not politicians, frequently wield the real power.

"If you scratch the surface, guess what you're going to find? They have other causes but they're also debit card issuers," Durbin says of the NAACP and many of the other progressive groups siding with the banks. "They have a financial interest in keeping the status quo."

The NAACP doesn't have its own debit card, but does have a relationship with Visa and U.S. Bank through its credit card. And its top corporate donors include players on both sides of the debate—Bank of America, Walmart, Wachovia, Best Buy, and Target have all given generously in recent years. And like Ellmers, the NAACP has changed its position on swipe-fee reform multiple times and is having a hard time explaining it.

In recent weeks, NAACP Washington bureau director Hilary Shelton has been besieged by lobbyists on swipe fees, meeting with as many as four groups about the issue in a single day. After backing the Durbin amendment throughout 2010, Shelton penned a letter to House Speaker John Boehner (R-Ohio) in March, saying the NAACP supported a study on the Fed's swipe-fee rule to ensure that it would have no harmful effects on consumers.

Immediately after the letter became public knowledge, Shelton says he got a call from Durbin's office. Two days later, he was meeting with an official from Walmart. In April, Shelton clarified his letter to Boehner, insisting that the NAACP continues to support swipe-fee reform, but wants to see a study completed prior to July 21.

Shelton says his organization faces no conflicts of interest on the swipe fees and insists that the NAACP has never in fact changed its position on the issue.

"We have relationships and friends with Walmart, we have relationships and friends with Bank of America and Wachovia. We have friends at McDonald's, the hamburger people," Shelton says, before emphasizing that their concern is first and foremost for consumers. "Sometimes," he says, "you have to do things your friends don't like."

In the run-up to this vote, both banks and merchants have swarmed Hill staffers with a seemingly endless barrage of meetings on swipe fees.

In February, BofA associate general counsel Karl Kaufman held a private briefing for staffers on the Financial Services Committee. The Merchant Payments Coalition, a retailer group, gave their own briefing. House staffers were also treated to a separate private briefing that included both sides debating each other.

On the Senate side, things could move more quickly, as Carper noted. When the Senate returns next week, the climate may be right for a vote. Even if banks come up short, the vote will give them a firmer count of just who is on their side and who still needs to be worked.

Democrat Joe Manchin (W. Va.) could wind up being the deciding vote on the swipe-fee bill. On the morning of April 14, Manchin booked a big room in the Senate Hart Office Building more often used for hearings than for lobbying—a symbol of how thoroughly business fights have come to dominate the agenda, that they now must be waged in hearing rooms with the doors closed. Manchin was undecided as the meeting broke up.

On April 18, while Congress was in recess, credit unions flooded Hill staffers with scripted phone calls from customers worrying that the Durbin amendment will kill their rewards points. The bank lobby named April 21, the deadline the Fed missed, "Save My Debit Card Day" and launched a Twitter campaign using the hashtag #savemydebitcard. The mid-March ABA convention in Washington prompted the type of personal glad-handing that lands cosponsors for bills. It was one of at least three major bank fly-ins since February.

The merchants have been everywhere, too. Five hundred restaurant owners flew in last week; 7-Eleven owners, a Hill staple during the initial fight, came the week before that. Grocers and beer wholesalers have also visited.

The next few weeks and months could mean millions for merchants if Durbin can hold back the banks.

Whatever happens the next few weeks or months, Charlie Chung of Cups & Co. isn't confident that he'll wind up paying less money to the banks. He guesses that the banks will find a way to increase unregulated fees: "It's like, you'd scratch your head, 'I thought they were going to charge me two cents per transaction?'"

Mark Pryor, one of the senators from Walmart, is equally pessimistic that consumers will see any benefit. "Either way, the consumer probably ends up paying for it," he says. "They'll get you. You're going to pay for it one way or another."

*Elise Foley and Paul Blumenthal contributed reporting.*

***The New York Times*** | Before there was the Buffett Rule, there was the game-changing Buffett op-ed column, challenging the unfairness of generous tax breaks that he and his rich friends enjoy. "While the poor and middle class fight for us in Afghanistan, and while most Americans struggle to make ends meet," Buffett wrote, "we mega-rich continue to get our extraordinary tax breaks." Buffett was writing specifically about lower tax rates for capital gains and for hedge fund managers. Before long, President Barack Obama had adopted some of Buffett's rhetoric—that the rich guy who runs the office should pay more in taxes than lower-paid coworkers.

Warren Buffett

# 14. Stop Coddling the Super-Rich

Our leaders have asked for "shared sacrifice." But when they did the asking, they spared me. I checked with my mega-rich friends to learn what pain they were expecting. They, too, were left untouched.

While the poor and middle class fight for us in Afghanistan, and while most Americans struggle to make ends meet, we mega-rich continue to get our extraordinary tax breaks. Some of us are investment managers who earn billions from our daily labors but are allowed to classify our income as "carried interest," thereby getting a bargain 15 percent tax rate. Others own stock index futures for 10 minutes and have 60 percent of their gain taxed at 15 percent, as if they'd been long-term investors.

These and other blessings are showered upon us by legislators in Washington who feel compelled to protect us, much as if we were spotted owls or some other endangered species. It's nice to have friends in high places.

Last year my federal tax bill—the income tax I paid, as well as payroll taxes paid by me and on my behalf—was $6,938,744. That sounds like a lot of money. But what I paid was only 17.4 percent of my taxable income—and that's actually a lower percentage than was paid by any of the other twenty people in our office. Their tax burdens ranged from 33 percent to 41 percent and averaged 36 percent.

If you make money with money, as some of my super-rich friends do, your percentage may be a bit lower than mine. But if you earn money from a job, your percentage will surely exceed mine—most likely by a lot.

To understand why, you need to examine the sources of government revenue. Last year about 80 percent of these revenues came from personal income taxes and payroll taxes. The mega-rich pay income taxes at a rate of 15 percent on most of their earnings but pay practically nothing in payroll taxes. It's a different story for the middle class: typically, they fall into the 15 percent and 25 percent income tax brackets, and then are hit with heavy payroll taxes to boot.

Back in the 1980s and 1990s, tax rates for the rich were far higher, and my percentage rate was in the middle of the pack. According to a theory I sometimes hear, I should have thrown a fit and refused to invest because of the elevated tax rates on capital gains and dividends.

I didn't refuse, nor did others. I have worked with investors for sixty years and I have yet to see anyone—not even when capital gains rates were 39.9 percent in 1976–77—shy away from a sensible investment because of the tax rate on the potential gain. People invest to make money, and potential taxes have never scared them off. And to those who argue that higher rates hurt job creation, I would note that a net of nearly 40 million jobs were added between 1980 and 2000. You know what's happened since then: lower tax rates and far lower job creation.

Since 1992, the IRS has compiled data from the returns of the 400 Americans reporting the largest income. In 1992, the top 400 had aggregate taxable income of $16.9 billion and paid federal taxes of 29.2 percent on that sum. In 2008, the aggregate income of the highest 400 had soared to $90.9 billion—a staggering $227.4 million on average—but the rate paid had fallen to 21.5 percent.

The taxes I refer to here include only federal income tax, but you can be sure that any payroll tax for the 400 was inconsequential compared to income. In fact, 88 of the 400 in 2008 reported no wages at all, though every one of them reported capital gains. Some of my brethren may shun work but they all like to invest. (I can relate to that.)

I know well many of the mega-rich and, by and large, they are very decent people. They love America and appreciate the opportunity this country has given them. Many have joined the Giving Pledge, promising to give most of their wealth to philanthropy. Most wouldn't mind being told to pay more in taxes as well, particularly when so many of their fellow citizens are truly suffering.

Twelve members of Congress will soon take on the crucial job of rearranging our country's finances. They've been instructed to devise a plan that reduces the ten-year deficit by at least $1.5 trillion. It's vital, however, that they achieve far more than that. Americans are rapidly losing faith in the ability of Congress to deal with our country's fiscal problems. Only action that is immediate, real, and very substantial will prevent that doubt from morphing into hopelessness. That feeling can create its own reality.

Job one for the twelve is to pare down some future promises that even a rich America can't fulfill. Big money must be saved here. The twelve should then turn to the issue of revenues. I would leave rates for 99.7 percent of taxpayers unchanged and continue the current two-percentage-point reduction in the employee contribution to the payroll tax. This cut helps the poor and the middle class, who need every break they can get.

But for those making more than $1 million—there were 236,883 such households in 2009—I would raise rates immediately on taxable income in excess of $1 million, including, of course, dividends and capital gains. And for those who make $10 million or more—there were 8,274 in 2009—I would suggest an additional increase in rate.

My friends and I have been coddled long enough by a billionaire-friendly Congress. It's time for our government to get serious about shared sacrifice.

**Washington Post**

Pulitzer Prize–winning columnist Steven Pearlstein holds corporate America to account for "the growth of a radical right-wing cabal that has now taken over the Republican Party and repeatedly made a hostage of the U.S. government." In a blistering attack, he excoriates corporate executives for creating "Frankenpols," who threaten massive damage to the economy and who have revived a form of McCarthyism in American politics. Corporate America helped to create new political organizations with "hundreds of millions of the shareholders' dollars, laundered through once-respected organizations such as the Chamber of Commerce and the National Association of Manufacturers," which are now roaming the landscape, scarily out of control even of those who helped give them birth.

Steven Pearlstein

# 15. Blame for Financial Mess Starts with the Corporate Lobby

Another great week for Corporate America!

The economy is flatlining. Global financial markets are in turmoil. Your stock price is down about 15 percent in three weeks. Your customers have lost all confidence in the economy. Your employees, at least the American ones, are cynical and demoralized. Your government is paralyzed.

Want to know who is to blame, Mr. Big Shot Chief Executive? Just look in the mirror because the culprit is staring you in the face.

J'accuse, dude. J'accuse.

You helped create the monsters that are rampaging through the political and economic countryside, wreaking havoc and sucking the lifeblood out of the global economy.

Did you see this week's cartoon cover of the *New Yorker*? That's you in top hat and tails sipping champagne in the lifeboat as the *Titanic* is sinking. Problem is, nobody thinks it's a joke anymore.

Did you presume we wouldn't notice that you've been missing in action? I can't say I was surprised. If you'd insisted on trotting out those old canards again, blaming everything on high taxes, unions, regulatory uncertainty, and the lack of free-trade treaties, you would have lost whatever shred of credibility you have left.

My own bill of particulars begins right here in Washington, where over the past decade you financed and supported the growth of a radical right-wing cabal that has now taken over the

Republican Party and repeatedly made a hostage of the U.S. government.

When it started out all you really wanted was to push back against a few meddlesome regulators or shave a point or two off your tax rate, but you were concerned it would look like special-interest rent seeking. So when the Washington lobbyists came up with the clever idea of launching a campaign against over-regulation and overtaxation, you threw in some money, backed some candidates, and financed a few lawsuits.

The more successful it was, however, the more you put in—hundreds of millions of the shareholders' dollars, laundered through once-respected organizations such as the Chamber of Commerce and the National Association of Manufacturers, phony front organizations with innocent-sounding names such as Americans for a Sound Economy, and a burgeoning network of Republican PACs and financing vehicles. And thanks to your clever lawyers and a Supreme Court majority that is intent on removing all checks to corporate power, it's perfectly legal.

Somewhere along the way, however, this effort took on a life of its own. What started as a reasonable attempt at political rebalancing turned into a jihad against all regulation, all taxes, and all government, waged by right-wing zealots who want to privatize the public schools that educate your workers, cut back on the basic research on which your products are based, shut down the regulatory agencies that protect you from unscrupulous competitors, and privatize the public infrastructure that transports your supplies and your finished goods. For them, this isn't just a tactic to brush back government. It's a holy war to destroy it—and one that is now out of your control.

For years you complained bitterly about the uncompetitive nature of an employer-based health-care system, the inexorable rise of health insurance premiums, the folly of medical malpractice, and the unfair burden of having to subsidize the uninsured.

But when your lobbyists and your bought-and-paid-for politicians had the chance to cut a deal that would have given you most of what you asked for, they walked away.

For years you complained bitterly about rising federal budget deficits and a corporate tax code that was too complex and burdensome. But when your crew had the chance to strike a grand bargain that would have fixed both those things, they not only rejected it but insisted on creating an unnecessary crisis that triggered a credit downgrade of U.S. Treasurys and a roller-coaster ride for stocks.

Please don't tell me about your mealy-mouthed letter warning Congress not to play politics with the debt ceiling. By that point, the Frankenpols you created were not interested in your advice. The only thing that might have got their attention was a threat to cut off the flow of political money. You didn't—and now they know they can ignore you with impunity.

I wonder how many of your fellow members of the Business Roundtable would accept a credible budget-balancing deal that had $10 of spending cuts for every $1 of tax increases. My guess is they all would. And what about the presidential candidates in the new, improved Republican Party that you helped create? In last week's Iowa debate, every last one of them promised to veto such a deal. Good luck with that!

Remember way back last fall when your big concern was with regulatory uncertainty, which you continue to use as the excuse for letting all those profits build up on your balance sheet rather than investing in equipment or hiring workers. Whatever uncertainty you can pin on the Obama administration and the Democratic Congress now looks like small potatoes given the uncertainty caused by your political shock troops as they challenge every new regulation all the way to the Supreme Court. They'll try to prevent or roll back implementation of others with appropriations riders, just like they did with the Federal Aviation Administration—and we know how well that worked out.

In your name, they are also refusing to confirm nominees to dozens of key vacancies in the executive branch and independent agencies. Among them is President Obama's choice for commerce secretary, John Bryson, who for eighteen years was chief executive of the largest electric utility in Southern California and served as a director at Boeing and Disney. His sin, apparently, is that he was cofounder of a respected environmental organization, the Natural Resources Defense Council, and—get this—actually believes the scientific community when it says global warming is a problem.

I can just hear it now: "Mr. Bryson, are you now, or were you ever, a member of an environmental organization?" How does it make you feel to know that you've helped to revive McCarthyism in American politics?

Your culpability, however, extends beyond the breakdown in Washington.

For the past thirty years, there has been a steady financialization of the American economy in which the interests of so-called shareholders have become the single-minded focus of large corporations, to the virtual exclusion of the interests of customers, employees, and the society at large.

Early on, some of your predecessors were willing to put up a fight against the Wall Street cabal, but in time they bought you off with exorbitant perks and pay packages that nearly rival their own. This occupation of Main Street by Wall Street was confirmed again last week as anonymous traders and hedge fund managers went on a riotous spree, wielding false rumors and high-frequency computerized trading to loot pension and retirement accounts and rob consumers and real investors of whatever confidence they had left.

I suppose there are some schnooks who actually believe that those wild swings in stock prices last week represented sober and serious concerns by thoughtful, sophisticated investors about the Treasury debt downgrade or European sovereign debt or a slowdown in global growth. But surely such perceptions don't radically change each afternoon between 2 and 4:30, when the market averages last week were gyrating out of control.

The only credible explanation for that is speculation, herd behavior, and market manipulation by traders looking to make a quick million—financial wiseguys who could not care less what impact it might have on the real economy. And other than JP Morgan's Jamie Dimon, I didn't hear a peep of protest from you on CNBC, or a speech to the Economic Club of Chicago, or even a simple letter to the editor of the *Wall Street Journal*. A cameo appearance at the White House doesn't quite cut it.

It's not just that you have remained silent as the financial sector has sucked away much of the profit generated by the private sector, stolen away much of the nation's best talent, and transformed the process of capital allocation and formation into a casino. Even worse, through organizations such as the Chamber and the Business Roundtable you reflexively provided them with crucial political support that allowed them to beat back regulators who tried to restrict their growth, curb their risk-taking, or put a stop to the kind of fraudulent activity that nearly sank the recovery, and from which it will take years to recover. Given your role in society and in the economy, your silence amounts to complicity.

The truth is you've become them. Instead of focusing your attention and ingenuity in developing new products and services, you're spending most of your own time on financial engineering—buying up companies at one moment because of synergies and cost saving, then spinning them off the next moment because they no longer fall in to your "core mission."

The big innovation at Kraft these days is to separate its overprocessed food (Jell-O, Velveeta, Oscar Meyer) and unhealthy snacks (Cadbury chocolates, Oreo cookies, saltine crackers) into two companies.

Conoco-Phillips, which embraced hyphenation when it decided to merge into a vertically integrated oil company, has now decided that the world would be a better place if it spun off its refining and distribution business from exploration and drilling.

And let's not forget Medco, the pharmacy benefit manager, which was bought and then spun off by Merck into an independent company again until it was scooped up by Express Scripts, one of its biggest competitors.

I'm not exactly sure how we're going to generate more jobs and generate stronger growth in this country, but I'm fairly certain those kinds of bold initiatives aren't going to do the trick.

Hey, but don't worry about us. Enjoy that fly fishing in Montana. You deserve it.

## Association of Alternative Newsweeklies

David Cay Johnston's crystalline excoriation of the U.S. tax code was perfectly timed for April 15, when Americans care even more than they usually do about the amount they're paying in taxes. The piece, which was commissioned by the Association of Alternative Newsweeklies and syndicated to forty different national alt-weeklies, caused a major national stir and acted as a wake-up call for anybody who thinks that the rich pay more taxes than the poor. Turns out, not so much: hedge-fund superstar John Paulson paid no tax at all on the $9 billion he made in 2008 and 2009.

David Cay Johnston

# 16. Nine Things the Rich Don't Want You to Know About Taxes

For three decades we have conducted a massive economic experiment, testing a theory known as supply-side economics. The theory goes like this: Lower tax rates will encourage more investment, which in turn will mean more jobs and greater prosperity—so much so that tax revenues will go up, despite lower rates. The late Milton Friedman, the libertarian economist who wanted to shut down public parks because he considered them socialism, promoted this strategy. Ronald Reagan embraced Friedman's ideas and made them into policy when he was elected president in 1980.

For the past decade, we have doubled down on this theory of supply-side economics with the tax cuts sponsored by President George W. Bush in 2001 and 2003, which President Obama has agreed to continue for two years.

You would think that whether this grand experiment worked would be settled after three decades. You would think the practitioners of the dismal science of economics would look at their demand curves and the data on incomes and taxes and pronounce a verdict, the way Galileo and Copernicus did when they showed that geocentrism was a fantasy because Earth revolves around the sun (known as heliocentrism). But economics is not like that. It is not like physics with its laws and arithmetic with its absolute values.

Tax policy is something the framers left to politics. And in politics, the facts often matter less than who has the biggest bullhorn.

The Mad Men who once ran campaigns featuring doctors extolling the health benefits of smoking are now busy marketing the dogma that tax cuts mean broad prosperity, no matter what the facts show.

As millions of Americans prepare to file their annual taxes, they do so in an environment of media-perpetuated tax myths. Here are a few points about taxes and the economy that you may not know, to consider as you prepare to file your taxes. (All figures are inflation-adjusted.)

## Trends Reverse

The bottom 90 percent saw their incomes grow faster than the top 1 percent before Reaganism, but since then, nearly all the gains have been at the top.

In 2008 dollars

**Income Percentiles—Where You Stand on the Income Ladder Statistically**

|  | 0–90 | 90–95 | 95–99 | 99–99.5 | 99.5–99.9 | 99.9–99.9 | 99.9–100 |
|---|---|---|---|---|---|---|---|
| Increased Income 1950 to 1980 | $13,222 | $48,041 | $61,352 | $73,950 | $90,175 | $137,764 | $2,419,070 |
| Growth | 75% | 97% | 78% | 43% | 29% | 16% | 80% |
| Increased Income 1980 to 2008 | $303 | $29,497 | $71,460 | $198,404 | $479,870 | $2,228,724 | $21,904,288 |
| Growth | 1% | 30% | 51% | 81% | 121% | 221% | 403% |

Credits: WW Chart. Source: Author analysis of Saez & Piketty table A6.

## 1. Poor Americans do pay taxes.

Gretchen Carlson, the Fox News host, said last year "47 percent of Americans don't pay any taxes." John McCain and Sarah Palin both said similar things during the 2008 campaign about the bottom half of Americans.

Ari Fleischer, the former Bush White House spokesman, once said "50 percent of the country gets benefits without paying for them."

Actually, they pay lots of taxes—just not lots of federal income taxes.

Data from the Tax Foundation show that in 2008, the average income for the bottom half of taxpayers was $15,300.

This year the first $9,350 of income is exempt from taxes for singles and $18,700 for married couples, just slightly more than in 2008. That means millions of the poor do not make enough to owe income taxes.

But they still pay plenty of other taxes, including federal payroll taxes. Between gas taxes, sales taxes, utility taxes, and other taxes, no one lives tax-free in America.

When it comes to state and local taxes, the poor bear a heavier burden than the rich in every state except Vermont, the Institute on Taxation and Economic Policy calculated from official data. In Alabama, for example, the burden on the poor is more than twice that of the top 1 percent. The one-fifth of Alabama families making less than $13,000 pay almost 11 percent of their income in state and local taxes, compared with less than 4 percent for those who make $229,000 or more.

### Population Grew Almost Five Times More Than Jobs in the Aughts

| Year | Number With Any Work | Change From Previous Year |
|---|---|---|
| 2000 | 148,113,768 | 3,052,929 |
| 2001 | 148,282,344 | 168,576 |
| 2002 | 148,069,056 | −213,288 |
| 2003 | 147,722,206 | −346,850 |
| 2004 | 149,438,752 | 1,716,546 |
| 2005 | 151,603,359 | 2,164,607 |
| 2006 | 153,852,734 | 2,249,375 |
| 2007 | 155,570,422 | 1,717,688 |
| 2008 | 155,434,562 | −135,860 |
| 2009 | 150,917,735 | −4,516,827 |
| 2000 to 2009 Increase in People With Any Work | | 2,803,967 |
| Percentage | | 1.9% |
| 2000 to 2009 Increase in Population | | 25,584,644 |
| Percentage | | 9.1% |
| Ratio | | 5 to 1 |

Credits: WW Chart. Source: Medicare Tax Database; Census.

## 2. The wealthiest Americans don't carry the burden.

This is one of those oft-used canards. Sen. Rand Paul, the Tea Party favorite from Kentucky, told David Letterman recently that "the wealthy do pay most of the taxes in this country."

The Internet is awash with statements that the top 1 percent pays, depending on the year, 38 percent or more than 40 percent of taxes.

It's true that the top 1 percent of wage earners paid 38 percent of the federal income taxes in 2008 (the most recent year for which data is available). But people forget that the income tax is less than half of federal taxes and only one-fifth of taxes at all levels of government.

Social Security, Medicare, and unemployment insurance taxes (known as payroll taxes) are paid mostly by the bottom 90 percent of wage earners. That's because, once you reach $106,800 of income, you pay no more for Social Security, though the much smaller Medicare tax applies to all wages. Warren Buffett pays the exact same amount of Social Security taxes as someone who earns $106,800.

### The Wage Gap Widens

The gap between the median wage (half make more, half less) and the average wage is growing four times faster than median wage because pay increases are going mostly to the workers at the top. (*In 2009 dollars*)

| Year | Median Wage | Average Wage | Gap |
| --- | --- | --- | --- |
| 1990 | $23,799 | $33,112 | $9,313 |
| 1991 | $23,747 | $32,958 | $9,211 |
| 1992 | $23,870 | $33,644 | $9,773 |
| 1993 | $23,296 | $32,947 | $9,651 |
| 1994 | $23,333 | $32,987 | $9,654 |
| 1995 | $23,439 | $33,363 | $9,924 |
| 1996 | $23,797 | $33,991 | $10,195 |
| 1997 | $24,431 | $35,168 | $10,737 |
| 1998 | $25,215 | $36,441 | $11,226 |
| 1999 | $25,887 | $37,640 | $11,754 |
| 2000 | $26,298 | $38,708 | $12,409 |
| 2001 | $26,369 | $38,258 | $11,889 |
| 2002 | $26,418 | $38,040 | $11,622 |
| 2003 | $26,324 | $38,102 | $11,778 |
| 2004 | $26,526 | $38,839 | $12,313 |
| 2005 | $26,322 | $38,941 | $12,618 |
| 2006 | $26,489 | $39,458 | $12,969 |
| 2007 | $26,630 | $40,106 | $13,476 |
| 2008 | $26,420 | $39,511 | $13,091 |
| 2009 | $26,261 | 39,269 | $13,008 |
| 1990-2009 | +$2,462 | +$6,157 | +$3,695 |
| Percentage Change | 10% | 19% | 40% |
| G.H.W. Bush (3 years) | $71 | $532 | $461 |
| Clinton (8 years) | $2,428 | $5,064 | $2,636 |
| G.W. Bush (8 years) | $122 | $804 | $682 |
| Obama (1 year) | $(159) | $(243) | $(84) |

Credits: WW Chart. Source: Social Security Medicare Tax Database.

### 3. In fact, the wealthy are paying less taxes.

The Internal Revenue Service issues an annual report on the 400 highest income-tax payers. In 1961, there were 398 taxpayers who made $1 million or more, so I compared their income tax burdens from that year to 2007.

Despite skyrocketing incomes, the federal tax burden on the richest 400 has been slashed, thanks to a variety of loopholes, allowable deductions and other tools. The actual share of their income paid in taxes, according to the IRS, is 16.6 percent. Adding payroll taxes barely nudges that number.

Compare that to the vast majority of Americans, whose share of their income going to federal taxes increased from 13.1 percent in 1961 to 22.5 percent in 2007.

(By the way, during seven of the eight George W. Bush years, the IRS report on the top 400 taxpayers was labeled a state secret, a policy that the Obama administration overturned almost instantly after his inauguration.)

### Working Stiffs Taxed Much More Than Plutocrats

Income and tax information from 2007, latest available for top 400.

|  | Median Wage, Single Worker | Average of Top 400 | Percentage Higher Burden of Median-Wage Worker |
|---|---|---|---|
| Income | $26,000 | $344,759,000 | |
| Income and Payroll Tax | ($6,084) | ($58,176,761) | |
| Share of Income Paid in Tax | 23.4% | 16.9% | 38.5% |
| Less Charitable Gifts | $0 | ($28,512,000) | |
| Share of Income Paid in Tax | 23.4% | 18.7% | 25.1% |

Credits: WW Chart. Source: Author calculations from IRS.

## 4. Many of the very richest pay no current income taxes at all.

John Paulson, the most successful hedge-fund manager of all, bet against the mortgage market one year and then bet with Glenn Beck in the gold market the next. Paulson made himself $9 billion in fees in just two years. His current tax bill on that $9 billion? Zero.

Congress lets hedge-fund managers earn all they can now and pay their taxes years from now.

In 2007, Congress debated whether hedge-fund managers should pay the top tax rate that applies to wages, bonuses, and other compensation for their labors, which is 35 percent. That tax rate starts at about $300,000 of taxable income—not even pocket change to Paulson, but almost twelve years of gross pay to the median-wage worker.

The Republicans and a key Democrat, Sen. Charles Schumer of New York, fought to keep the tax rate on hedge-fund managers at 15 percent, arguing that the profits from hedge funds should be considered capital gains, not ordinary income, which got a lot of attention in the news.

What the news media missed is that hedge-fund managers don't even pay 15 percent. At least, not currently. So long as they leave their money, known as "carried interest," in the hedge fund, their taxes are deferred. They only pay taxes when they cash out, which could be decades from now for younger managers. How do these hedge-fund managers get money in the meantime? By borrowing against the carried interest, often at absurdly low rates—currently about 2 percent.

Lots of other people live tax-free, too. I have Donald Trump's tax records for four years early in his career. He paid no taxes for two of those years. Big real-estate investors enjoy tax-free living under a 1993 law President Clinton signed. It lets "professional" real-estate investors use paper losses like depreciation on their buildings against any cash income, even if they end up with negative incomes like Trump.

Frank and Jamie McCourt, who own the Los Angeles Dodgers, have not paid any income taxes since at least 2004, their divorce case revealed. Yet they spent $45 million one year alone. How? They just borrowed against Dodger ticket revenue and other assets. To the IRS, they look like paupers.

In Wisconsin, Terrence Wall, who unsuccessfully sought the Republican nomination for U.S. Senate in 2010, paid no income taxes on as much as $14 million of recent income, his disclosure forms showed. Asked about his living tax-free while working people pay taxes, he had a simple response: Everyone should pay less.

### It Wasn't Always Like This

Before Reaganism, the vast majority saw their incomes grow, but since then they've been virtually flat.

|  | Start | End | Increased Income | Percentage Change |
|---|---|---|---|---|
| 1950 to 1980 | $17,719 | $30,941 | $13,222 | 75% |
| 1980 to 2008 | $30,941 | $31,244 | $303 | 1% |

Credits: WW Chart. Source: Author calculations from IRS.

## 5. And (surprise!) since Reagan, only the wealthy have gained significant income.

The Heritage Foundation, the Cato Institute and similar conservative marketing organizations tell us relentlessly that lower tax rates will make us all better off.

"When tax rates are reduced, the economy's growth rate improves and living standards increase," according to Daniel J. Mitchell, an economist at Heritage until he joined Cato. He says that supply-side economics is "the simple notion that lower tax rates will boost work, saving, investment and entrepreneurship."

When Reagan was elected president, the top marginal tax rate (the tax rate paid on the last dollar of income earned) was

70 percent. He cut it to 50 percent and then 28 percent starting in 1987. It was raised by George H. W. Bush and Clinton, and then cut by George W. Bush. The top rate is now 35 percent.

Since 1980, when Reagan won the presidency promising prosperity through tax cuts, the average income of the vast majority—the bottom 90 percent of Americans—has increased a meager $303, or 1 percent. Put another way, for each dollar people in the vast majority made in 1980, in 2008 their income was up to $1.01.

Those at the top did better. The top 1 percent's average income more than doubled to $1.1 million, according to an analysis of tax data by economists Thomas Piketty and Emmanuel Saez. The really rich, the top one-tenth of 1 percent, each enjoyed almost $4 in 2008 for each dollar in 1980.

The top 300,000 Americans now enjoy almost as much income as the bottom 150 million, the data show.

### Tax Havens and Corporate Profits

In 2007, U.S. multinational corporations took a fourth of their offshore profits to five tax havens: Bermuda, the Cayman Islands, Ireland, Singapore and Switzerland.

| | Pre-Tax Profit of All Foreign Affiliates | Share of Profits Paid in Taxes | Profit as a Share of Assets* |
|---|---|---|---|
| U.S. Multinationals' Worldwide Profits | $430.2 billion | 29.6% | 44% |
| U.S. Multinational Profits in Five Tax Havens* | $101.9 billion | 7.2% | 173% |
| Share in the Five Tax Havens | 24% | | |
| Ratio Tax Havens to all U.S. Corporate Profits Earned Outside the U.S. | | 4-to-1 | 4-to-1 |

*Most assets in tax havens are intangibles, such as patents or property physically located somewhere else, but technically owned in the tax-haven country.

Credits: WW Chart. Source: Martin Sullivan, tax analysts economist, from data at bea.gov.

### 6. When it comes to corporations, the story is much the same—less taxes.

Corporate profits in 2008, the latest year for which data are available, were $1,830 billion, up almost 12 percent from $1,638.7 billion in 2000. Yet even though corporate tax rates have not been cut, corporate income-tax revenues fell to $230 billion from $249 billion—an 8 percent decline, thanks to a number of loopholes. The official 2010 profit numbers are not added up and released by the government, but the amount paid in corporate taxes is: In 2010 they fell further, to $191 billion—a decline of more than 23 percent compared with 2000.

#### Corporate Profits Rise, Taxes Fall

(in billions of 2010 dollars)

| Year | Corporate Profits | Tax Paid | Real Tax Rate |
| --- | --- | --- | --- |
| 2000 | $1,638.7 | $249.9 | 15.2% |
| 2008 | $1,830.0 | $230.1 | 12.6% |

Credits: WW Chart. Source: IRS.

### 7. Some corporate tax breaks destroy jobs.

Despite all the noise that America has the world's second-highest corporate tax rate, the actual taxes paid by corporations are falling because of the growing number of loopholes and companies shifting profits to tax havens like the Cayman Islands.

And right now America's corporations are sitting on close to $2 trillion in cash that is not being used to build factories, create jobs, or anything else, but acts as an insurance policy for managers unwilling to take the risk of actually building the businesses they are paid so well to run. That cash hoard, by the way, works out to nearly $13,000 per taxpaying household.

A corporate tax rate that is too low actually destroys jobs. That's because a higher tax rate encourages businesses (who don't want to pay taxes) to keep the profits in the business and reinvest, rather than pull them out as profits and have to pay high taxes.

The 2004 American Jobs Creation Act, which passed with bipartisan support, allowed more than 800 companies to bring profits that were untaxed but overseas back to the United States. Instead of paying the usual 35 percent tax, the companies paid just 5.25 percent.

The companies said bringing the money home—"repatriating" it, they called it—would mean lots of jobs. Sen. John Ensign, the Nevada Republican, put the figure at 660,000 new jobs.

Pfizer, the drug company, was the biggest beneficiary. It brought home $37 billion, saving $11 billion in taxes. Almost immediately it started firing people. Since the law took effect, Pfizer has let 40,000 workers go. In all, it appears that at least 100,000 jobs were destroyed.

Now Congressional Republicans and some Democrats are gearing up again to pass another tax holiday, promoting a new Jobs Creation Act. It would affect ten times as much money as the 2004 law.

### Average Incomes Fell During Bush Years

In 2000, candidate George W. Bush promised voters his tax-cut plan would make us all better off than we were by spurring çinvestment, creating more jobs, and raising incomes.

Figures below for all taxpayers are the number of returns filed each year multiplied by the increase (decrease) in average income. The total line shows the difference between actual results and what would have happened had 2000 average adjusted gross incomes continued for eight more years.

| Year | Average AGI (2008$) | Change in $ Per Taxpayer from 2000 | Total Income Change from 2000 |
|---|---|---|---|
| 2000 | $61,517.00 | | |
| 2001 | $57,592.00 | $3,925.00 | −$511,251,805,225.00 |
| 2002 | $55,513.00 | −$6,004.00 | −$780,978,963,772.00 |
| 2003 | $55,688.00 | −$5,829.00 | −$760,239,315,954.00 |
| 2004 | $58,519.00 | −$2,998.00 | −$396,413,673,916.00 |
| 2005 | $60,896.00 | −$621.00 | −$83,445,433,038.00 |
| 2006 | $61,973.00 | $456.00 | −$63,108,007,824.00 |
| 2007 | $63,096.00 | $1,579.00 | $225,763,534,674.00 |
| 2008 | $58,005.00 | −$3,512.00 | −$500,286,398,328.00 |
| Bush-era average income | $58,910.25 | −$2,606.75 | |
| TOTAL | | −$20,854.00 | −$2,743,744,047,735.00 |
| **2000 to 2008** | | | |
| $ change | | −$3,512.00 | |
| % change | | −5.7% | |

Credits: WW Chart. Source: IRS table 1.4 in 2008 dollars.

## 8. Republicans like taxes too.

President Reagan signed into law 11 tax increases, targeted at people down the income ladder. His administration and the Washington press corps called the increases "revenue enhancers." Reagan raised Social Security taxes so high that by the end of 2008, the government had collected more than $2 *trillion* in surplus tax.

George W. Bush signed a tax increase, too, in 2006, despite his written ironclad pledge never to raise taxes on anyone. It raised taxes on teenagers by requiring kids up to age seventeen, who earned money, to pay taxes at their parents' tax rate, which would almost always be higher than the rate they would otherwise pay. It was a story that ran buried inside the *New York Times* one Sunday, but nowhere else.

In fact, thanks to Republicans, one in three Americans will pay higher taxes this year than they did last year.

First, some history. In 2009, President Obama pushed his own tax cut—for the working class. He persuaded Congress to enact the Making Work Pay Tax Credit. Over the two years 2009 and 2010, it saved single workers up to $800 and married heterosexual couples up to $1,600, even if only one spouse worked. The top 5 percent or so of taxpayers were denied this tax break.

The Obama administration called it "the biggest middle-class tax cut" ever. Yet last December the Republicans, poised to regain control of the House of Representatives, killed Obama's Making Work Pay Credit while extending the Bush tax cuts for two more years—a policy Obama agreed to.

By doing so, Congressional Republican leaders increased taxes on a third of Americans, virtually all of them the working poor, this year.

As a result, of the 155 million households in the tax system, 51 million will pay an average of $129 more this year. That is $6.6 billion in higher taxes for the working poor, the nonpartisan Tax Policy Center estimated.

In addition, the Republicans changed the rate of workers' FICA contributions, which finances half of Social Security. The result:

If you are single and make less than $20,000, or married and less than $40,000, you lose under this plan. But the top 5 percent, people who make more than $106,800, will save $2,136 ($4,272 for two-career couples).

### Average Wages Declined in the Aughts

America's population grew five times faster than jobs from 2000 to 2009, but in 2010 dollar wages per capita declined, the opposite of President George W. Bush's repeated statements that lower tax rates would make everyone better off. Congressional Republicans say more tax cuts will improve the economy.

| Year | Population (in millions) | Total Wages in 2010 $ | Number of Workers | Avg. Wage in 2010 (actual) | Avg. Wage Per Capita |
|---|---|---|---|---|---|
| 2000 | 281.4 | $5,805,167 | 148,113,768 | $39,194 | $20,268 |
| 2009 | 308.7 | $5,894,034 | 150,917,733 | $39,055 | $19,283 |
| Change | 27.3 | $88,867 | $2,803,965 | (139) | (1,345) |
| Percentage Change | 9.7% | 1.5% | 1.9% | −0.4% | −6.5% |

Credits: WW Chart. Source: Medicare Tax Database; census.gov.

## 9. Other countries do it better.

We measure our economic progress, and our elected leaders debate tax policy, in terms of a crude measure known as gross domestic product. The way the official statistics are put together, each dollar spent buying solar energy equipment counts the same as each dollar spent investigating murders.

We do not give any measure of value to time spent rearing children or growing our own vegetables or to time off for leisure and community service.

And we do not measure the economic damage done by shocks, such as losing a job, which means not only loss of income and depletion of savings, but loss of health insurance, which a Harvard Medical School study found results in 45,000 unnecessary deaths each year.

Compare this to Germany, one of many countries with a smarter tax system and smarter spending policies.

Germans work less, make more per hour, and get much better parental leave than Americans, many of whom get no fringe benefits such as health care, pensions, or even a retirement savings plan. By many measures the vast majority live better in Germany than in America.

To achieve this, unmarried Germans on average pay 52 percent of their income in taxes. Americans average 30 percent, according to the Organization for Economic Cooperation and Development.

At first blush the German tax burden seems horrendous. But in Germany (as well as in Britain, France, Scandinavia, Canada, Australia and Japan), tax-supported institutions provide many of the things Americans pay for with after-tax dollars. Buying wholesale rather than retail saves money.

A proper comparison would take the 30 percent average tax on American workers and add their out-of-pocket spending on health care, college tuition and fees for services, and compare that with taxes that the average German pays. Add it all up and the combination of tax and personal spending is roughly equal in both countries, but with a large risk of catastrophic loss in America, and a tiny risk in Germany.

Americans take on $85 billion of debt each year for higher education, while college is financed by taxes in Germany and tuition is cheap to free in other modern countries. While soaring medical costs are a key reason that since 1980 bankruptcy in America has increased fifteen times faster than population growth, no one in Germany or the rest of the modern world goes broke because of accident or illness. And child poverty in America is the highest among modern countries—almost twice the rate in Germany, which is close to the average of modern countries.

On the corporate tax side, the Germans encourage reinvestment at home and the outsourcing of low-value work, like auto assembly, and German rules tightly control accounting so that profits earned at home cannot be made to appear as profits earned in tax havens.

Adopting the German system is not the answer for America. But crafting a tax system that benefits the vast majority, reduces risks, provides universal health care and focuses on diplomacy rather than militarism abroad (and at home) would be a lot smarter than what we have now.

Here is a question to ask yourself: We started down this road with Reagan's election in 1980 and upped the ante in this century with George W. Bush.

How long does it take to conclude that a policy has failed to fulfill its promises? And as you think of that, keep in mind George Washington. When he fell ill his doctors followed the common wisdom of the era. They cut him and bled him to remove bad blood. As Washington's condition grew worse, they bled him more. And like the mantra of tax cuts for the rich, they kept applying the same treatment until they killed him.

Luckily we don't bleed the sick anymore, but we are bleeding our government to death.

### Starving Our Government

Supply-siders said lower tax rates would mean more revenue, yet tax revenues rose after Clinton's 1993 tax-rate hikes and fell after Bush's 2001 and 2003 tax-rate cuts. Incomes through 2008 (latest data) are up 4.3 percent; corporate profits through 2009 were up 60 percent.

| | Individual Income Tax | | | Corporate Income Tax | | |
|---|---|---|---|---|---|---|
| Year | Population | Total | Per Capita | Total | Per Capita | |
| 2000 | 281,421,906 | 1,276.3 | 4,535 | 263 | 936 | |
| 2010 | 308,745,538 | 898.5 | 2,910 | 191 | 620 | |
| Change | 27,323,632 | (377.8) | (1,625) | (72) | (316) | |
| Percentage Change | 9.7% | −30% | −36% | −27% | −34% | |

| Year | Social Security & Medicare Tax | | Gross Domestic Product | |
|---|---|---|---|---|
| | Total | Per Capita | GDP | Per Capita |
| 2000 | 830 | 2,948 | 12,645 | 44,931 |
| 2010 | 865 | 2,801 | 14,660 | 47,483 |
| Change | 35 | (147) | 2,016 | 2,552 |
| Percentage Change | 4% | -5% | 16% | 6% |

(in 2010 dollars; billions for totals, actual for per capita).

Credits: WW Chart. Sources: OMB; census.gov; bea.gov; calculations by author.

**The New York Times**

Paul Krugman has argued for years now that the bond market's potential worries about government debt were far less important than the actual existing crisis of unemployment. He writes here that the political elite still don't get that the theoretical bond vigilantes are in full retreat and in fact are begging for government spending to stimulate a depressed economy. The budget deficit and national debt dominated economic discussions in 2011, in large part because of fears that soaring U.S. debt would cause government borrowing costs to skyrocket. Instead, the opposite has happened: Treasury bond rates have plummeted to record lows, making it cheaper than ever for the government to attempt to get the economy going again. That has helped Krugman cement his status as the most important liberal columnist.

Paul Krugman

# 17. The Hijacked Crisis

as market turmoil left you feeling afraid? Well, it should. Clearly, the economic crisis that began in 2008 is by no means over.

But there's another emotion you should feel: anger. For what we're seeing now is what happens when influential people exploit a crisis rather than try to solve it.

For more than a year and a half—ever since President Obama chose to make deficits, not jobs, the central focus of the 2010 State of the Union address—we've had a public conversation that has been dominated by budget concerns, while almost ignoring unemployment. The supposedly urgent need to reduce deficits has so dominated the discourse that on Monday, in the midst of a market panic, Mr. Obama devoted most of his remarks to the deficit rather than to the clear and present danger of renewed recession.

What made this so bizarre was the fact that markets were signaling, as clearly as anyone could ask, that unemployment rather than deficits is our biggest problem. Bear in mind that deficit hawks have been warning for years that interest rates on U.S. government debt would soar any day now; the threat from the bond market was supposed to be the reason that we must slash the deficit now now now. But that threat keeps not materializing. And, this week, on the heels of a downgrade that was supposed to scare bond investors, those interest rates actually plunged to record lows.

What the market was saying—almost shouting—was, "We're not worried about the deficit! We're worried about the weak economy!" For a weak economy means both low interest rates and a lack of business opportunities, which, in turn, means that government bonds become an attractive investment even at very low yields. If the downgrade of U.S. debt had any effect at all, it was to reinforce fears of austerity policies that will make the economy even weaker.

So how did Washington discourse come to be dominated by the wrong issue?

Hard-line Republicans have, of course, played a role. Although they don't seem to truly care about deficits—try suggesting any rise in taxes on the rich—they have found harping on deficits a useful way to attack government programs.

But our discourse wouldn't have gone so far off track if other influential people hadn't been eager to change the subject away from jobs, even in the face of 9 percent unemployment, and to hijack the crisis on behalf of their preexisting agendas.

Check out the opinion page of any major newspaper, or listen to any news-discussion program, and you're likely to encounter some self-proclaimed centrist declaring that there are no short-run fixes for our economic difficulties, that the responsible thing is to focus on long-run solutions and, in particular, on "entitlement reform"—that is, cuts in Social Security and Medicare. And when you do encounter such a person, you should be aware that people like that are a major reason we're in so much trouble.

For the fact is that right now the economy desperately needs a short-run fix. When you're bleeding profusely from an open wound, you want a doctor who binds that wound up, not a doctor who lectures you on the importance of maintaining a healthy lifestyle as you get older. When millions of willing and able workers are unemployed, and economic potential is going to waste to the tune of almost $1 trillion a year, you want policy makers who work on a fast recovery, not people who lecture you on the need for long-run fiscal sustainability.

Unfortunately, giving lectures on long-run fiscal sustainability is a fashionable Washington pastime; it's what people who want to sound serious do to demonstrate their seriousness. So when the crisis struck and led to big budget deficits—because that's what happens when the economy shrinks and revenue plunges—many members of our policy elite were all too eager to seize on those deficits as an excuse to change the subject from jobs to their favorite hobbyhorse. And the economy continued to bleed.

What would a real response to our problems involve? First of all, it would involve more, not less, government spending for the time being—with mass unemployment and incredibly low borrowing costs, we should be rebuilding our schools, our roads, our water systems, and more. It would involve aggressive moves to reduce household debt via mortgage forgiveness and refinancing. And it would involve an all-out effort by the Federal Reserve to get the economy moving, with the deliberate goal of generating higher inflation to help alleviate debt problems.

The usual suspects will, of course, denounce such ideas as irresponsible. But you know what's really irresponsible? Hijacking the debate over a crisis to push for the same things you were advocating before the crisis, and letting the economy continue to bleed.

**The Motley Fool**

*The Motley Fool* hilariously and scathingly calls to account once-esteemed financial leaders who enabled or took part in the excesses of the mortgage bacchanal then later misremembered their roles. Morgan Housel here puts in the dock Alan Greenspan, Robert Rubin, and Tom Maheras, who ran the investment-banking division of Citigroup. In congressional testimony, Maheras defended his piling-up of way too much risk, saying he relied on the advice of outside experts. "It's worth asking," writes Housel, "If Maheras wasn't an 'expert in the business,' why was he running the business?"

# 18. Greenspan, Rubin, and a Roomful of Hypocrites

"There is a lot of amnesia that's emerging, apparently," former Federal Reserve chairman Alan Greenspan told the Financial Crisis Inquiry Commission on Wednesday. He's appalled that we don't remember the Alan Greenspan who fought for more regulation and led a crusade to stomp out predatory lending.

And we don't. Because he didn't. Greenspan's testimony, along with cameos by former treasury secretary Robert Rubin and Citigroup executive Tom Maheras, are classic examples of soaking up adulation and nine-figure paydays during the run-up of a bubble only to plead ignorance after it pops.

### Exhibit A: Alan Greenspan

Throughout Greenspan's two-hour testimony, committee members persistently asked why the Fed sat on its hands while subprime lending ran wild.

Greenspan's rambling reply was that he and the Fed actually tried to warn everyone of its hazards and even attempted to do something about it to no avail. He backs up his regulator-in-chief stance by noting:

> In 2001, we issued our "Expanded Guidance for Subprime Lending Programs." This guidance warned regulated institutions

that loans designed to serve borrowers with impaired credit "may be prone to rapid deterioration in the early stages of an economic downturn," and imposed requirements for internal controls to protect against such risks.

This took me off guard—it didn't sound like something laissez-faire commander Greenspan would say. So I looked up the report and quote in full context and found this:

Although subprime lending is generally associated with higher inherent risk levels, properly managed, this can be a sound and profitable business. Because of the elevated risk levels, the quality of subprime loan pools may be prone to rapid deterioration, especially in the early stages of an economic downturn. Sound underwriting practices and robust effective control systems can provide the lead time necessary to react to deteriorating conditions, while sufficient allowance and capital levels can reduce its impact.

All the report says is that subprime can be safe and sound provided it's done in a safe and sound manner . . . which it isn't, wasn't, and never will be. Subprime and "sound underwriting practices" is oxymoron to the extreme. Like a prudent round of Russian roulette.

But more importantly, the report Greenspan mentions is simply a guidelines statement. The word "should" is mentioned fifty-eight times in the report, and specifically states, "we expect institutions to recognize that the elevated levels of credit and other risks arising from these activities require more intensive risk management." Just expect banks to behave, bow to your Ayn Rand shrine, and call it good.

At any rate, we know how Greenspan felt about subprime when he used blunter language. In 2005, he wrote:

Where once more-marginal applicants would simply have been denied credit, lenders are now able to quite efficiently judge the risk posed by individual applicants and to price that risk appropriately. These improvements have led to rapid growth in subprime mortgage lending; indeed, today subprime mortgages account for roughly 10 percent of the number of all mortgages outstanding, up from just 1 or 2 percent in the early 1990s.

But apparently we're the ones suffering from amnesia.

Next, Greenspan tackled credit derivatives. Brooksley Born, the former chairwoman of the Commodity Futures Trading Commission who was famously ostracized for her derivatives warnings a decade ago, asked Greenspan to comment on AIG's fatal use of credit default swaps (CDSes). His answer is a spectacle of denial:

> [AIG] was selling insurance. They could just as easily have sold and gotten into the same trouble by issuing insurance instruments rather than credit default swaps. My understanding is the reason they did that is because there were [different] capital requirements, but that is not an issue of the credit default swaps per se.

No, that's exactly the issue per se. Banks love credit default swaps because they can gamble their brains out behind closed doors without setting aside a penny to cover losses like regular insurance products. Had CDSes been regulated like insurance, issuers like AIG would have only been able to sell them to investors actually insuring something (not "naked" swaps that are purely speculative), and regulators would have forced issuers to set aside enough money to cover probable losses. But they weren't, and taxpayers paid dearly.

## Exhibit B: Robert Rubin

Next in the hot seat was Rubin, a former Goldman Sachs boss who became treasury secretary under President Clinton. While in office, Rubin was instrumental in repealing Glass-Steagall regulations, which paved the way for the creation of Frankenstein financial behemoths—particularly Citigroup. After leaving Washington in 1999, Citigroup named Rubin chairman of the executive committee, where he was paid $126 million over the next eight years—call it $43,000 a day. Rolling Stone columnist Matt Taibbi gets the award for explaining this relationship: "They don't call it bribery in this country when they give you the money post factum."

Rubin's defense for Citigroup's misery boils down to the claim that he had no operational duties, and didn't realize the bank was choking to death on toxic mortgages until it was too late. He was more of a highly paid face, and "wasn't a substantive part of the decision-making process."

Others disagree. In November 2008, the Wall Street Journal reported that "Mr. Rubin was deeply involved in a decision in late 2004 and early 2005 to take on more risk to boost flagging profit growth." The New York Times quotes a former Citi executive as saying, "Rubin had always been an advocate of being more aggressive in the capital markets arena. He would say, 'You have to take more risk if you want to earn more.'"

And earn more he did, which gets to the heart of the matter. When you're making $15 million a year as the head of the executive committee, you're not an innocent bystander. You're responsible for the outcome whether it makes you look good or not.

### Exhibit C: Tom Maheras

This one's short and sweet. Maheras, who ran Citigroup's toxic-asset campaign, was asked by the committee what led him to pile on so much risk. The reason, he claims, was that's what the pros told him to do. "Based in part on a careful study from outside consultants . . ." he explained, "the company decided to expand certain areas of our fixed income business that we believed at the time offered opportunities for long-term growth."

He went on. "Even in the summer and fall of 2007, I continued to believe, based upon what I understood from the experts in the business, that the bank's [CDO] holdings were safe."

It's worth asking: If Maheras wasn't an "expert in the business," why was he running the business? And if he wasn't an expert, why was he paid $97 million—ninety-seven million—during the three years before Citigroup disintegrated? Makes you wonder what kind of money the experts made.

## Suck It Up and Say It Like It Is

I'd like to have sympathy for these people. But every time we hear their side, it's the same story. They didn't know. They were blindsided. It was someone else's fault. They tried to warn, but no one would listen. What's sad is they were the first to accept full responsibility for the bubble's success on the way up, but largely claim ignorance now that the cat's out of the bag. I'd call that hypocrisy.

Part V

# The Big Picture

**The Atlantic**

Politicians (Democrats, at least) and others have been talking about the rise in the divide between the very wealthy and everyone else for years now, but the financial crisis threw it into such stark relief that the conversation has broadened, spiking fears that we are living in "a plutocracy, in which the rich display outsize political influence, narrowly self-interested motives, and a casual indifference to anyone outside their own rarefied economic bubble," writes Chrystia Freeland in *The Atlantic*. Months later those fears were being acted out in demonstrations around the nation, sparked by the Occupy Wall Street movement. Unlike earlier elites, today's super-wealthy are more likely to come from modest backgrounds and to have made their fortunes, rather than inheriting them; to still be working; to think globally; to be surrounded by their own kind; and to think that the trials of the middle and working classes are their own fault.

Chrystia Freeland

# 19. The Rise of the New Global Elite

f you happened to be watching NBC on the first Sunday morning in August last summer, you would have seen something curious. There, on the set of *Meet the Press*, the host, David Gregory, was interviewing a guest who made a forceful case that the U.S. economy had become "very distorted." In the wake of the recession, this guest explained, high-income individuals, large banks, and major corporations had experienced a "significant recovery"; the rest of the economy, by contrast—including small businesses and "a very significant amount of the labor force"—was stuck and still struggling. What we were seeing, he argued, was not a single economy at all, but rather "fundamentally two separate types of economy," increasingly distinct and divergent.

This diagnosis, though alarming, was hardly unique: drawing attention to the divide between the wealthy and everyone else has long been standard fare on the left. (The idea of "two Americas" was a central theme of John Edwards's 2004 and 2008 presidential runs.) What made the argument striking in this instance was that it was being offered by none other than the former five-term Federal Reserve chairman Alan Greenspan: iconic libertarian, preeminent defender of the free market, and (at least until recently) the nation's foremost devotee of Ayn Rand. When the high priest of capitalism himself is declaring the growth in economic inequality a national crisis, something has gone very, very wrong.

This widening gap between the rich and nonrich has been evident for years. In a 2005 report to investors, for instance, three analysts at Citigroup advised that "the World is dividing into two blocs—the Plutonomy and the rest":

> In a plutonomy there is no such animal as "the U.S. consumer" or "the UK consumer", or indeed the "Russian consumer". There are rich consumers, few in number, but disproportionate in the gigantic slice of income and consumption they take. There are the rest, the "non-rich", the multitudinous many, but only accounting for surprisingly small bites of the national pie.

Before the recession, it was relatively easy to ignore this concentration of wealth among an elite few. The wondrous inventions of the modern economy—Google, Amazon, the iPhone—broadly improved the lives of middle-class consumers, even as they made a tiny subset of entrepreneurs hugely wealthy. And the less-wondrous inventions—particularly the explosion of subprime credit—helped mask the rise of income inequality for many of those whose earnings were stagnant.

But the financial crisis and its long, dismal aftermath have changed all that. A multi-billion-dollar bailout and Wall Street's swift, subsequent reinstatement of gargantuan bonuses have inspired a narrative of parasitic bankers and other elites rigging the game for their own benefit. And this, in turn, has led to wider—and not unreasonable—fears that we are living in not merely a plutonomy but a plutocracy, in which the rich display outsize political influence, narrowly self-interested motives, and a casual indifference to anyone outside their own rarefied economic bubble.

Through my work as a business journalist, I've spent the better part of the past decade shadowing the new super-rich: attending the same exclusive conferences in Europe, conducting interviews over cappuccinos on Martha's Vineyard or in Silicon Valley meeting rooms, observing high-powered dinner parties in Manhattan.

Some of what I've learned is entirely predictable: the rich are, as F. Scott Fitzgerald famously noted, different from you and me.

What is more relevant to our times, though, is that the rich of today are also different from the rich of yesterday. Our light-speed, globally connected economy has led to the rise of a new super-elite that consists, to a notable degree, of first- and second-generation wealth. Its members are hardworking, highly educated, jet-setting meritocrats who feel they are the deserving winners of a tough, worldwide economic competition—and many of them, as a result, have an ambivalent attitude toward those of us who didn't succeed so spectacularly. Perhaps most noteworthy, they are becoming a transglobal community of peers who have more in common with one another than with their countrymen back home. Whether they maintain primary residences in New York or Hong Kong, Moscow or Mumbai, today's super-rich are increasingly a nation unto themselves.

## The Winner-Take-Most Economy

The rise of the new plutocracy is inextricably connected to two phenomena: the revolution in information technology and the liberalization of global trade. Individual nations have offered their own contributions to income inequality—financial deregulation and upper-bracket tax cuts in the United States, insider privatization in Russia, rent-seeking in regulated industries in India and Mexico. But the shared narrative is that, thanks to globalization and technological innovation, people, money, and ideas travel more freely today than ever before.

Peter Lindert is an economist at the University of California at Davis and one of the leaders of the "deep history" school of economics, a movement devoted to thinking about the world economy over the long term—that is to say, in the context of the entire sweep of human civilization. Yet he argues that the economic changes we are witnessing today are unprecedented. "Britain's classic industrial revolution was far less impressive than what has been going on in the past thirty years," he told me. The current productivity gains are larger, he explained, and the waves of disruptive innovation much, much faster.

From a global perspective, the impact of these developments has been overwhelmingly positive, particularly in the poorer parts of the world. Take India and China, for example: between 1820 and 1950, nearly a century and a half, per capita income in those two countries was basically flat. Between 1950 and 1973, it increased by 68 percent. Then, between 1973 and 2002, it grew by 245 percent, and continues to grow strongly despite the global financial crisis.

But within nations, the fruits of this global transformation have been shared unevenly. Though China's middle class has grown exponentially and tens of millions have been lifted out of poverty, the super-elite in Shanghai and other east-coast cities have steadily pulled away. Income inequality has also increased in developing markets such as India and Russia, and across much of the industrialized West, from the relatively laissez-faire United States to the comfy social democracies of Canada and Scandinavia. Thomas Friedman is right that in many ways the world has become flatter; but in others it has grown spikier.

One reason for the spikes is that the global market and its associated technologies have enabled the creation of a class of international business megastars. As companies become bigger, the global environment more competitive, and the rate of disruptive technological innovation ever faster, the value to shareholders of attracting the best possible CEO increases correspondingly. Executive pay has skyrocketed for many reasons—including the prevalence of overly cozy boards and changing cultural norms about pay—but increasing scale, competition, and innovation have all played major roles.

Many corporations have profited from this economic upheaval. Expanded global access to labor (skilled and unskilled alike), customers, and capital has lowered traditional barriers to entry and increased the value of an ahead-of-the-curve insight or innovation. Facebook, whose founder, Mark Zuckerberg, dropped out of college just six years ago, is already challenging Google, itself hardly an old-school corporation. But the biggest winners have been individuals, not institutions. The hedge-fund manager John Paulson, for instance, single-handedly profited almost as much from the crisis of 2008 as Goldman Sachs did.

Meanwhile, the vast majority of U.S. workers, however devoted and skilled at their jobs, have missed out on the windfalls of this winner-take-most economy—or worse, found their savings, employers, or professions ravaged by the same forces that have enriched the plutocratic elite. The result of these divergent trends is a jaw-dropping surge in U.S. income inequality. According to the economists Emmanuel Saez of Berkeley and Thomas Piketty of the Paris School of Economics, between 2002 and 2007, 65 percent of all income growth in the United States went to the top 1 percent of the population. The financial crisis interrupted this trend temporarily, as incomes for the top 1 percent fell more than those of the rest of the population in 2008. But recent evidence suggests that, in the wake of the crisis, incomes at the summit are rebounding more quickly than those below. One example: after a down year in 2008, the top 25 hedge-fund managers were paid, on average, more than $1 billion each in 2009, quickly eclipsing the record they had set in pre-recession 2007.

## Plutocracy Now

If you are looking for the date when America's plutocracy had its coming-out party, you could do worse than choose June 21, 2007. On that day, the private-equity behemoth Blackstone priced the largest initial public offering in the United States since 2002, raising $4 billion and creating a publicly held company worth $31 billion at the time. Stephen Schwarzman, one of the firm's two cofounders, came away with a personal stake worth almost $8 billion, along with $677 million in cash; the other, Peter Peterson, cashed a check for $1.88 billion and retired.

In the sort of coincidence that delights historians, conspiracy theorists, and book publishers, June 21 also happened to be the day Peterson threw a party—at Manhattan's Four Seasons restaurant, of course—to launch *The Manny*, the debut novel of his daughter, Holly, who lightly satirizes the lives and loves of financiers and their wives on the Upper East Side. The best-seller fits neatly into the genre of modern "mommy lit"—*USA Today* advised readers to take it to the beach—but the author told me that she was inspired to write it in part by her belief that "people have no clue about how much money there is in this town."

Holly Peterson and I spoke several times about how the super-affluence of recent years has changed the meaning of wealth. "There's so much money on the Upper East Side right now," she said. "If you look at the original movie *Wall Street*, it was a phenomenon where there were men in their thirties and forties making $2 and $3 million a year, and that was disgusting. But then you had the Internet age, and then globalization, and you had people in their thirties, through hedge funds and Goldman Sachs partner jobs, who were making $20, $30, $40 million a year. And there were a lot of them doing it. I think people making $5 million to $10 million definitely don't think they are making enough money."

As an example, she described a conversation with a couple at a Manhattan dinner party: "They started saying, 'If you're going to buy all this stuff, life starts getting really expensive. If you're going to do the NetJet thing'"—this is a service offering "fractional aircraft ownership" for those who do not wish to buy outright—"'and if you're going to have four houses, and you're going to run the four houses, it's like you start spending some money.'"

The clincher, Peterson says, came from the wife: "She turns to me and she goes, 'You know, the thing about twenty'"—by this, she meant $20 million a year—" 'is twenty is only ten after taxes.' And everyone at the table is nodding."

As with the aristocracies of bygone days, such vast wealth has created a gulf between the plutocrats and other people, one reinforced by their withdrawal into gated estates, exclusive academies, and private planes. We are mesmerized by such extravagances as Microsoft cofounder Paul Allen's 414-foot yacht, the *Octopus*, which is home to two helicopters, a submarine, and a swimming pool.

But while their excesses seem familiar, even archaic, today's plutocrats represent a new phenomenon. The wealthy of F. Scott Fitzgerald's era were shaped, he wrote, by the fact that they had been "born rich." They knew what it was to "possess and enjoy early."

That's not the case for much of today's super-elite. "Fat cats who owe it to their grandfathers are not getting all of the gains," Peter Lindert told me. "A lot of it is going to innovators this time around. There is more meritocracy in Bill Gates being at the top than the Duke of Bedford." Even Emmanuel Saez, who is deeply worried about the social and political consequences of rising income inequality, concurs that a defining quality of the current crop of plutocrats is that they are the "working rich." He has found that in 1916, the richest 1 percent of Americans received only one-fifth of their income from paid work; in 2004, that figure had risen threefold, to 60 percent.

Peter Peterson, for example, is the son of a Greek immigrant who arrived in America at age seventeen and worked his way up to owning a diner in Nebraska; his Blackstone cofounder, Stephen Schwarzman, is the son of a Philadelphia retailer. And they are hardly the exceptions. Of the top ten figures on the 2010 *Forbes* list of the wealthiest Americans, four are self-made, two (Charles and David Koch) expanded a medium-size family oil business into a billion-dollar industrial conglomerate, and the remaining four are all heirs of the self-made billionaire Sam

Walton. Similarly, of the top ten foreign billionaires, six are self-made, and the remaining four are vigorously growing their patrimony rather than merely living off it. It's true that few of today's plutocrats were born into the sort of abject poverty that can close off opportunity altogether—a strong early education is pretty much a precondition—but the bulk of their wealth is generally the fruit of hustle and intelligence (with, presumably, some luck thrown in). They are not aristocrats, by and large, but rather economic meritocrats, preoccupied not merely with consuming wealth but with creating it.

## The Road to Davos

To grasp the difference between today's plutocrats and the hereditary elite, who (to use John Stuart Mill's memorable phrase) "grow rich in their sleep," one need merely glance at the events that now fill high-end social calendars. The debutante balls and hunts and regattas of yesteryear may not be quite obsolete, but they are headed in that direction. The real community life of the twenty-first-century plutocracy occurs on the international conference circuit.

The best-known of these events is the World Economic Forum's annual meeting in Davos, Switzerland, invitation to which marks an aspiring plutocrat's arrival on the international scene. The Bilderberg Group, which meets annually at locations in Europe and North America, is more exclusive still—and more secretive—though it is more focused on geopolitics and less on global business and philanthropy. The Boao Forum for Asia, convened on China's Hainan Island each spring, offers evidence of that nation's growing economic importance and its understanding of the plutocratic culture. Bill Clinton is pushing hard to win his Clinton Global Initiative a regular place on the circuit. The TED conferences (the acronym stands for "Technology, Entertainment, Design") are an important stop for the digerati;

Herb Allen's Sun Valley gathering, for the media moguls; and the Aspen Institute's Ideas Festival (cosponsored by this magazine), for the more policy-minded.

Recognizing the value of such global conclaves, some corporations have begun hosting their own. Among these is Google's Zeitgeist conference, where I have moderated discussions for several years. One of the most recent gatherings was held last May at the Grove Hotel, a former provincial estate in the English countryside, whose 300-acre grounds have been transformed into a golf course and whose high-ceilinged rooms are now decorated with a mixture of antique and contemporary furniture. (Mock Louis XIV chairs—made, with a wink, from high-end plastic—are much in evidence.) Last year, Cirque du Soleil offered the 500 guests a private performance in an enormous tent erected on the grounds; in 2007, to celebrate its acquisition of YouTube, Google flew in overnight Internet sensations from around the world.

Yet for all its luxury, the mood of the Zeitgeist conference is hardly sybaritic. Rather, it has the intense, earnest atmosphere of a gathering of college summa cum laudes. This is not a group that plays hooky: the conference room is full from nine A.M. to six P.M., and during coffee breaks the lawns are crowded with executives checking their BlackBerrys and iPads.

Last year's lineup of Zeitgeist speakers included such notables as Archbishop Desmond Tutu, London mayor Boris Johnson, and Starbucks CEO Howard Schultz (not to mention, of course, Google's own CEO, Eric Schmidt). But the most potent currency at this and comparable gatherings is neither fame nor money. Rather, it's what author Michael Lewis has dubbed "the new new thing"—the insight or algorithm or technology with the potential to change the world, however briefly. Hence the presence last year of three Nobel laureates, including Daniel Kahneman, a pioneer in behavioral economics. One of the business stars in attendance was the thirty-six-year-old entrepreneur Tony Hsieh, who had sold his Zappos online shoe retailer to Amazon for more than $1 billion the previous summer. And the most popular session of all was the one in which Google showcased some of its new inventions, including the Nexus phone.

This geeky enthusiasm for innovation and ideas is evident at more-intimate gatherings of the global elite as well. Take the elegant Manhattan dinner parties hosted by Marie-Josée Kravis, the economist wife of the private-equity billionaire Henry, in their elegant Upper East Side apartment. Though the china is Sèvres and the paintings are museum quality (Marie-Josée is, after all, president of the Museum of Modern Art's board), the dinner-table conversation would not be out of place in a graduate seminar. Mrs. Kravis takes pride in bringing together not only plutocrats such as her husband and Michael Bloomberg but also thinkers and policy makers such as Richard Holbrooke, Robert Zoellick, and *Financial Times* columnist Martin Wolf, and leading them in discussion of matters ranging from global financial imbalances to the war in Afghanistan.

Indeed, in this age of elites who delight in such phrases as *outside the box* and *killer app*, arguably the most coveted status symbol isn't a yacht, a racehorse, or a knighthood; it's a philanthropic foundation—and, more than that, one actively managed in ways that show its sponsor has big ideas for reshaping the world.

### Philanthrocapitalism

George Soros, who turned eighty last summer, is a pioneer and role model for the socially engaged billionaire. Arguably the most successful investor of the postwar era, he is nonetheless proudest of his Open Society Foundations, through which he has spent billions of dollars on issues as diverse as marijuana legalization, civil society in central and eastern Europe, and rethinking economic assumptions in the wake of the financial crisis.

Inspired and advised by the liberal Soros, Peter Peterson—himself a Republican and former member of Nixon's cabinet—has spent $1 billion of his Blackstone windfall on a foundation dedicated to bringing down America's deficit and entitlement spending. Bill Gates, likewise, devotes most of his energy and intellect today to his foundation's work on causes ranging from supporting charter schools to combating disease in Africa. Facebook's Zuckerberg has yet to reach his thirtieth birthday, but last fall he donated $100 million to improving the public schools of Newark, New Jersey. Insurance and real-estate magnate Eli Broad has become an influential funder of stem-cell research; Jim Balsillie, a cofounder of BlackBerry creator Research in Motion, has established his own international-affairs think tank; and on and on. It is no coincidence that Bill Clinton has devoted his postpresidency to the construction of a global philanthropic "brand."

The super-wealthy have long recognized that philanthropy, in addition to its moral rewards, can also serve as a pathway to social acceptance and even immortality: Andrew "The Man Who Dies Rich Dies Disgraced" Carnegie transformed himself from robber baron to secular saint with his hospitals, concert halls, libraries, and university; Alfred Nobel ensured that he would be remembered for something other than the invention of dynamite. What is notable about today's plutocrats is that they tend to bestow their fortunes in much the same way they made them: entrepreneurially. Rather than merely donate to worthy charities or endow existing institutions (though they of course do this as well), they are using their wealth to test new ways to solve big problems. The journalists Matthew Bishop and Michael Green have dubbed the approach "philanthrocapitalism" in their book of the same name. "There is a connection between their ways of thinking as businesspeople and their ways of giving," Bishop told me. "They are used to operating on a grand scale, and so they operate on a grand scale in their philanthropy as well. And they are doing it at a much earlier age."

A measure of the importance of public engagement for today's super-rich is the zeal with which even emerging-market plutocrats are developing their own foundations and think tanks. When the oligarchs of the former Soviet Union first burst out beyond their own borders, they were Marxist caricatures of the nouveau riche, purchasing yachts and sports teams and surrounding themselves with couture-clad supermodels. Fifteen years later, they are exploring how to buy their way into the world of ideas.

One of the most determined is the Ukrainian entrepreneur Victor Pinchuk, whose business empire ranges from pipe manufacturing to TV stations. With a net worth of $3 billion, Pinchuk is no longer content merely to acquire modern art: in 2009, he began a global competition for young artists, run by his art center in Kiev and conceived as a way of bringing Ukraine into the international cultural mainstream. Pinchuk hosts a regular lunch on the fringes of Davos and has launched his own annual "ideas forum," a gathering devoted to geopolitics that is held, with suitable modesty, in the same Crimean villa where Stalin, Roosevelt, and Churchill attended the Yalta Conference. Last September's meeting, where I served as a moderator, included Bill Clinton, International Monetary Fund head Dominique Strauss-Kahn, Polish president Bronislaw Komorowski, and Russian deputy prime minister Alexei Kudrin.

As an entrée into the global super-elite, Pinchuk's efforts seem to be working: on a visit to the United States last spring, the oligarch met with David Axelrod, President Obama's top political adviser, in Washington and schmoozed with Charlie Rose at a New York book party for *Time* magazine editor Rick Stengel. On a previous trip, he'd dined with Caroline Kennedy at the Upper East Side townhouse of HBO's Richard Plepler. Back home, he has entertained his fellow art enthusiast Eli Broad at his palatial estate (which features its own nine-hole golf course) outside Kiev and has partnered with Soros to finance Ukrainian civil-society projects.

## A Nation Apart

Pinchuk's growing international Rolodex illustrates another defining characteristic of today's plutocrats: they are forming a global community, and their ties to one another are increasingly closer than their ties to hoi polloi back home. As Glenn Hutchins, cofounder of the private-equity firm Silver Lake, puts it, "A person in Africa who runs a big African bank and went to Harvard might have more in common with me than he does with his neighbors, and I could well share more overlapping concerns and experiences with him than with my neighbors." The circles we move in, Hutchins explains, are defined by "interests" and "activities" rather than "geography": "Beijing has a lot in common with New York, London, or Mumbai. You see the same people, you eat in the same restaurants, you stay in the same hotels. But most important, we are engaged as global citizens in cross-cutting commercial, political, and social matters of common concern. We are much less place-based than we used to be."

In a similar vein, the wife of one of America's most successful hedge-fund managers offered me the small but telling observation that her husband is better able to navigate the streets of Davos than those of his native Manhattan. When he's at home, she explained, he is ferried around town by a car and driver; the snowy Swiss hamlet, which is too small and awkward for limos, is the only place where he actually walks. An American media executive living in London put it more succinctly still: "We are the people who know airline flight attendants better than we know our own wives."

America's business elite is something of a latecomer to this transnational community. In a study of British and American CEOs, for example, Elisabeth Marx, of the head-hunting firm Heidrick & Struggles, found that almost a third of the former were foreign nationals, compared with just 10 percent of the latter. Similarly, more than two-thirds of the Brits had worked abroad for at least a year, whereas just a third of the Americans had done so.

But despite the slow start, American business is catching up: the younger generation of chief executives has significantly more international experience than the older generation, and the number of foreign and foreign-born CEOs, while still relatively small, is rising. The shift is particularly evident on Wall Street: in 2006, each of America's eight biggest banks was run by a native-born CEO; today, five of those banks remain, and two of the survivors—Citigroup and Morgan Stanley—are led by men who were born abroad.

Mohamed El-Erian, the CEO of Pimco, the world's largest bond manager, is typical of the internationalists gradually rising to the top echelons of U.S. business. The son of an Egyptian father and a French mother, El-Erian had a peripatetic childhood, shuttling between Egypt, France, the United States, the United Kingdom, and Switzerland. He was educated at Cambridge and Oxford and now leads a U.S.-based company that is owned by the German financial conglomerate Allianz SE.

Though El-Erian lives in Laguna Beach, California, near where Pimco is headquartered, he says that he can't name a single country as his own. "I have had the privilege of living in many countries," El-Erian told me on a recent visit to New York. "One consequence is that I am a sort of global nomad, open to many perspectives." As he talked, we walked through Midtown, which El-Erian remembered fondly from his childhood, when he'd take the crosstown bus each day to the United Nations International School. That evening, El-Erian was catching a flight to London. Later in the week, he was due in St. Petersburg.

Indeed, there is a growing sense that American businesses that don't internationalize aggressively risk being left behind. For all its global reach, Pimco is still based in the United States. But the flows of goods and capital upon which the super-elite surf are bypassing America more often than they used to. Take, for example, Stephen Jennings, the fifty-year-old New Zealander who cofounded the investment bank Renaissance Capital. Renaissance's roots are in Moscow, where Jennings maintains his primary residence, and his business strategy involves positioning the firm to capture the investment flows between the emerging markets, particularly Russia, Africa, and Asia. For his purposes, New York is increasingly irrelevant. In a 2009 speech in Wellington, New Zealand, he offered his vision of this post-unipolar business reality: "The largest metals group in the world is Indian. The largest aluminum group in the world is Russian. . . . The fastest-growing and largest banks in China, Russia, and Nigeria are all domestic."

As it happens, a fellow tenant in Jennings's high-tech, high-rise Moscow office building recently put together a deal that exemplifies just this kind of intra-emerging-market trade. Last year, Digital Sky Technologies, Russia's largest technology investment firm, entered into a partnership with the South African media corporation Naspers and the Chinese technology company Tencent. All three are fast-growing firms with global vision—last fall, a DST spin-off called Mail.ru went public and immediately became Europe's most highly valued Internet company—yet none is primarily focused on the United States. A similar harbinger of the intra-emerging-market economy was the acquisition by Bharti Enterprises, the Indian telecom giant, of the African properties of the Kuwait-based telecom firm Zain. A California technology executive explained to me that a company like Bharti has a competitive advantage in what he believes will be the exploding African market: "They know how to provide mobile phones so much more cheaply than we do. In a place like Africa, how can Western firms compete?"

The good news—and the bad news—for America is that the nation's own super-elite is rapidly adjusting to this more global perspective. The U.S.-based CEO of one of the world's largest hedge funds told me that his firm's investment committee often discusses the question of who wins and who loses in today's economy. In a recent internal debate, he said, one of his senior colleagues had argued that the hollowing-out of the American middle class didn't really matter. "His point was that if the transformation of the world economy lifts four people in China and India out of poverty and into the middle class, and meanwhile means one American drops out of the middle class, that's not such a bad trade," the CEO recalled.

I heard a similar sentiment from the Taiwanese-born, thirty-something CFO of a U.S. Internet company. A gentle, unpretentious man who went from public school to Harvard, he's nonetheless not terribly sympathetic to the complaints of the American middle class. "We demand a higher paycheck than the rest of the world," he told me. "So if you're going to demand ten times the paycheck, you need to deliver ten times the value. It sounds harsh, but maybe people in the middle class need to decide to take a pay cut."

At last summer's Aspen Ideas Festival, Michael Splinter, CEO of the Silicon Valley green-tech firm Applied Materials, said that if he were starting from scratch, only 20 percent of his workforce would be domestic. "This year, almost 90 percent of our sales will be outside the U.S.," he explained. "The pull to be close to the customers—most of them in Asia—is enormous." Speaking at the same conference, Thomas Wilson, CEO of Allstate, also lamented this global reality: "I can get [workers] anywhere in the world. It is a problem for America, but it is not necessarily a problem for American business . . . American businesses will adapt."

## Revolt of the Elites

Wilson's distinction helps explain why many of America's other business elites appear so removed from the continuing travails of the U.S. workforce and economy: the global "nation" in which they increasingly live and work is doing fine—indeed, it's thriving. As a consequence of this disconnect, when business titans talk about the economy and their role in it, the notes they strike are often discordant: for example, Goldman Sachs CEO Lloyd Blankfein waving away public outrage in 2009 by saying he was "doing God's work"; or the insistence by several top bankers after the immediate threat of the financial crisis receded that their institutions could have survived without TARP funding and that they had accepted it only because they had been strong-armed by Treasury Secretary Henry Paulson. Nor does this aloof disposition end at the water's edge: think of BP CEO Tony Hayward, who complained of wanting to get his life back after the Gulf oil spill and then proceeded to do so by watching his yacht compete in a race off the Isle of Wight.

It is perhaps telling that Blankfein is the son of a Brooklyn postal worker and that Hayward—despite his U.S. caricature as an upper-class English twit—got his start at BP as a rig geologist in the North Sea. They are both, in other words, working-class boys made good. And while you might imagine that such backgrounds would make plutocrats especially sympathetic to those who are struggling, the opposite is often true. For the super-elite, a sense of meritocratic achievement can inspire high self-regard, and that self-regard—especially when compounded by their isolation among like-minded peers—can lead to obliviousness and indifference to the suffering of others.

Unsurprisingly, Russian oligarchs have been among the most fearless in expressing this attitude. A little more than a decade ago, for instance, I spoke to Mikhail Khodorkovsky, at that moment the richest man in Russia. "If a man is not an oligarch, something is not right with him," Khodorkovsky told me. "Everyone had the same starting conditions, everyone could have done it." (Khodorkovsky's subsequent political travails—his oil company was appropriated by the state in 2004 and he is currently in prison—have tempered this Darwinian outlook: in a jail-cell correspondence last year, he admitted that he had "treated business exclusively as a game" and "did not care much about social responsibility.")

Though typically more guarded in their choice of words, many American plutocrats suggest, as Khodorkovsky did, that the trials faced by the working and middle classes are generally their own fault. When I asked one of Wall Street's most successful investment-bank CEOs if he felt guilty for his firm's role in creating the financial crisis, he told me with evident sincerity that he did not. The real culprit, he explained, was his feckless cousin, who owned three cars and a home he could not afford. One of America's top hedge-fund managers made a near-identical case to me—though this time the offenders were his in-laws and their subprime mortgage. And a private-equity baron who divides his time between New York and Palm Beach pinned blame for the collapse on a favorite golf caddy in Arizona, who had bought three condos as investment properties at the height of the bubble.

It is this not-our-fault mentality that accounts for the plutocrats' profound sense of victimization in the Obama era. You might expect that American elites—and particularly those in the financial sector—would be feeling pretty good, and more than a little grateful, right now. Thanks to a $700 billion TARP bailout and hundreds of billions of dollars lent nearly free of charge by the Federal Reserve (a policy Soros himself told me was a "hidden gift" to the banks), Wall Street has surged back to precrisis levels of compensation even as Main Street continues to struggle. Yet many of America's financial giants consider themselves under siege from the Obama administration—in some cases almost literally. Last summer, for example, Blackstone's Schwarzman caused an uproar when he said an Obama proposal to raise taxes on private-equity-firm compensation—by treating "carried interest" as ordinary income—was "like when Hitler invaded Poland in 1939."

However histrionic his imagery, Schwarzman (who subsequently apologized for the remark) is a Republican, so his antipathy toward the current administration is no surprise. What is more striking is the degree to which even former Obama support-ers in the financial industry have turned against the president and his party. A Wall Street investor who is a passionate Democrat recounted to me his bitter exchange with a Democratic leader in Congress who is involved in the tax-reform effort. "Screw you," he told the lawmaker. "Even if you change the legislation, the govern-ment won't get a single penny more from me in taxes. I'll put my money into my foundation and spend it on good causes. My money isn't going to be wasted in your deficit sinkhole."

He is not alone in his fury. In a much-quoted newsletter to investors last summer, the hedge-fund manager—and 2008 Obama fund-raiser—Dan Loeb fumed, "So long as our leaders tell us that we must trust them to regulate and redistribute our way back to prosperity, we will not break out of this economic quagmire." Two other former Obama backers on Wall Street—both claim to have been on Rahm Emanuel's speed-dial list—told me that the president is "antibusiness"; one went so far as to worry that Obama is "a socialist."

Much of this pique stems from simple self-interest: in addi-tion to the proposed tax hikes, the financial reforms that Obama signed into law last summer have made regulations on Ameri-can finance more stringent. But as the Democratic investor's angry references to his philanthropic work suggest, the rage in the C-suites is driven not merely by greed but by a perceived af-front to the plutocrats' amour propre, a wounded incredulity that anyone could think of them as villains rather than heroes. Aren't they, after all, the ones whose financial and technological innovations represent the future of the American economy? Aren't they "doing God's work"?

You might say that the American plutocracy is experiencing its John Galt moment. Libertarians (and run-of-the-mill high-school nerds) will recall that Galt is the plutocratic hero of Ayn Rand's 1957 novel, *Atlas Shrugged*. Tired of being dragged down by the parasitic, envious, and less-talented lower classes, Galt and his fellow capitalists revolted, retreating to "Galt's Gulch," a refuge in the Rocky Mountains. There, they passed their days in secluded natural splendor, while the rest of the world, bereft of their genius and hard work, collapsed. (G. K. Chesterton suggested a similar idea, though more gently, in his novel *The Man Who Was Thursday*: "The poor man really has a stake in the country. The rich man hasn't; he can go away to New Guinea in a yacht.")

This plutocratic fantasy is, of course, just that: no matter how smart and innovative and industrious the super-elite may be, they can't exist without the wider community. Even setting aside the financial bailouts recently supplied by the governments of the world, the rich need the rest of us as workers, clients, and consumers. Yet, as a metaphor, Galt's Gulch has an ominous ring at a time when the business elite view themselves increasingly as a global community, distinguished by their unique talents and above such parochial concerns as national identity, or devoting "their" taxes to paying down "our" budget deficit. They may not be isolating themselves geographically, as Rand fantasized. But they appear to be isolating themselves ideologically, which in the end may be of greater consequence.

## The Backlash

The cultural ties that bind the super-rich to everyone else are fraying from both ends at once. Since World War II, the United States in particular has had an ethos of aspirational capitalism. As Soros told me, "It is easier to be rich in America than in Europe, because Europeans envy the billionaire, but Americans hope to emulate him." But as the wealth gap has grown wider, and the rich have appeared to benefit disproportionately from government bailouts, that admiration has begun to sour.

One measure of the pricklier mood is how risky it has become for politicians to champion Big Business publicly. Defending Big Oil and railing against government interference used to be part of the job description of Texas Republicans. But when Congressman Joe Barton tried to take the White House to task for its post-spill "shakedown" of BP, he was immediately silenced by party elders. New York's Charles Schumer is sometimes described as "the senator from Wall Street." Yet when the financial-reform bill came to the Senate last spring—a political tussle in which each side furiously accused the other of carrying water for the banks—on Wall Street, Schumer was called the "invisible man" for his uncharacteristic silence on the issue.

In June, when I asked Larry Summers, then the president's chief economic adviser, about hedge funds' objections to the carried-interest tax reform, he was quick to disassociate himself from Wall Street's concerns. "If that's been the largest public-policy issue you've encountered," he told me, "you've been traveling in different circles than I have been over the last several months." I reminded him that he had in fact worked for a hedge fund, D. E. Shaw, as recently as 2008, and he emphasized his use of the qualifier *over the last several months.*

Critiques of the super-elite are becoming more common even at gatherings of the super-elite. At a *Wall Street Journal* conference in December 2009, Paul Volcker, the legendary former head of the Federal Reserve, argued that Wall Street's claims of wealth creation were without any real basis. "I wish someone," he said, "would give me one shred of neutral evidence that financial innovation has led to economic growth—one shred of evidence."

At Google's May Zeitgeist gathering, Desmond Tutu, the opening speaker, took direct aim at executive compensation. "I do have a very real concern about capitalism," he lectured the gathered executives. "The Goldman Sachs thing. I read that one of the directors general—whatever they are called, CEO—took away one year as his salary $64 million. *Sixty-four million dollars.*" He sputtered to a stop, momentarily stunned by this sum (though, by the standards of Wall Street and Silicon Valley compensation, it's not actually that much money). In an op-ed in the *Wall Street Journal* last year, even the economist Klaus Schwab— founder of the World Economic Forum and its iconic Davos meeting—warned that "the entrepreneurial system is being perverted," and businesses that "fall back into old habits and excesses" could "undermin[e] social peace."

## Bridging the Divide

Not all plutocrats, of course, are created equal. Apple's visionary Steve Jobs is neither the moral nor the economic equivalent of the Russian oligarchs who made their fortunes by brazenly seizing their country's natural resources. And while the benefits of the past decade's financial "innovations" are, as Volcker noted, very much in question, many plutocratic fortunes—especially in the technology sector—have been built on advances that have broadly benefited the nation and the world. That is why, even as the TARP-recipient bankers have become objects of widespread anger, figures such as Jobs, Bill Gates, and Warren Buffett remain heroes.

And, ultimately, that is the dilemma: America really does need many of its plutocrats. We benefit from the goods they produce and the jobs they create. And even if a growing portion of those jobs are overseas, it is better to be the home of these innovators—native and immigrant alike—than not. In today's hypercompetitive global environment, we need a creative, dynamic super-elite more than ever.

There is also the simple fact that someone will have to pay for the improved public education and social safety net the American middle class will need in order to navigate the wrenching transformations of the global economy. (That's not to mention the small matter of the budget deficit.) Inevitably, a lot of that money will have to come from the wealthy—after all, as the bank robbers say, that's where the money is.

It is not much of a surprise that the plutocrats themselves oppose such analysis and consider themselves singled out, unfairly maligned, or even punished for their success. Self-interest, after all, is the mother of rationalization, and—as we have seen—many of the plutocracy's rationalizations have more than a bit of truth to them: as a class, they are generally more hardworking and merito-cratic than their forebears; their philanthropic efforts are inno-vative and important; and the recent losses of the American mid-dle class have in many cases entailed gains for the rest of the world.

But if the plutocrats' opposition to increases in their taxes and tighter regulation of their economic activities is under-standable, it is also a mistake. The real threat facing the super-elite, at home and abroad, isn't modestly higher taxes but rather the possibility that inchoate public rage could cohere into a more concrete populist agenda—that, for instance, middle-class Ameri-cans could conclude that the world economy isn't working for them and decide that protectionism or truly punitive taxation is preferable to incremental measures such as the eventual repeal of the upper-bracket Bush tax cuts.

Mohamed El-Erian, the Pimco CEO, is a model member of the super-elite. But he is also a man whose father grew up in rural Egypt, and he has studied nations where the gaps between the rich and the poor have had violent resolutions. "For successful people to say the challenges faced by the lower end of the income dis-tribution aren't relevant to them is shortsighted," he told me. Noting that "global labor and capital are doing better than their strictly national counterparts" in most Western industrialized nations, El-Erian added, "I think this will lead to increasingly inward-looking social and political conditions. I worry that we risk ending up with very insular policies that will not do well in a global world. One of the big surprises of 2010 is that the protec-tionist dog didn't bark. But that will come under pressure."

The lesson of history is that, in the long run, super-elites have two ways to survive: by suppressing dissent or by sharing their wealth. It is obvious which of these would be the better outcome for America, and the world. Let us hope the plutocrats aren't already too isolated to recognize this. Because, in the end, there can never be a place like Galt's Gulch.

**The Wall Street Journal**

Brian M. Carney of the *Wall Street Journal* editorial board sat down with the chairman of Nestlé last year for a chat on how government subsidies and energy policies threaten fragile global food resources. A calorie is a calorie, says Peter Brabeck-Letmathe, arguing that the world can't afford to redirect relatively scarce food sources to an energy market that uses twenty times as many of them. Carney threads together his asides on urbanization, the industrialization of food, and water rights to argue why we should let markets feed the world.

Brian M. Carney

# 20. Can the World Still Feed Itself?

As befits the chairman of the world's largest food-production company, Peter Brabeck-Letmathe is counting calories. But it's not his diet that the chairman and former CEO of Nestlé is worried about. It's all the food that the United States and Europe are converting into fuel while the world's poor get hungrier.

"Politicians," Mr. Brabeck-Letmathe says, "do not understand that between the food market and the energy market, there is a close link." That link is the calorie.

The energy stored in a bushel of corn can fuel a car or feed a person. And increasingly, thanks to ethanol mandates and subsidies in the United States and biofuel incentives in Europe, crops formerly grown for food or livestock feed are being grown for fuel. The U.S. Department of Agriculture's most recent estimate predicts that this year, for the first time, American farmers will harvest more corn for ethanol than for feed. In Europe some 50 percent of the rapeseed crop is going into biofuel production, according to Mr. Brabeck-Letmathe, while "world-wide about 18 percent of sugar is being used for biofuel today."

In one sense, this is a remarkable achievement—five decades ago, when the global population was half what it is today, catastrophists like Paul Ehrlich were warning that the world faced mass starvation on a biblical scale. Today, with nearly seven billion mouths to feed, we produce so much food that we think nothing of burning tons of it for fuel.

Or at least we think nothing of it in the West. If the price of our breakfast cereal goes up because we're diverting agricultural production to ethanol or biodiesel, it's an annoyance. But if the price of corn or flour doubles or triples in the Third World, where according to Mr. Brabeck-Letmathe people "are spending 80 percent of [their] disposable income on food," hundreds of millions of people go hungry. Sometimes, as in the Middle East earlier this year, they revolt.

"What we call today the Arab Spring," Mr. Brabeck-Letmathe says over lunch at Nestlé's world headquarters, "really started as a protest against ever-increasing food prices."

Mr. Brabeck-Letmathe has extensive experience at the intersection of food, politics, and development. He spent most of his first two decades at Nestlé in Latin America. In 1970, he was posted to Chile, where Salvador Allende's socialist government was threatening to nationalize milk production, and Nestlé's Chilean operations along with it. He knows that most of the world is not as fortunate as we are.

"There is a huge difference," he says, "between how we live this crisis and what the reality of today is for hundreds of millions of people, who we have been pushing back into extreme poverty with wrong policy making." First there's the biofuels craze, driven by concerns over energy independence, oil supplies, global warming, and, ironically, Mideast political stability.

Add to that, especially in Europe, a paralyzing fear of genetically modified crops, or GMOs. This refusal to use "available technology" in agriculture, Mr. Brabeck-Letmathe contends, has halted the multidecade rise in agricultural productivity that has allowed us, so far, to feed more mouths than many people believed was possible.

Then there is demographics. Recent decades have seen "the creation of more than a billion new consumers in the world who have had the opportunity to move from extreme poverty into what we would call today a moderate middle class," thanks to economic growth in places like China and India. This means a billion people who have "access to meat" for the first time, Mr. Brabeck-Letmathe says.

"And the demand for meat," he says, "has a multiplier effect of ten. You need ten times as much land, ten times as much [feed], ten times as much water to produce one calorie of meat as you do to have one calorie of vegetables or grain." Even so, we are capable of satisfying this increased demand—if we choose to. "If politicians of this world really want to tackle food security," Mr. Brabeck-Letmathe says, "there's only one decision they have to make: No food for fuel. . . . They just have to say 'No food for fuel,' and supply and demand would balance again."

If we don't do that, we can never hope to square the drive for biofuels with the world's food needs. The calories don't add up. "The energy market," Mr. Brabeck-Letmathe argues, "is twenty times as big, in calories, as the food market." So "when politicians say, 'We want to replace 20 percent of the energy market through the food market,'" this means "we would have to triple food production" to meet that goal—and that's before we eat the first kernel of what we've grown.

Even if we could pull this off, we will never get there by turning our backs on genetically modified crops and holding up "organic" food as the new gold standard of safety, purity, and health. Organic production is all the rage in the rich West, but we can't "feed the world with this stuff," he says. Agricultural productivity with organics is too low.

"If you look at those countries that have introduced GMOs," Mr. Brabeck-Letmathe says, "you will see that the yield per hectare has increased by about 30 percent over the past few years. Whereas the yields for non-GMO crops are flat to slightly declining." And that gap, he says, "is a voluntary gap. . . . It's just a political decision."

And it's one thing for rich, well-fed Europe to say, as Mr. Brabeck-Letmathe puts it, "I don't want to produce GMO [crops] because frankly speaking I don't want to produce so much food." That, he says, he can understand.

What's harder for him to understand is that Europe's policies effectively forbid poor countries in places like Africa from using genetically modified seed. These countries, he says, urgently need the technology to increase yields and productivity in their backward agricultural sectors. But if they plant GMOs, then under Europe's rules the EU "will not allow you to export anything—anything. Not just the [crop] that has GMO—anything," because of European fears about cross-contamination and almost impossibly strict purity standards. The European fear of genetically modified crops is, he says, "purely emotional. It's becoming almost a religious belief."

This makes Mr. Brabeck-Letmathe, a jovial man with a quick smile, get emotional himself. "How many people," he asks with a touch of irritation, "have died from food contamination from organic products, and how many people have died from GMO products?" He answers his own question: "None from GMO. And I don't have to ask too long how many people have died just recently from organic," he adds, referring to the *E. coli* outbreak earlier this year in Europe.

Nestlé itself has at times been painted as an enemy of the world's poor—for thirty years it has contended with a sporadic boycott movement over the sale and marketing of infant formula in the Third World, a push that some rich Westerners find unethical. On the other hand, under Mr. Brabeck-Letmathe, Nestlé's corporate strategy has emphasized that all food markets are intensely local. Americans may increasingly buy all drinks by the gallon and chocolate bars by the pound, but in many parts of the world a trip to the store might yield a single Maggi cube—the Nestlé-made bullion cubes that are ubiquitous in many countries. In these countries, single servings of many products are sold in little foil packets to allow people to match their spending to their cash flow.

This is, Mr. Brabeck-Letmathe contends, an extension of Nestlé's original reason for being. Nestlé exists, Mr. Brabeck-Letmathe says, because as Europe's population "urbanized," as people moved to the cities and traded their ploughshares for time cards, "somebody had to ensure that people" who worked twelve hours a day in a factory could feed themselves. For the first time in history, "you need[ed] a food industry. You need[ed] somebody who takes a product, who treats it so that its shelf life allows it to be transported, to be brought into the consumption center. That's why we have canning, that's why we have pasteurization, that's why we have all these things."

The vast majority of us would have no idea any longer how to feed ourselves if we turned up one day to find the supermarket empty. We rely on industrialized food production, distribution, preservation, and storage to make our urban lifestyles, our very lives, possible. And "it was not the state that took care of this thing. It was private initiative." Today, Nestlé employs some 300,000 people, takes in some $100 billion a year in revenue—and yet represents just 1.5 percent of a global food industry that feeds billions.

But for private initiative to work that kind of miracle, you need a market. Mr. Brabeck-Letmathe even worries about the absence of a functioning market for water. Some 98.5 percent of the fresh water the world uses every year goes to agricultural or industrial use. And in most cases, there is no market for how that water is allocated and used. The result is waste, overuse, and misuse of the water we have. If we don't do something about that, Mr. Brabeck-Letmathe fears, we will soon run ourselves dry.

Up to now, he says, our response to water shortages has focused "on the supply side": We build another dam, or a canal to bring water from one place to another. But "the big issue," he contends, "is on the demand side," and the "best regulator" of demand is prices.

"If oil becomes scarce," he notes, "the oil price goes up. But if water does, well, we still pump the same amount. It doesn't matter because it doesn't cost. It has no value." He drives this point home by connecting it back to biofuels: "We would never have had a biofuel policy—never," he contends, "if we would have given water any value." It takes, Mr. Brabeck-Letmathe says, "9,100 liters of water to produce one liter of biodiesel. You can only do that because water has no price."

He cites Spain as an example of an agricultural sector in need of adjustment. "The total [output] of the Spanish agricultural system," he says, "is less in value than the subsidies they receive between the Common Agricultural Policy, the subsidies for tax relief, the subsidies for water."

"Take away the emotion of the water issue," Mr. Brabeck-Letmathe argues. "Give the 1.5 percent of the water [that we use to drink and wash with], make it a human right. But give me a market for the 98.5 percent so the market forces are able to react, and they will be the best guidance that you can have. Because if the market forces are there the investments are going to be made."

The world's population is projected to hit nine billion by midcentury, up from 6.7 billion today. So, can we feed all those people? Mr. Brabeck-Letmathe doesn't hesitate. "We can feed nine billion people," he says, with a wave of the hand. And we can provide them with water and fuel. But only if we let the market do its thing.

**The New York Times**

The business of law school is a racket—one that David Segal explored at great length in a *New York Times* article in January 2011. In this follow-up piece, he looks at the invidious position of the law schools themselves: how even a reformist with the best will in the world is forced by the crazy economics of law school to overcharge his students and lie about their fortunes.

David Segal

# 21. Law School Economics: Ka-Ching!

With apologies to show business, there's no business like the business of law school.

The basic rules of a market economy—even golden oldies, like a link between supply and demand—just don't apply.

Legal diplomas have such allure that law schools have been able to jack up tuition four times faster than the soaring cost of college. And many law schools have added students to their incoming classes—a step that, for them, means almost pure profits—even during the worst recession in the legal profession's history.

It is one of the academy's open secrets: law schools toss off so much cash they are sometimes required to hand over as much as 30 percent of their revenue to universities, to subsidize less profitable fields.

In short, law schools have the power to raise prices and expand in ways that would make any company drool. And when a business has that power, it is apparently difficult to resist.

How difficult? For a sense, take a look at the strange case of New York Law School and its dean, Richard A. Matasar. For more than a decade, Mr. Matasar has been one of the legal academy's most dogged and scolding critics, and he has repeatedly urged professors and fellow deans to rethink the basics of the law school business model and put the interests of students first.

"What I've said to people in giving talks like this in the past is, we should be ashamed of ourselves," Mr. Matasar said at a 2009 meeting of the Association of American Law Schools. He ended with a challenge: If a law school can't help its students achieve their goals, "we should shut the damn place down."

Given his scathing critiques, you might expect that during Mr. Matasar's eleven years as dean, he has reshaped New York Law School to conform with his reformist agenda. But he hasn't. Instead, the school seems to be benefitting from many of legal education's assorted perversities.

NYLS is ranked in the bottom third of all law schools in the country, but with tuition and fees now set at $47,800 a year, it charges more than Harvard. It increased the size of the class that arrived in the fall of 2009 by an astounding 30 percent, even as hiring in the legal profession imploded. It reported in the most recent *US News & World Report* rankings that the median starting salary of its graduates was the same as for those of the best schools in the nation—even though most of its graduates, in fact, find work at less than half that amount.

Mr. Matasar declined to be interviewed for this article, though he agreed to answer questions e-mailed through a public relations representative.

Asked if there was a contradiction between his stand against expanding class sizes and the growth of the student population at NYLS, Mr. Matasar wrote: "The answer is that we exist in a market. When there is demand for education, we, like other law schools, respond."

This is a story about the law school market, a singular creature of American capitalism, one that is so durable it seems utterly impervious to change. Why? The career of Richard Matasar offers some answers. His long-time and seemingly sincere ambition is to "radically disrupt our traditional approach to legal education," as it says on his NYLS webpage. But even he, it seems, is engaged in the same competition for dollars and students that consumes just about everyone with a financial and reputational stake in this business.

"The broken economic model Matasar describes appears to be his own template," wrote Brian Z. Tamanaha, a professor at Washington University Law School in St. Louis, in a blog posting about Mr. Matasar last year. "Are his increasingly vocal criticisms of legal academia an unspoken mea culpa?"

.     .     .

A private, stand-alone institution located in the TriBeCa neighborhood of downtown Manhattan, New York Law School was founded in 1891 and counts Justice John Marshall Harlan among its most famous graduates. The school—which is not to be confused with New York University School of Law—is housed in a gleaming new 235,000-square-foot building at the corner of West Broadway and Leonard Street.

That building puts NYLS in the middle of a nationwide trend: the law school construction boom. As other industries close offices and downsize plants, the manufacturing base behind the doctor of jurisprudence keeps growing. Fordham Law School in New York recently broke ground on a $250 million, twenty-two-story building. The University of Baltimore School of Law and the University of Michigan Law School are both working on buildings that cost more that $100 million. Marquette University Law School in Wisconsin has just finished its own $85 million project. A bunch of other schools have built multimillion dollar additions.

NYLS has participated in another national law school trend: the growth in the number of enrollees. Last year, law schools across the country matriculated 49,700 students, according to the Law School Admission Council, the largest number in history, and 7,000 more students than in 2001. NYLS grew at an even faster clip. In 2000, the year Mr. Matasar took over, the school had a total of 1,326 full- and part-time students. By 2009, the figure had risen to 1,596.

The jump seems to contradict one of Mr. Matasar's core tenets.

"Can class size be increased without damaging quality?" he asked in a 1996 *Florida Law Review* article. "Can class size be increased without assurances that jobs will be available for the increased number of graduates? Can class size be increased without also providing more staff, faculty, books and service? Increase class size? No!"

Did Mr. Matasar change his mind? In an e-mail, he cited the unpredictability of yield rates, which is the percent of students who accept an offer of admission. There was more than one year of yield surprises under Mr. Matasar, the largest of which came in 2009, when the incoming class leapt by 171 students.

It was a very profitable surprise, worth about $6.7 million in gross revenue. Mr. Matasar would not discuss the added costs of teaching what became known at the school as "the bulge class." But faculty members, some of whom were offered the chance to take on additional courses, estimate that, at most, the school had to spend about $500,000 more that year on teaching.

This windfall, it turns out, was perfectly timed. Because as all those students were signing up for their first year at NYLS, a little-noticed drama was unfolding that involved the financing for that brand-new building.

•    •    •

Three years earlier, in 2006, the school had floated $135 million worth of bonds to finance construction of the new building, at 185 West Broadway. At the time, Moody's rated the bonds A3, placing them squarely in the "come and get 'em" category for investors. The rating reflected NYLS's strong balance sheet and the quality of its management, Moody's said.

Equally important, NYLS was—and is—in a very lucrative business. Like business schools and some high-profile athletic programs, law schools subsidize other fields in universities that can't pay their own way.

"If my president were to say 'We'll never take more than 10 percent of your revenue,' I'd say 'God bless you,' and we'd never have to talk again," says Lawrence E. Mitchell, the incoming dean of the Case Western Reserve University School of Law in Cleveland. "But having just come from a two-day meeting of new and current deans organized by the American Bar Association, I can tell you that some law schools pay 25 or even 30 percent."

Among deans, the money surrendered to the administration is known informally as "the tax." Even in the midst of a merciless legal downturn, the tax still pumps huge sums into universities, in part because the price of a law degree continues to climb.

From 1989 to 2009, when college tuition rose by 71 percent, law school tuition shot up 317 percent.

There are many reasons for this ever-climbing sticker price, but the most bizarre comes courtesy of the highly influential *US News* rankings. Part of the *US News* algorithm is a figure called expenditures per student, which is essentially the sum that a school spends on teacher salaries, libraries, and other education expenses, divided by the number of students.

Though it accounts for just 9.75 percent of the algorithm, it gives law schools a strong incentive to keep prices high. Forget about looking for cost efficiencies. The more that law schools charge their students, and the more they spend to educate them, the better they fare in the *US News* rankings.

"I once joked with my dean that there is a certain amount of money that we could drag into the middle of the school's quadrangle and burn," said John F. Duffy, a George Washington School of Law professor, "and when the flames died down, we'd be a top ten school. As long as the point of the bonfire was to teach our students. Perhaps what we could teach them is the idiocy in the *US News* rankings."

For years, it made economic sense for smart, ambitious twenty-two-year-olds to pay the escalating price for a legal diploma. Law schools have had a monopolist's hold on the keys to corporate lawyerdom, which pays graduates six-figure salaries.

But borrowing $150,000 or more is now a vastly riskier proposition given the scarcity of Big Law jobs. Of course, that scarcity hasn't been priced into the cost of law school. How come? In part, it's because schools have managed to convey the impression that those jobs aren't very scarce.

For instance, although NYLS is ranked no. 135 out of the roughly 200 schools in the *US News* survey, it asserts in figures provided to the publisher that nine months after graduation, the median private-sector salary of alums who graduated in 2009—which is the class featured in the most recent *US News* annual law school issue—was $160,000. That is exactly the same figure cited by Yale and Harvard, the top law schools in the country.

Mr. Matasar stood by that number, but acknowledged that it did not give a complete picture of the prospects for NYLS grads. He noted that the school takes the over-and-above step of posting more granular salary data on its website.

"In these materials and in our conversations with students and applicants," he wrote, "we explicitly tell them that most graduates find work in small to medium firms at salaries between $35,000 and $75,000."

Determining exactly how many graduates make even those relatively modest salaries isn't easy. The information posted online by NYLS about the class of 2010 says that only 26 percent of those employed reported their salaries. The nearly 300 students who reported being employed but said nothing about their salaries—who knows?

Like all other law schools, NYLS collects this job information without anyone else looking at the raw data or double-checking the math. Which gets to another dimension of the law school business that other companies might envy: a lack of independent auditing, at least when it comes to these crucial employment stats. It's kind of like makers of breakfast cereal reporting the nutrition levels of their products, without worrying that anyone will actually count the calories.

．　　　．　　　．

Though astoundingly resilient as businesses, law schools have always had a glaring liability: they generally sell just one product, legal diplomas. This lack of diversification means that if enrollment drops, a school's balance sheet will suffer.

Like all stand-alone institutions, NYLS is even more dependent on student tuition than those attached to universities, and Moody's highlighted this fact in its 2006 appraisal of the school's bonds. Under a section about potential "challenges" that could lead to a downgrade, Moody's cited "significant and sustained deterioration of student market position."

A downgrade would be expensive for the school because it would mark the bonds as riskier, which would force the school to pay higher interest rates in the future.

In May of 2009, a month before the official end of the recession, Moody's issued a new report and suddenly, a downgrade seemed like a real possibility. One problem was that applications to the school for the upcoming class of 2009, Moody's reported, were down 28 percent compared with the volume the year before. The rating agency changed its outlook on the bonds from "stable" to "negative," which is bond-speak for "If current trends continue, a downgrade is coming."

But just three months later, the enrollment scare was over. In the fall of 2009, the incoming class was NYLS's largest ever—736 students. (Only one law school in the country, Thomas M. Cooley in Michigan, matriculated a greater number.)

Some faculty members were happy to enhance their salaries by teaching another course. Others were appalled at what the super-sized class would mean for students.

"At a school like New York Law, which is toward the bottom of the pecking order, it's long been difficult for our students to find high-paying jobs," said Randolph N. Jonakait, a professor at NYLS and a frequent critic of Mr. Matasar's. "Adding more than 100 students to an incoming class harms their employments prospects. It's always been tough for our graduates. Now it's tougher."

Was Mr. Matasar more worried about bond ratings than the fortunes of his new students? Several faculty members said, and he confirmed, that the bonds were part of discussions about the financial health of the school in 2009.

"However," Mr. Matasar wrote, "N.Y.L.S. never promised (nor needed to promise) anyone that it would increase enrollment to meet debt service obligations." The size of the 2009 class, he went on, was "unplanned," again referring to a surprise in yield.

But given that interest in graduate school typically spikes during economic slumps, wasn't a sharp rise in yield foreseeable? It was to NYLS's rivals. There are about 40 other schools in what *US News* has long categorized as its third tier, and the average increase in class size at those schools in 2009 was just 6 percent. (At ten of those schools, enrollment declined.) That is dwarfed by the 30 percent uptick at NYLS.

Whether Mr. Matasar had bond ratings in mind at the time, Moody's liked what it saw. In August of 2010, the company issued a new report that included news of the 736-student class, which was described, in the classic understated style of bond reporting, as "particularly large." The Moody's outlook for the NYLS bonds changed once again—this time from negative to stable.

· · ·

The incoming class of 2009 won't hit the job market until next year, but if the experience of recent NYLS graduates is an indication, many of them are in for a lengthy hunt. Mr. Matasar offered an inventory of NYLS's career services office, which he says includes fifteen employees and provides development and mentoring programs and oversees a series of networking events.

There are those, he wrote, "who rave about the career services office." But he added that a recent poll of law schools found that a little more than half of third-year students were unsatisfied with the job search help. "We have a similar experience," he wrote.

Among the unsatisfied is Katherine Greenier, of NYLS's class of 2010. As she neared graduation, she organized an informational meeting for students interested in public-interest law, the kind of get-together she thought the career services office should have offered. To her amazement, a rep from that office showed up, took a seat and asked questions.

"She was asking about the process, like how you go about applying for public-interest fellowships," Ms. Greenier says. "Things that you would have hoped she already knew."

Ms. Greenier, who wound up with a job at the American Civil Liberties Union in Richmond, Va., ultimately decided that the school had what she called a "factory feel."

The size of the incoming class of 2009 only sharpened that conclusion.

"There were people wondering, why did the school take on this many people in a job market this terrible?" she asked. "How many of these folks are going to find jobs? And what does it say about the school?"

. . .

In April, Mr. Matasar stood in a lecture hall on the third floor at NYLS and delivered the keynote at Future Ed, the third of three conferences about legal education that he'd helped organize, in partnership with Harvard Law School. A few dozen professors and deans were in attendance as he argued for a more student-centric approach to education.

"The focus shifts from us—we the faculty, we the administration, we the permanent employees of the school—to those we serve, our students," he said. "Things are seen through a lens that says 'What will this do for the students?'"

Nearly all the people who have worked with Mr. Matasar say he means what he says about reforming legal education. NYLS professors recall meetings where he urged the faculty to be more responsive to students—to return calls faster, meet more often, whatever would help.

"He put a huge, beautiful student dining area in the top floor of that new building," says Tanina Rostain, a former NYLS professor, now at Georgetown University Law Center. "But it doesn't have a faculty lounge. We were a little nonplussed, but it was clear that the students were Rick's priority."

How does one square that priority with the inexorable rise of NYLS's tuition, its population growth, its eyebrow-arching job data?

The question has puzzled more than a few academics and has produced a variety of theories. Perhaps the most compelling is that as both a crusader and a dean, Mr. Matasar has conflicting, even incompatible missions. The crusader thinks that law school costs too much. The dean has to raise the price of tuition or get murdered in the *US News* rankings. The crusader worries about the future of all those unemployed graduates. The dean has interest payments to make on a gorgeous new building.

"I'm 100 percent convinced that Matasar believes in his reformist agenda," says Paul F. Campos, a professor at the University of Colorado at Boulder School of Law and a Future Ed attendee. "But all reformers discover that they can't change a system by themselves. And by trying to survive in the current structure, he has ended up participating in the perpetuation of its most indefensible elements."

The tale of Mr. Matasar's career is not primarily about a gap between words and actions. Rather, it is a measure of how all-consuming competition in the legal academy has become, and how unlikely it is that the system will be reformed from within.

To be clear, there is little about the way NYLS operates that is drastically different from other American law schools. What's happened there is, for the most part, standard operating procedure. What sets NYLS apart is that it is managed by a man who has criticized many of the standards and much of the procedure.

In fact, Mr. Matasar has been quoted about wanting to upend legal education for so long it is impossible to believe he is doesn't mean it. But he can't act unilaterally. And what industry has ever decided that for the good of its customers, it ought to charge less money, or shrink?

"My salary," Mr. Campos said, "is paid by the current structure, which is in many ways deceptive and unjust to a point that verges on fraud. But as a law professor, I understand that what is good for me is that the structure stay the way it is."

·       ·       ·

Decrying a business and benefitting from it at the same time—it puts you in a tough spot, Mr. Campos said, and one he speculated is even tougher for a dean. But it is not a spot that Mr. Matasar will be in for much longer.

Several weeks ago, Mr. Matasar sent an e-mail to his faculty stating that he would step down in the next academic year. He was considering a few different job options, he explained, all of them "outside of legal education."

**This American Life**

In this radio piece, Alex Blumberg and Laura Sydell investigate how patent lawyers have run amok in the digital age, hindering innovation and costing companies and consumers billions of dollars. They weave their reporting into the narrative itself, adding tension as they track down shell companies in East Texas and a source's inconsistencies in Silicon Valley. In "When Patents Attack!" *This American Life* reveals how one big patent firm is not what it wants us to believe—and what that means for the American tech industry. Ira Glass, who narrates the piece's prologue, has built *This American Life* into a storytelling institution over the last decade and a half, and this episode, a collaboration with National Public Radio's *Planet Money*, shows why.

Alex Blumberg and
Laura Sydell

# 22. When Patents Attack!

IRA GLASS: Back during the rise of the dot-coms and the Internet, Jeff Kelling and a few friends were working as programmers together at this company in Dallas, and they decided they want to get together the way that tech geeks were doing all over the world at the time and come up with an idea for their own Internet company to start.

JEFF KELLING: One of my business partners, Andy, his wife had just had a baby, and we started thinking about photo-sharing. You know, Andy could share his photos of his new baby with, you know, the grandparents that live across the state.

GLASS: Now this is 1999. This is before Flickr, this is before Shutterfly. But Jeff and his friends weren't the first people to try to make a business out of photo sharing. There were other companies out there trying to make a go of that. And it is not easy. It took Jeff and his partners years, working nights, working weekends until finally in 2006, their start-up was doing well enough that they all could quit their day jobs and do that full-time. Their company was called FotoTime, it's FotoTime with a "F." Jeff says that they were living the dream, entrepreneurship, their own business. Until . . .

KELLING: We got a letter in May of 2008 and it wasn't a friendly letter. I mean, if you take a letter from the IRS that says "we're going to audit you," this letter was even less friendly than that. It pretty much said, "You're in violation of three of the patents that our company holds. You must contact us immediately to arrange payment and settlement or we will be taking you to court."

And we were wondering, you know, what is all this? I mean, this whole thing was developed internally, it's not like we went through the Patent Office and stole people's ideas. And it's also not like we were the first to do this. And we looked up this lawsuit online and we saw there were over 130 companies named in this lawsuit.

GLASS: All the big names were there. Yahoo, which owns Flickr, as well as Shutterfly and Photobucket, and lots of small companies like Jeff's as well.

The company suing Jeff was a company called FotoMedia. Jeff was FotoTime with an "F." This was FotoMedia with an "F." And one thing that was odd: they weren't actually a competitor of Jeff's. They didn't have a website where you could upload or share photos. And it wasn't clear to Jeff what in the world he had stolen from them.

Had he accidentally come up with, you know, a way to upload files or maybe see photos online or do the credit card transactions that already somebody had some sort of patent on? Or was it that he hadn't stolen anything and they were just looking for a payout, scamming him for some money?

And what was especially galling to Jeff? When he called them to ask, "What am I stealing from you guys?" they wouldn't tell him.

KELLING: That was a question they wouldn't answer. They said they wouldn't answer that until we got into court. So they wouldn't even identify what parts of our business or what they thought we were doing to use . . . to use their technology.

GLASS: But to go to court, to answer that question, was gonna cost money. A lot of money.

KELLING: It was between two and five million dollars and that's more than our company could handle, honestly. We knew we had to settle this thing somehow. There would be no more FotoTime today if we had to do that.

GLASS: Amazingly, it wasn't just Jeff and the other companies getting sued over these three patents who were upset. Out there in the world was an inventor who came up with the original ideas that got patented for two of these three patents, and he wasn't that happy about the lawsuit either. The guy's name was David Rose, and he was issued these patents back when he started his own photo-sharing company, back in the mid-nineties, just a couple years before Jeff Kelling started his.

And he'd gotten the patents in part because having a patent was just one of those things you did to raise money from investors, a check box you checked to prove you were serious, and to protect yourself from some company swooping in and stealing your ideas.

He sold his company in 2000, and the patents he got along with it. He thought the people who bought his company would expand the company, make it prosper. Hopefully turn it into a household name. He has some problems with what they chose to do instead. He talked to *This American*

*Life* producer Alex Blumberg and reporter Laura Sydell.

DAVID ROSE: It's the hoarding and nonoperating of the technology that doesn't feel good because they didn't become the brand that they could have become. They had the protection. They could have built Flickr.

ALEX BLUMBERG: Right, and instead they waited for somebody else to build Flickr and then they sued Flickr.

ROSE: Yes.

GLASS: Companies that make no products but go around suing other companies that do make products, over supposed patent infringement, are so common in Silicon Valley these days that there's a derogatory term for it. Trolls. Or patent trolls. David Rose explains trolls . . .

ROSE: You don't know that there's one under the bridge. They pop up. They have unreasonable demands. They can charge monopoly tolls or monopoly rents.

GLASS: So the guy who came up with two of these patents doesn't want the lawsuit. And the guy getting sued for the patent doesn't want the lawsuit. And yet, the lawsuit happens.

FotoMedia, by the way, denies being a patent troll. Its CEO told us that "patent troll" is a term that people throw around very loosely when they're in litigation over patent rights. As far as we can tell, and not a lot of this information is public, most of the companies being sued ended up doing what Jeff did and agreed to pay FotoMedia money. Some of them were put out of business.

Jeff felt like he had no choice but to settle. He told Laura and Alex that reaching a settlement ended up taking six months, a very rough six months.

KELLING: It feels like if they're not reasonable, OK, our venture of ten years is going to be gone. They have to be reasonable or we will just plain be gone. And we're talking about ten years of our life. You know, honestly, as I'm talking about it now, it's kind of raising my heartbeat a little bit because I just remember how I personally felt. Just the huge amount of anxiety and lack of control over the whole situation. It was just an awful feeling.

LAURA SYDELL: Can I ask what that final settlement was? How much it was?

KELLING: No, no. Unfortunately, part of the terms of our settlement agreement is that we don't discuss the amount.

BLUMBERG: Did it put your business in danger?

KELLING: It did. And they knew that. The settlement they wanted to get was just enough to put us in danger but not to close us. And I'll stop there.

GLASS: Patents are so foundational to the American way of life that they're in the Constitution. Their purpose is, quote, "to promote the useful arts and sciences." In other words, to get people to share their ideas and inventions to say to somebody like Eli Whitney, OK, you have this amazing invention, the cotton gin. If you tell everybody how it works and how to make their own, in exchange anytime someone uses the idea, you get paid.

If there were no such thing as a patent, Eli Whitney would have to keep his invention hidden in a dark room with no windows, so nobody would steal the idea, and then people would bring him their cotton and he'd spit it out for them, all processed, on the other side. Instead of that we had thousands of cotton gins, everywhere. Patents make it safe to share and to innovate.

But today, lots of investors and innovators in Silicon Valley, maybe the majority, would tell you the patent system is doing the exact opposite of what it's supposed to. It's not promoting innovation. It's stifling it. Because patent lawsuits are on the rise. Patent trolls are on the move. Patent lawsuits are so common now that it's hard to find even one semi-successful startup in Silicon Valley that has not been hit with a suit, which slows innovation, makes it harder for companies to prosper, hurts our global competitiveness (is this getting big enough for you?), costs us all more money when we buy the stuff these companies sell.

## Act One

SYDELL: The term "patent troll" was first coined by a guy named Peter Detkin, who at the time was one of the top lawyers at one of the biggest tech companies in the world, the computer chip maker Intel.

BLUMBERG: Around 1999, Intel found itself in the position that Jeff Kelling, the guy we heard from at the top of the show, was in—getting approached by a company that didn't build anything.

PETER DETKIN: Simply saying "I have a patent that covers semiconductors generally. You make a semiconductor. And therefore, you should pay me some money." And there were a lot of claims like that.

SYDELL: One lawsuit in particular made Peter Detkin so mad that he called the lawyer who filed it a "patent extortionist." The lawyer turned around and sued

Peter Detkin for libel. So, Detkin needed a better name.

DETKIN: So I had a contest inside Intel. The contest itself was named "The Terrorist." And the suggestions, we got a lot of suggestions but none really fit. But at the time my daughter was four or five, and she liked playing with those troll dolls. The original one, in fact, is still in my office. And so I turned to her and said, "Oh, the story of a troll kind of fits 'cause the whole Billy Goats Gruff thing, it's someone lying under a bridge they didn't build, demanding payment from anyone who passed. I said, "How about a patent troll?"

BLUMBERG: The name stuck. And if anything, the problem of patent trolls just got worse. From 2004 to 2009, the number of patent infringement lawsuits jumped by 70 percent. Licensing fee requests, like what happened to Peter Detkin and to FotoTime, went 650 percent. Today, pretty much any time you talk to a computer or tech person in Silicon Valley, and the subject of patents comes up, everyone groans.

SYDELL: I hear these groans a lot. I live out here in San Francisco. And just to get a flavor of this, the other day I went down to a park called South Park, around noon. It's a place where a lot of tech workers eat their lunch. And the sentiment was universal . . .

SYDELL: If I say patent system, what do you say?

MAN 1: I think it's just a way for lawyers to make money, and basically it's a killer for creativity.

MAN 2: Complicated. Broken.

MAN 3: It's basically a flim-flam game that anybody who knows how to take advantage of it, is doing.

SYDELL: Do you kind of groan when you hear the word?

MAN 4: I do, yeah. You wanna hear a groan for the radio?

SYDELL: Yeah, let's hear a groan.

MAN 4: Grrr.

SYDELL: If I say the word "patent troll," does any company or any entity come to mind in particular?

MAN 4: Nathan Myhrvold, I guess, and, like, whatever his company is. It has some stupid name like Associate Associates or something like that. I don't know.

SYDELL: The name he's searching for is Intellectual Ventures, the company Nathan Myhrvold founded in 2000. Nathan Myhrvold used to be the chief technology officer at Microsoft, where he made a lot of money, hundreds of millions of dollars. Even if you haven't heard of Intellectual Ventures, you might have heard of Nathan Myhrvold

STEVEN COLBERT: My guest tonight has written a six-volume book on cutting-edge food made with modern science. Please welcome Nathan Myhrvold!

[applause]

BLUMBERG: This is Myhrvold on the *Colbert Report*, talking about another one of his ventures, an opus on the science of cooking, which teaches you how to do things like make ice cream with liquid nitrogen. Myhrvold is the kind of guy the press loves to profile.

COLBERT: You are a polymath. You're a Renaissance man. You're a world BBQ champion now. You've discovered T-Rex fossils. You've studied quantum physics with Stephen Hawking. And you have a new six-volume, forty-pound, $625 book called *Modernist Cuisine*.

SYDELL: But this image of Nathan Myhrvold, who gives TED Talks and generally plays the role of an avuncular elder statesman for the tech industry, is at odds with the image of his company, Intellectual Ventures.

BLUMBERG: There's an influential blog in Silicon Valley called *TechDirt* that regularly refers to Intellectual Ventures as a patent troll. Another blog, *IP Watchdog*, called Intellectual Ventures "patent troll public enemy #1." And the *Wall Street Journal*'s law blog had an article about Intellectual Ventures titled "Innovative Invention Company or Giant Patent Troll?"

SYDELL: These articles talk about how IV has amassed one of the largest patent portfolios in existence. How it's going around to technology companies demanding money to license these patents. But the thing is, people at companies that have been approached by Intellectual Ventures won't talk about it.

CHRIS SACCA: There is a lot of fear about Intellectual Ventures. You don't want to make yourself a target.

SYDELL: This is Chris Sacca. An entrepreneur and venture capitalist in Silicon Valley, who was an early investor in companies like Twitter and FanBridge and lots of other startups. He wouldn't say if Intellectual Ventures had been in contact with his companies.

SACCA: I tried to put you in touch with other people in this community to talk to you about this, and they almost uniformly said they couldn't talk to you. They were afraid to.

BLUMBERG: And we should just cut in here and say, when Chris says "this community," he's talking about the community of multimillionaire venture capitalists that he hangs around with. Not a timid crowd. Back to Chris.

SACCA: They almost uniformly said they couldn't talk to you. They were afraid to. And they didn't even hem and haw about it. They just said they're afraid to talk about this on the record. It's such a mismatched fight that your best defensive option is security by obscurity. They have the potential to literally obliterate startups.

NATHAN MYHRVOLD: Intellectual Ventures is a company that invests in invention.

SYDELL: This, of course, is Nathan Myhrvold. I went to talk to him and spent a day at his company. And not surprisingly, Nathan Myhrvold had a very different story about what he's up to.

SYDELL: Are you a patent troll?

MYHRVOLD: [laughs] Well, that's a term that has been used by people to mean someone they don't like, who has patents. I think you would find almost anyone who stands up for their patent rights has been called a patent troll.

BLUMBERG: Intellectual Ventures, says Myhrvold, is just the opposite. They're on the side of the inventors. They pay inventors for patents. Then gather patents together into this huge warehouse of invention that companies can use if they want. Sort of like a department store for patents. Whatever technology you're looking for, Intellectual Ventures has it.

SYDELL: And when reporters come to visit Myhrvold, to underline this idea that IV is all about invention, he takes them to see this . . .

GEOFF DEAN: Out here we're standing on the brink of our machine shop.

SYDELL: I'm on a tour with Geoff Dean, who runs the Intellectual Ventures Invention Lab. About one

hundred people work here. The lab is massive.
There are people walking around in white lab coats
mixing chemicals in beakers and looking at stuff
under microscopes. There's a machine shop, a
nanotechnology section. It's like a playground for
scientists and engineers.

BLUMBERG: And if you ask them what have they invented so
far, there's a couple things they point to: a nuclear
technology they say is safer and greener than
existing technologies; a cooler that can keep
vaccines cold for months without electricity.

SYDELL: And, the world's most high-tech mosquito zapper,
which senses mosquitoes from hundreds of feet
away by detecting the speed of their wings.

DEAN: Where on one side you have a reflector, on the other
side you have something that's looking down range
at the reflector. And any time a mosquito flies
between there, it finds the mosquito and shoots it
out of the air as fast as you can imagine. So it takes
about a tenth of a second for it to find the mosquito,
identify it as a mosquito, and kill it.

BLUMBERG: Like a missile defense shield, for mosquitoes.

SYDELL: But the fact is, this lab is a tiny fraction of what the
company does. Intellectual Ventures has received a
little over 1,000 patents on stuff they've come up
with here, which pales in comparison to the more
than 30,000 patents they've bought from other
people. In fact, nothing that's come out of this
lab—not the mosquito zapper, not the nuclear
technology—nothing has made it into commercial
use.

BLUMBERG: But Intellectual Venture says, that's not our job.
Our job, they say, is to encourage invention. For
example, imagine an inventor out there, someone

with a brilliant idea, a breakthrough. This inventor has a patent, but still, companies are stealing his idea. And he doesn't have the money or legal savvy to stop them. That's where Intellectual Ventures comes in. They buy this inventor's patent, and they make sure that companies who are using the idea pay for it.

SYDELL: A lot of people I met at IV told me some version of this story. We are promoting innovation by supporting inventors. And when I asked for an example of an inventor in this situation, someone with a breakthrough, who wasn't getting paid for it, two separate people pointed me to the same guy.

JOE CHERNESKY: There's one story I can think of, a gentleman named Chris Crawford.

SYDELL: This is one of the people who mentioned Chris Crawford, Joe Chernesky, a vice president at Intellectual Ventures.

CHERNESKY: The neat thing about Chris is, he had no idea how to get money for his patents. He had this great idea. These patents were immensely valuable because every technology company was adopting the technology. Yet he didn't know how to get paid. He eventually found Intellectual Ventures. So we bought those patents.

SYDELL: So, I figured, I want to talk to this guy. Not so simple. It turned out trying to talk to Chris Crawford led us on a five-month odyssey, where things didn't exactly fit the story Intellectual Ventures was telling us.

It started when I called Intellectual Ventures to get Chris Crawford's contact info. I got a strange e-mail back in response. I was told they no longer owned Chris Crawford's patent. And, I was told, he

> probably wouldn't want to talk to me right now because he was in the middle of litigation.

BLUMBERG: That just made us curious, so we started digging around. We found Chris Crawford in Clearwater, Florida, but as predicted, he never responded to our many e-mails and phone calls. You will never hear from him in this story. We were able, though, to locate his patent.

SYDELL: Patent number 5771354. He got it in 1998, back in the relatively early days of the Internet. And the way IV explained the patent to us, Chris Crawford invented something that we all do all the time now. He figured out a way to upgrade the software on your home computer over the Internet. So in other words, when you turn on your computer and a little box pops up and says, "Click here to upgrade to the newest version of iTunes"—that was Chris Crawford's idea.

BLUMBERG: But when we looked at the patent, it seemed to claim a lot more than that. The patent says this invention makes it possible to connect to an online service provider to do a bunch of stuff: software purchases, online rentals, data back ups, information storage. The patent makes it seem like this one guy—Chris Crawford—invented a lot of what we do on the Internet every day. We weren't sure what to make of all this, so we turned to an expert.

DAVID MARTIN: You're going to start by looking at the left- and right-hand screens.

SYDELL: This is David Martin, who runs a company called M-CAM. They're hired by governments, banks, businesses to assess patent quality, which they do with this fancy software program. We asked him to assess Chris Crawford's patent.

MARTIN: Now if you would, please just click on the patent number itself, Laura.

BLUMBERG: The software program actually scans through millions of patents and analyzes them to see if any of them overlap

MARTIN: That's a bad number.

SYDELL: An idea being patented is supposed to be non-obvious to a person of ordinary skill in the art. What that means is you shouldn't be able to get a patent just for a commonsense, good idea. It has to be a breakthrough.

MARTIN: That's correct.

SYDELL: In other words, we shouldn't be seeing what we are seeing on David Martin's computer screen.

MARTIN: 5,303 patents that were issued while his was being prosecuted, which covered the same material. 5,303.

BLUMBERG: And so that means at the same time Chris Crawford's patent was getting issued . . .

MARTIN: Only 5,303 people were pursuing the same thing.

BLUMBERG: And when you say the same thing . . .

MARTIN: I mean: The. Same. Thing.

SYDELL: David Martin may be exaggerating a little here for effect, but as we look through some of the patents that are on his screen, the resemblances are pretty clear. Remember, Chris Crawford's patent is for "an online back-up system."

BLUMBERG: And on David Martin's computer screen, we see lots of patents with slightly different language but covering essentially the same idea. For example, patent number 6003044 for "efficiently backing up files using multiple computer systems." Patent 5933653 for "mirroring data in a remote data storage system." And then there were three different patents with three different patent numbers but that all had the same title, "System and Method for Backing Up Computer Files Over a Wide Area Computer Network."

SYDELL: David Martin says when he first started looking into this stuff and saw all these patents that were granted for essentially the same thing.

MARTIN: We thought that would be an anomaly. And then we were told, "Oh no it's not an anomaly. That happens." So that's what got us into the rabbit hole you're about to see, which is to say, "let's see how many times that happens." And as I've testified in Congress, that happens about 30 percent of the time in U.S. patents.

BLUMBERG: That is, 30 percent of U.S. patents are essentially for things that have already been invented.

MARTIN: So, for example, toast becomes the "thermal re-freshening of a bread product."

SYDELL: These are real patents?

MARTIN: Yes.

BLUMBERG: There's a patent on toast?

MARTIN: Yes, thermally freshened bread, not on toast.

SYDELL: Ladies and gentlemen, patent number 6080436, "Bread Refreshing Method," issued in . . . 2000.

BLUMBERG: And we talked to another expert who told us Chris Crawford's patent was similar to the toast patent in one respect.

RICK MCLEOD: None of this was actually new.

BLUMBERG: Rick McLeod is a patent lawyer and former software engineer, who we also asked to evaluate Chris Crawford's patent. So he went on a search. This is how patent lawyers research this kind of thing. He looked to see if anyone else in the field was already doing the thing Chris Crawford claimed to invent in 1993, when he first filed his patent.

McLeod: There were institutions, both academic and businesses, that used computers in this way, and I think it's a very interesting collection of things that were well known in the 1980s. With the exception that it adds on the word "Internet."

Sydell: Do you think this patent should have been issued in the first place?

McLeod: No. I don't.

Blumberg: And in fact, for a long time, the Patent Office wouldn't have agreed with Rick

McLeod: The Patent Office used to be very reluctant to grant patents for software. For decades, it considered software to be like language. Software programs were more like books or articles. You could copyright them. But you couldn't patent them. They weren't inventions, like the cotton gin.

Sydell: But then the federal courts stepped in and started chipping away at this interpretation. There was a big decision in 1994, and another one in 1998, which rejected the Patent Office's view. The Patent Office got the memo and a flood of software patents followed. A lot of people in Silicon Valley wish that that had never happened, including a very surprising group—software engineers.

Stephan Brunner: I have to say, I worked on a whole bunch of patents in my career over the years, and I have to say that every single patent is nothing but crap.

Sydell: This is Stephan Brunner, a programmer. He said something we heard from a lot of software engineers. His software patents don't even make sense to him.

Brunner: I can't tell you for the hell of it what they're actually supposed to do. The company said we have to do a patent on this. Then they send in a lawyer and you basically say, "That's probably right, that's probably wrong." And they just write something that makes no sense. I personally, when I look at them, I'm not proud at all because most of them, it's just like mungo-mumbo-jumbo, which nobody understands and makes no sense from an engineering standpoint whatsoever.

BLUMBERG: Stephan Brunner, patent 7650296, "a configurator using structure and rules to provide a user interface." One sample section—and trust me, the whole thing's like this—"According to one embodiment of the invention, a customizable product class is created. . . . A component product class is added to the customizable product class, where the component product class is a subclass of the customizable product."

SYDELL: In polls, as many as 80 percent of software engineers say the patent system actually hinders innovation. In other words, it does exactly the opposite of what it's supposed to do. It doesn't encourage them to come up with new ideas and create new products; it actually gets in their way. Here's another programmer, Adam Cohen.

ADAM COHEN: I worked for a company, which I'm not gonna say, that at the end of the company we tried to patent—we did successfully patent—our software that we made, and that patent is really meaningless because everybody that has an Internet website basically almost today, breaks, uses the stuff we patent to make their website work. Almost everybody.

BLUMBERG: This, we heard, happens all the time. Patents that are so broad, everyone's guilty of infringement, which causes huge problems for almost anyone trying to start or grow a business on the Internet.

SACCA: We're at a point in the state of intellectual property where existing patents probably cover every behavior that's happening on the Internet or our mobile phones today.

SYDELL: This again is Chris Sacca, the investor you heard from earlier who helped lots of companies, including Twitter, get off the ground.

SACCA: So I have no doubt that the average Silicon Valley start-up or even medium-sized company, no matter how truly innovative they are, I have no doubt that aspects of whatever they're doing violate patents that are out there right now. And that's what's fundamentally broken about this system right now.

BLUMBERG: And this brings us back to patent 5771354, Chris Crawford's patent, the patent Intellectual Ventures pointed us to as an example of how they encourage innovation. As we've said, this patent also seems to cover a big chunk of what's happening on the Internet—upgrading software, buying stuff online, what's called cloud storage (storing data on the Internet). If you have a patent on all that, you could sue a lot of people. Make a lot of money.

SYDELL: And in fact, that's what's happening with Chris Crawford's patent. Intellectual Ventures sold it to another company, a company called Oasis Research, in June of 2010. Less than a month later, Oasis Research used the patent to sue sixteen different tech companies. Companies like Rackspace, Go Daddy, and AT&T. Companies that do cloud storage.

OPERATOR: You have reached Oasis Research. At the tone please leave your name, your telephone number . . .

SYDELL: I called the number on Oasis's website numerous times. But an actual human being never picked up. For a while the message directed all questions to a lawyer in New York, named John Desmarais. He also didn't return our phone calls. Although I did track him down, at a conference in San Francisco. I ran up to him right after a talk and asked him what he could tell me about Oasis Research.

JOHN DESMARIS: I can't talk about folks I represent.

SYDELL: Do you know who owns Oasis Research to reach them?

DESMARIS: Yes, I do. Yes, but I'm not going to tell you.

SYDELL: I mean, they're bringing a suit and you literally can't tell us who owns the company?

DESMARIS: I'm not gonna answer questions about pending lawsuits for you.

SYDELL: Another question: is there any chance at a later date of talking to you more generally?

DESMARIS: I don't think so. But thanks for asking. Although I love NPR and I love the work you guys do.

BLUMBERG: Behavior like this makes it hard not to think, are you hiding something? When someone says, "Yes I know, but I'm not going to tell you," it really makes you want to find stuff out. There was hardly any public information about Oasis Research. Minimal corporate filings. No way to know who owned it, how many employees it had. If it even had employees at all.

One of the few details that was available: an address, in Marshall Texas. 104 East Houston Street, Suite 190.

MICHAEL SMITH: Right now we're going into the first floor of the Baxter Building, which is 104 East Houston.

SYDELL: This is Michael Smith. He's an attorney in
Marshall, Texas, who does mostly patent cases.
He agreed to show us the offices of Oasis Research.
They're in a nondescript two-story building on
the town's main square, two doors down from
the federal courthouse. He led us into a narrow
corridor lined with doors with gold and black
office name plates.

SMITH: And we here go. Suite 190. Oasis Research, LLC.

BLUMBERG: We arrived on a weekday, not a holiday, but the
door was locked. Through the crack under the door
you could see there were no lights were on inside.
Marshall is a very small town, 24,000 people.
Michael was born and raised here, so we started
quizzing him about Oasis:

SYDELL: Does it have any employees that you know about?

SMITH: Not that I know of.

SYDELL: Have you ever seen any people coming in and out of
that office?

SMITH: No, I haven't.

BLUMBERG: Is this office ever occupied?

SMITH: I doubt that it is.

SYDELL: If you don't mind, I'm gonna knock on the door and
see if there's anyone here today.

BLUMBERG: I know this is kind of a cliche at this point,
knocking on the door of the suspected fake office.

SYDELL: Nothing.

BLUMBERG: But we'd flown a long way.

SYDELL: But I will say, standing in that corridor was eerie.
All the other doors looked exactly the same: locked,
nameplates over the door, no light coming out. It
was a corridor of silent, empty offices.

SMITH: Right next to Software Rights Archive, Bulletproof
Technology of Texas, Jellyfish Technology of Texas,

and a couple of others that I recognize as plaintiffs in cases that we're involved in here.

SYDELL: Are there a lot of companies like this here in east Texas?

SMITH: Yes.

BLUMBERG: And we're standing in a whole corridor of them it seems like.

SMITH: Yes. This would be ground zero, yes.

SYDELL: So what's going on here? It turns out, a lot of those companies in that corridor, maybe every single one of them are doing exactly what Oasis Research is doing. They appear to have no employees. They are not making new inventions here. They're filing lawsuits for patent infringement.

Patent lawsuits, says Michael Smith, are big business in Marshall, part of the eastern district of Texas.

Walking back across the town square, past the Eastern District Court House, Michael explained it.

SMITH: The Eastern District, in the last few years, has been either number one or number two or three in the nation in numbers of patent cases. The list of the patent cases at this courthouse would be about 2,000 cases long.

SYDELL: As we walk past the courthouse, as if to drive the point home, a gaggle of lawyers emerges. Dozens and dozens of dark suits in the hot Texas sun.

SMITH: They're taking their midmorning break during a patent trial that started yesterday morning in front of Magistrate Judge Everingham.

SYDELL: It's quite something to see. In this case, it's mostly men in suits, a couple women, just streaming out of that court house one after another, this little federal courthouse.

SMITH: Oh yeah, they travel in packs.

BLUMBERG: We talked to many people about why this is so, why do all these New York– and San Francisco–based companies come to tiny Marshall to battle in court.

SYDELL: Many people say that it has to do with juries in Marshall; they're famously plaintiff-friendly, friendly to patent owners trying to get a large verdict. But Michael Smith, who's argued on both sides of numerous patent cases, says that might have been true once, but not anymore.

BLUMBERG: He says they're in Marshall because of the drug war. Basically in the nineties, federal courts everywhere were clogged with drug cases. Civil cases like patent cases couldn't get in front of a judge because criminal cases take precedence. So companies with patent suits had to find a spot with fewer criminals to prosecute. Hence, sleepy Marshall Texas.

Our visit to Marshall made us realize something big is going on here in Texas, and Oasis research is part of it. Two thousand lawsuits making the same essential claim Intellectual Ventures makes—there's an inventor whose invention is being stolen, used without permission. But there were no inventors here, just corridors of empty offices and a lot of lawyers. That made us wonder: what else about Intellectual Ventures is not what it appears to be?

## Act Two

GLASS: A quick review of where we are in our story. OK, there's this company called Intellectual Ventures.

They told our reporters they, if they wanted to understand what the company was all about, should talk to this inventor that Intellectual Ventures helped out. The guy is a patent holder named Chris Crawford. But when our reporters tried to contact Chris Crawford, he won't return any phone calls, he won't return e-mails. We find out his patent has actually been sold by Intellectual Ventures. They no longer own it. It is now being used to sue over a dozen different tech businesses.

And the company doing the suing, called Oasis Research, has no researchers, no employees of any kind that we can find, and it's only place of business seems to be an empty office in a corridor of empty offices in a small town in Texas. So our reporters, Laura Sydell and Alex Blumberg, had a lot of questions.

SYDELL: Some of the questions seemed like they should have been simple to answer, but they weren't. For example, when did Intellectual Ventures actually buy the patent from Chris Crawford? There's a document that's publicly available on the U.S. Patent Office website; it traces a patent's ownership history. In the case of Chris Crawford's patent, though, the ownership history is really hard to understand.

BLUMBERG: The first owner is clear, it's Chris Crawford, who was granted the patent in 1998. And then it's clear that a company named Intellectual Ventures Computing Platforce Assets, LLC—no one could actually tell us what a "platforce" is—bought the patent in July of 2010. But in between those two dates, there are two other owners. A company called Kwon Holdings and another one named

Enhanced Software, LLC. And what was odd, Kwon Holdings, Enhanced Software, and Intellectual Ventures all have the same address.

SYDELL: We went back to Intellectual Ventures to clear some of this stuff up. Now, there's one thing we need to explain before we tell you what happened there. Remember the guy at the very beginning of our story? Peter Detkin, the guy who coined the term "patent troll" after his daughter's doll, the guy who hates patent trolls. You'll never guess what he's doing now.

DETKIN: I'm a founder and vice chairman of Intellectual Ventures here in Silicon Valley.

BLUMBERG: That's right, the guy who coined the term patent troll teamed up with Nathan Myhrvold to start a company that many people call the biggest patent troll out there. Peter Detkin obviously disagrees with this characterization.

SYDELL: So anyway, we went to Peter Detkin to ask our questions, and we started off by showing him that publicly available page on the U.S. Patent Office website and we asked him what seemed like a pretty straightforward question. When exactly did Intellectual Ventures buy Chris Crawford's patent? Turns out this was the question that completely threw him off, and led the PR women who was in the room with us to jump in and to try and shut down the interview. You'll hear her voice in the background.

BLUMBERG: This is just the patent history of Chris's patent. So could you just . . . so here . . . and honestly we just don't understand this, so if you could explain what, what we're looking at here? So he invented it in 1998 . . .

DETKIN: Let me put on my reading glasses on. So I'm
struggling a little bit here.

SYDELL: Right, so he invented this first . . .

PR WOMAN: I don't know that going into the history of this
patent is necessary or useful.

DETKIN: Well, I don't know where you're going with this.
What's the question? What are you trying to find
out?

BLUMBERG: If you could explain . . . the story you're telling is
that you bought this patent from this inventor Chris
Crawford and then you sold it a little bit later. But
then if actually you look at the history, it's very
different story. It seems very different. So I'm trying
to figure out like if you could explain to us . . .

DETKIN: I won't be able to tell you by looking at this. I mean
I'd have to talk . . . I'm not an expert . . . you're on
the USPTO website? I haven't looked at this
particular website in a while. I don't know how it's
organized. So I mean, I'm trying to be helpful, but
the fact is I know we bought it from some entity of
his and apparently we then sold it. And again, I
have some vague recollection of us doing that deal.

BLUMBERG: Wait, are you telling me you're the . . . you run a
patent company and you were the head council for
Intel in the patent department and you don't know
the Patent Office website . . . you don't know how to
read this?

DETKIN: Look, I mean I could look at this if you want. I
could . . . but I haven't looked at this particular
website, and I don't know how it's organized. And
I'm not exactly sure what it is you're trying to get at.
I'm happy to answer questions, but if you're going
to cross-examine me on the record—

BLUMBERG: It's just, it's just confusing . . .

DETKIN: . . . about a patent website, I don't think that's quite fair.

BLUMBERG: So, for example, one question is when was it sold to Intellectual Ventures because it's sold a number of times, but it sold a number of times to different companies with the same address as Intellectual Ventures. Does that mean it was sold to Intellectual Ventures or not?

PR WOMAN: It's a little different, and we're not gonna talk about this.

DETKIN: Yeah, I have no idea. There's no way without knowing the details of this particular deal I could ever possibly answer that question.

BLUMBERG: Laura, we were honestly surprised at this response. It wasn't like this was a secret document or something. What was the big deal about answering this seemingly simple question?

SYDELL: Part of it certainly was that we took him a little bit by surprise. I take him at his word that they do a lot of deals and he doesn't know the details of every one. But we talked to another guy, an intellectual property lawyer named Tom Ewing, who suggested there might have been more to it than that.

BLUMBERG: Tom Ewing told us those other companies listed on that Patent Office document, Kwon Holdings and Enhanced Software, they might very well be Intellectual Ventures. What he calls Intellectual Ventures' "shell companies."

Tom Ewing makes a business of tracking them. He started it as a sort of a private challenge to himself.

TOM EWING: I heard for the longest time when they first started that they hid everything in shell companies and no one could ever find it. And I kept hearing

SYDELL: that so much and it irritated me because I figured that I could, if I just sat down and started looking. So I did.

SYDELL: How many shell companies do you personally believe that Intellectual Ventures has, based on your research?

EWING: Very close to 1,300.

SYDELL: So we asked Tom Ewing what seemed like an obvious question. Is Oasis Research a shell company of Intellectual Ventures? And he said, probably not.

BLUMBERG: Tom said Oasis more likely falls into a second category, companies that are independently owned but with close links to Intellectual Ventures. For example, John Desmarais, the lawyer representing Oasis, also represents Intellectual Ventures in lots of cases and has links to that company going back almost a decade.

SYDELL: And, Tom said, there's evidence that Intellectual Ventures might be getting a cut of whatever money Oasis receives from its lawsuits. He shows us a document that's called a Certification of Interested Parties.

BLUMBERG: The court in Texas required that Oasis list all the entities who have a financial stake in the outcome of the case. This is a standard form that pretty much all plaintiffs in civil cases have to file. Oasis listed the parties that most people list: the plaintiff, the defendants, the attorneys involved. But it added one other name: Intellectual Ventures.

SYDELL: So we went back to Intellectual Ventures one more time to talk to Peter Detkin. We picked up where we left off the last time. When did Intellectual Ventures actually buy Chris Crawford's patent? And this time, he had no hesitation about explaining it. It turns out, Tom Ewing had been right. Those other mysterious companies, Kwon Holdings and Enhanced Software, they were Intellectual Ventures' shell companies:

DETKIN: This is when we bought it. October of 2007 from CMC Software to Kwon Holdings. And Kwon is a company that we created to purchase these assets. Then when we actually struck a deal and prepared to sell it in the name of transparency, we changed it to the Intellectual Ventures Computing Platforce Assets, please don't ask me what a "platforce" is. I don't know what it is. Then in August of 2010 we sold it to Oasis Research.

BLUMBERG: We showed Detkin that court document from the Oasis case, listing Intellectual Ventures as an interested party.

DETKIN: OK, and it does list the Intellectual Ventures Computing Platforce Assets as an interested party. I see that.

BLUMBERG: And you don't know why in this instance you're listed?

DETKIN: I believe it's because we likely have a back-end arrangement here.

BLUMBERG: What does a back-end deal mean?

DETKIN: We sell for some amount of money up front and we get some percentage of the royalty stream down the road that is generated from the monetization of these assets.

BLUMBERG: So just to spell this out: Peter Detkin is saying it's likely that Intellectual Ventures is taking a cut of whatever money Oasis gets from its lawsuits. Oasis, a company with no operations, no products, and as far as we can tell no employees, whose only activity seems to be taking a very broad patent from 1998 and using it to sue over a dozen Internet companies today.

SYDELL: And so we asked him. How does it feel making money from an entity which is behaving a lot like the patent trolls that he once condemned?

DETKIN: These are patents we used to hold, we no longer hold. And we ensure that we have no control over the actions of these third parties. They are independent actors. They're not Intellectual Ventures. They may be monetizing in ways that we disagree with, but it's not our call. It's theirs.

BLUMBERG: But you're also still getting paid.

SYDELL: Yeah, I sort of feel like, 'Yeah well, but what do you expect?' You must have some knowledge that it's highly likely these people are gonna go and bring lawsuits, especially since they're companies that only have these largely run by attorneys.

DETKIN: Sure, no, I understand and I'm not disputing any of that. What I'm trying to say, and I apologize if I'm not being clear, is that we do believe, we believe in our heart that litigation is a highly inefficient way to do licensing. But let's not lose sight that litigation is just licensing by other means.

BLUMBERG: In other words, we try to license these patents in a friendly way. But sometimes you have to sue.

SYDELL: Peter Detkin then repeated the company line that'd we heard from a lot of people at IV—that the mission of Intellectual Ventures is to help inventors bring great ideas into the world. That lots of inventors, they're like great artists, brilliant but not brilliant at business. So their patents languish. IV gets their ideas into the hands of companies who'll actually build what they've invented.

BLUMBERG: So can you point me to a patent that you acquired that was languishing but then got licensed to somebody and built in a way that I could see?

DETKIN: I can tell you that it's happened, but unfortunately the deal is confidential. There are two deals that were done. One was with a toy company. The other was, I can't remember the technology of the other one but they came to us and they said we're interested in this particular patent. We'd like to take it out into the world. Will you give us a license? And we did. And they put it out there. It was out there for last Christmas. I actually don't know how it's done. I would be curious to find out myself. But I agree, that's an anomaly. I see where you're going with your question, and I don't mean to fight you on it. The fact is the bulk of our patents, the bulk of our revenue is from people using inventions . . . they were using it before we bought it and they were using it after we bought it, but we provided an efficient way for them to get access to those invention rights.

BLUMBERG: The way I hear what you're saying, the way I translate it in my head, is they were using it before without paying a license and nobody was bothering them. And now they are paying a license to you. Why is that a better situation?

DETKIN: Well, because we want to incentivize the guy who invented it.

BLUMBERG: That is, if companies pay their licenses, inventors make more money. Which in turn gives them incentive to invent more stuff. This is the rhetorical cul-de-sac where every argument with Peter Detkin ends. But here's the problem with that argument. IV is not buying inventions. They're buying patents.

And as we've heard, as most software engineers will tell you, at least when it comes to computers and the Internet, a patent and an invention are not the same. Lots of patents cover things that people in the field wouldn't consider inventions at all.

SYDELL: And these patents out there that aren't for something novel or are so broad they can cover anything? Every single one of them can be used to bring lawsuits. In response, all the big tech companies have started amassing troves of software patents, not to build anything but to defend themselves. If a company's patent horde is big enough, it can say, essentially, if you try to sue me with your patents, I'll sue you with mine.

BLUMBERG: It is the old mutually assured destruction. Except instead of arsenals of nuclear weapons it's arsenals of patents. And this was a problem Intellectual Ventures founder Nathan Myhrvold said he was trying to solve when he first started his company. A problem that he and others from Intellectual Ventures talked about at investor meetings all around Silicon Valley. Chris Sacca was there at one of them.

SACCA: I think I saw Nathan for the first time present the idea of Intellectual Ventures in either the fall of 2007 or the spring of 2008.

BLUMBERG: And the pitch he heard was basically, Intellectual Ventures helps defend against lawsuits. Intellectual Ventures has this horde of 35,000 patents—35,000 patents that, for a price, companies can access and use to defend themselves.

SACCA: They pay administrative fees ranging from the tens of thousand to the millions and millions of dollars, all into this entity to kind of buy themselves insurance that protects them from being sued by any harmful, you know, malevolent outsiders.

BLUMBERG: In other words, Intellectual Ventures goes around to companies and says, "Hey, you wanna protect yourself from lawsuits? We own tons of patents. Make a deal with us. Our patents will not only cover everything you're doing in your business, no one will dare to sue you."

SYDELL: But to Chris Sacca, there's an implication in there: "If you don't join us, who knows what'll happen?" Which reminds him of the business practices of another organization.

SACCA: A mafia-style shakedown, where someone comes in the front door of your building and says, "It would be a shame if this place burnt down. I know the neighborhood really well and I can make sure that doesn't happen." And saying, "Pay us up." Now here's, here's what's funny. If you talk to . . . when I've seen Nathan speak publicly about this and when I've seen spokespeople from Intellectual Ventures, they constantly remind us that they themselves don't bring lawsuits, that they themselves are not litigators, that they're a defensive player. But the truth is that the threat of their patent arsenal can't actually be realized, that it can't be taken seriously unless they have that offensive posture, unless they're willing to assert those patents. And so it's this very delicate balancing act that is quite reminiscent of scenes you see in movies when the mafia comes to visit your butcher shop and they say to you, "Hey, it would be a real shame if somebody else came and sued you. Tell you what, pay us an exorbitant membership fee into our collective and we'll keep you protected that way." A protection scheme isn't that credible unless some butcher shops burn down now and then.

BLUMBERG: We told Intellectual Ventures that Chris Sacca compared their business to a mafia shakedown, and in an e-mail, Peter Detkin called that ridiculous and offensive. He then reiterated some of the arguments you've heard about how IV protects inventors and went on to say, "We're a disruptive company that's providing a way for patent-holders to recognize value." (By "recognize value," he means "make money.") "That wasn't available before we came on the scene, and we are making a big impact on the market. That obviously makes people uncomfortable. But no amount of name-calling changes the fact that ideas have value."

SYDELL: True enough, but lately it seems like a lot of butcher shops have been burning. As we were reporting this story, more and more Intellectual Ventures patents started showing up in the hands of companies like Oasis, companies without employees or operations, who were formed for the purpose of filing lawsuits. They're known as nonpracticing entities or NPE's.

BLUMBERG: One former IV patent was used by an NPE to sue nineteen different companies, a seemingly random assortment, which included Dell computers, Abercrombie & Fitch, Visa, UPS. What's the suit about? These companies all have websites that when you scroll your mouse over certain sections, pop-up boxes appear. This NPE said, "We have a patent on that."

SYDELL: Another group of former IV patents is being used in one of the most controversial and most talked about cases in Silicon Valley right now. An NPE called Lodsys is suing almost three dozen companies and counting. These are small- and medium-sized companies developing apps for iPhone and Android smartphones. Lodsys says every time you buy something within a smartphone app, they own the patent on that.

BLUMBERG: And one interesting wrinkle about that case. The address of Lodsys? 104 East Houston Street, Marshall, Texas, Suite 190. The same exact address, down to the suite number, as Oasis Research.

SYDELL: Tom Ewing, the lawyer who keeps track of Intellectual Ventures, says that all this behavior has led people to come up with a special name for the company.

EWING: "The troll on steroids."

SYDELL: Do you think it's a troll on steroids?

EWING: You know, I don't want to complicate things, but I personally think there's a whole lot of gray. For example, they've already collected $2 billion dollars worth of royalties, so they say. And you have to ask yourself of the $2 billion dollars in royalties they've collected, how much of those royalties that they've collected are based on sort of reasonable licensing fees that the people they received it from should have paid? And how much of it is simply based on trying to avoid litigation? And I would say it's probably a mix of both.

SYDELL: The problem is: to try and figure out what that actually mix looks like is virtually impossible. We called dozens of people. We called people who had licensing arrangements with Intellectual Ventures. We called people who were defendants in lawsuits involving Intellectual Ventures' patents. We called every single company being sued by Oasis Research, all sixteen of them. No one would talk to us. Partly this is fear. Partly, Intellectual Ventures is said to have the strictest nondisclosure agreement in Silicon Valley.

BLUMBERG: The Oasis Research case is still ongoing, but many of the original defendants seem to have settled. Michael Smith, the attorney in Marshall, Texas, who showed us the Oasis offices, represented one of those defendants. He was pretty sure they would have won the case if they'd gone to trial. But his client settled anyway. He says sometimes it makes more sense to settle and pay a license fee than to spend $2 to $5 million on a court case.

SYDELL: Tom Ewing, the lawyer who tracks Intellectual Ventures, says it's likely we're going to see plenty more of these cases in the future. And that's based just on the math of IV's business model. In order to purchase its 35,000 patents, Intellectual Ventures got money from investors. A lot of money. More than $5 billion dollars.

SYDELL: And a lot of these investors are venture capitalists who expect very high returns. These are people who are looking for the next Google, the next Apple. People who want to get back many times what they put in. Since its founding in 2000, Intellectual Ventures has generated $2 billion dollars in revenue. But to keep its investors happy, over the next ten years, says Tom Ewing, they're going to have to do a lot better than that.

EWING: So if you calculate this out, that means that over say a ten-year period they're going to need to collect about $35 billion dollars in licensing revenue, in order for them to be successful among the people who they're trying to compare themselves with. IV seems to have signed a number of deals. If the stream of deals they're signing doesn't increase significantly, then I would imagine they will be forced to file more litigations in order to achieve their revenue targets.

SYDELL: Tom's prediction already seems to be coming true. Earlier this month, Intellectual Ventures itself filed a patent-infringement suit in federal court against several companies it claimed were infringing some patents it owns.

SYDELL: In early July, the bankrupt tech company Nortel put its 6,000 patents up for auction as part of a liquidation. A bidding war broke out between the Silicon Valley powerhouses. Google said in press accounts that it wanted the patents purely to defend itself against lawsuits and it was willing to spend over $3 billion dollars to get them. But that wasn't enough. The portfolio eventually sold to Apple and a strange consortium of other tech companies, including Apple competitor Microsoft. The price tag? Four point five billion dollars. Five times the opening bid. More than double what most people were expecting. The largest patent auction in history.

BLUMBERG: Think of that—4.5 billion dollars on patents that these companies almost certainly don't want for their technical secrets. That 4.5 billion dollars won't build anything new, won't bring new products to the shelves, won't open up new factories that can hire people who need jobs. That's 4.5 billion dollars that adds to the price of every product these companies sell you—4.5 billion dollars essentially wasted, buying arms for an ongoing patent war. The big companies, Google, Apple, Microsoft, will probably survive this war. The likely casualties, the companies out there now that no one's ever heard of that could one day take their place.

**The New York Review of Books**

One of the hardest things for any journalist to do is to talk clearly and compellingly about that murkiest of sciences, medical statistics. Doctors and drug companies have every incentive to make us believe that they know what they're doing and that the drugs they're prescribing are effective. In reality, however, debates are constantly raging, especially in the area of antidepressants. Marcia Angell has a rare ability to elucidate the massive conflicts of interest here and is unsparing in her treatment of the overprescription epidemic. This is the second installation of her two-part *New York Review of Books* series on the subject.

Marcia Angell

# 23. The Illusions
# of Psychiatry

In my article in the last issue, I focused mainly on the recent books by psychologist Irving Kirsch and journalist Robert Whitaker, and what they tell us about the epidemic of mental illness and the drugs used to treat it.[1] Here I discuss the *American Psychiatric Association's Diagnostic and Statistical Manual of Mental Disorders* (*DSM*)—often referred to as the bible of psychiatry, and now heading for its fifth edition—and its extraordinary influence within American society. I also examine *Unhinged*, the recent book by Daniel Carlat, a psychiatrist, who provides a disillusioned insider's view of the psychiatric profession. And I discuss the widespread use of psychoactive drugs in children and the baleful influence of the pharmaceutical industry on the practice of psychiatry.

One of the leaders of modern psychiatry, Leon Eisenberg, a professor at Johns Hopkins and then Harvard Medical School, who was among the first to study the effects of stimulants on attention deficit disorder in children, wrote that American psychiatry in the late twentieth century moved from a state of "brainlessness" to one of "mindlessness."[2] By that he meant that before psychoactive drugs (drugs that affect the mental state) were introduced, the profession had little interest in neurotransmitters or any other aspect of the physical brain. Instead, it subscribed to the Freudian view that mental illness had its roots in unconscious conflicts, usually originating in childhood, that affected the mind as though it were separate from the brain.

But with the introduction of psychoactive drugs in the 1950s, and sharply accelerating in the 1980s, the focus shifted to the brain. Psychiatrists began to refer to themselves as psychopharmacologists, and they had less and less interest in exploring the life stories of their patients. Their main concern was to eliminate or reduce symptoms by treating sufferers with drugs that would alter brain function. An early advocate of this biological model of mental illness, Eisenberg in his later years became an outspoken critic of what he saw as the indiscriminate use of psychoactive drugs, driven largely by the machinations of the pharmaceutical industry.

When psychoactive drugs were first introduced, there was a brief period of optimism in the psychiatric profession, but by the 1970s, optimism gave way to a sense of threat. Serious side effects of the drugs were becoming apparent, and an antipsychiatry movement had taken root, as exemplified by the writings of Thomas Szasz and the movie *One Flew Over the Cuckoo's Nest*. There was also growing competition for patients from psychologists and social workers. In addition, psychiatrists were plagued by internal divisions: some embraced the new biological model, some still clung to the Freudian model, and a few saw mental illness as an essentially sane response to an insane world. Moreover, within the larger medical profession, psychiatrists were regarded as something like poor relations; even with their new drugs, they were seen as less scientific than other specialists, and their income was generally lower.

·     ·     ·

In the late 1970s, the psychiatric profession struck back—hard. As Robert Whitaker tells it in *Anatomy of an Epidemic*, the medical director of the American Psychiatric Association (APA),

Melvin Sabshin, declared in 1977 that "a vigorous effort to re-medicalize psychiatry should be strongly supported," and he launched an all-out media and public relations campaign to do exactly that. Psychiatry had a powerful weapon that its competitors lacked. Since psychiatrists must qualify as MDs, they have the legal authority to write prescriptions. By fully embracing the biological model of mental illness and the use of psychoactive drugs to treat it, psychiatry was able to relegate other mental health care providers to ancillary positions and also to identify itself as a scientific discipline along with the rest of the medical profession. Most important, by emphasizing drug treatment, psychiatry became the darling of the pharmaceutical industry, which soon made its gratitude tangible.

These efforts to enhance the status of psychiatry were undertaken deliberately. The APA was then working on the third edition of the *DSM*, which provides diagnostic criteria for all mental disorders. The president of the APA had appointed Robert Spitzer, a much-admired professor of psychiatry at Columbia University, to head the task force overseeing the project. The first two editions, published in 1952 and 1968, reflected the Freudian view of mental illness and were little known outside the profession. Spitzer set out to make the *DSM-III* something quite different. He promised that it would be "a defense of the medical model as applied to psychiatric problems," and the president of the APA in 1977, Jack Weinberg, said it would "clarify to anyone who may be in doubt that we regard psychiatry as a specialty of medicine."

When Spitzer's *DSM-III* was published in 1980, it contained 265 diagnoses (up from 182 in the previous edition), and it came into nearly universal use not only by psychiatrists but by insurance companies, hospitals, courts, prisons, schools, researchers, government agencies, and the rest of the medical profession. Its main goal was to bring consistency (usually referred to as "reliability") to psychiatric diagnosis, that is, to ensure that psychiatrists who saw the same patient would agree on the diagnosis. To do that, each diagnosis was defined by a list of symptoms, with numerical thresholds. For example, having at least five of nine particular symptoms got you a full-fledged diagnosis of a major depressive episode within the broad category of "mood disorders." But there was another goal—to justify the use of psychoactive drugs. The president of the APA last year, Carol Bernstein, in effect acknowledged that. "It became necessary in the 1970s," she wrote, "to facilitate diagnostic agreement among clinicians, scientists, and regulatory authorities given the need to match patients with newly emerging pharmacologic treatments."[3]

The *DSM-III* was almost certainly more "reliable" than the earlier versions, but reliability is not the same thing as validity. Reliability, as I have noted, is used to mean consistency; validity refers to correctness or soundness. If nearly all physicians agreed that freckles were a sign of cancer, the diagnosis would be "reliable" but not valid. The problem with the *DSM* is that in all of its editions, it has simply reflected the opinions of its writers, and in the case of the *DSM-III* mainly of Spitzer himself, who has been justly called one of the most influential psychiatrists of the twentieth century.[4] In his words, he "picked everybody that [he] was comfortable with" to serve with him on the fifteen-member task force, and there were complaints that he called too few meetings and generally ran the process in a haphazard but high-handed manner. Spitzer said in a 1989 interview, "I could just get my way by sweet talking and whatnot." In a 1984 article entitled "The Disadvantages of *DSM-III* Outweigh Its Advantages," George Vaillant, a professor of psychiatry at Harvard Medical School, wrote that the *DSM-III* represented "a bold series of choices based on guess, taste, prejudice, and hope," which seems to be a fair description.

Not only did the *DSM* become the bible of psychiatry, but like the real Bible, it depended a lot on something akin to revelation. There are no citations of scientific studies to support its decisions. That is an astonishing omission, because in all medical publications, whether journal articles or textbooks, statements of fact are supposed to be supported by citations of published scientific studies. (There are four separate "sourcebooks" for the current edition of the *DSM* that present the rationale for some decisions, along with references, but that is not the same thing as specific references.) It may be of much interest for a group of experts to get together and offer their opinions, but unless these opinions can be buttressed by evidence, they do not warrant the extraordinary deference shown to the *DSM*. The *DSM-III* was supplanted by the *DSM-III-R* in 1987, the *DSM-IV* in 1994, and the current version, the *DSM-IV-TR* (text revised) in 2000, which contains 365 diagnoses. "With each subsequent edition," writes Daniel Carlat in his absorbing book, "the number of diagnostic categories multiplied, and the books became larger and more expensive. Each became a best seller for the APA, and *DSM* is now one of the major sources of income for the organization." The *DSM-IV* sold over a million copies.

. . .

As psychiatry became a drug-intensive specialty, the pharmaceutical industry was quick to see the advantages of forming an alliance with the psychiatric profession. Drug companies began to lavish attention and largesse on psychiatrists, both individually and collectively, directly and indirectly. They showered gifts and free samples on practicing psychiatrists, hired them as consultants and speakers, bought them meals, helped pay for them to attend conferences, and supplied them with "educational" materials. When Minnesota and Vermont implemented "sunshine laws" that require drug companies to report all payments to doctors, psychiatrists were found to receive more money than physicians in any other specialty. The pharmaceutical industry also subsidizes meetings of the APA and other psychiatric conferences. About a fifth of APA funding now comes from drug companies.

Drug companies are particularly eager to win over faculty psychiatrists at prestigious academic medical centers. Called "key opinion leaders" (KOLs) by the industry, these are the people who through their writing and teaching influence how mental illness will be diagnosed and treated. They also publish much of the clinical research on drugs and, most importantly, largely determine the content of the *DSM*. In a sense, they are the best sales force the industry could have and are worth every cent spent on them. Of the 170 contributors to the current version of the *DSM* (the *DSM-IV-TR*), almost all of whom would be described as KOLs, ninety-five had financial ties to drug companies, including all of the contributors to the sections on mood disorders and schizophrenia.[5]

The drug industry, of course, supports other specialists and professional societies, too, but Carlat asks, "Why do psychiatrists consistently lead the pack of specialties when it comes to taking money from drug companies?" His answer: "Our diagnoses are subjective and expandable, and we have few rational reasons for choosing one treatment over another." Unlike the conditions treated in most other branches of medicine, there are no objective signs or tests for mental illness—no lab data or MRI findings—and the boundaries between normal and abnormal are often unclear. That makes it possible to expand diagnostic boundaries or even create new diagnoses, in ways that would be impossible, say, in a field like cardiology. And drug companies have every interest in inducing psychiatrists to do just that.

In addition to the money spent on the psychiatric profession directly, drug companies heavily support many related patient-advocacy groups and educational organizations. Whitaker writes that in the first quarter of 2009 alone,

> Eli Lilly gave $551,000 to NAMI [National Alliance on Mental Illness] and its local chapters, $465,000 to the National Mental Health Association, $130,000 to CHADD (an ADHD

[attention deficit/hyperactivity disorder] patient-advocacy group), and $69,250 to the American Foundation for Suicide Prevention.

And that's just one company in three months; one can imagine what the yearly total would be from all companies that make psychoactive drugs. These groups ostensibly exist to raise public awareness of psychiatric disorders, but they also have the effect of promoting the use of psychoactive drugs and influencing insurers to cover them. Whitaker summarizes the growth of industry influence after the publication of the *DSM-III* as follows:

> In short, a powerful quartet of voices came together during the 1980's eager to inform the public that mental disorders were brain diseases. Pharmaceutical companies provided the financial muscle. The APA and psychiatrists at top medical schools conferred intellectual legitimacy upon the enterprise. The NIMH [National Institute of Mental Health] put the government's stamp of approval on the story. NAMI provided a moral authority.

.    .    .

Like most other psychiatrists, Carlat treats his patients only with drugs, not talk therapy, and he is candid about the advantages of doing so. If he sees three patients an hour for psychopharmacology, he calculates, he earns about $180 per hour from insurers. In contrast, he would be able to see only one patient an hour for talk therapy, for which insurers would pay him less than $100. Carlat does not believe that psychopharmacology is particularly complicated, let alone precise, although the public is led to believe that it is:

Patients often view psychiatrists as wizards of neurotransmitters, who can choose just the right medication for whatever chemical imbalance is at play. This exaggerated conception of our capabilities has been encouraged by drug companies, by psychiatrists ourselves, and by our patients' understandable hopes for cures.

His work consists of asking patients a series of questions about their symptoms to see whether they match up with any of the disorders in the *DSM*. This matching exercise, he writes, provides "the illusion that we understand our patients when all we are doing is assigning them labels." Often patients meet criteria for more than one diagnosis because there is overlap in symptoms. For example, difficulty concentrating is a criterion for more than one disorder. One of Carlat's patients ended up with seven separate diagnoses. "We target discrete symptoms with treatments, and other drugs are piled on top to treat side effects." A typical patient, he says, might be taking Celexa for depression, Ativan for anxiety, Ambien for insomnia, Provigil for fatigue (a side effect of Celexa), and Viagra for impotence (another side effect of Celexa).

As for the medications themselves, Carlat writes that "there are only a handful of umbrella categories of psychotropic drugs," within which the drugs are not very different from one another. He doesn't believe there is much basis for choosing among them. "To a remarkable degree, our choice of medications is subjective, even random. Perhaps your psychiatrist is in a Lexapro mood this morning, because he was just visited by an attractive Lexapro drug rep." And he sums up:

Such is modern psychopharmacology. Guided purely by symptoms, we try different drugs, with no real conception of what we are trying to fix, or of how the drugs are working. I am perpetually astonished that we are so effective for so many patients.

While Carlat believes that psychoactive drugs are sometimes effective, his evidence is anecdotal. What he objects to is their overuse and what he calls the "frenzy of psychiatric diagnoses." As he puts it, "if you ask any psychiatrist in clinical practice, including me, whether antidepressants work for their patients, you will hear an unambiguous 'yes.' We see people getting better all the time." But then he goes on to speculate, like Irving Kirsch in *The Emperor's New Drugs*, that what they are really responding to could be an activated placebo effect. If psychoactive drugs are not all they're cracked up to be—and the evidence is that they're not—what about the diagnoses themselves? As they multiply with each edition of the *DSM*, what are we to make of them?

·     ·     ·

In 1999, the APA began work on its fifth revision of the *DSM*, which is scheduled to be published in 2013. The twenty-seven-member task force is headed by David Kupfer, a professor of psychiatry at the University of Pittsburgh, assisted by Darrel Regier of the APA's American Psychiatric Institute for Research and Education. As with the earlier editions, the task force is advised by multiple work groups, which now total some 140 members, corresponding to the major diagnostic categories. Ongoing deliberations and proposals have been extensively reported on the APA website (www.DSM5.org) and in the media, and it appears that the already very large constellation of mental disorders will grow still larger.

In particular, diagnostic boundaries will be broadened to include precursors of disorders, such as "psychosis risk syndrome" and "mild cognitive impairment" (possible early Alzheimer's disease). The term "spectrum" is used to widen categories, for example, "obsessive-compulsive disorder spectrum," "schizophrenia spectrum disorder," and "autism spectrum disorder."

And there are proposals for entirely new entries, such as "hyper-sexual disorder," "restless legs syndrome," and "binge eating."

Even Allen Frances, chairman of the *DSM-IV* task force, is highly critical of the expansion of diagnoses in the *DSM-V*. In the June 26, 2009, issue of *Psychiatric Times*, he wrote that the *DSM-V* will be a "bonanza for the pharmaceutical industry but at a huge cost to the new false positive patients caught in the excessively wide *DSM-V* net." As if to underscore that judgment, Kupfer and Regier wrote in a recent article in the *Journal of the American Medical Association* (*JAMA*), entitled "Why All of Medicine Should Care About *DSM-5*," that "in primary care settings, approximately 30 percent to 50 percent of patients have prominent mental health symptoms or identifiable mental disorders, which have significant adverse consequences if left untreated."[6] It looks as though it will be harder and harder to be normal.

At the end of the article by Kupfer and Regier is a small-print "financial disclosure" that reads in part:

Prior to being appointed as chair, *DSM-5* Task Force, Dr. Kupfer reports having served on advisory boards for Eli Lilly & Co, Forest Pharmaceuticals Inc, Solvay/Wyeth Pharmaceuticals, and Johnson & Johnson; and consulting for Servier and Lundbeck.

Regier oversees all industry-sponsored research grants for the APA. The *DSM-V* (used interchangeably with *DSM-5*) is the first edition to establish rules to limit financial conflicts of interest in members of the task force and work groups. According to these rules, once members were appointed, which occurred in 2006–2008, they could receive no more than $10,000 per year in aggregate from drug companies or own more than $50,000 in company stock. The website shows their company ties for three years before their appointments, and that is what Kupfer disclosed in the *JAMA* article and what is shown on the APA website, where 56 percent of members of the work groups disclosed significant industry interests.

· · ·

The pharmaceutical industry influences psychiatrists to prescribe psychoactive drugs even for categories of patients in whom the drugs have not been found safe and effective. What should be of greatest concern for Americans is the astonishing rise in the di-agnosis and treatment of mental illness in children, sometimes as young as two years old. These children are often treated with drugs that were never approved by the FDA for use in this age group and have serious side effects. The apparent prevalence of "juvenile bipolar disorder" jumped forty-fold between 1993 and 2004, and that of "autism" increased from one in five hun-dred children to one in ninety over the same decade. Ten per-cent of ten-year-old boys now take daily stimulants for ADHD— "attention deficit/hyperactivity disorder"—and 500,000 children take antipsychotic drugs.

There seem to be fashions in childhood psychiatric diagnoses, with one disorder giving way to the next. At first, ADHD, mani-fested by hyperactivity, inattentiveness, and impulsivity usually in school-age children, was the fastest-growing diagnosis. But in the mid-1990s, two highly influential psychiatrists at the Massachu-setts General Hospital proposed that many children with ADHD really had bipolar disorder that could sometimes be diagnosed as early as infancy. They proposed that the manic episodes character-istic of bipolar disorder in adults might be manifested in children as irritability. That gave rise to a flood of diagnoses of juvenile bi-polar disorder. Eventually this created something of a backlash, and the *DSM*-V now proposes partly to replace the diagnosis with a brand-new one, called "temper dysregulation disorder with dys-phoria," or TDD, which Allen Frances calls "a new monster."[7]

One would be hard pressed to find a two-year-old who is not sometimes irritable, a boy in fifth grade who is not sometimes inattentive, or a girl in middle school who is not anxious. (Imagine what taking a drug that causes obesity would do to such a girl.) Whether such children are labeled as having a mental disorder and treated with prescription drugs depends a lot on who they are and the pressures their parents face.[8] As low-income families experience growing economic hardship, many are finding that applying for Supplemental Security Income (SSI) payments on the basis of mental disability is the only way to survive. It is more generous than welfare, and it virtually ensures that the family will also qualify for Medicaid. According to MIT economics professor David Autor, "This has become the new welfare." Hospitals and state welfare agencies also have incentives to encourage uninsured families to apply for SSI payments, since hospitals will get paid and states will save money by shifting welfare costs to the federal government.

Growing numbers of for-profit firms specialize in helping poor families apply for SSI benefits. But to qualify nearly always requires that applicants, including children, be taking psychoactive drugs. According to a *New York Times* story, a Rutgers University study found that children from low-income families are four times as likely as privately insured children to receive antipsychotic medicines.

In December 2006 a four-year-old child named Rebecca Riley died in a small town near Boston from a combination of Clonidine and Depakote, which she had been prescribed, along with Seroquel, to treat "ADHD" and "bipolar disorder"—diagnoses she received when she was two years old. Clonidine was approved by the FDA for treating high blood pressure. Depakote was approved for treating epilepsy and acute mania in bipolar disorder. Seroquel was approved for treating schizophrenia and acute mania. None of the three was approved to treat ADHD or for long-term use in bipolar disorder, and none was approved for children Rebecca's age. Rebecca's two older siblings had been given the same diagnoses and were each taking three psychoactive drugs. The parents had obtained SSI benefits for the siblings and for themselves and were applying for benefits for Rebecca when she died. The family's total income from SSI was about $30,000 per year.[9]

Whether these drugs should ever have been prescribed for Rebecca in the first place is the crucial question. The FDA approves drugs only for specified uses, and it is illegal for companies to market them for any other purpose—that is, "off-label." Nevertheless, physicians are permitted to prescribe drugs for any reason they choose, and one of the most lucrative things drug companies can do is persuade physicians to prescribe drugs off-label, despite the law against it. In just the past four years, five firms have admitted to federal charges of illegally marketing psychoactive drugs. AstraZeneca marketed Seroquel off-label for children and the elderly (another vulnerable population, often administered antipsychotics in nursing homes); Pfizer faced similar charges for Geodon (an antipsychotic); Eli Lilly for Zyprexa (an antipsychotic); Bristol-Myers Squibb for Abilify (another antipsychotic); and Forest Labs for Celexa (an antidepressant).

Despite having to pay hundreds of millions of dollars to settle the charges, the companies have probably come out well ahead. The original purpose of permitting doctors to prescribe drugs off-label was to enable them to treat patients on the basis of early scientific reports, without having to wait for FDA approval. But that sensible rationale has become a marketing tool. Because of the subjective nature of psychiatric diagnosis, the ease with which diagnostic boundaries can be expanded, the seriousness of the side effects of psychoactive drugs, and the pervasive influence of their manufacturers, I believe doctors should be prohibited from prescribing psychoactive drugs off-label, just as companies are prohibited from marketing them off-label.

•   •   •

The books by Irving Kirsch, Robert Whitaker, and Daniel Carlat are powerful indictments of the way psychiatry is now practiced. They document the "frenzy" of diagnosis, the overuse of drugs with sometimes devastating side effects, and widespread conflicts of interest. Critics of these books might argue, as Nancy Andreasen implied in her paper on the loss of brain tissue with long-term antipsychotic treatment, that the side effects are the price that must be paid to relieve the suffering caused by mental illness. If we knew that the benefits of psychoactive drugs outweighed their harms, that would be a strong argument, since there is no doubt that many people suffer grievously from mental illness. But as Kirsch, Whitaker, and Carlat argue convincingly, that expectation may be wrong.

At the very least, we need to stop thinking of psychoactive drugs as the best, and often the only, treatment for mental illness or emotional distress. Both psychotherapy and exercise have been shown to be as effective as drugs for depression, and their effects are longer lasting, but unfortunately, there is no industry to push these alternatives and Americans have come to believe that pills must be more potent. More research is needed to study alternatives to psychoactive drugs, and the results should be included in medical education.

In particular, we need to rethink the care of troubled children. Here the problem is often troubled families in troubled circumstances. Treatment directed at these environmental conditions—such as one-on-one tutoring to help parents cope or after-school centers for the children—should be studied and compared with drug treatment. In the long run, such alternatives would probably be less expensive. Our reliance on psychoactive drugs, seemingly for all of life's discontents, tends to close off other options. In view of the risks and questionable long-term effectiveness of drugs, we need to do better. Above all, we should remember the time-honored medical dictum: first, do no harm (*primum non nocere*).

## Notes

1. See Marcia Angell, "The Epidemic of Mental Illness: Why?" *The New York Review of Books*, June 23, 2011.

2. Eisenberg wrote about this transition in "Mindlessness and Brainlessness," *British Journal of Psychiatry*, no. 148 (1986). His last paper, completed by his stepson, was published after his death in 2009. See Eisenberg and L. B. Guttmacher, "Were We All Asleep at the Switch? A Personal Reminiscence of Psychiatry from 1940 to 2010," *Acta Psychiatrica Scand.*, no. 122 (2010).

3. Carol A. Bernstein, "Meta-Structure in DSM-5 Process," *Psychiatric News*, March 4, 2011, 7.

4. The history of the DSM is recounted in Christopher Lane's informative book *Shyness: How Normal Behavior Became a Sickness* (Yale University Press, 2007). Lane was given access to the American Psychiatric Association's archive of unpublished letters, transcripts, and memoranda, and he also interviewed Robert Spitzer. His book was reviewed by Frederick Crews in *The New York Review of Books*, December 6, 2007, and by me, January 15, 2009 .

5. See L. Cosgrove et al., "Financial Ties Between DSM-IV Panel Members and the Pharmaceutical Industry," *Psychotherapy and Psychosomatics* 75 (2006).

6. David J. Kupfer and Darrel A. Regier, "Why All of Medicine Should Care About DSM-5," *JAMA*, May 19, 2010.

7. Greg Miller, "Anything But Child's Play," *Science*, March 5, 2010.

8. Duff Wilson, "Child's Ordeal Reveals Risks of Psychiatric Drugs in Young," *New York Times*, September 2, 2010.

9. Patricia Wen, "A Legacy of Unintended Side-Effects: Call It the Other Welfare," *Boston Globe*, December 12, 2010.

## Representational Pictures

Probably the most engrossing movie ever released on credit default swaps, collateralized debt obligations, and conflicts of interest in academia, *Inside Job* takes a withering look at the institutional causes of the financial crisis. In this segment, director Charles Ferguson grills famed economists from Columbia and Harvard on their undisclosed conflicts of interest, capturing fascinating exchanges of the kind that mainstream journalism rarely produces. It's no accident that Ferguson is no Wall Street beat reporter: He's a software entrepreneur, MIT lecturer, and movie director—and his film is one of the best pieces of journalism to emerge from the crisis.

Charles Ferguson,
Adam Bolt, and
Chad Beck

# 24. From
## *Inside Job*

CHARLES FERGUSON: Do you think the financial-services
industry has too much, uh, political power in the
United States?

GLENN HUBBARD: I don't think so, no. You certainly, you
certainly wouldn't get that impression by the
drubbing that they regularly get, uh, in Washington.

NARRATOR: Many prominent academics quietly make
fortunes while helping the financial industry shape
public debate and government policy. The Analysis
Group, Charles River Associates, Compass Lex-
econ, and the Law and Economics Consulting
Group manage a multi-billion-dollar industry that
provides academic experts for hire.

Two bankers who used these services were
Ralph Ciofi and Matthew Tannin, Bear Stearns
hedge fund managers prosecuted for securities
fraud. After hiring the Analysis Group, both were
acquitted.

Glenn Hubbard was paid 100,000 dollars to
testify in their defense.

CHARLES FERGUSON: Do you think that the economics
discipline has, uh, a conflict of interest problem?

GLENN HUBBARD: I'm not sure I know what you mean.

CHARLES FERGUSON: Do you think that a significant fraction of the economics discipline, a number of economists, have financial conflicts of interests that in some way might call into question or color—

GLENN HUBBARD: Oh, I see what you're saying. I doubt it. You know, most academic economists, uh, you know, aren't wealthy businesspeople.

NARRATOR: Hubbard makes 250,000 dollars a year as a board member of Met Life, and was formerly on the board of Capmark, a major commercial mortgage lender during the bubble, which went bankrupt in 2009. He has also advised Nomura Securities, KKR Financial Corporation, and many other financial firms.

Laura Tyson, who declined to be interviewed for this film, is a professor at the University of California, Berkeley. She was the chair of the Council of Economic Advisers, and then director of the National Economic Council in the Clinton administration.

Shortly after leaving government, she joined the board of Morgan Stanley, which pays her 350,000 dollars a year.

Ruth Simmons, the president of Brown University, makes over 300,000 dollars a year on the board of Goldman Sachs.

Larry Summers, who as treasury secretary played a critical role in the deregulation of derivatives, became president of Harvard in 2001. While at Harvard, he made millions consulting to hedge funds and millions more in speaking fees, much of it from investment banks.

According to his federal disclosure report, Summers's net worth is between 16.5 million and 39.5 million dollars.

Frederic Mishkin, who returned to Columbia Business School after leaving the Federal Reserve, reported on his federal disclosure report that his net worth was between 6 million and 17 million dollars.

CHARLES FERGUSON: In 2006, you coauthored a study of Iceland's financial system.

FREDERIC MISHKIN: Right, right.

CHARLES FERGUSON: Iceland is also an advanced country with excellent institutions, low corruption, rule of law. The economy has already adjusted to financial liberalization—while prudential regulation and supervision is generally quite strong.

FREDERIC MISHKIN: Yeah. And that was the mistake. That it turns out that, uh, that the prudential regulation and supervision was not strong in Iceland. And particularly during this period—

CHARLES FERGUSON: So what led you to think that it was?

FREDERIC MISHKIN: I think that, uh, you're going with the information you have at, and generally, uh, the view was that, that, uh, that Iceland had very good institutions. It was a very advanced country—

CHARLES FERGUSON: Who told you that?

FREDERIC MISHKIN: —and [they had not]—

CHARLES FERGUSON: Who did, what kind of research—

FREDERIC MISHKIN: Well, it—

CHARLES FERGUSON: —did you do?

FREDERIC MISHKIN: —you, you talk to people, you have faith in, in, uh, the Central Bank, which actually did fall down on the job. Uh, that, uh, clearly, it, this, uh—

CHARLES FERGUSON: Why do you have "faith" in a central bank?

FREDERIC MISHKIN: Well, that faith, you, ya, d—, because you ha—, go with the information you have.

CHARLES FERGUSON: Um, how much were you paid to write it?

FREDERIC MISHKIN: I was paid, uh, I think the number was, uh, it's public information.

{Frederic Mishkin was paid $124,000 by the Icelandic Chamber of Commerce to write this paper.}

CHARLES FERGUSON: Uh, on your CV, the title of this report has been changed from "Financial Stability in Iceland" to "Financial Instability in Iceland."

FREDERIC MISHKIN: Oh. Well, I don't know, if, itch—, whatever it is, is, the, uh, the thing—if it's a typo, there's a typo.

GLENN HUBBARD: I think what should be publicly available is whenever anybody does research on a topic, that they disclose if they have any financial conflict with that research.

CHARLES FERGUSON: But if I recall, there is no policy to that effect.

GLENN HUBBARD: I can't imagine anybody not doing that—in terms of putting it in a paper. You would, there would be significant professional sanction for failure to do that.

CHARLES FERGUSON: I didn't see any place in the study where you indicated that you had been paid, uh, by the Icelandic Chamber of Commerce to produce it. Um—

FREDERIC MISHKIN: No, I {mumble}—

CHARLES FERGUSON: Okay.

NARRATOR: Richard Portes, the most famous economist in Britain, and a professor at London Business School, was also commissioned by the Icelandic Chamber of Commerce in 2007 to write a report which praised the Icelandic financial sector.

RICHARD PORTES: The banks themselves are highly liquid. They've actually made money on the fall of the Icelandic krona.

These are strong banks; their funding, their market funding is assured for the coming year. These are well-run banks.

NEWSMAN: Richard, thank you so much.

NARRATOR: Like Mishkin, Portes's report didn't disclose his payment from the Icelandic Chamber of Commerce.

{John Campbell, chairman, Harvard Economics Department}

CHARLES FERGUSON: Does Harvard require disclosures of financial conflict of interest in publications?

JOHN CAMPBELL: Um, not to my knowledge.

CHARLES FERGUSON: Do you require people to report the compensation they've received from outside activities?

JOHN CAMPBELL: No.

CHARLES FERGUSON: Don't you think that's a problem?

JOHN CAMPBELL: I don't see why.

CHARLES FERGUSON: Martin Feldstein being on the board of AIG; Laura Tyson going on the board of Morgan Stanley; uh, Larry Summers making 10 million dollars a year consulting to financial services firms; irrelevant.

JOHN CAMPBELL: Hm, ye—, well—yeah; basically irrelevant.

CHARLES FERGUSON: You've written a very large number of articles, about a very wide array of subjects. You never saw fit to investigate the risks of unregulated credit default swaps?

MARTIN FELDSTEIN: I never did.

CHARLES FERGUSON: Same question with regard to executive compensation; uh, the regulation of corporate governance; the effect of political contributions—

MARTIN FELDSTEIN: What, uh, what, uh, w—, I don't know that I would have anything to add to those discussions.

CHARLES FERGUSON: I'm looking at your résumé now. It looks to me as if the majority of your outside activities are, uh, consulting and directorship arrangements with the financial services industry. Is that, would you not agree with that characterization?

GLENN HUBBARD: No, to my knowledge, I don't think my consulting clients are even on my CV, so—

CHARLES FERGUSON: Uh, who are your consulting clients?

GLENN HUBBARD: I don't believe I have to discuss that with you.

CHARLES FERGUSON: Okay. Uh, uh—

GLENN HUBBARD: Look, you have a few more minutes, and the interview is over.

CHARLES FERGUSON: Do you consult for any financial services firms?

FREDERIC MISHKIN: Uh, the answer is, I do.

CHARLES FERGUSON: And—

FREDERIC MISHKIN: And, but I d—, I do not want to go into details about that.

CHARLES FERGUSON: Do they include other financial services firms?

GLENN HUBBARD: Possibly.

CHARLES FERGUSON: You don't remember?

GLENN HUBBARD: This isn't a deposition, sir. I was polite enough to give you time; foolishly, I now see. But you have three more minutes. Give it your best shot.

NARRATOR: In 2004, at the height of the bubble, Glenn Hubbard coauthored a widely read paper with William C. Dudley, the chief economist of Goldman Sachs. In the paper, Hubbard praised credit derivatives and the securitization chain, stating that they had improved allocation of capital, and were enhancing financial stability. He cited reduced volatility in the economy and stated that recessions had become less frequent and milder. Credit derivatives were protecting banks against losses, and helping to distribute risk.

CHARLES FERGUSON: A medical researcher writes an article, saying: to treat this disease, you should prescribe this drug. It turns out doctor makes 80 percent of personal income from manufacturer of this drug. Does not bother you.

JOHN CAMPBELL: I think, uh, it's certainly important to disclose the, um—the, um—

Well, I think that's also a little different from cases that we are talking about here. Because, um—um—

{The presidents of Harvard University and Columbia University refused to comment on academic conflicts of interest. Both declined to be interviewed for this film.}

CHARLES FERGUSON: So, uh, what do you think this says about the economics discipline?

CHARLES MORRIS: Well, heh heh heh, it has no relevance to anything, really. And, and fe—, indeed, I think, um, it's a part of the, it's a s—, important part of the problem.

Part VI

# Corporate Stories

**Fortune**

This deeply reported *Fortune* story takes readers inside the boardroom and executive suites at Pfizer, a company beset by indecision, infighting, and dimming prospects for future growth—all with the backdrop of the decline of blockbuster pharmaceuticals. Peter Elkind, Jennifer Reingold, and Doris Burke write around the central character, former CEO Jeff Kindler, who wouldn't comment on the record for the piece. That it doesn't suffer from his absence shows how rich the reporting really is. Corporate infighting can be a business journalist's best friend, and *Fortune* takes full advantage here to turn out one of the year's best stories.

Peter Elkind and
Jennifer Reingold, with
Doris Burke

# 25. Inside Pfizer's Palace Coup

For Jeff Kindler, it was a humiliating moment. The CEO of Pfizer, the world's largest pharmaceutical company, had been summoned to the airport in Fort Myers, Fla., on Saturday, December 4, 2010, for a highly unusual purpose: to plead for his job.

Three stone-faced directors, representing the company's board, sat inside a drab airport conference room as the CEO, trained as a trial lawyer, struggled to argue his most important case. Alerted to this meeting less than twenty-four hours earlier, Kindler detailed his accomplishments, speaking nonstop for the better part of an hour. He touted his bold reorganizations, praised his administration's sweeping cost reductions, and rhapsodized about his reinvention of Pfizer's crucial research-and-development operations.

But the three board members, Constance Horner, a former deputy secretary at the U.S. Department of Health and Human Services; George Lorch, an ex-CEO of Armstrong World Holdings; and Bill Gray, a former Philadelphia congressman, weren't there to debate the direction of the company. The board had spent a frantic week in an urgent investigation: A revolt had erupted against Kindler among a handful of senior managers, and the directors were trying to figure out what was going on. One possibility: an internal power grab. Another: a CEO who was unraveling.

Led by Horner, they confronted Kindler with questions about his management and his behavior. Had he routinely berated subordinates? Did he really bring senior executives to tears? And how did he respond to charges that his leadership style, a sort of micro-micro-management, had paralyzed Pfizer?

A questioner of prosecutorial intensity, Kindler was used to being the interrogator. But this time he had to respond, and his answers seemed only to harden the board members. Kindler insisted that just two executives were truly unhappy. Most of his team thought he was a good boss and had done great things for the company. What was the directors' basis for concluding otherwise? Had they reviewed his sterling performance evaluations? Spoken to his executive coach?

As the meeting continued—it lasted more than two hours—it became clear that Kindler had little chance of saving his job. Perhaps, he finally said, it was time for him to resign. The directors, who seemed ready for this suggestion, told Kindler they were prepared to give him a far more generous settlement package if he didn't take the fight to the full board. Kindler agreed to think it over and flew home.

A day later, in an unusual Sunday night announcement, the fifty-five-year-old CEO retired, effective immediately. Pfizer's press release offered a surprisingly candid explanation, which was inserted by Kindler himself: "The combination of meeting the requirements of our many shareholders around the world and the 24/7 nature of my responsibilities has made this period extremely demanding on me personally."

As revealing as it was, that statement only hinted at the turmoil inside Pfizer. Indeed, what has occurred at the company—whose $68 billion in annual sales are built on blockbuster drugs such as Lipitor and Viagra—is extraordinary. Once a Wall Street darling and corporate icon, Pfizer has tumbled into disarray. In the decade that ended with Kindler's departure, its stock price sagged from a high of $49 down to $17, and its drug pipeline dried up (problems the company continues to grapple with today). Pfizer lost its way, stumbling through a frantic series of zig-zags in the hopes of finding new blockbusters to sustain its prodigious profits in the future.

## Pfizer's Palace Coup: The Cast

Meanwhile, its managers descended into behavior that would do Shakespeare—or Machiavelli—proud. There was the ex-CEO who couldn't relinquish his power and quietly maneuvered to undercut two successors he had helped install. Then there was the human resources chief who divided the staff rather than uniting it. Most of all, there was Kindler himself, a bright man with some fresh ideas for reforming Pfizer but a person who agonized over decisions even as he second-guessed everybody else's actions. The story of Jeff Kindler's tumultuous tenure at Pfizer is a saga of ambition, intrigue, backstabbing, and betrayal—all of it exacerbated by a board that allowed the problems to fester for years.

The full story of Kindler's downfall has never before been told. Fortune reported this article for four months, interviewing 102 people, including executives and directors who worked closely with him at Pfizer and at previous stages of his career. For their parts, both Kindler and the company say that they are bound by a confidentiality agreement they signed as part of Kindler's departure.

Kindler declined to speak about Pfizer, but a representative provided a written statement: "Pfizer is a great company I was privileged to serve for nine years. I am proud of what our team accomplished and delighted to see [new CEO Ian Read], together with the business and scientific leaders we brought together, continue to build on these achievements." In its own statement, the drug company told *Fortune*: "We thank Jeff Kindler for his many years of service to Pfizer," noting that "Jeff came into the industry at a tumultuous time and faced significant challenges such as patent expirations of some of our major products. . . . We wish Jeff well in all of his future endeavors."

In the end, the story of Jeff Kindler's time at Pfizer provides a window into the challenges facing a mammoth company in an essential industry—and the people who aspire to govern it. Pfizer is an enterprise with the noble calling of easing pain and curing disease. Yet its leaders spent much of their time in the tawdry business of turf wars and political scheming.

## A Star Who Wanted to Be in Charge

Jeffrey Bruce Kindler has the sort of background that marked him for success—but perhaps not as CEO of a giant pharmaceutical company. He boasts a sterling résumé. The son of a New Jersey dermatologist, Kindler graduated with high honors from Tufts University and Harvard Law School and went on to clerk for the late Supreme Court Justice William Brennan. Kindler then became a litigator at the pugnacious Washington law firm Williams & Connolly, where he defended the *National Enquirer* in a libel suit and represented late oilman Marvin Davis in a contracts case.

"In our world, Jeff was a star," says Ben Heineman, the former general counsel of General Electric, who lured Kindler to that company in 1990. But Kindler was the sort of star who mostly wanted to be an even bigger star. And he wanted to be in charge.

In 1996, at age forty, he became general counsel at Mc-Donald's, with a clear eye toward moving up. Everyone at the fast-food company recognized Kindler's abilities. He juggled complex intellectual issues with ease, made dazzling presentations, wielded a self-deprecating charm, and worked longer hours than anyone else. He brought GE-style rigor to a place that lacked that sort of discipline. Says longtime board member Rick Hernandez: "McDonald's as a culture benefited from having Jeff around."

But genial as he could be, Kindler also had an aggressive, combative side. He cleaned house at McDonald's, sacking inside and outside lawyers. He rarely trusted experienced subordinates to perform their jobs without his scrutiny. And when he was unhappy about something, he made his feelings bluntly known— sometimes through angry voicemails left late at night.

From the moment he entered management, Kindler was marked by two traits. First, he remained a confrontational trial lawyer: He sought knowledge through interrogation; he was skeptical of what he was told, even when it came from people who knew far more about a subject than he did; and he bored in relentlessly on small details, always searching for the sort of nuance that could make or break a legal case—but seemed trivial in other contexts. The second: For all Kindler's talents, he remained palpably insecure, acutely sensitive to anything or anyone he feared might undermine his standing. Some years later, after Kindler was named CEO of Pfizer, a CNBC reporter asked him on-air whether "a guy who sold chicken"—Kindler—was qualified to run a pharma company. He didn't talk to CNBC again for more than a year.

"Jeff didn't take a lot of prisoners," says Shelby Yastrow, who preceded Kindler as general counsel at McDonald's and worked with him for two years. When Yastrow retired in 1998, Kindler was master of ceremonies at his retirement dinner. "He couldn't have been funnier or more gracious," Yastrow recalls. After Kindler finished, Yastrow took the podium and jabbed: "Where has *this* Jeff Kindler been?"

Still, Kindler's behavior seemed like a minor detail in a career that was soaring. In 2000, after McDonald's purchased the Boston Market chicken chain in bankruptcy, Kindler developed a plan for reviving the business and breathed fresh life into it. He was rewarded with the presidency of McDonald's Partner Brands, the company's five nonburger chains, which included Boston Market.

Soon after, Pfizer came courting. The company offered him a job as its general counsel, overseeing 330 lawyers worldwide. Pfizer also held out the prospect that even bigger things might lie ahead for him.

## Pfizer's Glory Years

The company that Kindler joined in January 2002 was just ending its golden age, though it wasn't apparent at the time. In the 1990s Pfizer, once a second-tier chemical and drug company founded in Brooklyn in 1849, had become a global pharma powerhouse.

Pfizer's greatest strength wasn't developing drugs—it was selling them. The company was a marketing juggernaut, staffed with the industry's most potent army of sales reps. Other companies began striking lucrative partnership deals for Pfizer to market their medicines. So it was with Lipitor, the mother of all blockbusters. Pfizer's aggressive promotion and pricing strategy helped Lipitor, discovered by Warner-Lambert, take off on launch in 1997 and become the world's first $10-billion-a-year drug. Lipitor was so big that Pfizer ultimately bought Warner-Lambert for $115 billion.

Every move seemed to be paying off. Pfizer was ranked among America's "best managed" and "most admired" companies. And the stock! Its price multiplied tenfold in a decade.

The executive who led Pfizer through the Lipitor and Viagra glory years was William Campbell Steere Jr. A biology major at Stanford, he joined the company in 1959 as a drug salesman. Lean and wily, Steere didn't have the extroverted personality of a salesman. He was quiet and hated confrontation—indeed, Pfizer itself had a genteel culture that frowned on open disputation—but he found ways to build alliances and influence people.

Starting as CEO in 1991, Steere placed all his chips on pharmaceuticals, selling off dozens of unrelated businesses, pouring money into R&D, and audaciously declaring his intention to make Pfizer the industry giant. The company thrived by relying on a handful of billon-dollar-a-year blockbusters: By 2001 just eight drugs generated more than half its revenues. The Warner-Lambert deal assured Pfizer's rise to no. 1.

In January 2001, Steere, by then sixty-four and a company legend, retired as CEO. He handed the job to his handpicked no. 2, Hank McKinnell. Steere stepped aside—but not out. He received a consulting contract, with an office and secretary at Pfizer headquarters. Most important, Steere was granted the title of chairman emeritus and retained his seat on the Pfizer board. Governance experts widely regard such lingering as a recipe for trouble. Steere would remain a potent influence for another decade, outlasting his two successors.

## "The Only Smart Guy in the Room" Emerges

When Henry "Hank" McKinnell Jr. took over in 2001, Pfizer was perched on the mountaintop. It seemed the company had nowhere to go but down. A fit, cerebral British Columbia native, McKinnell joined Pfizer in 1971 and earned a reputation as a brilliant but brusque leader. He favored lightning-fast meetings—"What's next?" was his trademark line—set ambitious goals for the company, and refused to dwell on setbacks.

He would face many of them. Pfizer's pipeline simply couldn't support the growth the company had promised investors. Three of its blockbusters were about to lose patent protection and face generic competition, meaning their profits would plummet. The biggest issue, of course, was Lipitor—by 2005, it was bringing in a staggering $12 billion a year, more than a quarter of Pfizer's revenues. The company wouldn't lose its exclusive rights to Lipitor until late 2011, but already Wall Street was wondering how Pfizer could possibly replace it.

McKinnell kept boosting R&D budgets, maintaining Pfizer's "shots on goal" approach—the more compounds you explored, in theory, the more drugs you'd generate. But drugs can take a full decade to be developed and approved, and nothing big would be ready for years.

So McKinnell fell back on the refuge of the desperate pharma CEO: In July 2002 he announced the acquisition of Pharmacia, the industry's seventh-largest company, for $60 billion in stock. But even as Pfizer struggled to digest this latest meal, McKinnell seemed to spend less and less time at headquarters, becoming head of industry trade groups, funding an institute in Africa to combat AIDS, even writing a book about reforming health care.

That left a power vacuum, and Bill Steere, the former CEO, seemed more than willing to fill it. He was a familiar figure at Pfizer's New York headquarters, where he worked out in the basement fitness center and ate lunch in the cafeteria. Steere was always happy to lend an ear and share his views. His retired status and public reserve concealed tremendous influence. "He says almost nothing," says a person familiar with Pfizer's board. "But people look to him to see how he nods and how he moves, because he knows the company better than anyone."

With Pfizer no longer soaring, internal squabbling intensified. Vexed by what he viewed as Steere's meddling, McKinnell even tried to terminate his consulting contract. Steere fended off that move. Support for him ran deep on the board: Later, when Steere turned seventy-two, the mandatory retirement age for directors, the board raised it to seventy-three so he could stick around, then amended the provision again when he hit that limit.

Steere and McKinnell, former friends and colleagues, became mortal enemies. "You've got a guy who's absent from the office, and you've got a guy who can't let go," says former senior vice president Greg Vahle, who retired in 2008 after thirty-two years at Pfizer. "It's a disaster."

By 2005, McKinnell was already making plans for his succession. He promoted three executives to vice chairman, setting off what would become a long and increasingly bitter contest to choose the next CEO. Two names were no surprise: Karen Katen and David Shedlarz. Both were longtime Pfizer stars. Katen, then fifty-five, had run Pfizer's global pharmaceutical business since 2001. Shedlarz, fifty-six, was a numbers man and a keen strategist; he'd been CFO since 1995. The winner was to take over in 2008, when McKinnell turned sixty-five.

There was also a dark horse: Kindler. He had been at Pfizer, an insular organization whose leaders typically spent their entire careers at the company, for only three years. Unlike Katen and Shedlarz, he was a pharma neophyte.

But with Steere's help, Kindler outmaneuvered both rivals. He had plenty going for him. Kindler was outgoing, energetic, and a quick study. Aware that colleagues snickered at his fast-food background, he joked that he'd gone from causing America's cholesterol problem to trying to solve it.

But Kindler's less appealing traits had also begun to show, including his ultra-hands-on style. For example, with his promotion to vice chairman in 2005, he assumed oversight of Pfizer's communications department. After phone conversations about one impending press statement, Kindler suddenly appeared on the floor to join the discussion—then sat down at the keyboard and started typing, telling his startled media team: "I've got to do this myself."

That turned out to be a succinct statement of Kindler's management philosophy. "Jeff seemed to believe he was the only smart guy in the room," says Kent Bernard, a Pfizer lawyer for twenty-eight years.

The CEO horserace divided Pfizer into camps. Each contender huddled regularly with a circle of advisers, plotting strategy. Kindler conducted his campaign the way he did everything: methodically and aggressively. About one hundred pages of campaign strategy notes—everything from how he planned to woo various directors to his view that he should acknowledge his lack of operating experience—were later found in Kindler's files.

In an attempt to defuse growing tensions, McKinnell's chief of staff took the three contenders to Maria's Mont Blanc, a Manhattan restaurant, for a fondue dinner. There, they sat around a bubbling pot, making awkward small talk while stabbing their forks into chunks of meat and bread.

To curb campaigning, the board and McKinnell decreed that none of the contenders could have discussions about the succession with any Pfizer director. But Kindler and Steere blithely ignored the rule, meeting for dinner at Oceana, a seafood restaurant in Midtown. The secret summit came to light only after a company driver tattled. Katen and Shedlarz were livid. But the board brushed the matter aside.

By 2006, Steere had grown increasingly disenchanted with the drift of the company—and the steady decline in value of his 2 million Pfizer shares (and 4.4 million options). In his view, Katen's marketing operation had sputtered, and she seemed unwilling to fire anyone. Shedlarz, skeptical about pharma's prospects, was advocating a diversification strategy that Steere had never liked. Kindler's relative outsider status was starting to look like an advantage.

Steere threw his support to Kindler, the change candidate. He also began to wonder whether McKinnell's retirement, still two years off, was too far away.

This feeling crystallized at Pfizer's annual meeting that April in Lincoln, Neb. The central issue: Pfizer stock was down 46 percent since McKinnell had taken over—and the company had disclosed that the CEO would receive an $83 million pension. As shareholders walked in, they were buzzed by an airplane flying overhead, pulling a banner that read: "Give it back, Hank." Protesters picketed. Pfizer's CEO had become the latest public example of excessive executive compensation.

By July 2006, the Pfizer board was ready to give McKinnell the boot, though he didn't realize it. But in the days before it met to decide who would succeed him later that month, the board received an anonymous letter castigating Kindler from someone who identified himself as a senior Pfizer employee. A second anonymous letter, claiming to be from "responsible, long and loyal Legal Division employees," arrived on the very day of the board meeting. It complained of "micromanagement," "constant" internal reorganization, and a "chaotic" decision-making process. "A decision is made, then reconsidered and changed. Decisions, even minor . . . are picked apart and often directed to be undone. Then re-studied. Then the decision-making group expands. Paranoia results. Autonomy is sapped." These were some of the very complaints that would become the subject of board alarm in late 2010.

The board dismissed any warnings. "You almost always get these kinds of letters," says University of Illinois president emeritus Stanley Ikenberry, then Pfizer's lead director. "We did a careful analysis of that, and did not see any reason to abort the course." Kindler got the job, and McKinnell left the board seven months later. "It was a very tough choice," recalls Ikenberry. "It was the desire of the board to chart a new direction."

Kindler's selection came as a shock. One of his direct reports had a particularly dramatic reaction. George Evans was a low-key, respected lawyer who had worked at Pfizer twenty-six years. He'd been a candidate for the top legal job when Kindler was hired and was general counsel for the pharmaceutical division. On Saturday, Evans read of his boss's elevation in the *New York Times*. On Monday he resigned. "At the end of the day, you have to have some level of respect for the person you are working for," Evans tells *Fortune*. "Having watched Jeff in action over a number of years, I just couldn't work for a company that had him as its CEO."

## The Blockbuster Pipeline Dries Up

When Kindler took the helm as CEO in July 2006, the board wasn't fretting about a few disaffected lawyers. Pfizer faced much graver challenges. Yes, it was still generating billions in profits. But the company was bitterly divided, its business model imperiled, its stock in the dumps. Everyone wanted action.

Kindler, it seemed, might be just the man to reenergize Pfizer. He promised to "transform virtually every aspect of how we do business." He had laudable goals: to modernize the company and, most of all, improve its ability to develop profitable new drugs.

That was ever harder to do, in part because generic drugs now made up 63 percent of the U.S. prescription market. It would take a major advance to persuade consumers and insurers to pony up for an expensive brand-name drug. All of Big Pharma faced this problem, but Lipitor's heft meant it was especially acute at Pfizer.

Kindler had inherited McKinnell's two foremost new-drug hopes. But both would end in disaster. The biggest disappointment was torcetrapib, a medication aimed at boosting "good cholesterol." Pfizer had spent $800 million to develop the drug and another $90 million on a plant expansion to manufacture the pill.

In November 2006, Kindler declared that torcetrapib "will be one of the most important compounds of our generation." Two days later it was history. Ongoing trials revealed that patients taking the drug suffered a 60 percent increase in deaths compared with a control group. After being roused early on a Saturday morning with a call about the calamitous results, Kindler acted decisively, immediately canceling the drug.

The second big hope was Exubera, an inhalable delivery system for insulin. Pfizer had for years touted Exubera as a future blockbuster, spending $1.4 billion to buy out its partner, Sanofi-Aventis. But consumers rejected the cumbersome inhaler, which had an unfortunate resemblance to a bong, and 2007 sales were a measly $12 million. Kindler finally put the project out of its misery, accepting a $2.8 billion write-off.

These failures placed the new CEO in an even tighter vise. Suddenly desperate to shrink the company—which had just completed two giant mergers—Kindler announced plans for brutal layoffs that included axing 20 percent of the vaunted U.S. sales force.

Yet even as he was making massive cuts, Kindler was also pondering acquisitions, toying with alternative strategies. The first was a "string of pearls" approach—a handful of smaller purchases, each aimed at filling a single strategic gap, such as biotech. The second strategy was yet another megadeal—namely, buying Wyeth. That company had $23 billion in sales, strength in vaccines and biotech, a large over-the-counter products division, and several blockbusters of its own, including Prevnar, an antibacterial vaccine for children.

But after more than a year of on-and-off debate, Kindler just couldn't make up his mind. "Jeff was really afraid of making a mistake," says one person who worked on the deal. "Everything had to be analyzed and re-analyzed. You'd close a meeting and he'd say, 'Okay, here's what we're going to do.' You'd sharpen your swords. And the next morning, it'd be off." Finally, in January 2009, Kindler announced a $68 billion deal to buy Wyeth. Pfizer, the company he'd been working to shrink, was now going to be bigger than ever.

Kindler's attempts to figure out what to do about research were even more anguished. He was right that the old Pfizer model wasn't working. Bigger wasn't better when it came to producing new drugs. Studies by Bernard Munos, a retired strategist at Eli Lilly, show that both massive increases in research spending and corporate mergers have failed to increase R&D productivity. Between 2000 and 2008, according to Munos, Pfizer spent $60 billion on research and generated nine drugs that won FDA approval—an average cost of $6.7 billion per product. At that rate, Munos concluded, the company's internal pipeline simply couldn't sustain its profits.

Kindler thought the era of the big blockbuster was over. He came to recognize the need to streamline the company's internal research operation and supplement it by exploiting partnerships with biotech companies and academic centers.

But the process of overhauling R&D was a messy one. Kindler shuffled through three research chiefs during his four and a half years as CEO. He closed six R&D sites, then halted research in ten disease areas even while setting a new goal of launching four new internally developed drugs a year by 2010. He split the research operation in two—setting up a separate unit for biologic drugs (and launching an expensive new facility in San Francisco)—only to reverse the decision thirty months later after taking on Wyeth's big biotech operation.

Among the shuttered Pfizer sites was one at Ann Arbor, the birthplace of Lipitor. Says Bruce Roth, the scientist known as "the father of Lipitor," who lost his job when the Ann Arbor site closed and now works for Genentech: "When every eighteen months you throw the organization up in the air and are shifting therapeutic areas or closing sites, you have this period of turmoil when everybody in the organization is paralyzed. You need some continuity to do science."

Kindler was struggling for answers in a complex industry where his own experience was limited. In an effort to bring in fresh thinking, Kindler spun his leadership team like a top. Company veterans Shedlarz, chief medical officer Dr. Joseph Feczko, and CFO Alan Levin departed. Frank D'Amelio, Kindler's new CFO, arrived from Lucent. Sally Susman, his new communications chief, had worked at Estée Lauder. His new general counsel, Allen Waxman, resigned abruptly for "personal reasons" after just one year; replacing him was Amy Schulman, a high-profile litigator at DLA Piper.

For all of Kindler's lack of pharma experience, he didn't seem to trust Pfizer veterans that did have it. He often turned to outsiders, including experts and former colleagues, for counsel on business issues. And he employed swarms of consultants, working on initiatives to reorganize Pfizer into business units (instead of geographical regions), change reporting lines, and trim bureaucracy. As long-time staffers saw it, everything—and everyone— associated with the old Pfizer was under attack.

## Enter, Mary McLeod

Perhaps the only thing as destructive to Kindler as his inability to trust his colleagues was the one Pfizer executive in whom he did place his trust: Mary McLeod. The head of human resources under Kindler, McLeod would leverage her relationship to the CEO to become both his emissary and a power in her own right. Kindler's loyalty to her would undercut him at a crucial moment. McLeod, fifty-one when she joined Pfizer, had an unusual career trajectory. She had started as a dental hygienist before going back to school and pursuing a career in human resources. She had worked with GE Capital, Cisco, and Charles Schwab. She was a no-nonsense type who seemed to relish difficult environments.

Her tenure at Schwab had ended disastrously, though there's no sign Kindler knew that when he brought McLeod in. As Schwab's head of HR and chief of staff to CEO David Pottruck in the early 2000s, McLeod had proved toxic, according to six members of Pottruck's executive team. They say she isolated him from other points of view and went to extraordinary lengths to remove rivals. Meanwhile she criticized him behind his back and bragged that she had the CEO under her thumb.

After an internal investigation, Pottruck fired McLeod in 2004, he confirms. In an e-mail sent to McLeod the day of her termination, read aloud to *Fortune*, Pottruck wrote: "The issues are about the perceptions others have of you around character, integrity and divisiveness. . . . There is a perception that you do not tell the truth."

Nine days later, Pottruck himself was gone, forced out by the board over strategic differences. The McLeod situation, says one executive, "affected his credibility dramatically." Says Pottruck, who still sounds stung years later: "Why purposely undermine me and our entire team? Mary's behavior and motivations are hard to understand, even to this day." McLeod says *Fortune*'s account of her time at Schwab is "false" but declines to offer any specifics, noting that she is bound by a confidentiality agreement with the company.

McLeod managed to rebound from her firing and make her way back up the corporate ladder. By the time she became Pfizer's HR chief in early 2007, the company was preparing for wholesale layoffs. McLeod's job was critical.

Although she moved rapidly to shrink the bloated HR group, McLeod seemed uninterested in the details of how the streamlined department would actually function. Even top deputies say she was virtually unapproachable, preferring to communicate by e-mail and quarterly videocast.

McLeod's primary focus was the care and feeding of the CEO. She became Kindler's protector and surrogate, whispering in his ear, controlling access to him, delivering his blunt messages. Kindler admiringly called her "Neutron Mary," after his hero, Jack Welch. McLeod seemed to encourage his harshest nature, telling him, according to a person who was present, that one senior executive was "a B player," another too ambitious, someone else a "crybaby."

McLeod also publicly denigrated her employees, announcing at one town hall meeting in 2008 that two big positions would have to be filled from outside because no one inside Pfizer was capable of doing the job. Another episode, in which one of McLeod's lieutenants unsuccessfully attempted to make an outside consultant turn over so-called 360° reviews of Pfizer's top brass—which were intended only for the executives' personal development, not to assess performance—fed paranoia in the senior ranks. Says a former Pfizer HR exec: "There were a lot of comments to the effect of 'What is Jeff thinking?' Everybody questioned his judgment." (McLeod would not discuss any events at Pfizer, citing a confidentiality agreement with the drug company.)

Even as McLeod alienated staffers with her behavior, she was attracting notice for her perks. McLeod had negotiated a special deal, personally approved by Kindler and later ratified by the Pfizer board. First, she received a $125,000 cost-of-living adjustment to compensate for moving to the New York area from her home in Delaware (while getting another $238,000 to cover a loss on the sale of a second home she owned on Long Island).

But McLeod didn't move—at least not anytime soon. Instead, she began traveling back and forth regularly on a company helicopter from Delaware to Manhattan. Under Pfizer policy, top executives such as McLeod were entitled to business travel on company aircraft and twenty hours of free personal use each year of both jets and helicopters. But McLeod's employment agreement, signed by Kindler, was more generous. It allowed her to commute on a "weekend" basis between Delaware and Manhattan for a three-month period starting in April 2007. When McLeod failed to move to New York during that period, Kindler extended the deal through the end of 2007. Ultimately, even after buying a house in New Jersey, she continued using company helicopters for business travel into and out of Delaware until she left the company.

Apart from the terrible impression conveyed by an HR chief choppering to work in the midst of massive layoffs, someone soon realized that this arrangement posed another problem: McLeod's emoluments were so lavish they might make her one of the company's five most compensated employees, which would require Pfizer to disclose the details in its annual proxy statement. In early 2008 company governance chief Peggy Foran investigated the issue and tallied nearly $1 million in payments to McLeod, including those relating to her various houses, the helicopter use, and a large bonus to buy her out of a consulting partnership. Then there was McLeod's salary and regular bonus of $900,000 and restricted stock and options.

The prospect of revealing those details was disturbing for the board, which had been pilloried for McKinnell's severance package. Foran and Kindler were called before an executive session to discuss the aviation policy. The compensation committee reviewed McLeod's package in detail before ratifying Kindler's approval of exceptions to Pfizer's compensation policies. Ultimately Pfizer concluded that it did not need to disclose McLeod's pay.

Still, rumors of McLeod's perks spread around the company. Word also leaked to Pharmalot, an industry blog, and a cartoon circulated on the web showing a sinking Pfizer ocean liner and a helicopter hovering overhead. Asks the pilot: "Ms. McLeod, are you ready to head home?"

## A "Prosecutor Mindset"

Life at the top of Pfizer had become increasingly stressful. In September 2009 the company paid a $2.3 billion civil and criminal fine for the illegal marketing of the pain medication Bextra and other drugs. Kindler had been Pfizer's general counsel and chief compliance officer or CEO during the period when some of this behavior occurred. It was the largest criminal sanction in U.S. history, in part because companies that Pfizer acquired had committed previous violations. "These were viewed as individual instances until it dawned on everybody that this was more pervasive," says Feczko, Pfizer's chief medical officer until 2009. But few at the company held Kindler responsible for this particular problem.

Still, with Pfizer floundering, Kindler turned up the heat on his deputies even higher. He bombarded them with long Black-Berry messages filled with questions at all hours of the day and night. He regularly scheduled conference calls on weekends. He seemed oblivious to executive vacations. He expected immediate responses to his questions, making no distinctions between urgent matters and routine ones.

All that didn't just make life miserable for Kindler's team; it also clogged the company's decision-making process. Kindler was a voracious consumer of information—often a strength but increasingly a weakness. "Jeff heard something or read something," one former HR executive recounts, "and there would be a barrage of e-mails in the middle of the night." The next morning, staffers would have to divvy up the directives. "It was triage."

Kindler's friends defend his style. "He's very demanding" says Matthew Paull, a friend who worked with him at McDonald's and served as its CFO, "but he demands less from others than he would from himself." Paull and others say they view what some, in Pfizer's nonconfrontational culture, saw as anger instead as passion or intensity. (They say that same intensity helped Kindler play a key role in persuading Big Pharma to back President Obama's health care plan.)

Still, Kindler's tendency to grill people in public made other team members cringe. At a 2008 retreat he browbeat Ian Read, head of the pharma division, in front of colleagues. "He was just crushing onto Ian in a way that made everybody feel uncomfortable," recalls one witness. Kindler had an issue with the budget, the witness recalls, but his cross-examination seemed aimed at "breaking" Read. "That *can't* be true!" Kindler insisted. "You just said something different to me two minutes ago."

Bill Ringo, a retired Eli Lilly strategist whom Kindler added to his executive team in 2008, says Kindler's "prosecutor mindset" impaired his "ability to listen. . . . If he did wait for the answer, he didn't always hear it."

Kindler could be remorseful after letting loose—he'd send women flowers the day after bringing them to tears—but that didn't prevent the next explosion. Says an executive who worked closely with him: "Don't call me at five o'clock in the morning and rip my face off, then call me at eleven o'clock at night and tell me how much you love me."

Kindler even unloaded on a Pfizer board member at a party celebrating the retirement of another director in early 2010. The target that night was Bob Burt, retired CEO of a chemicals company called FMC. Burt had pressed Read on whether his division's cost targets were aggressive enough. Read mentioned it to Kindler.

In the middle of the retirement party, Kindler made a beeline for Burt. "If you don't think I'm challenging our people enough," Kindler shouted, according to one director present, "I'll quit and *you* can run the company." Witnesses were flabbergasted. Kindler later apologized. But everyone heard about the incident.

Steere had been Kindler's biggest fan. He'd helped him become CEO and regularly counseled him on everything from acquisitions to his weight. Steere had warned him early on that his temper was "a silent weakness." After the Burt incident, Steere took him aside again. "You can't do that," he told him. "Screaming at board members is not a good business plan."

## The Executive Leadership Team Falls Apart

Ultimately it wasn't just the board that would prove Kindler's undoing. It was that loyalty to the CEO among members of his "executive leadership team," or ELT, was growing tenuous. One catalyst for the disaffection was Mary McLeod. With the CEO's support, she had become feared inside Pfizer. Kindler seemed blind to her shortcomings, opening up a divide within the ELT. Says one executive: "There was Mary and Jeff, and then there was the rest of us."

Two of the eleven members of the ELT would play key roles in what a retired director would later call "just a tragedy." The first was general counsel Amy Schulman. She was a master networker and litigator who'd handled Pfizer cases at DLA Piper, where she'd been the top-paid lawyer. She actively courted media attention and had even been the subject of an eighteen-page Harvard Business School case study.

Shortly after hiring her in 2008, Kindler started to sour on Schulman. He criticized her knowledge of corporate law, her attentiveness to his requests, and her preparation for board presentations. He refused to award her a bonus for the Wyeth deal, saying she didn't deserve it. Schulman was deeply upset by this snub. (Kindler rewarded only CFO D'Amelio, Read—and McLeod, who got $600,000.)

Kindler also criticized Schulman for being overly ambitious and for her desire to gain operating experience in addition to her legal duties. Kindler, of course, had followed just such a path at McDonald's. But he wouldn't expand Schulman's portfolio. He told her she needed to learn to be a good general counsel first. (Counters one former director: "Amy is a great general counsel.")

The second principal in the drama was Ian Read. Born and raised in Scotland, the fifty-six-year-old Read was an accountant, not a revolutionary. A short, bald, bespectacled man, he'd begun his career at Pfizer in 1978 as an auditor, and had run the core pharmaceutical business since 2006. He had a reputation as a steady, astute operator.

That November, Read knew, he'd reach the "rule of ninety," where the combination of his age and years at Pfizer meant he could retire with a hefty pension. Read was tired of the Kindler treatment; his wife wanted him to quit. He began talking about leaving, even mentioning it to Kindler before the CEO went on a rare vacation to Vietnam in July.

Kindler returned from that trip with what a friend called "an epiphany." He needed to run the company in a less frenetic manner. He now realized Pfizer couldn't afford to lose Read. The Scotsman was in charge of businesses that accounted for 90 percent of Pfizer's sales, and the pharmaceutical division, after years of bloodletting, didn't have anyone ready to replace him. Kindler also needed to develop a succession plan.

Working closely with McLeod, he hatched a scheme to share power—but not too much. He would promote Read into a newly established "office of the chairman," but he wouldn't officially designate him as the company's no. 2. That role would be shared with CFO D'Amelio, who was closer to Kindler.

Kindler resolved to present this plan to the board at its September meeting in La Jolla, Calif. But first he and McLeod had much work to do with his two lieutenants, who were both on long-planned vacations. The executives began what seemed like an endless string of discussions about Kindler's complex vision, dubbed "Project Jett," as spelled out in PowerPoint decks with tables and charts. Both had issues about their proposed duties, insisting on more autonomy than Kindler offered. They were furious that these discussions, much of them involving arcane organizational matters, repeatedly intruded on their vacations. For his part, Kindler thought Read and D'Amelio were seeking to turn him into a figurehead. He fumed about their reluctance to interrupt their vacations to do the detailed work required for their promotions.

By the time of the September board meeting, one big issue remained unresolved. Kindler had agreed to name Read chief operating officer but wouldn't give him control over Pfizer's R&D, which Read wanted. The directors, recognizing Read's value, liked the plan. Some, including Steere, wanted Read named COO quickly. But Kindler insisted he couldn't make the move before February—there were far too many details to work out.

Read's growing unhappiness was no secret to members of Pfizer's board. After thirty-two years with the company, he knew all of them. Read's Florida vacation home was less than three miles from the residences of Steere and two other directors in Bonita Springs, where he sometimes played golf with the former Pfizer CEO.

There was another area of conflict in La Jolla: Kindler's new plan to slash the research budget. Even with the billions in cost cutting, Pfizer's research spending had continued to grow; it stood at a staggering $9.4 billion for 2010. So Kindler created a secret project to examine big R&D reductions, code-named

Project Copernicus. He ultimately proposed shrinking the budget to as little as $6.5 billion. This angered the board's two medical researchers, Nobel Prize–winner Dr. Michael Brown and Dr. Dennis Ausiello, who insisted it was too much. They accused Kindler of mortgaging Pfizer's future for short-term profits. Brown even stormed out of the La Jolla meeting where Kindler was discussing the cuts.

As this was happening, Schulman began letting her own feelings about Kindler be known. She told colleagues (with perhaps a touch of melodrama) that she felt like "a battered housewife." Weighing the option of leaving Pfizer, Schulman secretly interviewed for the general counsel's job at PepsiCo.

Then, on November 9, something happened that amplified the growing sense of disarray at Pfizer, setting in motion the events that would lead to Kindler's departure: Mary McLeod sent out an e-mail. The HR director had recently received the abysmal results of a survey of her direct subordinates. More than a third of them rated her performance as a one or two out of five in key areas.

She reacted by writing a strange, meandering e-mail to her top staff. "I just wanted to say how sad and embarrassed I am by these results," McLeod began. "I'm sad for all of you that you work in an environment that clearly is making you so unhappy." One option she proposed: "I can leave the company and/or this particular job. . . . This will allow Jeff to hire someone that is more in sync with all of you and a better leader for you." She added: ". . . if any one of you spent 48 hours in my job, you would understand."

On November 14, someone forwarded McLeod's e-mail to both Kindler and the Pfizer board, with a detailed (but unsigned) cover note. While McLeod's e-mail was itself "troubling," the author wrote, the state of the Pfizer HR department should be "cause for serious concern. . . . The real issue is Mary's leadership. She has very little interest in the HR function itself, offers little guidance and focuses mainly on the CEO and his needs." The writer urged a thorough investigation, conducted by someone independent because McLeod's deputies feared retaliation.

The letter was discussed at a board call on November 16. Given the retaliation assertion, Schulman wanted to name an independent outside investigator. Kindler defended McLeod, praising her for connecting HR to the company's businesses instead of focusing on "touchy-feely" stuff. But he went along with Schulman's recommendation.

The two-week investigation was conducted by Bart Friedman, an attorney with Cahill Gordon & Reindel who specializes in corporate governance work. After interviewing all of McLeod's direct reports, Friedman found nothing illegal. He did, however, conclude that HR was thoroughly dysfunctional and riven by inept management. In his view, this was a simple case of incompetence.

On Wednesday, December 1, Pfizer's executive team gathered for a day of meetings with the CEO. Mary McLeod was missing. After hearing Friedman's report, Kindler had finally parted ways with his controversial HR chief—though not without a generous severance package.

Now it was Kindler whose job was threatened.

### The Ouster

The problems with Pfizer's HR chief had sharpened board concern about its CEO. Why had Kindler defended McLeod? How could he be so blind to all the trouble that she was causing? Just as had happened at Schwab, McLeod's issues had morphed into a crisis for her boss.

Now Pfizer's board shifted into action. Around Thanksgiving, Steere and Connie Horner, the lead outside director, began speaking to a few of Kindler's deputies to assess the situation. By this point, Schulman had a formal job offer from PepsiCo. Read also had let it be known that he was planning to retire—COO job or no COO job.

All this created a nightmare scenario for the board. Were Read and Schulman threatening to leave so that the directors would oust Kindler? The board didn't think so. But could it really afford to find out? Investors were already howling; Pfizer's stock had dropped 36 percent since Kindler had taken over. Imagine the uproar if both Read and Schulman suddenly left.

Over Thanksgiving weekend, Horner called the other board members. "She told me that she and one or two other directors had heard very disturbing things about Jeff and we talked about what we should do about it," says one former director.

That Sunday, Horner contacted Wachtell Lipton lawyer Marty Lipton, the go-to man for corporate boards in a giant mess. Lipton agreed to advise them, and the entire board convened in secret in his office the following Wednesday, December 1. Half the directors were there in person; half participated by phone. Horner reported what she knew. She pointed out that, in addition to Read and Schulman, a third senior executive, communications chief Sally Susman, was deeply frustrated and might also leave Pfizer.

One former board member summed up the issue this way: "Do we have three brave souls who have risked their lives to come forward, or do we have three disgruntled employees?"

To many of the directors, the stories about Kindler's management style rang true. They remembered how he'd lost it with Burt at the board retirement party. And there were reports that other top executives were unhappy. Even D'Amelio, the even-keeled CFO, seemed to think Jeff's behavior was a big problem. Or did he? Another director had spoken to him, too, and provided a conflicting account, leading to a debate about the accuracy of the incoming reports.

Lipton advised them that they needed to make absolutely sure they weren't responding to one or two executives. The board resolved to survey all eleven members of Kindler's management.

Kindler's ELT was in a horribly awkward situation. On Wednesday, they had spent the day meeting with their boss about the business. Mary McLeod had disappeared. Hours later, they were getting calls from the board's lead director, swearing them to secrecy, questioning them about incidents involving Kindler.

Kindler had caught wind of what was up. He'd begun making his own calls, desperately trying to assess his support. Steere, his longtime ally, didn't return his call. D'Amelio anguished about being in the middle of it all. He refused his boss's request that he tell the board he would resign if Kindler were fired, according to a person who spoke to D'Amelio. (A source close to Kindler denies this.)

When Horner had completed her inquiries, she passed on her conclusion: No one was standing 100 percent behind Kindler. All confirmed the situation was untenable. A few of the eleven executives made it explicitly clear that they believed Jeff needed to go. The directors agreed to summon Kindler down to the airport conference room in Florida for a private reckoning.

At that meeting, Kindler talked and talked, blaming others for the entire imbroglio. That evening, after he returned home to Westport, Conn., Kindler arranged for Judd Burstein, a close friend and trial lawyer, to represent him. Kindler briefly considered whether to fight on.

The next morning, Sunday, December 5, 2010, Kindler and Pfizer quickly agreed on a generous exit package. He was getting $16 million in cash and stock, another $6.9 million in retirement benefits, and various other forms of stock compensation. Burstein made one final request: Could Kindler stay on till the end of the year? The directors said no.

At noon, Pfizer's board convened in Lipton's office to replace the company's CEO for the second time in five years. "Basically, everybody was quite sympathetic to Jeff," says one participant. "They just felt he was no longer capable of leading the company."

The Kindler era at Pfizer had ended the way it had begun—with turmoil, backstage maneuvering, and trauma. The latest CEO was gone, leaving Pfizer once again in search of a cure.

**London Review of Books**

The review-essay is one of the hardest forms of journalism, and Daniel Soar provides a master class in his take on Google. The trick is to downplay the books under review, and instead to synthesize their wisdom, adding your own insight at the same time, in something much more compact and powerful. Once you've read Soar's explanation of how everything that Google does is driven by data gathering, you'll never think about the company quite the same way again.

Daniel Soar

# 26. It Knows

This spring, the billionaire Eric Schmidt announced that there were only four really significant technology companies: Apple, Amazon, Facebook, and Google, the company he had until recently been running. People believed him. What distinguished his new "gang of four" from the generation it had superseded—companies like Intel, Microsoft, Dell, and Cisco, which mostly exist to sell gizmos and gadgets and innumerable hours of expensive support services to corporate clients—was that the newcomers sold their products and services to ordinary people. Since there are more ordinary people in the world than there are businesses, and since there's nothing that ordinary people don't want or need, or can't be persuaded they want or need when it flashes up alluringly on their screens, the money to be made from them is virtually limitless. Together, Schmidt's four companies are worth more than half a trillion dollars. The technology sector isn't as big as, say, oil, but it's growing, as more and more traditional industries—advertising, travel, real estate, used cars, new cars, porn, television, film, music, publishing, news—are subsumed into the digital economy. Schmidt, who as the ex-CEO of a multi-billion-dollar corporation had learned to take the long view, warned that not all four of his disruptive gang could survive. So—as they all converge from their various beginnings to compete in the same area, the place usually referred to as "the cloud," a place where everything that matters is online—the question is: who will be the first to blink?

If the company that falters is Google, it won't be because it didn't see the future coming. Of Schmidt's four technology juggernauts, Google has always been the most ambitious, and the most committed to getting everything possible onto the internet, its mission being "to organize the world's information and make it universally accessible and useful." Its ubiquitous search box has changed the way information can be got at to such an extent that ten years after most people first learned of its existence you wouldn't think of trying to find out anything without typing it into Google first. Searching on Google is automatic, a reflex, just part of what we do. But an insufficiently thought-about fact is that in order to organize the world's information Google first has to get hold of the stuff. And in the long run "the world's information" means much more than anyone would ever have imagined it could. It means, of course, the totality of the information contained on the World Wide Web, or the contents of more than a trillion webpages (it was a trillion at the last count, in 2008; now, such a number would be meaningless). But that much goes without saying, since indexing and ranking webpages is where Google began when it got going as a research project at Stanford in 1996, just five years after the Web itself was invented. It means—or would mean, if lawyers let Google have its way—the complete contents of every one of the more than 33 million books in the Library of Congress or, if you include slightly varying editions and pamphlets and other ephemera, the contents of the approximately 129,864,880 books published in every recorded language since printing was invented. It means every video uploaded to the public Internet, a quantity—if you take the Google-owned YouTube alone—that is increasing at the rate of nearly an hour of video every second.

It means the location of businesses, religious institutions, schools, libraries, community centers and hospitals worldwide—

a global Yellow Pages. It means the inventories of shops, the archives of newspapers, the minute by minute performance of the stock market. It means, or will mean, if Google keeps going, the exact look of every street corner and roadside on the planet, photographed in high resolution and kept as up to date as possible: the logic, if not yet the practice, of Google Street View, means that city streets should be under ever more regular photographic surveillance, since the fresher and more complete the imagery the more useful people will find it, and the more they will therefore use it. If it doesn't already have a piece of data, you can be sure that Google is pursuing a way of getting it, of gathering and sorting every kind of public information there is.

But all this is just the stuff that Google makes publicly searchable, or "universally accessible." It's only a small fraction of the information it actually possesses. I know that Google knows, because I've looked it up, that on 30 April 2011 at 4:33 P.M. I was at Willesden Junction station, traveling west. It knows where I was, as it knows where I am now, because like many millions of others I have an Android-powered smartphone with Google's location service turned on. If you use the full range of its products, Google knows the identity of everyone you communicate with by e-mail, instant messaging, and phone, with a master list—accessible only by you, and by Google—of the people you contact most. If you use its products, Google knows the content of your e-mails and voicemail messages (a feature of Google Voice is that it transcribes messages and e-mails them to you, storing the text on Google servers indefinitely). If you find Google products compelling—and their promise of access-anywhere, conflagration- and laptop-theft-proof document creation makes them quite compelling—Google knows the content of every document you write or spreadsheet you fiddle or presentation you construct. If as many Google-enabled robotic devices get installed as Google hopes, Google may soon know the contents of your fridge, your heart rate when you're exercising, the weather outside your front door, the pattern of electricity use in your home.

Google knows or has sought to know, and may increasingly seek to know, your credit card numbers, your purchasing history, your date of birth, your medical history, your reading habits, your taste in music, your interest or otherwise (thanks to your searching habits) in the First Intifada or the career of Audrey Hepburn or flights to Mexico or interest-free loans, or whatever you idly speculate about at 3:45 on a Wednesday afternoon. Here's something: if you have an Android phone, Google can guess your home address, since that's where your phone tends to be at night. I don't mean that in theory some rogue Google employee could hack into your phone to find out where you sleep; I mean that Google, as a system, explicitly deduces where you live and openly logs it as "home address" in its location service, to put beside the "work address" where you spend the majority of your daytime hours.

Some people find all this frightening. Since Google still makes more than 95 percent of its money through selling advertising—that's $30 billion a year, or about twice the annual global revenue of the entire recorded music industry—the fear is that all the information about us it has hoovered up is used to create scarily exact user profiles which it then offers to advertisers, as the most complete picture of billions of individuals it's currently possible to build. The fear seems be based on the assumption that if Google is gathering all this information then it must be doing so in order to sell it: it is a profit-making company, after all. "We are not Google's customers," Siva Vaidhyanathan writes in *The Googlisation of Everything*. "We are its product. We—our fancies, fetishes, predilections and preferences—are what Google sells to advertisers." Vaidhyanathan, who likes alliteration but isn't so big on facts, doesn't explain what he means by "sells" (or whether "to sell a fancy" could mean anything at all), but if he's implying that Google makes the information it has about us available to advertisers then he's wrong. It isn't possible, using Google's tools, to target an ad to thirty-two-year-old single heterosexual men living in London who work at Goldman Sachs and like skiing, especially at Courchevel. You can do exactly that using Facebook, but the options Google gives advertisers are, by comparison, limited: the closest it gets is to allow them to target display ads to people who may be interested in the category of "skiing and snowboarding"—and advertisers were always able to do that anyway by buying space in *Ski & Snowboard* magazine. The rest of the time, Google decides the placement of ads itself, using its proprietary algorithms to display them wherever it knows they will get the most clicks. The advertisers are left out of the loop.

So why doesn't Google market its personal information, when it has so much of it? One answer might be that to do so would be "evil." "Don't be evil" is Google's geeky corporate motto—a hostage to fortune if ever there was one, though it usually seems to mean "don't do anything to upset the users." We'd be upset—we might even choose to use a competing service—if Google released information about us that we didn't know it had, or that we didn't even know ourselves, such as the likelihood, revealed by our searches, that we might be suffering from a particular illness. Facebook gets away with being evil—or does it?—because the personal information it makes available for targeting is information that users have voluntarily surrendered by filling in their profiles: birthday, relationship status, hometown, workplace; every time they click on a "Like" button on the Web they are deemed to have declared an interest that can be used for targeting. But another answer might be that the information Google has is too valuable to give away, that it has another reason for collecting every piece of data it possibly can, that the stuff it's amassing is worth more than just money.

The reason is that Google is learning. The more data it gathers, the more it knows, the better it gets at what it does. Of course, the better it gets at what it does the more money it makes, and the more money it makes the more data it gathers and the better it gets at what it does—an example of the kind of win-win feedback loop Google specializes in—but what's surprising is that there is no obvious end to the process. Thanks to what it has learned so far, Google is no longer the merely impressive search engine it was a decade ago. Back then, it was assumed that the key to its success in delivering its (as it once seemed) uncannily accurate results was its first and best-known invention, Page-Rank, the algorithm that assigns to every page on the Web a value indicating how authoritative it is, based on the number and the authoritativeness of the pages linking to it. Its inventor was Larry Page (hence, cunningly, PageRank), one of Google's founders and now once more its CEO; and his model, as Steven Levy explains in *In the Plex*, was the system of scholarly citation, by which journal articles and books are considered important if they are referred to by other important journal articles and books. Levy is big on origins. Not everyone will think much of the suggestion that Page and Sergey Brin, his cofounder, got where they are today because they were both "Montessori kids" who were taught from an early age to believe anything was possible. But he may be on to something when he says that Page's academic family background—his father taught at Michigan State, and he hung out at Stanford as a child—meant that when he faced the problem of how to rank importance he recognized that the economy of the Web was very similar to the economy of academia. Those at the bottom of the ladder (the junior academics, the lowly website owners) seek recognition from those above them (the celebrated professors, the global Internet portals) and use citations in the hope that some of the gold dust will rub off on them if they get cited back. Rankings based on citations aren't necessarily a measure of excellence—if they were, we wouldn't hear so much about Steven Pinker—but they do reflect where humans have decided that authority lies.

PageRank, however, has always been just one of the factors determining how Google's search results are ordered. In 2007, Google told the *New York Times* that it was now using more than 200 signals in its ranking algorithm, and the number must now be higher. What every one of those signals is and how they are weighted is Google's most precious trade secret, but the most useful signal of all is the least predictable: the behavior of the person who types their query into the search box. A click on the third result counts as a vote that it ought to come higher. A "long click"—when you select one of the results and don't come back—is a stronger vote. To test a new version of its algorithm, Google releases it to a small subset of its users and measures its effectiveness through the pattern of their clicks: more happy surfers and it's just got cleverer. We teach it while we think it's teaching us. Levy tells the story of a new recruit with a long managerial background who asked Google's senior vice president of engineering, Alan Eustace, what systems Google had in place to improve its products. "He expected to hear about quality assurance teams and focus groups"—the sort of set-up he was used to. "Instead Eustace explained that Google's brain was like a baby's, an omnivorous sponge that was always getting smarter from the information it soaked up." Like a baby, Google uses what it hears to learn about the workings of human language. The large number of people who search for "pictures of dogs" and also "pictures of puppies" tells Google that "puppy" and "dog" mean similar things, yet it also knows that people searching for "hot dogs" get cross if they're given instructions for "boiling puppies." If Google misunderstands you and delivers the wrong results, the fact that you'll go back and rephrase your query, explaining what you mean, will help it get it right next time. Every search for information is itself a piece of information Google can learn from.

By 2007, Google knew enough about the structure of queries to be able to release a U.S.-only directory inquiry service called GOOG-411. You dialed 1-800-4664-411 and spoke your question to the robot operator, which parsed it and spoke you back the top eight results, while offering to connect your call. It was free, nifty, and widely used, especially because—unprecedentedly for a company that had never spent much on marketing—Google chose to promote it on billboards across California and New York State. People thought it was weird that Google was paying to advertise a product it couldn't possibly make money from, but by then Google had become known for doing weird and pleasing things. In 2004, it launched Gmail with what was for the time an insanely large quota of free storage—1GB, five hundred times more than its competitors. But in that case it was making money from the ads that appeared alongside your e-mails. What was it getting with GOOG-411? It soon became clear that what it was getting were demands for pizza spoken in every accent in the continental United States, along with questions about plumbers in Detroit and countless variations on the pronunciations of "Schenectady," "Okefenokee," and "Boca Raton." GOOG-411, a Google researcher later wrote, was a phoneme-gathering operation, a way of improving voice recognition technology through massive data collection.

Three years later, the service was dropped, but by then Google had launched its Android operating system and had released into the wild an improved search-by-voice service that didn't require a phone call. You tapped the little microphone icon on your phone's screen—it was later extended to Blackberries and iPhones—and your speech was transmitted via the mobile Internet to Google servers, where it was interpreted using the advanced techniques the GOOG-411 exercise had enabled. The baby had learned to talk. Now that Android phones are being activated at a rate of more than half a million a day, Google suddenly has a vast and growing repository of spoken words, in every language on earth, and a much more powerful learning machine. If your phone mistranscribes what you say, you correct it by typing it in, and Google's algorithms—once again—are taught how to get better still. It's a frustratingly faultless learning loop. It's easy to assume that the end result of this increasing perfection will be a Google machine in the cloud that can correctly transcribe all speech in all languages from Afrikaans to Xhosa, however badly you mumble: useful when you're driving or have your hands full. But that's to think small.

Before Google bought YouTube in 2006 for $1.65 billion, it had a fledgling video service of its own, predictably called Google Video, that in its initial incarnation offered the—it seemed—brilliant feature of answering a typed phrase with a video clip in which those words were spoken. The promise was that, for example, you'd be able to search for the phrase "in my beginning is my end" and see T. S. Eliot, on film, reciting from the *Four Quartets*. But no such luck. Google Video's search worked by a kind of trickery: it used the hidden subtitles that broadcasters provide for the hard of hearing, which Google had generally paid to use, and searched against the text. The service is just one of the many experiments that Google over the years has killed, but a presumably large reason for its death was that although it appeared to work it was really very limited. Not everything is tailored for the deaf, and subtitles are often wrong. If, however, Google is able to deploy its newly capable voice recognition system to transcribe the spoken words in the two days' worth of video uploaded to YouTube every minute, there would be an explosion in the amount of searchable material. Since there's no reason Google can't do it, it will.

A thought experiment: if Google launched satellites into orbit it could record all terrestrial broadcasts and transcribe those too. That may sound exorbitant, but it's not obviously crazier than some of the ideas that Google's founders have dreamed up and found a way of implementing: the idea of photographing all the world's streets, of scanning all the world's books, of building cars that drive themselves. It's the sort of thing that crosses Google's mind. An April Fool's joke a few years ago advertised job opportunities at Google's research center on the Moon, where listening equipment would provide an "ear on the chatter of the universe, the vast web of electromagnetic pulses that may contain signals from intelligent life forms in other galaxies, as well as a complete record of every radio or television signal broadcast from our own planet." Google takes its April Fool's jokes very seriously, as the marketing man who wrote some of them, Douglas Edwards, explains in *I'm Feeling Lucky: The Confessions of Google Employee Number 59*: big arguments broke out when the founders felt that proposed jokes weren't true to Google's sense of its mission. The jokes—like the friendly logo, and the homepage doodles—are carefully designed to hint at the scale of Google's ambition without scaring the world to death.

There seem to be no large Google initiatives—however seemingly tangential to the company's core competency, and unhelpful to its bottom line—that don't bring as a side benefit, or as the main benefit, an enormous amount of data to Google. They also threaten to put whole industries out of business by being free. In 2009, Google updated its Maps application for Android to include free turn-by-turn navigation: on-screen and spoken directions to whatever destination you choose. The cost to Google was negligible, and the damage to existing businesses was enormous: companies like Garmin and TomTom had been getting large margins on hundred-pound satnav hardware, and then charging for monthly subscriptions. Not any more. Naturally, those threatened don't always give up without a fight. That a more esoteric battle has been taking place over Android was revealed earlier this year when a little company called Skyhook took Google to court for alleged unfair business practices. Skyhook makes its money by licensing location-detection technology to hardware manufacturers, and—in an impressive coup—had succeeded in persuading Motorola, among others, that its system was better than Google's. Motorola agreed to pay to use Skyhook's service on its Android phones in preference to Google's built-in free one. When Google executives found out what had happened—as subpoenaed e-mails between them showed—they were incredulous, and alarmed:

This feels like a disaster :(

I think this is worth a postmortem and maybe a code yellow or something like that to really focus here.

What they were alarmed about was not that their system might not be the best—they didn't quite believe that—but that if manufacturers started using a competitor's product they would no longer be getting the data they needed to improve their own. In other words, Google faced the unfamiliar problem of the negative feedback loop: the fewer people that used its product, the less information it would have and the worse the product would get. So the executives swung into action and reminded Motorola of various contractual obligations that went with the Android license. Google got to keep its data. Coincidentally, last month, it announced its plan to buy Motorola Mobility—along with 19,000 employees, nearly doubling Google's workforce—for $12.5 billion.

Google isn't invincible. Eric Schmidt likes to say that its competitors are only one click away: if you don't like Google's search results, or its business practices, you can always use Bing. But Google is currently facing antitrust scrutiny by Senate subcommittees, and the bigger it gets the less answerable the regulatory threat will become. Google is getting cleverer precisely because it is so big. If it's cut down to size then what will happen to everything it knows? That's the conundrum. It's clearly wrong for all the information in all the world's books to be in the sole possession of a single company. It's clearly not ideal that only one company in the world can, with increasing accuracy, translate text between 506 different pairs of languages. On the other hand, if Google doesn't do these things, who will?

*Financial Times*

When Neflix CEO Reed Hastings announced that he was splitting his company in two, with the popular DVD-by-mail service being rebranded as Qwikster, John Gapper lost no time in nailing exactly where he had gone wrong. Hastings had clearly spent too much time reading too many business books and had lost sight of what his customers wanted. And indeed, only a couple of weeks later, Hastings ate humble pie and scrapped the Qwikster plan—proving that Gapper and other critics were right on the money.

John Gapper

# 27. Innovators Don't Ignore Customers

According to the business textbooks, Reed Hastings is a visionary and innovator. But thousands of his customers, and many of his investors, think the chief executive of Netflix is an idiot.

The DVD rental and online film service is "going to be held up as a gold standard of how to avoid being disrupted." Clayton Christensen, the Harvard Business School professor and author of *The Innovator's Dilemma*, tweeted this week. As he opined, Netflix shares were dropping rapidly and 25,000 of its customers were posting irate protests at having their service disrupted.

I'm with them. Mr. Hastings is the latest chief executive to blow up his company in response to changes sweeping the media and technology industries—Léo Apotheker was just as explosive at Hewlett-Packard last month. But no matter how solid the logic and brave the strategy, it has to carry people with it.

In practice, there was a vast gulf between what customers wanted—largely what they had already—and Mr. Hastings' vision of his company's future. He rebranded its declining DVD rental operation Qwikster (yes, seriously), confined the Netflix name to its high-growth but immature online streaming service, and imposed a 60 percent price increase on subscribers to both.

He did not help matters with his online apology—"I messed up. I owe everyone an explanation"—in which he claimed that the problem was that Netflix "lacked respect and humility" in how it had explained the price rise, rather than the rise itself. He antagonized his audience further with the rebranding.

The fall in the shares—13 percent on Monday and Tuesday and by more than half in two months—does not matter so much. They had risen sixfold in three years on hopes that Netflix was seamlessly adapting to the digital era, and even if Mr. Hastings had not clumsily made that error clear, they would have adjusted eventually. But the customer revolt has long-term consequences.

Mr. Hastings is not alone in struggling with upheaval. Many technology and media companies—from Microsoft to Time Warner and News Corp—now own businesses that produce plenty of cash but grow slowly, if at all, alongside promising digital operations.

Such divergence of activities under one roof is nothing new. The Boston Consulting Group came up with its famous matrix dividing businesses into cash cows, question marks, stars, and dogs (now politely renamed "pets") in 1968. On that matrix, Netflix has a cash cow in Qwikster and a star with trailing question marks in streaming.

The traditional prescription was for businesses to reinvest the proceeds of cash cows into stars, which is what Netflix did until now. It launched a free streaming service in 2007 and later bundled it with its monthly DVD subscriptions for $2 extra a month. In July, however, it abruptly abandoned bundling and forced those who wanted both services to pay twice.

Mr. Hastings was influenced by Prof. Christensen's work, which has rightly become a set text in Silicon Valley. As Prof. Christensen noted in 1996, well-managed companies can fall prey to new technologies that are "simpler, cheaper and more convenient" than their own.

He recommended that those faced with the dilemma of whether to stick with incremental improvement of products or act radically by cannibalizing their business before someone else did should choose the latter. Companies often lost their way "precisely because they listened to their [existing] customers".

Mr. Hastings added this week: "Most companies that are great at something—like AOL dial-up or Borders book stores—do not become great at new things people want (streaming for us) because they are afraid to hurt their initial business. . . . Companies rarely die from moving too fast and they frequently die from moving too slowly."

Leaving aside the fallacy in the last sentence (many companies die from making things that too few people yet want; that's how markets work) his missive felt squarely aimed at the wrong audience—business strategists, professors, and managers, rather than customers.

Customers don't care about corporate structures, cash flows, technologies, and growth ratings. They care about whether the familiar envelope containing a DVD arrives on time and whether they can stream a good selection of films at a decent price without their television screens freezing. They were not holding Netflix back from streaming—they were adopting it.

Netflix has been extremely good at providing its service, which is why it flourished while competitors fell away. Its disruption of the Blockbuster business model of charging high fees for late returns of DVDs to stores is one of the biggest reasons why that company filed for bankruptcy last year.

Now Mr. Hastings faces new challenges—the rising costs of leasing films; new competition from Apple, Amazon, and others; and a fading DVD business which Netflix last year predicted would keep growing until 2013. His response has been to leap into the chasm.

But Netflix subscribers liked both DVDs and streaming and saw them as complementary—they wanted both the traditional product and the disruptive one. Even if it made sense to split the two in financial reports and even to separate them into business divisions, there was no need to force Netflix customers to snap to the organization chart.

From a business strategy perspective, I admire Mr. Hastings' quest to revolutionize his company. From a customer's perspective, however, I canceled my Netflix subscription on Tuesday. I suspect the second matters more.

**The New Yorker**

With its LACK tables and KARLSTAD chairs, Ikea has quietly insinuated its "global functional minimalist aesthetic" into middle-class homes from Beijing to Boston. We try to resist, but it's hard! In this wry and thoughtful piece, Lauren Collin recounts how in 1943 young Igvar Kamprad conceived the retailer at his uncle's kitchen table in remote Älmhult, Sweden, and proceeded to turn it into a global phenomenon, "a sort of borderless state, with seats of power, redoubts of conservatism, second cities, imperial outposts, creative hubs, and administrative backwaters." If you think shopping there is disorienting, read what it's like to work in this peculiar, utopian corporate culture.

Lauren Collins

# 28. House Perfect

On a recent Sunday, I woke up around 8 A.M. I had slept on a SULTANA HAGAVIK mattress. I smoothed the DVALA fitted sheet and tucked the HENNY CIRKEL quilt beneath four pillows sheathed in matching polka-dot cases. In the kitchen, some lettuce clung to the meniscus of a BLANDA BLANK salad bowl. Rouged RÄTTVIK wineglasses and dirty DRAGON forks waited to be washed. In the living room, I sat down on the KIVIK sofa. Because it is a few years old, its lines are leaner than those of current models, which have been expanded to accommodate the modern habit of perching a laptop on the armrest.

KIVIK—along with a profusion of things I use every day—is made by IKEA, the Swedish home-furnishings company. IKEA has three hundred and twenty-six stores in thirty-eight countries. In the fiscal year 2010, it sold $23.1 billion worth of goods, a 7.7 percent increase over the year before. IKEA calls itself the Life Improvement Store. The invisible designer of domestic life, it not only reflects but also molds, in its ubiquity, our routines and our attitudes. When IKEA stopped selling incandescent light bulbs last year, 626 million people became environmentalists.

The prevalence of IKEA in my apartment is more the result of circumstance than of desire or discernment. Since graduating from college nine years ago, I have moved eight times, propelled by the usual vicissitudes of money, romance, and work. My first encounter with IKEA was in the freshman-year dormitory, where I marveled at the profligacy of classmates who, that September, and each one thereafter, ordered a new couch from IKEA—and paid the ninety-nine-dollar delivery fee! (My roommates and I settled for a hand-me-down, which we covered with a sleeping bag and doused in Febreze.) By the time I was a senior, I had my own room and had acquired my first piece of IKEA furniture, an only slightly shopworn navy-blue love seat. A shared apartment in Manhattan followed. It suffered from a plight that IKEA has acknowledged in an internal report titled "Life in Rental Accommodation": the tragedy of the common room is that it often is a dump. There were several apartments in the West Village, and one, farther south, in which my parents and I spent a long night trying to assemble an IKEA bookshelf with the guidance of only a stick man with a mute smirk. IKEA omits words from instruction booklets because words make instruction booklets thicker, which makes them more expensive. The screws strip easily. Amy Poehler once said that IKEA is Swedish for "argument." In Tribeca, I pridefully refused IKEA, like a child announcing that she no longer plays with dolls. IKEA can also be Swedish for feeling like you're never going to grow up.

The apartment I live in now is a rental in west London. Like many rentals here, it comes furnished—which means that instead of your having to go to IKEA and get the stuff yourself, the landlord goes to IKEA and gets it for you. IKEA offers more than 9,000 products, divided into four "style groups": Traditional, Scandinavian, Modern, and Popular. (These are subdivided into such categories as Continental Dark, Continental Light, Contemporary, and Ethnic.) I moved into the London apartment in January. The person I live with had added to the mostly Modern infrastructure a few personal touches, for an effect one might call Itinerant Indifferent: a picture frame with no picture, various gifts from his mother, no knife that could penetrate meat. I put the picture frame in a drawer. The knives I cared enough about to buy a decent set from a department store. In a paper called "On the IKEAnization of France," a sociologist named Tod Hartman suggests that IKEA resolves the conundrum posed by Georges Perec in his 1965 novel, *Les Choses*, about a young couple consumed with unhappiness at the discrepancy between the dismal home they have and the tasteful one they think they deserve. "Question your teaspoons," Perec later wrote.

Eventually, we drove to the IKEA store in Wembley, where we picked out some throw pillows and a phalaenopsis orchid. We liked the SNÄRTIG bud vase, the surface of which is dotted with tiny bubbles, like eyelet lace. It cost fifty-nine pence, which makes it what IKEA calls a "breathtaking item"—so affordable that you can't afford not to buy it. We took two. IKEA offers the serendipity of the yard sale without the mothballs.

Bill Moggridge, the director of the Cooper-Hewitt, National Design Museum, in New York, calls IKEA's aesthetic "global functional minimalism." He said, "It's modernist, and it's very neutral in order to avoid local preferences, to get the economies of scale they need in order to keep the prices good." IKEA products are intended to work as well in Riyadh as they do in Reykjavík. (Pigs and skeletons, for example, are banned motifs.) Last year, IKEA's business in China, where it has eight stores, grew by 20 percent. IKEA sells a few products (water fountains, chopsticks, mosquito nets) tailored to a Chinese clientele, but 95 percent of the product range is standard. It is said that one in ten Europeans is conceived in an IKEA bed.

People have cared intensely about the decoration of their houses since cavemen began painting on walls. We are attached to our belongings because they are vessels for our memories and for our aspirations. Freud wrote to Martha, his future wife, during their engagement:

> Tables and chairs, beds, mirrors, a clock to remind the happy
> couple of the passage of time, an armchair for an hour's pleas-
> ant daydreaming, carpets to help the housewife keep the
> floors clean, linen tied with pretty ribbons in the cupboard
> and dresses of the latest fashion and hats with artificial flow-
> ers, pictures on the wall, glasses for everyday and others for
> wine and festive occasions. . . . Are we to hang our hearts on
> such little things? Yes, and without hesitation.

Our curio cabinets and chesterfield sofas are the backdrops
of domesticity, forming the unchanging indoor landscape—
mahogany mountains, meadows of chintz—against which we go
about life. Choosing a piece of furniture was once a serious decision, because of the expectation that it was permanent. It is said
that Americans keep sofas longer than they keep cars and change
dining-room tables about as often as they trade spouses. IKEA
has made interiors ephemeral. Its furniture is placeholder furniture, the prelude to an always imminent upgrade. It works until
it breaks, or until its owners break up. It carries no traces. (Jonathan Coulton's song "IKEA": "Just some oak and some pine and
a handful of Norsemen / Selling furniture for college kids and
divorced men.") In David Fincher's 1999 movie *Fight Club*, the
character played by Edward Norton flips through an IKEA catalogue while sitting on the toilet. "Like so many others, I had become a slave to the IKEA nesting instinct," he says, in a voiceover.
"If I saw something clever, like a little coffee table in the shape of
a yin-yang, I had to have it." The ease of self-invention that IKEA
enables is liberating, but it can be sad to be able to make a life, or
to dispose of it, so cheaply.

•     •     •

IKEA stores, like Chihuahuas and cilantro, provoke extreme re-
actions. Some people, such as the members of the "Official IKEA

Is Hell on Earth" Facebook group, can't stand them. Others treat IKEA as a human-size doll house, hanging around its prettily furnished rooms just for entertainment. In recent months, middle-aged singles have taken to congregating in a Shanghai IKEA in such numbers that management has been forced to cordon off a designated "match-making corner." Shen Jinhua, an IKEA employee, told the *Shanghai Daily*, "Before we set up an isolated area for them, they occupied the seats in the dining area for a long time, and thus other guests could not find a seat."

Each IKEA store is carefully laid out to stimulate certain behaviors. Johan Stenebo, who worked at IKEA for twenty years, writes in *The Truth About IKEA* (2009), "One could describe it as if IKEA grabs you by the hand and consciously guides you through the store in order to make you buy as much as possible." In June, I visited IKEA's new store in Hyllie, a suburb of the Swedish city of Malmö. The store, which opened in September 2010, is IKEA's "everyday best practice" store. Martin Albrecht, the store's manager, agreed to give me a tour of the premises. "All the knowledge and wisdom of our stores is built into this one," he said.

A bin of blue-and-yellow tarpaulin bags stood at the store's entrance. Albrecht explained that a customer, wherever he is, should always be able to see the next bin of bags. We were standing on the gray path that guides customers through an IKEA store. "We call this the Main Aisle," Albrecht said. "You should feel safe that you can walk it and you won't miss anything." The Main Aisle is supposed to curve every fifty feet or so, to keep the customer interested. A path that is straight for any longer than that is called an Autobahn—a big, boring mistake. Those customers who would like to veer off the IKEA-approved route often cannot find the exit. IKEA stores have secret doors, like those in *The Lion, the Witch, and the Wardrobe*: one can step through them and go directly from Living Rooms (which an IKEA store always starts with) to Children's Rooms ("Cots are our ticket to building a lifelong relationship with our core customers," according to an internal report) without having to look at two hundred bath mats on the way. But the hidden portals are almost impossible to find: if sticky eyeballs are the metric of success on the Internet, then IKEA rules sticky feet. Alan Penn, a professor of architectural and urban computing at University College London, conducted a study of the IKEA labyrinth and deemed it sadomasochistic. The only comparably vast shopping environment he could think of, he told the *London Times*, was the Bazaar of Isfahan, a seventeenth-century Persian marketplace.

Albrecht, an affably earnest man in a blue and yellow polo shirt, led the way past several room sets. In the IKEA catalogue, the rooms are always perfectly done, but in stores the quality of their execution varies. Design experts love IKEA's products but consider going to retrieve them a necessary evil. Maxwell Gillingham-Ryan, a cofounder of the blog *Apartment Therapy*, praised IKEA for "the inventiveness of their designs" and "the usability of their furniture," but, he added, "a brand-new IKEA store that's fully stocked can be a happy place, but one that's been trampled by the crowds on a Saturday is an ugly place to be."

At the Malmö store, Albrecht and I ran into Gabrielle Granath and Linda Eriksson, who were tidying a room set.

"We find things all over the place," Granath said. "We find trash in the trash bins."

"Sometimes in the toilets," Eriksson added.

Granath and Eriksson explained that their job was to keep the room sets looking fresh. They change the slipcovers once a week. They cut wicks on candles and dust fake computer screens. They make sure that all the price tags aim to the left.

Albrecht indicated a box of green fleece blankets, meant to complement a couch on display. "This we would call an 'add-on,'" he explained. Add-ons are not the only way that IKEA encourages what it refers to, internally, as "unplanned purchasing." When we reached the Market Hall section of the store, where IKEA sells pots, pans, and other lightweight items, Albrecht declared, "Now it's the famous Open the Wallet section." There, an abundance of cheap goods—flowerpots, slippers, lint rollers— encourages the customer to make a purchase, any purchase, the thinking being that IKEA shoppers buy either nothing or a lot. There is art in the visual merchandising, too. Albrecht showed me how IKEA uses a technique called "bulla bulla," in which a bunch of items are purposely jumbled in bins, to create the impression of volume and, therefore, inexpensiveness.

.　　.　　.

IKEA constitutes a sort of borderless nation-state, with seats of power, redoubts of conservatism, second cities, imperial outposts, creative hubs, and administrative backwaters. In a letter that prefaces "A Furniture Dealer's Testament," the company's constitutional text, Ingvar Kamprad, IKEA's founder, wrote, "A well-known industrialist/politician once said that IKEA has had a greater impact on the democratization process than many political measures combined."

The capital of IKEA is Älmhult, a small village on Sweden's southern peninsula. Kamprad, who is eighty-five, opened the first IKEA store there in 1953. Älmhult lies halfway between the North Sea and the Baltic Sea, in Småland, a remote region of barren, rocky flatland. Smålanders are known, more or less, as the Scots of Sweden. Faced with the area's harsh winters and lack of arable soil, many of them immigrated to Minnesota in the nineteenth century. Those who didn't are renowned for their obstinacy and thrift. The Småland ethos is central to IKEA's self-mythology. "Like Småland's farmers, our values are down-to-earth," an IKEA ad from 1981 read. "We have toiled hard in a difficult field to produce sweet harvests." Clogs and a lip full of *snus* are still the favored uniform of Kamprad loyalists.

Kamprad's paternal grandparents, Achim and Franziska, arrived in Småland in the winter of 1896. Immigrants from Germany, they had bought a timber estate of four hundred and forty-nine hectares near Agunnaryd, about twelve miles from Älmhult, after seeing an advertisement in the back of a hunting magazine. They established a farm there. They didn't speak Swedish. The farm, called Elmtaryd, foundered. In the spring of 1897, after the local savings bank rejected his loan application, Achim Kamprad shot his hounds and then killed himself. His widow continued to run the farm, which in 1918 passed to her eldest son, Feodor. He married the daughter of the proprietor of the area's biggest country store, "the old kind with four or five assistants, the smell of herring and toffees and leather," as Ingvar Kamprad described it to Bertil Torekull in his authorized biography, *Leading by Design*, published in 1998. Ingvar was born in 1926. At Elmtaryd, Torekull writes, "the silence is still more likely to be broken by the bark of a roebuck than the sound of a tractor or a car." I.-B. Bayley, a Kamprad cousin, recalled young Ingvar's life there:

> We taught him to dance to the gramophone beneath the thick foliage of the oaks down by the church.... He caught fish and crayfish and was adventurous and bold, stuffing the crayfish he'd just caught down the back of his long johns.

For Christmas in 2007, IKEA employees received a DVD about the first sixty years of Kamprad's life. The cover featured an image of a stone wall built in the Småland style, along with a head shot of Kamprad, like a Mao or a Padre Pio. Kamprad has said that he engineered his first business deal at the age of five, when he contracted with an aunt in Stockholm to buy a hundred boxes of matches. "Then I sold the boxes at two or three öre each, sometimes even five öre," Kamprad told Torekull. "Talk about profit margins, but I still remember the lovely feeling." Eventually, Kamprad branched out into Christmas cards and wall hangings. He caught fish and picked lingonberries. At eleven, he made a killing in garden seeds. As Kamprad tells it, he was an Agunnarydian

Iacocca: "In my last year at middle school, my first rather childish business was beginning to look rather like a real firm."

Kamprad founded IKEA at his uncle Ernst's kitchen table in 1943. (The "I" is for "Ingvar," the "K" is for "Kamprad," the "E" is for "Elmtaryd," and the "A" is for "Agunnaryd.") He sold fountain pens, encyclopedias, table runners, udder balm, reinforced socks. In 1948, in imitation of a competitor, he added furniture to his portfolio. The business was mostly mail-order: at six-fifty every morning, the milk bus came by the farm's churn stand and picked up goods that had been ordered, carrying them on to the train station. In 1949, Kamprad published a circular in the national farmers' newspaper. His appeal, "To the People of the Countryside," read:

> You may have noticed that it is not easy to make ends meet. Why is this? You yourself produce goods of various kinds (milk, grain, potatoes, etc.), and I suppose you do not receive too much payment for them. No, I'm sure you don't. And yet everything is so fantastically expensive.
>
> To a great extent, that is due to the middlemen. Compare what you receive for a kilo of pork with what the shops ask for it. . . .
>
> In this price list we have taken a step in the right direction by offering you goods at the same price your dealer buys for, in some cases lower.

But the mail-order business proved tricky: customers were not always pleased with the items that arrived on their doorsteps. In 1952, Kamprad bought a joinery in Älmhult—his grandfather's general store had once occupied the site—and set up a showroom, where people could come and see the goods. "At that moment, the basis of the modern IKEA concept was created, and in principle it still applies: first and foremost, use a catalogue to tempt people to come to an exhibition, which today is our store,"

Kamprad later said. In 1963, IKEA opened its first store outside Sweden, in Oslo. Ten years later, IKEA was expanding so frantically that German executives accidentally opened a store in Konstanz when they had meant to open one in Koblenz.

·    ·    ·

In June, I flew to Copenhagen. From there, I look a train to Älmhult. Out the window, I glimpsed a series of glittering lakes that appeared to be populated by the hardy mothers and cherubic children of La Leche League literature. Abandoned crofts bordered wooden cottages painted Sweden's traditional Falu red. Two and a half hours later, I reached Älmhult's station. The town was quiet, as though a storm had just blown through. I walked across the tracks and, in five minutes, arrived at what is known as the "IKEA village": a large parking lot surrounded by IKEA corporate offices, an IKEA store, a museum, and an IKEA hotel. Twenty-five hundred of Älmhult's eighty-five hundred inhabitants work for IKEA. Spending time in Älmhult is a prerequisite for advancing one's career at IKEA, and the social scene is as intense as the professional one. "It's a very strange climate," Johan Stenebo, the former employee, told me. "Älmhult is pretty much what you get if you live in the middle of a dark, boring forest." It sounded like a mixture of Lowell, Massachusetts, summer camp, and *Ice Storm*–era New Canaan. According to an IKEA brochure, "At first sight, Älmhult seems very normal. But in time a sense of positive madness begins to surface."

My first appointment in Älmhult was at IKEA's "corporate culture centre," Tillsammans. (It means "together" in Swedish.) Michele Acuna, who had recently moved to Älmhult from Shanghai, was my guide. A native Californian in her forties, she spoke fluent IKEAn. IKEA's products offered "solutions" to "challenges." Its employees were "coworkers." Kamprad was "Ingvar" or "the founder." Rooms were "living situations," which, a circle graph explained, are occupied by eight categories of people: "baby," "toddler," "starting school," "tweens and teens," "living single/starting out," "living single/established," "living together/ starting out," and "living together/established." (The uncertainty I felt at deciding which label I qualified for reminded me why a trip to IKEA can induce existential dread.)

Inside the museum, I played a magnetic matching game, pairing products with their designers. Traditionally, the names of IKEA's bookcases derive from different occupations; curtains are given names from mathematics; and bathroom products are named for lakes and rivers. A file cabinet was filled with cards bearing unfortunate IKEA product names: ANIS, DICK, FANNY, BRACKEN (a homophone for "vomiting" in Dutch), GUTVIK (a child's bed; it sounds like "good fuck" in German). At a poker table, I perused cards inscribed with bits of Kampradiana: the time someone tried to sell the founder an intercom system and the founder yelled to a coworker, "We already have one!"; the time the founder was in Romania looking at a freezer case full of ducks, and wondered, What do they do with all the feathers? (He wanted to use them for pillows.) The feather story is to Kamprad as the cherry-tree tale is to George Washington. In another version I heard, it was China and chickens.

Near a display of LACK tables, we ran into an executive—a European with reading glasses and a sweater draped over his shoulders. "It is one of the most copied," he said, of LACK. "So many have tried to do the same. But they make it a little more ugly." He, Acuna, and the PR person who had accompanied us dissolved into a round of giggles.

On the way out the door, I noticed a video of Kamprad in a chambray shirt and gold chain playing on a nearby screen. It also showed men and women prying stones out of the Smålandian soil with what looked like a large spoon.

"As long as earth has houses for people, there will also be a need for a strong and efficient IKEA," a narrator intoned.

Acuna looked me in the eyes. "You know that's the vision of the company—to create a better life for the many?"

.　　　.　　　.

That night, I stayed at the IKEA hotel. Its website promises, "Guests sleep well and wake up refreshed, without art or frills." The lounge area was fresh and bright, like a scene from the IKEA catalogue. I sat on a candy-striped KARLSTAD chair and listened to supply managers discuss the respective turnaround times of China and Pakistan in global English. Swedish-speaking men with mustaches wore short-sleeved plaid shirts and drank Eriksberg beer. Ostensibly, this was a public space, but I felt as if I had walked into a bar where everybody had been at the same wedding. Behind the reception desk was a series of candy jars filled with gummy bears and caramels. Why was the receptionist smiling so broadly? Were the toasting salesmen bit players in some sort of Älmhultian *Truman Show*?

IKEA is obsessed with *lista*, which translates as "making do." IKEA employees, including the CEO, travel in coach. To save money, the company uses employees as models for its catalogues. "I'm tall, so the furniture looks too small when I'm standing by it," one told me. "So I usually have to be sitting or lying down on a couch." In "A Furniture Dealer's Testament," Kamprad writes, "It is not only for cost reasons that we avoid the luxury hotels. We don't need flashy cars, impressive titles, uniforms or other status symbols. We rely on our strength and our will!" (Don't order that ficus!) Kamprad drives a beat-up Volvo. He is reported to recycle tea bags. He is known to pocket the salt and pepper packets at restaurants. He has ranked as high as fifth on *Forbes*'s list of the world's richest people.

Ikea's utopian strain derives partly from Swedish tradition. In the nineteenth century, Carl Larsson's influential watercolors depicted halcyon scenes of family life—blond children, blond furniture, teapots, kittens, striped cotton rugs. In the 1930s, the social-democratic movement advanced the idea of the *folkhemmet*—"the people's home"—using the home as a metaphor for its vision of a harmonious, classless Sweden. After the war, the *folkhemmet* became manifest in the Scandinavian design movement, which envisaged a world in which beautiful things would be made accessible to everyone through mass production. The Swedish welfare state built more than a million new dwellings and issued advice on interior design, health, and hygiene.

"What IKEA did then was to commercialize this idea," Cilla Robach, a curator at the National Museum of Fine Arts in Stockholm, told me. "Ingvar Kamprad understood quite early how to change the social-democratic ideology into money and make an industry of it." IKEA is Legos for grownups, connecting the furniture of our adulthoods with the toys of our childhoods.

IKEA is proud of its egalitarianism. Perks such as special parking places and corporate dining rooms are not considered "IKEA-*mässigt*"—acceptable in the IKEA worldview —and co-workers who are thought to be snobbish are quickly disabused of their pretensions, or their positions: "If you don't fit, you quit." A recent edition of *ReadMe*, IKEA's internal magazine, featured an article entitled "Step Inside—into two co-workers' bathrooms," in which a human-resources employee from Lisbon discussed her bidet. The sense of informality extends to customers. A recent promotion instructed Britons, "Chuck Out Your Chintz." IKEA featured gay couples in its advertising as early as 1994. This year, it ran an ad, to accompany a store opening in Sicily, that featured two men holding hands, beneath the legend "We are open to all families."

There is a conviction within IKEA that the company is more than a mere purveyor of futons and meatballs. Last year, in October, IKEA issued its first annual report. It justified the company's scary-genius approach to cost-cutting, declaring, "Sustained profitability gives us resources to grow further and offer a better everyday life for more of the many people." Mikael Ohlsson, the CEO, promised a new era of transparency. He said that he had decided to publish the report in response to interest from coworkers. However, the *Financial Times* noted, "Mr. Ohlsson's drive for openness is long overdue, and intended to restore a corporate reputation sullied by a highly critical book by former senior IKEA executive Johan Stenebo."

Ohlsson, a smiling blond man in rumpled khakis, told me that the purpose of the report was to diffuse some of the mystery surrounding IKEA, the ownership of which Kamprad transferred to a private foundation in 1982. "If you don't tell, people start to wonder," he said.

Ohlsson seemed almost wounded by the suggestion that IKEA was a multi-billion-dollar business, rather than an altruistic concern. "IKEA was and will remain value-driven," he said. "You see, this is to create a better life for the many people." IKEA attempts to resolve the paradox of its devotion to cost-cutting and its altruistic self-image with team spirit. The near-messianic faith that IKEA employees have in the rightness of their cause can lead to an odd insularity. "One cannot help feeling sorry for those who cannot or will not join us," Kamprad wrote in 1976 in "A Furniture Dealer's Testament." IKEA's internal communications feature morality tales, with Kamprad as exemplar:

As a youngster, Ingvar Kamprad was always reluctant to drag himself out of bed in the morning to milk the cows on his father's farm. "You sleepy head! You'll never make anything of yourself!" his father would say. Then, one birthday, Ingvar got an alarm clock. "Now by jiminy, I'm going to start a new life," he determined, setting the alarm for twenty to six and removing the "off button."

The *ReadMe* newsletter also contained the story of Nicole Wiesmüller, who had moved with the company from Vienna to Salzburg to Vienna to Linz and back to Salzburg. "Store manager Nicole Wiesmüller has moved around a lot," the article read. "Cost: Her private life. Reward: Success with Her Co-workers."

"IKEA at its worst is like a sect," Goran Carstedt, a former head of IKEA North America, once said. According to Stenebo, employees parse Kamprad's frequent handwritten faxes as if they were pages from the Talmud: "If he starts with 'Dear,' it is neutral. If he starts with only your first name it is a sharp request. If the fax starts with 'Dearest' you are in his good books." The atmosphere at IKEA reminded me of that of a political campaign, with true believers, whispering skeptics, inside jokes, and deflection of even the most innocuous questions. A former senior executive told me that although he still admired the company, he had found it suffocating. He said, "For me, it was like North Korea."

When I was at the IKEA hotel, the sun stayed up until midnight. In Tillsamans, I wandered into a sort of rec room (it is used for conferences), which was equipped with a karaoke machine. On the wall, someone had painted the lyrics to an IKEA version of Frank Sinatra's "My Way": "As long as there's human life on earth / A strong IKEA has its worth / We satisfy the many needs / A strong IKEA that succeeds / Our culture leads us on our way / That's the IKEA way!" Eventually, I went to my room. It was furnished with a pair of spartan single beds. Two books sat on top of a pine desk: the IKEA catalogue and the New Testament.

·     ·     ·

The LACK table is one of those commodities, like salt or cod, through which one could tell the story of the world. LACK, along with the BILLY bookshelf, is IKEA's most iconic product. You may not know that you've seen it, but you have: it's the twenty-two-by-twenty-two-inch side table that looks a bit like one of those plastic things which come in a pizza box.

LACK, which was introduced in 1979, sells for seven dollars and ninety-nine cents. IKEA's designers begin, rather than end, with a price. "Normally, you get a brief with a price and a style matrix," Marcus Arvonen, one of IKEA's twelve staff designers, explained. "It's 'OK, can you make this plastic spatula? It cannot cost more than one euro and has to function as a spatula, and it has to be gray and plastic.'"

A LACK table begins as a tree, or part of one. (IKEA is the world's third-largest consumer of wood, behind Home Depot and Lowe's, and ahead of Walmart.) Wood is used for IKEA's more expensive products. Its by-products go into the making of particleboard, which is cut into the twenty-two-by-twenty-two-inch squares that form a LACK tabletop. Meanwhile, the table's interior is being fabricated: IKEA uses a construction technique called "board-on-frame," in which solid-wood exteriors are stuffed with paper innards. Scott made paper dresses; IKEA makes cardboard furniture.

IKEA invented flat-packed furniture in 1951, when an employee named Gillis Lundgren, struggling to squeeze a table into the back of his Volvo, decided to remove the legs. The company's goal is to design products that can be packed as tightly as possible, minimizing damage and maximizing profit as they are transported over the oceans. Its motto: "We hate air!"

LACK tables are made in China and Poland and in Danville, Virginia, at a plant owned by Swedwood, IKEA's manufacturing subsidiary. The plant opened in 2008. As the *Los Angeles Times* reported, locals were, at first, mostly thrilled to hear that IKEA had chosen to build the plant—its only one in the United States—in Danville, a former textile town where the average annual income is $29,000.

Although the company had a reputation as a conscientious employer—it has ranked in *Fortune*'s list of the "Top 100 Companies to Work For"—there was trouble in Danville from the start. Six former employees filed grievances with the Equal Employment Opportunity Commission, alleging racial discrimination. Employees complained that they were required to work mandatory overtime, often with no notice. Mike Ward, the head of IKEA USA, acknowledged, when we spoke in July, that mandatory overtime had been a problem. He said, "At this moment, 95 percent of the overtime is voluntary, and so they've made great improvements there." IKEA commissioned an internal audit of the plant, and found no further cause for concern.

But this summer Danville's workers threatened to unionize. I asked Ward whether he felt that it was fair that the minimum pay for IKEA workers in Danville is eight dollars an hour, and that they receive twelve days' vacation (eight of them selected by Swedwood), while their counterparts in Sweden make at least nineteen dollars an hour and get five weeks off. "I think that when we really dig and look, the situation in Danville meets our standards, the things that are concerns are being worked on actively, and we'll respect the decisions that our coworkers make," he said.

On July 27, the Danville workers decided, by a vote of 221-69, to join the International Association of Machinists and Aerospace Workers. (IKEA's code of conduct stipulates that workers be allowed to join unions if they choose to do so.) Several days later, I spoke to Bill Street, who leads the woodworkers' division of the IAMAW He said that conditions in Danville were still unacceptable. "I truly believe that Danville management has a plantation mentality," he said. "They think that they own these workers and it's their right to use them any way they so choose."

Tawanda Tarpley, a union member who has worked at Swedwood since 2008, was less combative, but her complaints were the same. Swedwood's managers, Tarpley said, hired their white friends and family members, overlooking black workers, even when they were more qualified. "I think it's more of a structural unfairness, because they're not mean." She continued, "The plant manager, he came to me on Wednesday and he told me, 'Tawanda, we are willing to do whatever we can to work together and to make this a better working environment for everyone.' He told me that, so I'm praying that that will be an outcome."

•    •    •

Each year, IKEA conducts thousands of "home visits," in which coworkers go and nose around people's houses—a "come as you are" party in which the party comes to your living room. In July, I joined Kerrice Hayward, an interior designer at one of London's IKEA stores, and Tom James, a sales coworker, on such a mission. "Basically, we go out and find what frustrates our customers," Hayward said.

We drove for half an hour before arriving in Chatham, a village in Kent. Hayward parked on a sharply sloped street. We made our way to a 1930s-era terraced house, built of brick and pebble dash. It had a large bay window, with stained-glass panels depicting red roses.

A woman wearing leggings and a striped tunic greeted us.

"Shoes off?" Hayward asked. "Yes, please," the woman, who introduced herself as Sandra Denbow, said, ushering us into the house's front room.

Denbow is a full-time mother. Her husband, Paul, works for a company that recycles high-voltage transformers. (They are members of IKEA's loyalty program and had agreed to host the home visit in exchange for a seventy-five-pound voucher.) They live with their twenty-four-year-old son and their four-year-old daughter, who was drawing at the coffee table with colored pencils.

The daughter's bedroom was pink and immaculate; the son's, in the attic, was fluorescent green and surprisingly tidy. Sandra and Paul's bedroom had blue carpeting, a water bed, and a wallpaper border of a tropical scene, with palm trees and schools of angelfish. "We had a son who died ten years ago, and this was his bedroom, so we really didn't want to redecorate," Sandra said.

Downstairs, we examined a small multipurpose room. Hayward politely pointed out to the Denbows that they were using a task light to illuminate the entire room. She wondered if they had considered IKEA lighting products.

"See, IKEA's like, it's too far to just pop in for a light," Paul said.

"Could you tell me more?"

"I hate IKEA," Paul said. "You walk round and round, and you're never gonna get out."

Hayward nodded.

"But I do like the products."

As Denbow answered Hayward's questions, I wanted to yell, "Fix the feet!"—those unfinished pine blocks on which many an otherwise attractive IKEA sofa sits, the Reeboks to its Armani suit.

This fall, in response to feedback from customers, IKEA will introduce a new version of the Billy bookcase, which Gawker has described as "the bookshelf that everyone in every city with an IKEA is required to have in their apartments, because we are all pitiful sheep." The new version will have deeper shelves, the better to display bobbleheads and wedding pictures in a time when people's reading material increasingly resides on hard drives.

.     .     .

In 2002, Spike Jonze directed an ad for IKEA, in which an apartment dweller unplugs an ugly lamp—it's orange, with one of those bendy, strawlike necks—takes it outside, and deposits it on the curb. The lamp sits in the rain. A man approaches. "Many of you feel bad for this lamp," he says, with a Swedish Chef–type accent. "That is because you're crazy. It has no feelings! And the new one is much better."

IKEA has a largely excellent environmental record. But there are two caveats. IKEA builds its stores where land is cheap and you have to drive to get to them, and the company more or less invented disposable furniture. Movers have been known to advise their clients that IKEA items are not worth the cost of transport. I compare my apartment, full of IKEA, with my parents' home, bereft of it, with some discomfort. There is the fact that I have added dozens of possessions to the world's landfills, while they have been careful stewards of theirs. IKEA things are fresh, but they have no stories. Think of the beauty of classroom desks.

In *Cheap: The High Cost of Discount Culture*, Ellen Ruppel Shell argues that IKEA's low prices exact untold environmental, aesthetic, and social tolls. IKEA, she writes, has managed to perpetrate "one of the great marketing gambits of the twenty-first century: the discreet transfer of costs from seller to buyer." (She means labor costs.)

Still, IKEA offers irresistible deals. In 2007, BJURSTA, an extendable oak-veneer dining table, cost two hundred and ninety-nine dollars. Mindful of the recession and of rising wood prices, IKEA hollowed out the legs (which reduced the weight, making transport cheaper) and consolidated the manufacture of parts (bigger orders cost less). Customers appreciated that the table was lighter and less expensive. The more tables they bought, the more IKEA lowered the price. By 2011, BJURSTA cost a hundred and ninety-nine dollars. A Harvard Business School professor has written of "the IKEA effect," in which the requirement of a little bit of labor enhances affection for its results. The Allen wrench is the egg to IKEA's instant cake mix.

In Älmhult, I asked Jeanette Skjelmose, IKEA's sustainability manager, whether IKEA was at least partially culpable for having created a throwaway culture. She resorted to false humility. "I think the trend of using products for a short life span comes from consumers," she said. "I wish we had that much influence. I hope that our products have enough quality that they can have second and third lives in other people's homes."

The advantage of the IKEA approach is that its products don't lag behind the way that people actually use them. Visiting the store at Wembley one day, I came across an interesting item: a black half-moon of polypropylene, with a gray beanbag-ish underbelly. Inspection revealed that it was BRÄDA, a "laptop support." The TV tray of our moment, BRÄDA was developed in 2004 by Hanna Ahlberg, then a student at Lund Technical University. For her thesis in industrial design, she decided to make a soft piece of furniture that would allow teenagers to do their homework in their beds. It also prevents the laptop from burning the leg (a condition that is technically known as "toasted skin syndrome"). Upon Ahlberg's graduation, IKEA hired her as a product developer.

IKEA's employees are some of the world's foremost anthropologists of home life. From them I learned that people want twice the storage in bathrooms because men now have as many grooming products as women do. They want food containers, as the IKEA catalogue puts it, "For all those recipes that call for five olives, half a can of tomatoes, and an ounce of couscous." The British peer Michael Jopling once dismissed Michael Heseltine, the deputy prime minister at the time, saying, "The trouble with Michael is that he had to buy his own furniture." But Michael Heseltine didn't have to drill holes in the back of the family Chippendale armoire to plug in the television.

·     ·     ·

The IKEA catalogue is a primer for the sort of "good, clean living" of which IKEA approves. The company published a 197 million catalogues last year, in twenty-nine languages and sixty-one editions. As reading material, the IKEA catalogue is only slightly less popular than Harry Potter books. It combines the voyeuristic pleasures of browsing albums on Facebook (peeping into other people's houses) with the aspirational ones of *Architectural Digest* (we are all a $39.99 bookshelf away from being well-read Swedish architects). The IKEA catalogue is a self-help manual for a certain kind of life. The French singer Renaud observes, in "Les Bobos," "Their bedtime reading is . . . next to the IKEA catalogue / They like Japanese restaurants and Korean cinema." They used to like ferns, but now they like orchids.

In Älmhult, I visited the offices of IKEA Communications, where the catalogue is made. Selin Hult, an information manager, and Henrik Palmberg, who said he was a "competence matrix owner," showed me around. We enjoyed *fika*, the Swedish coffee break, with summer cake and mugs of tea, and then set off on a tour. First, we walked through a vast warehouse lined with towering racks of IKEA products—a sort of furniture lending library, where an interior designer can check out whatever crib or dresser he needs. It looked as though an entire high-rise had disgorged its contents. All around us, I could see three-sided rooms, like sitcom sets. "At full capacity, we can do twenty-five at once," Palmberg said.

In a far corner, a room set had been built and furnished to resemble a bed-and-breakfast in the Swedish countryside. Whenever an IKEA designer creates a room set, for the catalogue or in a store, he or she writes up a detailed treatment. The treatment for the bed-and-breakfast read, "Story: a weekend hobby that turned into a full-time business, this B. and B. is nestled in the countryside untroubled by tourists. It is popular among those taking a break from the city and looking for peace and quiet. Despite its rural setting, this B. and B. is tastefully decorated to appeal to its urban guests." The room's designer, Sara Bohlin, had appointed the time of day "Morning/Breakfast." The price, "Medium." She had even mocked up a brochure for the place, which she had named Alanda. She was still putting on final touches. "I'm in a bit of a panic," she said.

The kitchen looked rustically inviting, with wide white floorboards and white walls. The focal point was a large STORNÄS dining table, in gray, with STEFAN chairs and a MÅNLJUS pendant lamp. There were board games and a stack of woolen blankets on shelves for the guests. A spotlight simulated a beam of morning light hitting the table. (You will find three types of lighting schemes in the IKEA catalogue: Let the Sun In, Lamps Lit, and Middle of the Day.) A carpenter had installed a real wood-burning stove, which the designer had found, into a "brick" hearth made of plywood. On the table sat a ceramic milk pitcher. To complete the tableau, Bohlin had gone out to fetch fresh bread and marmalade.

Just as the goal of a real room is to look like a fake one, the goal of a fake room is to look like a real one. At the catalogue headquarters, Hult and Palmberg showed me into a large room filled with kitchen supplies. I marveled at bins of plastic food: mushrooms, strawberries, apples, lemons, bell peppers, bunches of green grapes. "When we go close, we go fresh," Palmberg said. "Otherwise, we go fake." A loaf of sourdough in the IKEA catalogue will have a slice taken out. If the photograph shows something frying, there ought to be grease in the pan, but not all over the stove. Some splashes in the sink are nice.

"Pillows should be a bit squished," Bohlin said. "If you have a teacup, maybe there should be some smoke showing."

Palmberg added, "And water on the floor outside the bathroom!"

IKEA attempts to make the room sets generically pleasing, but in some cases cultural differences necessitate tweaks. "We say we need to be as global as possible and as local as necessary," Palmberg said. You'll see a friendly golden retriever curled up by the dining-room table in the British catalogue, but not in the Emirati one. Europeans like to sit on their furniture while Americans prefer to sit *in* it. "A Swedish bed should be soft and inviting and open, so that you almost want to crawl in," Hult explained. (Despite the influx of duvets in the seventies, most Americans remain wedded to the top sheet.) In the kitchen-supplies room, I counted fifteen coffee machines. Hult said, "For example, in Sweden we brew our own coffee, but perhaps if it's in Italy you want an espresso machine. It's these things that can make a difference. Small things, but quite important."

IKEA believes that it can make your sleep better and that it can enhance your family life. All you have to do is buy IKEA products, such as the FLÖRT pen and pencil organizer, which you can hang on your bed, "so you won't forgot those brilliant business ideas you have just before falling asleep. Or the title of your next novel!" IKEA's vision of life in its environs is a safe and haimish one. In its rooms, people don't run late, they don't bicker; they have children, but they don't have sex. The pedagogical impulse can get a bit overweening. "We want to be the leader in life at home," Albrecht told me, in Malmö. "Not just be the leader in home furnishings, but show you how to live!" A few minutes later, he was pointing out an item that, he said, had not sold very well, because IKEA had not sufficiently illuminated its use. "If you don't show the customer the function, the customer won't understand it," he said. The item was a broom.

·     ·     ·

IKEA is not really a Swedish company. It is controlled by a company called INGKA Holding, which, in turn, is controlled by the Dutch *stitchting*—a tax-exempt, nonprofit foundation—to which Ingvar Kamprad transferred his ownership shares in 1982. On its website, IKEA bills the *stitchting* structure as a means of creating "an ownership structure and an organization that stand for independence and a long-term approach," but the move minimized IKEA's tax burden and the financial oversight to which the company is subjected.

In 1982, Kamprad also set up a company called Inter IKEA Systems B.V., which owns the IKEA concept and trademark. Three percent of the revenues of each IKEA store go to Inter IKEA, as a kind of royalty. Those revenues then feed into the accounts of a series of offshore holding companies. "Few tasks are more exasperating than trying to assemble flat-pack furniture from IKEA," *The Economist* wrote in 2006. "But even that is simple compared with piecing together the accounts of the world's largest home-furnishing retailer." *The Economist* pointed out that IKEA's charitable giving through the Dutch foundation had been paltry—"barely a rounding error in the foundation's assets." More recently, IKEA has increased its commitment to philanthropy. Last month, the IKEA foundation pledged to donate 62 million dollars over three years to help Somali refugees in Kenya.

Kamprad has been a tax exile since the 1970s. He lives in the Swiss village of Epalinges, near Lausanne. "Kamprad has only very little taxes to pay," Yvan Tardy, the mayor of Epalinges, told the Dutch newspaper *Algemeen Dagblad*. "Unfortunately, he has never done anything for our village." Kamprad's nickname in town is the Miser.

A bigger blow to Kamprad's reputation came in 1994, when the Swedish newspaper *Expressen* published evidence revealing that Kamprad had once been active in the Swedish Nazi movement. The stories, by Pelle Tagesson, showed that Kamprad, between the ages of sixteen and twenty-five, had been a disciple of Per Engdahl, the leader of the Neo-Swedish movement. In 1948, Kamprad paid to publish a book of Engdahl's political writings. In 1950, he invited Engdahl to his wedding, writing that he was proud to be a part of the Neo-Swedish circle. After *Expressen*'s revelations, Kamprad faxed a handwritten letter to his employees, entitled "MY GREATEST FIASCO." "Dear IKEA family," it read. "You have been young yourself, and perhaps you find something in your youth now, so long afterward, that was ridiculous and stupid. In that case, you will understand me better. In hindsight, I know that early on I should have included this in my fiascos, but that is now spilled milk." The employees responded with a letter, signed by hundreds. "Ingvar, we are here whenever you need us." Bertil Torekull, Kamprad's handpicked biographer, writes, "Then the father of the family broke down and wept like a child."

After more revelations of Nazi associations, Kamprad wrote an apology, which appeared in Torekull's book, in a section entitled "A Youth and His Errors." He explained that, growing up at Elmtaryd, he had been especially close to his grandmother, Grossmutter Franziska, who was from the Sudetenland. (Torekull writes that Kamprad didn't come clean about all of his Nazi affiliations because he had forgotten about them.) Kamprad concludes the chapter by asking, "As I have lain awake at night pondering this dismal affair, I have asked myself: when is an old man forgiven for the sins of his youth? Is it a crime that I was brought up by a German grandmother and a German father?"

Still, Kamprad enjoys a hero's status in Sweden. "Everything that is about Ingvar Kamprad is big news," Fredrik Sjöshult, a reporter for *Expressen*, told me. "He's lived, like our version of the American dream, the Swedish dream." Last year, the Malmö City Theatre premièred *Ingvar! A Musical Furniture Saga*. In the production, the Kamprad character is crucified on a Maypole. He sings, "Do you think this can stop Ingvar?"

In 2009, Sweden's largest television station, SVT, revealed that IKEA's money—the 3 percent collected from each store—does not actually go to a charitable foundation in Holland, as IKEA had led people to believe. Rather, as Magnus Svenungsson reported, Inter IKEA is owned by a foundation in Liechtenstein, called Interogo, a corporate rainy-day fund. Interogo, which has amassed 12 billion dollars, is controlled by the Kamprad family.

IKEA is in the midst of a succession crisis. With his second wife, Margaretha, Kamprad has three sons, Peter, Jonas, and Matthias. None has any public profile. None has distinguished himself particularly within the company. In earlier years, Kamprad spoke of a sort of battle royal in which the son who proved himself most capable would inherit control of the company. More recently, he and his associates have suggested that none of them possess sufficient mettle.

IKEA would tell me only, "Peter, Jonas, and Matthias Kamprad will continue to occupy important board positions and actively participate in the future governance of the IKEA sphere companies. How they will exactly divide up the roles among them is under discussion."

Even Bertil Torekull, who has likened Kamprad, as a leader, to "some venerable African freedom fighter," admitted that Kamprad's reluctance to anoint a successor endangered the stability of IKEA. "What he's doing is risky," Torekull told me. "It's definitely time that other people must be more decisive or play a larger role." He concluded, "Anything can happen when the strong Ingvar Kamprad is gone."

Kamprad's legacy in the dining room has never been in question. The Sunday that I bummed around on my living-room couch, I went over to a friend's house for lunch. She served lamb on an IKEA platter and poured wine into IKEA wineglasses like the ones that I had earlier neglected to wash. At the end of September, she's moving in with her boyfriend. She wrote to me, "I'm really torn about the IKEA question. Inevitably, there will be a trip there, but I'm actually really keen to take a bit more time this time around, and not do the 'quick fix house kit-out' and try and get some more bits and pieces from antique auctions and so on. But, then, who has the time and the patience (and the money!) to do that?"

**The New York Times**

James B. Stewart made his name getting deep inside companies for stories like his book *Den of Thieves*. In this column, he's all over the boardroom and executive suites at Hewlett-Packard, which fired chief executive Léo Apotheker after a year of miscues cut its value in half. Stewart traces the company's problems back to its board of directors, which hired Apotheker amid intramural squabbling over the dismissal of its previous CEO. Most of HP's board, "tired" after the tussle, never even met Apotheker before they hired him, and his disastrous tenure leads one former director to call its board, with only a little hyperbole, "the worst board in the history of business."

James B. Stewart

# 29. Voting to Hire a Chief Without Meeting Him

The mystery isn't why Hewlett-Packard is likely to part ways with its chief executive, Léo Apotheker, after just a year in the job. It's why he was hired in the first place. The answer, say many involved in the process, lies squarely with the troubled Hewlett board. "It has got to be the worst board in the history of business," Tom Perkins, a former HP director and a Silicon Valley legend, told me.

Interviews with several current and former directors and people close to them involved in the search that resulted in the hiring of Mr. Apotheker reveal a board that, while composed of many accomplished individuals, as a group was rife with animosities, suspicion, distrust, personal ambitions, and jockeying for power that rendered it nearly dysfunctional.

Among their revelations: when the search committee of four directors narrowed the candidates to three finalists, no one else on the board was willing to interview them. And when the committee finally chose Mr. Apotheker and again suggested that other directors meet him, no one did. Remarkably, when the twelve-member board voted to name Mr. Apotheker as the successor to the recently ousted chief executive, Mark Hurd, most board members had never met Mr. Apotheker.

"I admit it was highly unusual," one board member who hadn't met Mr. Apotheker told me. "But we were just too exhausted from all the infighting." During Mr. Apotheker's brief tenure, once-proud HP has become a laughingstock in Silicon Valley. Its results have weakened, its stock has plummeted, and his strategy shifts have puzzled people inside and outside the company. Hewlett did not respond to an e-mail seeking comment.

The immediate cause of dissension was the board's decision in August 2010 to demand the resignation of Mr. Hurd, who had himself assumed the top position in the midst of board leaks and a phone pretexting scandal surrounding efforts to determine the source of the leaks that had laid bare irreconcilable differences among directors. He had replaced Carly Fiorina, who was also summarily ousted by the board.

Though not without detractors, Mr. Hurd pulled off one of the great rescue missions in American corporate history, refocusing the strife-ridden company and leading it to five years of revenue gains and a stock that soared 130 percent. Then came an incendiary letter from the activist lawyer Gloria Allred, charging that Mr. Hurd had sexually harassed a former soft-core pornography actress named Jodie Fisher, whom he had hired as a consultant for HP. The accusations set off another fierce board battle.

The board named a committee headed by Robert L. Ryan, a former Medtronic executive and H.P.'s lead director, and Lucille Salhany, another director who was a former chairwoman of Fox Broadcasting, to investigate the accusations. An outside law firm did not find that that Mr. Hurd was guilty of the harassment charges but had submitted false expense reports in what seemed an effort to conceal the relationship. Mr. Hurd denied having an affair with Ms. Fisher (as he has since done publicly) and said his assistant had first contacted her after seeing her on a reality television program.

As one director told me, "We said, 'Mark, just tell us the truth.'" He stuck to this story. He interviewed the woman twice, there was no search firm, no job posting, no discussion with anyone else. He met with her alone on more than one occasion. To be the hostess at a party? Give me a break." Complicating matters was evidence HP obtained from Mr. Hurd's office computer showing that he had viewed videos of Ms. Fisher.

Once some board members became convinced that Mr. Hurd had not been totally truthful, they insisted he had to be fired. Mr. Ryan convened a meeting to decide Mr. Hurd's fate by saying that he wanted to give every director an opportunity to speak, but that he would begin.

"I don't believe him," he said bluntly, and noted that under HP's employee guidelines, any other employee who lied to the board would be fired. He was strongly backed by Ms. Salhany.

Two other members, Joel Z. Hyatt, a media executive and founder of Hyatt Legal Plans, and John Joyce, a former private equity partner, were adamant that Mr. Hurd should stay, at least long enough to groom a successor and arrange for an orderly transition.

"They were very vocal about it," said one director. "It's healthy to have differing opinions, but this went too far. It became fractious. There were so many hard feelings. It became difficult to conduct business in a civil manner."

Still grappling with Mr. Hurd's messy departure (HP sued him after he joined the rival Oracle as its president, later dropping the case), the company began a search for his successor. Four directors—Lawrence Babbio, John Hammergren, Marc Andreessen, and Mr. Hyatt—volunteered to form the search committee.

Some other directors were immediately distrustful. They suspected that some colleagues hoped to advance their own ambitions, including in at least one case to be the next chairman. Others were so angry over Mr. Hyatt's support for Mr. Hurd that they declined to participate in any committee he was on.

Running HP might seem to be one of the best jobs in corporate America. But the committee quickly discovered that a company whose board had summarily fired its last two chief executives was a hard sell to top candidates, said people involved in the search.

Among those who rebuffed HP, they said, was Virginia Rometty, a senior vice president at IBM. Ray Lane, a managing partner at Kleiner Perkins and a former president of Oracle, also rebuffed their approach but indicated he might be interested in being chairman.

According to directors, the committee narrowed the field to three candidates. Mr. Babbio favored an internal candidate. But before Mr. Hurd's ouster, he had told the board that he did not feel anyone at HP was ready to assume the top job. Mr. Andreessen favored Scott McNealy, a cofounder and chief executive of Sun Microsystems.

Mr. McNealy was a candidate who worried other directors, given his outspoken personality and his track record at Sun Microsystems, whose stock had dropped precipitously with him at the helm. That left Mr. Apotheker, who had lasted just seven months as chief executive of the German software giant SAP. While reasonably well known in Europe and in software circles, he was relatively unknown in Silicon Valley.

As one executive said, "We had a joke: the code name for the search was Léo Apotheker. Because no one had heard of him."

"Léo had a lot in his favor, and a lot of deficiencies," said one board member. Everyone thought he was extremely smart and knew the global software business. Among the deficiencies may have been the circumstances under which he left SAP, but when I pressed various directors, no one seemed able to recall just what those were.

"I know there was a satisfactory explanation, and we did look into it," one person told me. Others did not want to comment. (It has subsequently been reported that while Mr. Apotheker was at SAP, the German company was sued and admitted that it had infringed on Oracle software copyrights after stealing them. SAP has said he was not responsible for the part of the company where the theft occurred.)

Before a final vote on Mr. Apotheker, HP search committee members again urged other directors to meet him. No one took them up. At least one director, Ms. Salhany, tried to slow the process, worrying aloud that "no one has ever met him. Are we sure?" But her concerns were brushed aside. "Among the finalists, he was the best of a very unattractive group," one director said.

However hasty the process, board members felt they had little choice. "I believe the search committee did a good job. They worked hard. There were very few choices," one participant said. "So many people they called said they weren't interested. People didn't want to follow in Mark's footsteps. But Mr. Apotheker was a mistake. We all made it. Sometimes you make a mistake."

Mr. Apotheker was named HP's chief executive, with Ray Lane as chairman, almost exactly one year ago. Almost from the day Mr. Apotheker arrived, HP's operating results declined with dizzying speed, climaxing a few weeks ago when HP announced that it might—or might not—sell or spin off its PC business, with its $30 billion in revenue and strong market share.

HP also said it was abandoning it its once-vaunted operating system and its much promoted new tablet computer. The unexpected announcements highlighted what critics say are Mr. Apotheker's weaknesses: little experience in HP's dominant hardware businesses, including printers and PCs; an inability to communicate effectively; and a tendency to make major decisions only in consultation with Mr. Lane, and not with HP's managers.

"The company is coming apart at the seams," said one person familiar with HP's operations. "Because they may or may not be selling the PC business, the enterprise side is completely frozen. The business customers who buy tens of thousands of these machines along with support contracts are shutting them out. Dell and Lenovo are all over these accounts. They're having a field day. HP is self-destructing." A full-page ad in major newspapers trying to reassure PC customers did little to assuage doubts.

Whatever the board does now, ultimately it is going to need to examine itself.

How did it let things get to this? That, at the very least, should be the subject for inquiry by yet another committee.

**Reuters**

At age fifty-three, Bill Ford Jr. has seen the auto company founded by his great-grandfather go from boom to bust and back and formerly skeptical industry executives begin to embrace the environmentalism that he preached from his early days. But he's not looking back: he's trying to anticipate future challenges, from traffic gridlock in rapidly growing markets to choosing the right successor for chief executive Alan Mulally when he retires. Reuters reporters Bernie Woodall and Kevin Krolicki talk to the chairman of the board and others about Ford's drive to protect the investment of his life.

Bernie Woodall and
Kevin Krolicki

# 30. How Ford Became Last Man Standing

B ill Ford Jr. just can't let the good times roll. In late December, Ford, fifty-three, was on a family ski vacation in Colorado but found himself unable to put aside dark visions of how too much success could lead to the next crisis for the auto industry.

As Ford Motor Co. prepared to close the books on its biggest comeback year for sales and earnings since the 1980s, Ford was talking to friends about the risk of gridlock choking booming urban centers from Sao Paolo to Shanghai—and potentially choking auto sales, too.

"I want us to start thinking now about how we're going to solve it," he said. "Nobody is thinking about it yet in our industry, but it's going to be upon us fast."

The risk of cars literally stacking up in the world's emerging megacities presents a threat to automakers like Ford, which are banking on the fast-growth markets of China, Brazil, India, and Russia to make up almost a third of global auto sales this year. That would be up from just 6 percent when Ford took over as Ford chairman in 1999.

On the slopes, Ford's friends got an earful. "I think he's thought quite a bit about this," former Ebay chief executive Meg Whitman told Reuters of her conversation with Ford, a longtime friend, at Telluride, Colorado, where both families have vacation homes.

"Cars are going to be with us forever, but in cities like Shanghai, Beijing, and Mumbai what is the ultimate answer here? Because it cannot be that everyone in Shanghai has two cars in the garage," she said.

Of course, any such impediment to surging car sales in emerging markets could be years away. But Bill Ford is determined not to be blindsided or to allow his company to coast back to complacency after a near-death experience and an against-all-odds recovery that has taken its stock up by over 80 percent since end 2009.

"One of the things people say is, 'OK, Ford, you made it this time, but how are you not going to slide back?'" Ford said in an interview with Reuters.

## Inside Looking Out

In the three decades he has worked at the company his great-grandfather founded, Ford has been known as much as an iconoclast as an industrialist. The ultimate Detroit insider, he still carries an outsider's deep-seated skepticism about the auto industry's accepted wisdom.

Over the years, Ford has also made headlines as an unwavering environmental advocate, an instinctive contrarian, and the rare chief executive willing to fire himself in order to save his company—as he did in 2006 by hiring Alan Mulally.

Now, with the carmaker roaring away in the third year of its turnaround, Ford finds himself in an unaccustomed, conservative role as the company's executive chairman.

He has become the Ford family's surviving statesman in the executive suite, the counterweight to any runaway optimism and the guardian determined to keep Ford from sliding back into bust after boom as it did in both the early 1990s and again in the last decade.

"I always think of myself as one of the young guys around here, but with thirty-one years, I guess I'm the old-timer," Ford said at his office at the automaker's Dearborn, Michigan headquarters, known in the company as the Glass House. "In a couple of years, I'm going to be the last man standing."

He added: "Part of my role here is to be the institutional memory here and never let people forget what it felt like and what it was like to go through those difficult times."

The determination to drive home the lessons of the crisis comes at a time when Ford is on a white-hot tear. A $100,000 investment in the company's stock at the bottom in late 2008—when its cross-town rivals GM and Chrysler were nearing government bailouts—would be worth $1.8 million today.

After losing more than $30 billion from 2006 to 2008, Ford has made back $9 billion since and is gathering momentum still. Analysts, on average, project another $8.7 billion in earnings this year as the U.S. recovery gains steam.

Ford's sales in its home market jumped 19 percent—the largest gain since 1984—and its market share rose to just over 16 percent, overtaking Toyota for the no. 2 spot.

A survey released this week by consulting firm KPMG showed that 43 percent of auto industry executives, including key suppliers, expect Ford to continue to see its market share grow in 2011. By contrast, just 40 percent thought Toyota would gain ground.

What's more, *Consumer Reports*, considered the most influential guide to car shopping, said in a survey of consumers that Ford had topped Toyota in consumer perception of safety, quality, and value—the three qualities that are ranked as most important.

By delivering a range of more fuel-efficient and electric vehicles, Ford expects to close the gap in the only area where Toyota still leads—the perception that its "green" cars like the Prius are world beaters.

Ford's counter-offensive features an all-electric version of its Focus small car to be launched later this year. The battery-powered car is expected to recharge in half the time of the competing Nissan Leaf.

As importantly, it will be built on the same platform as an estimated 2 million other Ford cars by 2013, driving down production and engineering costs and boosting margins in a trick that Ford took straight from the Toyota playbook.

Ford is confident that the no. 2 U.S. automaker can steer past the next known risks. Those include ensuring that positive changes in the way it operates under Mulally are made permanent and that the right successor inside Ford can be found to the charismatic CEO. More immediately, it means striking a new contract deal with the United Auto Workers later this year that will not cause investors to worry about the risk of shutting down the profit engine in the United States.

"I always believed we had the right plan. The question was did we have enough time? Would external events swamp us before our plan could get traction and get going?" Ford told Reuters. "Fortunately, we did have enough time—just enough time."

## The Education of Bill Clay

The organic cotton curtains in earth tones on Bill Ford's twelfth-floor corner office part to provide a panoramic view of Detroit—and by extension much of the Ford family's history and his own.

In the far distance are the gleaming towers of the Renaissance Center, now home to GM but originally a 1970s-era project spearheaded by Bill Ford's uncle, Henry Ford II, to revive Detroit's downtown.

From the other window, you can see Ford's test track, and a bit beyond that the practice facility of the other Ford family business, the Detroit Lions of the National Football League, where Ford also serves as an executive.

A little to the east in the gray winter sky is the outline of the sprawling Rouge complex built by Henry Ford in the 1920s, a landmark in modern manufacturing. The plant has also been a turning point in Bill Ford's career.

In 1999, it was the site of a fatal explosion that killed six workers. Ford, then forty-two and a recent arrival as chairman, bucked the advice of handlers who told them that a general does not go to the front lines. His response: "Then bust me down to private."

He also won over lifelong friends among Ford factory workers by attending the funerals for the victims and expressing his remorse.

"He's very decent, very approachable, just a regular Joe," said Jimmy Settles, a UAW vice president who saw Ford at the 1999 funerals and is now charged by union leadership with negotiating a 2011 contract with Ford that will win back some of the ground lost in concessions over the past four years.

"There was never any mention of protecting the Ford Motor Co. or anything," Settles said.

In 2004, Ford spearheaded a project to restore the Rouge, including a truck plant with a ten-acre "living roof" of sedum plants to clean the air and retain water, against the grumbling opposition of some in the company who saw it as a meaningless gesture.

"I've been the Green Bolshevik for thirty years in this industry," Ford said. "Through the years I was ridiculed from our competitors. It is particularly humorous to see some of those who were the most outspoken in terms of how crazy this was all of the sudden in recent years trying to wrap themselves in the green mantle."

From the moment he joined the carmaker after graduating from Princeton in 1979, Ford said he was stunned by the "head-in-the-sand" mentality he found on environmental questions in the early years. Executives assumed that tough emissions standards would be rolled back and that any regulation was hostile and threatening.

Ford, who has collected Civil War–era documents rather than muscle cars like many of his peers in Detroit, was the odd man out. "I did believe that society could just not continue to use natural resources at an unprecedented pace forever," he said. "I was surprised when I joined the company there wasn't that recognition. In fact, quite the opposite."

Although he wrote his college thesis on labor relations at Ford and says he felt he belonged to the company from birth, Ford still struggled to find his place in the Ford of the 1980s. Some executives were hostile, emboldened by his uncle Henry Ford II's insistence that there would be "no crown princes" at his company.

Early in his career, Ford used an abbreviated version of his name "Bill Clay"—dropping Ford—to shield himself from scrutiny from the hourly workers at the plant in Wayne, Michigan, where he was briefly assigned. "They kind of figured out fairly quickly who I was. I wasn't exactly very original."

By the time he took over as chairman in 1999, Ford was determined to push the organization toward a break with its past. He was forty-two. At the same age Henry Ford had been three years from developing the Model T.

As a symbolic gesture, Ford challenged a designer to make everything from the brown-leather chairs to the ceiling tiles in his office from biodegradable or environmentally smart materials. A conference room table was made from wood salvaged from the icy waters of Lake Superior.

But for almost five years after he took over as CEO in 2001 after ousting Jacques Nasser, Ford struggled from the corner office to drive his vision for more hybrids and fuel-efficient cars at an automaker mostly known for its more profitable pickup trucks and the Mustang muscle car.

In June 2006, as Ford's troubles mounted and he began to court Mulally from Boeing, he also backed down from a pledge to sell 250,000 hybrids by 2010. That prompted criticism from environmentalists but the target had been wildly unrealistic, a mark of how badly broken Ford's planning process had become.

In the end, the whole industry sold only about 275,000 hybrids made by all manufacturers in the U.S. market last year as gasoline prices hovered near $3 per gallon, too low to justify the additional cost for many drivers.

As Mulally took charge of the plan for saving Ford in 2006, a more pragmatic approach emerged for Ford's goal of saving the planet. Rather than bank on a big breakthrough, Ford would rely on small gains on hundreds of thousands of vehicles by taking steps like introducing smaller, turbocharged engines to boost fuel efficiency.

The strategy has allowed Ford to offer a V6 turbocharged "EcoBoost" engine to swap out for larger V8 in trucks and a four-cylinder variant to power a version of its new Explorer. That vehicle, once an iconic SUV in the 1990s boom, has been redesigned on a lighter car platform. Engineers have also developed a three-cylinder, turbocharged engine that could be used in emerging markets and the megacities that worry Bill Ford.

In the meantime, Ford engineers under product-development chief Derrick Kuzak are also scrambling to slash the weight of future versions of the Ford F-Series pickup truck by incorporating lighter—and more costly—materials like aluminum and magnesium, people involved in the effort say. The goal is to push the limits of fuel economy.

Taken together, Ford has pledged to win the battle for fuel efficiency in every market segment from the subcompact Fiesta to the F-150 truck.

As importantly, Ford is pushing hard for leadership in another area pioneered by Japanese automakers led by Toyota and Honda Motor Corp.: flexible manufacturing.

Nissan Motor Corp. has made a huge bet on its all-electric Leaf, including a battery plant built with $1.4 billion in U.S. government funding in Tennessee. That strategy carries a risk; the car needs to be a hit. "If that thing doesn't sell what are they going to do?" Ford says.

By contrast, Ford is going green but hedging its bet on how many electric cars customers will want. Its Wayne, Michigan, plant will build all kinds of Focus sedans—from pure electric to conventional gas-engine—depending on customer orders.

"We're going to have a plug-in, a conventional hybrid, a pure electric, and a gasoline engine all going down the same assembly line," he said. "It will be up to the customer then to decide what best fits for them."

At the same time, Kuzak's team has been chipping away at billions of dollars in costs by merging the vehicle platforms Ford had used in Europe and the United States. Before Mulally's relentless push to merge those operations under his mantra of "One Ford," the two operations had been largely independent for decades. Essentially, all the Ford Focus sold in Europe shared with the car sold in the United States had been the name.

That progress in unifying its own engineering efforts is part of the reason Bill Ford is confident that Ford can go it alone globally—without the kind of alliance partner that Chrysler has in Fiat or Nissan has in Renault.

"We really have had our own merger," Ford said. "We merged these disparate regional operations into one global operation. Before we were a large corporation but we lacked the economies of scale because we were very regional. I'm not sure a joint venture is a panacea when I look at the totality of it."

## The Right Man for the Job?

Many of Ford's backers say that the management system now in place sets the company up for success even after sixty-five-year-old CEO Alan Mulally retires.

Under Mulally, Ford's top management gathers every Thursday morning for a meeting on the eleventh floor of headquarters that covers updates on every aspect of its business. The meetings have become the symbol of a new culture of openness and collaboration at an automaker Ford himself once described as having "more intrigue than czarist Russia."

"There is no place to hide," Ford said of the weekly meetings. "But it also really creates a very deep bench of management talent. Before, you were just running your own silo."

That system, he vows, will continue whoever leads Ford. "In terms of culture and transparency, keeping the system alive is very important," Ford said. "In terms of ultimate succession, it's created a very, very strong bench."

Mulally shows no sign of being ready to step down, and Ford has joked about asking him to stay on for decades. "I really like serving at Ford," Mulally told Reuters this week. "I heard Bill Ford said I was staying until I'm ninety-nine."

On the other hand, Ford also acknowledges that the CEO post takes a toll and carries a "burnout factor," in explaining how he would not consider returning to the job himself. The average CEO tenure, Ford notes, has shortened to around four and a half years, according to one study. Mulally has been at Ford almost that long.

Just four years ago, when Ford was serving as chairman, CEO, president, and COO, he was growing overwhelmed. He also felt he had no choice but to go outside for a senior executive because most of his own team were young and "in their first big job." His hiring of Mulally in 2006 came after a failed earlier bid to woo Nissan-Renault's Carlos Ghosn to Ford.

"He said, 'I think I need help running this company. I need to bring in someone who has a different set of skills to help take Ford to an entirely different place,'" his friend Whitman recalls Ford saying in 2006 in a conversation around the time of a meeting of Ebay's board, where Ford serves as a director.

"He wanted a partner, knew he needed help," said Whitman. "[He] basically said, 'I'll be an executive president, we'll hire a president and CEO, and we've got to bring in outside perspective and someone who can take Ford to the next level.' I admired him a lot for doing that because . . . it's very rare."

With the crisis now behind, Ford says he expects to promote the next CEO from within the group reporting to Mulally. "I'm really happy with the talent that we have here," he said.

Possible candidates include Jim Farley, forty-eight, Ford's top marketing executive, a hire from Toyota who has pushed Ford into spending far more on social media marketing on sites like Facebook to win younger buyers.

Mark Fields, forty-nine, the head of Ford's operations in North and South America is also on that list. So is Joe Hinrichs, forty-four, now head of Ford's China operations, who had won cost-saving labor deals with the UAW during the depth of the crisis.

Chief financial officer Lewis Booth, sixty-two, a veteran insider who was brought to the Glass House from Ford Europe, is also seen as a possible CEO unless Mulally were to hold the job for years more.

"The group has been through a lot together," Ford said. "Nobody wants to go back to the horrific times, so that's great motivation to keep it going."

Vikas Sehgal, an auto industry consultant at Booz and Co., said he believes the momentum Ford has now can be sustained because Mulally and Ford have managed to change the way the company runs in areas like engineering, manufacturing, and working with suppliers.

"The most interesting thing is that Ford has done this in the worst possible time for the auto industry," he said. "That has required a fundamental change in the way that they operate, not just cosmetic changes."

Other Ford investors and partners say that Bill Ford presents a reassuring continuity at the top in his role as executive chairman. By taking the hard step to recognize his own limitations and hire Mulally in 2006, he showed the kind of judgment that will serve the company well down the road, they say.

"You tend to hear about Alan Mulally, but you've got to remember that Bill's the one that put him there and made the choice," said Bert Boeckmann, who owns Galpin Ford just outside Los Angeles, the top-selling Ford dealership.

Bernie McGinn, chief investment officer at McGinn Investment Management, holds Ford stock and remains bullish even at its current level near eight-year highs above $18. He expects the stock to top $25 this year as its profits grow, the U.S. economy recovers, and a cultural change within the company takes hold that makes "reaching your goals become habit."

"The goal from Mulally's standpoint is to make these changes all permanent. That would be my concern," he said. "But I think at this stage of the game, I would expect them to carry through."

## Lucky or Good?

Ford may have had the right plan, but executives, including Bill Ford, also concede it caught a lucky break from the stumbles of its largest rivals.

In 2009, GM and Chrysler were both put through government-funded bankruptcies and the stigma from that bailout drove some customers Ford's way. In 2010, Toyota was struggling to break free from a costly series of recalls that shook its reputation for quality and safety.

Meanwhile, Bill Ford was getting fan mail in the Glass House. "I have gotten countless letters that go something like this," he said. "'I'm a small business person. I've got issues. No one will ever bail me out. You guys did it the right way. I've never considered a Ford before, but I will now.'"

Ford, which was forced to borrow $23.6 billion from banks in 2006 to fund its turnaround and had supported the bailouts, did nothing from headquarters to capitalize on the backlash. But its dealers hammered home the message that Ford was different in local ads.

"We knew it was time for all hands on deck, not a bailout," said one dealer's radio ad playing in southern Georgia in early January.

Ford says the company recognizes the glow of goodwill will fade. "We know it's a temporary thing," he said. "It's not forever and ultimately we will succeed only on the strength of our products and technology."

The terms of the Obama administration bailout keep the UAW from striking at GM and Chrysler when the current labor contracts expire in September.

That has put the focus on Ford, where workers rejected a final round of proposed concessions in October 2009. Bob King, now the UAW's president, had negotiated that proposed deal, including a "no-strike" clause on wages and benefits.

In November, King said he would offer no new concessions. Instead, he said, he wanted to see workers at Ford, GM, and Chrysler start to "share in the upside." Ford, King said, was not at any disadvantage to the other Detroit automakers.

The UAW push for some kind of profit-sharing promises to test the good will that Bill Ford has built up with the union since his first trial by negotiation in 1982.

"I just want to make sure anything we do is fair to them and fair to us," Ford said of the upcoming contract round. "So, you know, I don't think anything is off the table."

Ford was a junior member of the Ford negotiating team that won concessions in exchange for job security in the 1982 talks that played out against the backdrop of a crushing recession.

He describes it as "one of the best jobs" he ever had at Ford although he also remembers a senior union negotiator calling him out because of his family standing: "'Young man! I knew your grandfather, and I knew your uncle. What the hell are you made of?'"

Ford hung in with the talks although he dreaded the daily harangues. Settles of the UAW, who was then a local union leader, led protests outside the headquarters where the negotiators were sitting on the second floor. ("He probably has all the reason to hate me," says Settles, who now talks regularly with Ford and has found common ground in their shared love of football.)

Ford remembers walking out of one all-night negotiation and seeing a team of UAW guys headed his way. "They said, 'Hey, want to go get a beer?' And I'm looking around to see who they were talking to."

"And so we went out, and they said, 'Hey, you passed the test. Good job.' I said, 'Really?' And they said, 'Yeah, you were great. We were just trying you on for size.'"

In a similar way, Ford said he is proud that his family, which controls 40 percent of the voting stock in the automaker through a separate class of shares, stuck with Ford when tested by the company's financial crisis of 2006.

Advisers had presented the family and the company with a range of scenarios, including a merger or asset sales. In the end, the Fords opted to bet everything on the turnaround plan led by Mulally and Bill Ford.

"So many families that you've seen in other industries blew apart as soon as difficulty arose. Our family hung together when it was looking really grim, and said 'How can we help?' rather than 'How do we get out?' or 'Who do we blame?'" he said. "It helped management to have their big shareholder unified behind them."

Ford sees that long-term interest of the Ford family giving him the mandate to work on problems like the big one that worries him now: What comes after the car for the millions who will live in the big cities set to emerge over the next thirty years? "They're not going to have garages. And they certainly won't have two cars or even a car? But how can we at Ford make their lives better?" Ford said.

Ford's focus on the gridlock problem captured by China's now-infamous, eleven-day traffic jam last summer represents a shift in his thinking. Electric car technology and other innovations, Ford believes, are on the verge of cracking the industry's last big problem: how to reduce gasoline consumption and emissions.

"We had one huge challenge called the environment if I can use an overarching term. But we're solving that now through technology," he said. "To me, there will always be long-term problems to take on. I think one of the things I can provide this company is that long-term vision so we don't get blindsided by issues when it's too late."

**Fast Company**

The resignation and subsequent death of Steve Jobs produced an avalanche of business writing. Cliff Kuang, writing in *Fast Company* the day after Jobs's resignation from Apple, provided one of the better professional eulogies. He identifies Jobs's world-changing talent: not as the greatest engineer or designer but rather history's best user of technology, the man who could develop and identify exactly the products that consumers of the future would fall in love with.

Cliff Kuang

# 31. What Made Steve Jobs So Great?

In the wake of Steve Jobs's resignation, let's consider the greatest decision he ever made. It didn't happen in a garage in Cupertino, sweating with Steve Wozniak as they dreamed up a computer for the common man. Or in a conference room, as managers told him that no one would ever pay $500 for a portable music player. Or in another conference room, as new managers told him no one would ever pay $400 for a cell phone. Rather, it was in a dusty basement of the Apple campus.

Jobs had just recently come back to the company, after a twelve-year layoff working for two of his own startups: NeXT, which made ultra-high-end computers, and Pixar. He was taking a tour of Apple, becoming reacquainted with what the company had become in the years since he'd left. It must have been a sobering, even ugly sight: Apple was dying at the hands of Microsoft, IBM, Dell, and a litany of competitors who were doing what Apple did, only cheaper, with faster processors.

His tour finally brought him to the workbench of a designer ready to quit after just a year on the job, languishing amid a stack of prototypes. Among them was monolithic monitor with a teardrop swoop, which managed to integrate all of a computer's guts into a single package. In that basement Jobs saw what middle managers did not. He saw the future. And almost immediately he told the designer, Jonathan Ive, that from here on out they'd be working side-by-side on a new line.

Steve Jobs may not be the greatest technologist or engineer of his generation. But he is perhaps the greatest *user* of technology to ever live, and it was Apple's great fortune that he also happened to be the company's founder.

Those computers that Ive and Jobs worked on became, of course, the iMac—a piece of hardware designed with an unprecedented user focus, all the way to the handle on top, which made it easy to pull out of the box. ("That's the great thing about handles," Ive told *Fast Company* in 1999. "You know what they're used for.") And while it seems condescending to say that Jobs's greatest moment was finding someone else who was great, it's not. That single moment in the basement with Ive tells you a great deal about what made Steve Jobs the most influential innovator of our time. It shows you the ability to see a company from the outside, rather than inside as a line manager. He didn't see the proto iMac as a liability or a boondoggle. He saw something that was simply better than what had preceded it, and he was willing to gamble based on that instinct. That required an ability to think first and foremost as someone who lives with technology rather than produces it.

People often say that Jobs is, first and foremost, a great explainer of technology—a charismatic, plainspoken salesman who is able to bend those around him into a "reality distortion field." But charisma can be bent to all sorts of purposes. Those purposes may very well be asinine. So what gives his plain-speaking such force? He always talks about how wondrous it will be to *use* something, to actually live with it and hold it in your hands. If you listen to Steve Jobs's presentations over the years, he comes across not as the creator of a product so much as its very first fan—the first person to digest its possibilities.

Of course, when Steve Jobs has fancied himself the chief creator, disastrous failures often ensued. His instincts were often wrong. For example, his much ballyhooed Apple Cube, which was in fact a successor to the NeXT cube he'd developed during his

Apple hiatus, was an $6,500 dud. He was also openly disdainful of the Internet in the late 1990s. And before his hiatus from Apple, in 1985, his meddling and micro-management had gotten out of control. But the years away reportedly helped him begin ceding more responsibilities to others, and become less of a technology freak and more of a user-experience savant. A reporter who asked Jobs about the market research that went into the iPad was famously told, "None. It's not the consumers' job to know what they want." Which isn't to say that he doesn't think like a consumer—he just thinks like one standing in the near future, not in the recent past. He is a focus group of one, the ideal Apple customer, two years out. As he told *Inc.* magazine in 1989, "You can't just ask customers what they want and then try to give that to them. By the time you get it built, they'll want something new."

People also often reduce Jobs's success to a ruthless perfectionism which sometimes led him to scrap a product simply because it didn't feel right or because some minor feature like a power button or a home screen seemed buggy and unresolved. (Famously, he tore through three prototypes of the iPhone in 2007 before the last passed muster; he also berated Ive early over the details of the USB port in the first iMac.) But that doesn't get to it either. A myopic focus on details can readily destroy as much value as it creates: Just think about the number of times you've sat through a meeting with a boss who harped on details, killing a project before you ever had a chance to explain what it *could* be.

It's almost certain that Jobs has killed far more great ideas than he ever let live—there are 313 patents under his name covering everything from packaging to user interfaces. But those that survived outweighed all the rest, simply because his focus was, continually, on what it would be like to come at some new product raw, with no coaching or presentation but simply as a dumb, weird new thing. Again, that's ability to see past internal debates and to look at a potential product with the fresh eyes of a user rather than a creator.

Perhaps the best example of this hides in plain sight and is a fundamental part of every Apple product. All throughout the 1970s to the 1990s, if you ever opened up a new gadget the first thing you were ever faced with was figuring how the damn thing worked. To solve that, you'd have to wade through piles of instruction manuals written in an engineer's alien English. But a funny thing happened with the iMac: Every year after, Apple's instruction manuals grew thinner and thinner, until finally, today, there are none. The assumption is that you'll be able to tear open the box and immediately start playing with your new toy. Just watch a three-year-old playing with an iPad. You're seeing a toddler intuit the workings of one of the most advanced pieces of engineering on the planet. At almost no time in history has that ever been possible. It certainly wasn't when the first home computers were introduced, or the first TV remotes, or the first radios. And it was something he was driving for, his entire career. Again from 1989, *Inc.* asked him, "Do you sometimes marvel at the effect you've had on people's lives?" And Jobs said: "There are some moments. I was in an elementary school just this morning, and they still had a bunch of Apple IIs, and I was kind of looking over their shoulders. Then I get letters from people about the Mac, saying, 'I never thought I could use a computer before I tried this one.'"

There is, however, one decisive factor that Steve Jobs couldn't control: Timing. Yet it was perfect for him. He was born just in time to become a founding father of the personal computer movement. But he was also still young enough that in 1997, he could lead while his own sense of a computer's potential could finally bear fruit.

Throughout the 1980s and 1990s, computers were being sold on their speed and features. This was the birthing period for computers, when their capabilities were just being limned. But by 2000, all of these had largely become commoditized—it no longer mattered how fast a computer was, when basic issues of usability and integration became so pressing. Just think back to your Windows machine of the time: What did speed matter if you didn't even know what all the menus meant, or if you were hit with some weird bug that flashed pop-ups at you every time you clicked your mouse?

Before 1997, Jobs was ahead of his time. The computers he made were overpriced for the market because he thought that usability was more important than capability. But as computers reached maturity and became a feature in every home, his obsessions became more relevant to the market. And in fact, many of Apple's recent signature products, such as the iPad or the iPhone, were based on products first conceived of in the 1990s or even the 1980s—they had to bide their time.

All of this isn't to say that Steve Jobs has been Apple's sole arbiter of success: He purportedly has a great eye for talent. Moreover, he has taught his entire organization to play in the span of product generations rather than just product introductions: Apple designers say that now, each design they create has to be presented alongside a mock-up of how that design might evolve in the second or third generation. That should ensure Apple's continued success for as long as a decade. But it's not totally clear that anyone else can equal his talent for being able to look at Apple's product's from the outside view of a user. Tim Cook, his anointed successor, proved his worth by totally revamping Apple's production processes and supply chain. That talent is vital to running the business, and has increased Apple's profits by untold billions. But being able to break apart the nuances of sourcing is the precise opposite of being a usability genius: Cook's career has largely been spent focusing on precisely those things the consumer *never* sees.

Does Cook have an in-house product critic, who could stand in Jobs's place? Will Cook have as close a working relationship with Ive as Jobs did? Will Ive even stay? And did Steve Jobs create an entire organization that shared his balance of concerns—for the back end, yes, but for usability first and foremost? The biggest risk is that Apple has taken for granted that its superior design should demand a price premium. That might lull them into thinking that Apple is great, rather than its products. But Apple, all along, has only been as good as its last "insanely great" thing.

# Permissions

# Contributors

**MARCIA ANGELL** is a senior lecturer in social medicine at Harvard Medical School and former editor in chief of *The New England Journal of Medicine*. Her latest book is *The Truth About the Drug Companies: How They Deceive Us and What to Do About It*.

**RICK BARRETT** has been a reporter at the *Milwaukee Journal Sentinel* since September 2000 and currently covers manufacturing companies and the telecom industry. Barrett and Raquel Rutledge received the Barlett & Steele silver award for Business Investigative Journalism for their series, "A Case of Shattered Trust." He previously worked at the *Wisconsin State Journal*, in Madison, as well as for newspapers in Michigan, Florida, Arkansas, and Texas.

**CHAD BECK** is a film editor and a cowriter of *Inside Job*, which won the Academy Award for Best Documentary Feature in 2011. He also worked with Charles Ferguson on the Oscar-nominated documentary *No End in Sight*. He is currently editing a documentary about *South Park*'s Trey Parker and Matt Stone.

**JAKE BERNSTEIN** is a business and financial reporter for *ProPublica* who shared the 2011 Pulitzer Prize with Jesse Eisinger. Before joining ProPublica, Bernstein worked at *The Texas Observer*, an investigative biweekly, for six years, and as its executive editor from 2004 to 2008. He has also worked as a staff writer for the *Pasadena* (Texas) *Citizen* and then for the *Miami New Times*.

**ALEX BLUMBERG** is a producer at the public radio program *This American Life* and a cofounder of Planet Money, an economics reporting collaboration between *This American Life* and NPR. He has won numerous major awards in broadcast journalism and his radio documentary "The Giant Pool of Money," was named one of top ten works of journalism of the decade by New York University.

**ADAM BOLT** is a producer and editor for *Dan Rather Reports*. He is a cowriter of *Inside Job*, which won the Academy Award for Best Documentary Feature in 2011. He previously edited and coproduced the HBO documentary *The Recruiter*, which won a Columbia duPont award for excellence in broadcast journalism.

**WARREN BUFFETT** is the chairman and chief executive of Berkshire Hathaway.

**BRIAN M. CARNEY** is a member of the *Wall Street Journal*'s editorial board and editor of the *Wall Street Journal Europe*'s editorial page. He won the Gerald Loeb Award for Commentary in 2009 and is the coauthor of *Freedom, Inc.*

**ZACH CARTER** is *The Huffington Post*'s senior political economy reporter.

**MAX CHAFKIN** is a senior contributing writer for *Inc.* magazine who has profiled companies including Yelp, Zappos, Twitter, Threadless, and Tesla.

**LAUREN COLLINS** has worked at *The New Yorker* since 2003, and is currently a staff writer. She writes frequently for "The Talk of the Town" and "Tables for Two" and also writes longer features for the magazine. Before arriving at *The New Yorker*, Collins was at *Vogue*.

**NICK DAVIES** is the best-selling author of *Flat Earth News*, on falsehood and distortion in the media, and a former Journalist of the Year.

**JESSE EISINGER** is a senior reporter at *ProPublica*, covering Wall Street and finance. In April 2011, he and Jake Bernstein were awarded the Pulitzer Prize for National Reporting for a series of stories on questionable Wall Street practices that led to the 2008 financial crisis. Before joining *ProPublica*, Eisinger was the Wall Street editor of Conde Nast *Portfolio* and worked at the *Wall Street Journal*, where he was the founding writer of two market commentary columns.

**PETER ELKIND** is an editor at large at *Fortune* magazine and an award-winning investigative reporter. Elkind is coauthor of the national best-seller *The Smartest Guys in the Room: The Amazing Rise and Scandalous Fall of Enron*; author of *The Death Shift: The True Story of Nurse Genene Jones and the Texas Baby Murders*; and author of the newly published *Rough Justice: The Rise and Fall of Eliot Spitzer*. He has written for the *New York Times Magazine*, the *Washington Post*, and *Texas Monthly* and is a former editor of the *Dallas Observer*.

**CHARLES FERGUSON** is the founder and president of Representational Pictures, Inc., and director and producer of *Inside Job*, which won the Academy Award for Best Documentary Feature in 2011, and *No End In Sight: The American Occupation of Iraq*, which was nominated in the same category in 2008. Ferguson spent several years as a senior fellow at the Brookings Institution, and he is a life member of the Council on Foreign Relations and has been an independent consultant to Apple, Xerox, Motorola, Intel, and Texas Instruments, among other technology companies. He is the author of four books, including *High Stakes, No Prisoners, and Computer Wars* (coauthored with Charles Morris) and is currently working on a book about the global financial crisis, to be released by Random House in Spring 2012.

**CHRYSTIA FREELAND** is the editor of Thomson Reuters Digital. Before that, she held various editorial positions at the *Financial Times* and FT.com. From 1999 to 2001, Freeland served as deputy editor of the *Globe and Mail*, Canada's national newspaper.

**JOHN GAPPER** is associate editor and chief business commentator of the *Financial Times*. He is coauthor, with Nicholas Denton, of *All That Glitters*, an account of the collapse of Barings in 1995. His new e-book, *How to Be a Rogue Trader*, was recently published.

**JEFF GOODELL** is a contributing editor at *Rolling Stone* and the author of five books, including *Big Coal: The Dirty Secret Behind America's Energy Future.*

**HUGH GRANT** is an actor and film producer.

**RYAN GRIM** is the Washington bureau chief for *The Huffington Post* and author of *This Is Your Country on Drugs: The Secret History of Getting High in America.*

**AMELIA HILL** is special investigations correspondent for the *Guardian*.

**MORGAN HOUSEL** is a columnist at *The Motley Fool*. He is a two-time winner of the Best in Business Award from the Society of Business Editors and Writers. His columns have covered financial markets, the dynamics of recessions, economic policy, behavioral finance, and financial history.

**MICHAEL HUDSON** is a reporter with the Center for Public Integrity's iWatch News and the author of *The Monster: How a Gang of Predatory Lenders and Wall Street Bankers Fleeced America—and Spawned a Global Crisis.* The former *Wall Street Journal* staff writer has been called the reporter who "beat the world on subprime abuses" and "the guru of all things predatory lending."

**DAVID CAY JOHNSTON** is a Reuters columnist and best-selling author. He also teaches tax, property, and regulatory law at Syracuse University's law and graduate business schools. In 2001, while at the *New York Times*, he received a Pulitzer Prize for his tax reporting.

**KEVIN KROLICKI** is Detroit bureau chief for Reuters since 2006. He has also worked in Los Angeles and Tokyo for Reuters.

**PAUL KRUGMAN** is a columnist at the *New York Times*, a professor of economics and international affairs at Princeton University, and the winner of the 2008 Nobel Prize in economics. He's the author of twenty books, including *The Conscience of a Liberal* and *The Return of Depression Economics and the Crisis of 2008*.

**CLIFF KUANG** is the founding editor of Fast Company's Co.Design, a website covering design, business, and innovation. In 2011, Co.Design won the National Magazine Award for best online department.

**GRETCHEN MORGENSON** is a Pulitzer Prize winner and assistant business and financial editor and columnist at the *New York Times*. She is the author of three books, including *Reckless Endangerment*, which she coauthored with Joshua Rosner.

**STEVEN PEARLSTEIN** is a business and economics columnist for the *Washington Post*. He won the Pulitzer Prize for commentary in 2008 and a Gerald R. Loeb Lifetime Achievement award in 2011.

**JENNIFER REINGOLD** is a senior editor at *Fortune*. Previously, she was at *Fast Company* and *Business Week*. She is the coauthor of three books: *Confessions of a Wall Street Analyst: A True Story of Inside Information and Corruption in the Stock Market; Final Accounting: Ambition, Greed and the Fall of Arthur Andersen;* and *Business Week's Guide to the Best Business Schools.*

**JAY ROSEN** has been on the journalism faculty at New York University since 1986 and is the author of PressThink, a blog about journalism. He is the author of *What Are Journalists For?*, a book about the rise of the civic-journalism movement.

**RAQUEL RUTLEDGE** is an investigative reporter with the *Milwaukee Journal Sentinel*'s Watchdog Team. Her recent series "Cashing In on Kids" won the 2010 Pulitzer Prize for local reporting as well as a George Polk Award, the Goldsmith Prize for Investigative Reporting, and the Worth Bingham Prize for Investigative Journalism. In May she was awarded a fellowship from the Nieman Foundation for Journalism at Harvard University for the 2011–12 academic year.

**DAVID SEGAL** is a reporter for the *New York Times*. He was previously at the *Washington Post*, first in the business section, then as the pop music critic, and finally as the New York–based writer for the style section.

**DANIEL SOAR** is a senior editor at the *London Review of Books.*

**JAMES B. STEWART** is a columnist for the *New York Times*, a contributor to *The New Yorker,* and the author of eleven books. He was formerly the Page One editor at the *Wall Street Journal* and won the Pulitzer Prize for Explanatory Journalism in 1988.

**LOUISE STORY** writes about Wall Street and finance for the *New York Times* and helped chronicle the financial crisis and the federal bailout of the banks and its aftermath.

**LAURA SYDELL** is a correspondent for NPR based in San Francisco. She reports regularly for NPR's major news magazines, *Morning Edition* and *All Things Considered*, on the impact of new technologies on all aspects of culture and daily life.

**MATT TAIBBI** is a contributing editor for *Rolling Stone* and a winner of the National Magazine Award for commentary. He is the author of five books, including *The Great Derangement*.

**JONATHAN WEIL** is a columnist for Bloomberg News and was previously managing director at Glass Lewis & Co, an investment research firm, and a reporter for the *Wall Street Journal*. Weil was a Gerald Loeb award finalist in 2002 and won Society of American Business Editors and Writers Best in Business Journalism Awards in 2009 and 2010. He has been credited as the first reporter to challenge Enron Corp.'s accounting practices, and his columns for Bloomberg in 2007 and 2008 focused on questionable accounting practices at Fannie Mae, Freddie Mac, Wachovia, Washington Mutual, Lehman Brothers, AIG, and Citigroup, among others.

**MARTIN WOLF** is the award-winning chief economics commentator at the London-based *Financial Times*. He was awarded the CBE (Commander of the British Empire) in 2000 "for services to financial journalism."

**BERNIE WOODALL** is a Detroit-based correspondent with Reuters. He joined Reuters in New York in 1998 and has also worked in Los Angeles. He has covered the United Nations and energy policy and markets in addition to the automobile industry. Before joining Reuters, he worked at Dow Jones and newspapers in North Carolina and Florida.